SACRIFICE YOUR LOVE

MEDIEVAL CULTURES

SERIES EDITORS
RITA COPELAND
BARBARA A. HANAWALT
DAVID WALLACE

Sponsored by the Center for Medieval Studies at the University of Minnesota

Volumes in this series study the diversity of medieval cultural histories and practices, including such interrelated issues as gender, class, and social hierarchies; race and ethnicity; geographical relations; definitions of political space; discourses of authority and dissent; educational institutions; canonical and noncanonical literatures; and technologies of textual and visual literacies.

Volume 31
L. O. Aranye Fradenburg
Sacrifice Your Love: Psychoanalysis, Historicism, Chaucer

Volume 30
Stephanie Trigg
Congenial Souls: Reading Chaucer from Medieval to Postmodern

Volume 29
Edited by Kathleen Ashley and Robert L. A. Clark
Medieval Conduct

For more books in the series, see pages 329–331.

Sacrifice Your Love

Psychoanalysis, Historicism, Chaucer

L. O. Aranye Fradenburg

Medieval Cultures, Volume 31
University of Minnesota Press
Minneapolis
London

Published with assistance from the Margaret S. Harding Memorial Endowment honoring the first director of the University of Minnesota Press.

The author is grateful to the University of California, Santa Barbara, for funding research; to Richard Morrison of the University of Minnesota Press, for shepherding this book along; to Paul Strohm, for reading it and making so many helpful suggestions; and to many research assistants and dear friends, who have given every kind of support.

Part of chapter 2 originally appeared as "'My Worldes Blisse': Chaucer's Tragedy of Fortune," *South Atlantic Quarterly* 98 (1999): 563–92; reprinted with permission of Duke University Press. A version of chapter 4 appeared as "Sacrificial Desire in Chaucer's Knight's Tale," *Journal for Medieval and Renaissance Studies* 27 (1997); reprinted with permission from Duke University Press. A version of chapter 5 appeared as "The Love of Thy Neighbor," in *Constructing Medieval Sexualities*, edited by Karma Lochrie, Peggy McCracken, and James A. Schultz (Minneapolis: University of Minnesota Press, 1997), 135–57. Chapter 6 originally appeared as "'Oure Owen Wo to Drynke': Loss, Gender, and Chivalry in *Troilus and Criseyde*," in Chaucer's *Troilus and Criseyde*: "Subgit to alle Poesye," *Essays in Criticism*, edited by R. A. Shoaf with Catherine S. Cox (Binghamton, N.Y.: Medieval and Renaissance Texts and Studies, 1992), 88–106. Part of the epilogue appeared as "'So that we may speak of them': Enjoying the Middle Ages," *New Literary History* (spring 1997); reprinted with permission of The Johns Hopkins University Press.

Copyright 2002 by the Regents of the University of Minnesota

All rights reserved. No part of this publication may be reproduced, stored in a retrieval system, or transmitted, in any form or by any means, electronic, mechanical, photocopying, recording, or otherwise, without the prior written permission of the publisher.

Published by the University of Minnesota Press
111 Third Avenue South, Suite 290
Minneapolis, MN 55401-2520
http://www.upress.umn.edu

Library of Congress Cataloging-in-Publication Data
Fradenburg, L. O. Aranye, 1953–
    Sacrifice your love : psychoanalysis, historicism, Chaucer / L. O. Aranye Fradenburg.
        p.   cm. — (Medieval cultures ; v. 31)
    Includes bibliographical references and index.
    ISBN 0-8166-3645-1 (HC : alk. paper) — ISBN 0-8166-3646-X (PB : alk. paper)
    1. Chaucer, Geoffrey, d. 1400—Knowledge—Psychology. 2. Psychoanalysis and literature—England—History—To 1500. 3. Literature and history—England—History—To 1500. 4. Poetry—Psychological aspects. 5. Historicism in literature. 6. Psychology in literature. 7. Love in literature. I. Title. II. Series.
    PR1933.P679 F73 2002
    821'.1—dc21
                                        2001006556

Printed in the United States of America on acid-free paper

The University of Minnesota is an equal-opportunity educator and employer.

12 11 10 09 08 07 06 05 04 03 02   10 9 8 7 6 5 4 3 2 1

For Lily Grover

Contents

Introduction: Sacrifice in Theory   1

1. Becoming Medieval: Psychoanalysis and Historicism   43

2. "My Worldes Blisse": Courtly Interiority in
   The Book of the Duchess   79

3. The Ninety-six Tears of Chaucer's Monk   113

4. Sacrificial Desire in Chaucer's *Knight's Tale*   155

5. Loving Thy Neighbor: *The Legend of Good Women*   176

6. "Oure Owen Wo to Drynke":
   Dying Inside in *Troilus and Criseyde*   199

   Epilogue. Some Thoughts on the Humanities:
   Enjoying the Middle Ages   239

   Notes   253

   Index   299

INTRODUCTION

SACRIFICE IN THEORY

"I am what is lacking in you; with my devotion to you, with my sacrifice for you, I will fill you out, I will complete you."
—Slavoj Žižek,
ventriloquizing an unnamed spirit

[A]n object, insofar as it is a created object, may fill the function that enables it not to avoid the thing as signifier, but to represent it.
—Jacques Lacan

Sublimate as much as you like; you have to pay for it with something. And this something is called jouissance. I have to pay for that mystical operation with a pound of flesh. That's the object, the good, that one pays for the satisfaction of one's desire.... It is, in effect, there that the religious operation lies.... That good which is sacrificed for desire—and you will note that that means the same thing as that desire which is lost for the good—that pound of flesh is precisely the thing that religion undertakes to recuperate.
—Jacques Lacan

The most important single assumption of this book is that what we think we ought to do—even the very idea that we ought to do certain things—is always intimately related to our desire. This linkage between desire and ethics is, in turn, at the center of my thinking about sacrifice. My reading of sacrifice as a form and activity of enjoyment has been inspired by the psychoanalytic principle that it is desire that drives human subjectivity, both group and individual. As Lacan puts it, "the genesis of the moral dimension in Freud's theoretical elaboration is located nowhere else than in desire itself."[1] This introductory chapter lays out the chief concepts at work in my view of sacrifice, which are derived chiefly from psychoanalytic writing about culture and sociality, from medieval understandings of desire, and from historicist commitments to the variability, heritability, and retroactive legibility of the past. I draw on several straightforward, readily available examples from medieval texts to illustrate the chief points of my argument, in the hope that readers of this book who may not be specialists might turn to medieval literature and culture more regularly in the course of attempts to understand desire and its vicissitudes. In the history of "Western" thought (which has been shaped by so much "Eastern" thought), present-day fascination with desire as a key to understanding subjectivity is, I believe, matched only by that of the Middle Ages. In fact, the amorous subjectivity of Europe is often dated to the twelfth century, and the rise of *amour courtoise*. This way of telling the history of our sensibilities is a problematic one, and will be returned to later. But it is a historical narrative that has helped me understand, or at least work out my understanding of, the intimacy between privation and desire in discourses of love then, now, and sometimes in between.

Pleasure Unreconciled to Virtue: The Satisfactions of Renouncing Satisfaction

Our moral sense is what Slavoj Žižek would call a "mode of enjoyment," one of the many shapes taken by desire.[2] For this reason, it can fall ill: become persecuting, obsessive, self-punishing. It can also be used to further desire—for example, to exalt certain objects of desire and abject others. And because of its interdependence with all other forms of desire, our moral sense has a much greater hold over us than most of our ethical traditions acknowledge. We are, Freud and Lacan would argue, much more likely to "give way" on our desire than we are to pursue it thoughtlessly—much more likely to live the way we think we are "expected" to live, driving no more than ten to fifteen miles over the speed limit, than we are to pursue every possibility of sexual pleasure to come our way, or revenge ourselves on everyone who annoys us, including our oppressors. Psychoanalysis reorients previous ethical thinking by asking why we so readily (if not always graciously) give way on our desire—not why we have so much trouble restraining it.

Most of our ethical systems, certainly those with strong debts to classical culture, were developed for and by elites: "masters" whose entitlement to pleasure was axiomatic. The moral thought inspired by Christianity considerably complicated the self-evidence of the classical values of strength, physical well-being, leisure, and wealth. Psychoanalysis is part of this "genealogy"—part of a long historical process of thinking ethically about the *many* vagaries and varieties and limitations of human agency. Where psychoanalysis makes a break with this history, however, is its conviction that the moral sense is a form of enjoyment rather than a means of restraining it. The moral sense can both cause, and ease, suffering; its relation to desire can be deciphered and perhaps, by such means, reconfigured. It is no less moral for all that, at least from the standpoint of psychoanalysis; or, to put it another way, this is what morality *is* from the standpoint of psychoanalysis, and its importance to us and to the other is not at all diminished thereby. One of the traditional concerns of ethics has been the problem our desire poses for the suffering of the other. Psychoanalysis distinctively insists that we are capable of *desiring* suffering, for ourselves, not just for our loved ones or our enemies, because the subject *tout court* is a function of desire. Further, it is because so much libidinal energy is organized in relation to the question of what we ought to do that we react so violently when "ought" is put in relation to "wish"—for example, when we fight against the notion that we have helped to put ourselves in the difficult positions we are always finding ourselves in. As analysis of desire and its vicissitudes, ethics asks us to interpret ourselves and our designs on others, but our interpretations (as many ethical systems realize) cannot be disengaged from the very designs and desires we are meant to be scrutinizing. Interpreting, or "*giving* meaning" (Kristeva suggests that "'To interpret' . . . means 'to make a connection'"), is something we are not neutral about; we love to do it, we dislike doing it, it ruins or is the sine qua non of enjoyment, and the same is true for being interpreted.³ The Other sees right into my very soul; this is good (at least God is interested in me, I can't be *all* bad) or not (why is my lover always, annoyingly, telling me what I am thinking?). But the specially powerful resistances psychoanalytic interpretation is capable of calling up in us—and let us be clear that psychoanalytic interpretation always tries to restore desire to the field of inquiry—is, as Kristeva has argued, the very reason for the distinctive interpretive edge of psychoanalysis.⁴ For these reasons, ethical systems that *oppose* desire to sacrifice require considerable rethinking, as do many of our explanations for why we care about ethics at all. This is not because such practices are wrong or in bad faith, but because the opposition of desire and sacrifice is an integral part of so many enormously successful structures of enjoyment and "techniques of living" that we have to understand it if we are to understand enjoyment at all.⁵

True, the "opposition" of pleasure and duty is rarely treated, in moral philosophy, as a simple matter. Often such oppositions are made to seem more apparent than real; or they can be "reconciled," as Jonson's masque *Pleasure Reconciled to Virtue* so beautifully illustrates. In early Christian psychology, the appetites, when ruled by Reason, lived together in harmony, and have the potential to do so again. The perfection of obedience might even be the supreme exercise of the will. To give is to receive. In Platonic thought, the Good *enables* rightful pleasure; rightful pleasure is the only kind of pleasure that can make us happy; and it is self-evident that man desires happiness.⁶ For example, Dante, commenting on Aristotle's *Politics,* explains that "[s]ince all [man's] ... efforts are directed towards securing happiness, the force of his intellect regulates and rules the rest of him."⁷ Such reconciliations offer two powerful lures. They make promises, thus giving the subject a future; and they offer a technique of self-care, valuable because of the wondrousness of its ability to reconcile tensions, even if they are the very tensions it requires and fabricates. The subject is given work to do, in short; and its efforts will be rewarded, according to the economy of sacrifice that, as Derrida points out, recovers by means of a suspension of calculation whatever it gives away.⁸

In contrast, the notion of the "tight bond between desire and the Law," fundamental to the interpretation of sacrifice explored in this book, resituates the moral dimension altogether. It does so, first of all, by presenting desire as self-perpetuating. Desire desires, above all, its own continuation, not its fulfillment. We need our discontent in order to feel and enjoy our desire, and if events do not conspire to make us feel dissatisfied, we will arrange our own privations. The laws that we invent to guide our behavior use lack as a principle of design, intervening on one score so as to pointedly ignore another, fixing us here so that we will stay away from there, and so on. The law creates and shapes desire by creating and shaping for us the *experience* of lack: without the vessel, we do not know the void inside that is pushing us on into the future by asking to be filled; without the injunction, we do not know the freedom we may now want to search for. As Žižek suggests, the law can function phantasmatically to conceal the impossibility of ever fulfilling desire; we convince ourselves that we feel dissatisfied because some unpleasant rule or forbidding authority figure stands in our way, not because fulfillment is simply out of the question.[9] But it is, of course, that very "lack" of fulfillment that creates newness, curiosity, and indeed culture.

Why is fulfillment—at least, lasting, stable fulfillment—out of the question? For a variety of reasons, some of which will sound familiar to those who know the rhetoric of *vanitas*. The object of desire is incapable of giving lasting satisfaction. It is always, so to speak, a "prop" for desire, never the thing desire "wants"—partly because what desire wants above all is to keep on desiring. Also, full possession is impossible for mortal creatures; our objects of desire are always, by definition, alienable. In the "imaginary" register ("imaginary" is the Lacanian term for modes of desire that try to supplement lack through fantasies of unity and constancy), we might be disturbed by these failures of satisfaction, preferring to blame them on others, and best of all, on the Other (the "unbarred O")—on a deity, or an order of things, or a natural Law, which we have imagined according to our needs.[10] We imagine the Other as full, so that the Other can explain and potentially supplement our lack. Perhaps, we say to ourselves, we are timid about pursuing desire, or feel that we never get what we want, not because there is something in the nature of desire that *prefers* frustration, but because the Other is punishing us, or wants us to suffer so that we will become a better person.

But we are capable of so valuing what *is not* fully knowable or reducible to our own image that we can even find therein the very meaning of divinity. In Lacanian terms, the Ōther—the "barred" O—is what lies behind the fantasy of the full, watchful Other. This "barred" O can never fully be accounted for, nor is its meaning exhausted in taking account of us. The Other is one way of designating the "symbolic order," the open-ended and unpredictable network of signifiers that constructs human subjectivity. It does so by designating signifiers for the subject ("I," "daughter," and so on), and patterning those signifiers in relation to others ("you," "mother," and so on). To submit to, accept, or identify with these signifiers is no easy matter, and psychoanalytic theory has emphasized the losses suffered by *jouissance* when the subject "enters" the symbolic order.[11] With no stable sense of self, no name to answer to, "I" am, first of all, not an "I," but a multiplicity of possibilities, for joy and despair, for welcome and aversion; with no stable sense of what is "interior" or "exterior" to "me," the thing that I will someday recognize as my toe could be as other to me, as deserving of curiosity and investigation, as the hand that holds me. Someday, "I" am organized; I recognize borderlines between myself and others, my desires tend to follow some paths and not others. I mourn these lost pathways; but when I had them, they were not "my" pathways, because there was no "me." To be a "me," I have to *not* be other things—I have to *not* be, at the same time, "you." Desire is the result. It is my response to the fact that "I" can come into being only by being differentiated from everything else, which "I" now feel that I "lack" (and which I can never recover).

But desire's futility can also be a joy. We can, as Deleuze and Guattari have argued, find ecstasy in the very experience of desire.[12] Undoubtedly, we shy away from the satisfaction of our yearnings because we do not relish a final confrontation with the impossibility of lasting bliss. But the *jouissance* produced by our endless evasions of satisfaction suggests that we have found a way to make it up to ourselves. Desire desires to continue—it is "change as such," says Lacan—and prohibition can intensify the *jouissance* of fulfillment forever deferred, not just explain to us why we have to endure the wait (*Ethics of Psychoanalysis*, 293). Rather than restraining desire, the law perpetuates it, sometimes jubilantly; and insofar as this is true, desire is in part *for* the law. We do not give up passion for the sake of the law's compensations; instead, as Saint Paul well knew, the renunciations demanded by the law keep desire going.[13] The more we renounce, the more difficult it is to stop renouncing; the more we exercise our moral sense, the harder it becomes to keep our imperfections in perspective. Rarely do our self-excoriations make us feel permanently improved; more often they make us need even more self-excoriation, so as to satisfy the demands of the previous ones. I blame myself for being a proud and selfish creature; then I try to repair the problem by telling myself that I have not begun to blame myself enough, because this helps me to feel more humble. But only for a while, because shortly, in order to continue feeling humble, I will have to reproach myself for feeling too contentedly humble. We do more devotional exercises, buy more self-help books. Discipline does not teach us the identity of pleasure with the good; rather, it drags desire out into the open, pours gasoline on it, and sets it on fire, which is why it so easily becomes desire's object as well as its means.

If desire is fundamental to subjectivity, then nothing emerges from us that is not produced by our desire, including the law. Further, insofar as desire has a vanishing point, that vanishing point is *jouissance*—an experience of (virtually) unbearable intensity, not pleasure in the possession of an object or a feeling of fulfillment. The concept of *jouissance* has little in common with the notion of satisfaction. It is libidinal rapture at or beyond the limit of our endurance—most obviously orgasm, but by extension, any ecstasy that depends in some way on the exacerbation of sensuous experience. *Jouissance* is not pleasure, because it involves unpleasurable excesses of sensation; it is not the good, insofar as it is not necessarily "good for us."[14] Nor does it satisfy "me"; "I" lose "myself" in it. "I" am even, all too often, averse to it, because "I" do not *want* to lose myself in it. Indeed, one of the many reasons we prolong desire through techniques of restraint is that we fear the shattering effects of *jouissance*. But we also find the approach to *jouissance* irresistible.

To sum up: restraint, sacrifice, duty, "containment," *are* forms taken by desire. Discipline enhances *jouissance*; it multiplies and extends its possibilities, its potential for the remaking of identities. As Deleuze and Guattari put it, "*Training axiom—destroy the instinctive forces in order to replace them with transmitted forces.*"[15] But the intimacy between desire and the law is not one we readily acknowledge. We are so accustomed to pitting morality against desire that it is simply hard to believe that morality *is* a form of desire, or desire is what morality *is*. Most of us prefer to think that we are split between restraint and passion, because doing so helps us to conceal the more radical splitting on which the subject is founded, the fact that the subject is founded on the "desire of the other."[16] Lacan's famous theory of the "mirror stage" tries to explain how the subject comes into being as a consequence of splitting, just as we might imagine a unicellular organism becoming aware of itself only after it splits into two. According to Lacan, the subject comes into being when the infant first sees—or recognizes—its image in a mirror. The image in the mirror seems to have some striking properties; it appears to be unified, shapely, and gravity-free. The infant learns at this moment that it has a distinctive shape, does not coincide with anything outside itself, and so on. But the infant also intuits that the image it sees is *not* itself; it is "other" because it is an image, suspended in space only now recognized as "outside" the infant. The subject "is" this image, but this image is also exterior to it. The fact that the subject can only come into being *by* being split questions the idea that we can come to know ourselves through self-care. The subject does not begin heedlessly, seamlessly, and then have to learn to reflect on itself; it starts *as* a split. The opposition between desire and sacrifice helps the subject to avoid its fundamental multiplicity by pretending that feelings of fragmentation come later, whereas the subject does not exist apart from its multiplicity, its lack of self-presence.

The Making of Knowledge as Enjoyment: Group Desire, Knowledge Production, and Medieval Studies

More important even than identifying with one or the other term of the morality/passion dichotomy is maintaining the dichotomy itself, and the artistry required to negotiate it. A culture's "modes of enjoyment" will present themselves as the "perfect" balance between discipline and pleasure, so that the U.S. company man could distinguish himself from the automaton he once liked to believe was the Japanese worker, as well as from the native welfare parasite who gobbled up his hard-earned money in taxes.[17] The delicacy of the "perfect balance," looked at another way, is a plasticity—necessary if the distinction between enjoyment and the law is to be broadly sustainable. Because the multiplicity of our being can never be fully or finally resolved or unified, we leave no stone unturned in the attempt; if we contradict ourselves, *tant pis*—after all, it seems to the subject that its life is at stake, which in a way it is. So, we try to make ourselves into a self-present oneness by treating our feelings of fragmentation as a disturbance "within" us (rather than the disturbance that *is* us). Then we can get to work on it, "ethicizing" it so that it becomes something we could choose *not* to feel. We excoriate ourselves for giving way to it, and so on. Finally, we sublime this inside space in which we have been excoriating ourselves as purified and made important by our very attention to it (Derrida discusses the affinity between secrecy, sacrifice, and the sacred in *The Gift of Death*). If none of this works—and it won't, not completely—we may try exteriorizing our multiplicity, refinding it in a bad *worldly* variance that contrasts with the unity of our own group. In this way, the opposition of desire and sacrifice is closely linked to "othering" or "dissociation," to the phantasmic contrast between the good and the bad multitudes familiar, for example, in apocalyptic discourse, when what Eugen Weber calls the "purified remnant" finally gets away from the insufficiently burnished swarms.[18]

The distinction between the law and enjoyment is constitutive of the group as well as the individual subject. Exploring whether and how this distinction works at a particular time can contribute substantially to scholarly inquiry. Study of the ethical theories and practices of a group should not be dismissed as mere history of (elite) ideas, because it attends directly to "desiring production"—to the ways a given culture transforms its desires into objects of exchange. We can ask why and how a group presents law and enjoyment as opposed, and when, and the same goes for attempts to mitigate or undo their opposition. Some discourses try to sever the tight bond between desire and the law, and some cinch the knot. Mechanisms (including talk) of repression are not smoke screens for the design and dissemination of enjoyment, but fundamental operators of this process, capable of producing a "really remarkable diversity" of effects and transformations. The bond between desire and the law is a *relationship,* not an identity. What opens up for us thereby is the possibility that there have been many different ways to conceptualize, and live out, that bond. There are probably just as many different ways to analyze these techniques of living. One analogy to the potential effects of defamiliarizing the distinction between the law and enjoyment is how the defamiliarizing of literary and ordinary language enabled the "new historicism," deconstruction, neo-Marxist theory, and humanist anthropology and geography. The value of such a shift is not pluralism, however. Thought is a group process. Methods have their real effects by engaging with other, often contrary, methods. This is why differences between methods are real but also have effects that elude, that "supplement," their specific formulations, because "exchanges" of ideas, however antagonistic, always transform the terms being defended.[19]

Michel de Certeau argues that "each 'discipline' maintains its ambivalence of being at once the law of a group and the law of a field of scientific research."[20] In fact, these two laws are interdependent and inseparable. The symbolic structure of subjectivity, and hence the tight bond between desire and the law, is the matrix of group activity in general and research in particular. Group desire makes what we call knowledge. *There is no other kind of knowledge than this; this is what knowledge is, and we make it*. It is neither illusory nor objective; it is an artifact, carefully crafted, tested, debated, within groups, between groups, over time, and across cultures. In the historical and cross-cultural processes of its adjudication, it changes, because different questions, responsibilities, and institutions arise.

The idea that knowledge is something we make over time and space may itself help us rethink how different moments connect and disconnect. Courtly love is part of the genealogy of psychoanalysis, and for this reason it is also part of contemporary theory, because of its turn to language (cybernetic and otherwise), its role in structuring desire and work, and hence its (re)placement of sacrifice at the center of the human question. Courtly love has attracted the interest of some of the most influential theorists of this century: Jacques Lacan, Kenneth Burke, Julia Kristeva, Deleuze and Guattari, Slavoj Žižek. Crisscrossing this revival of courtly love discourse and its theory-drive (e.g., Capellanus's *Art of Courtly Love*), psychoanalysis has been largely responsible for the recent return of the humanities to the topics of ethics and sexuality.[21] Just prior to that emergence, "new historicism" refound Norbert Elias's readings of the courtly arts as social practice, inspired by the thinking of Michel Foucault, Pierre Bourdieu, and Michel de Certeau to read the courtly arts as social discourse and practice. In Stephen Orgel's *The Illusion of Power* (1975), Jonathan Goldberg's *James I and the Politics of Literature* (1983), and Richard McCoy's, *The Rites of Knighthood* (1989), the new-historicist emphasis on the textuality of everything that counts as "history" made courtly discourse count again; the intimacy of pleasure and power therein inspired some new historicists to reread Freud and Derrida.[22] In Chaucer studies, these crossings have informed the most definitive and provocative work of recent decades—for example, Paul Strohm's recent work on Žižek and Lancastrian monarchy; David Wallace's use of gender theory in *Chaucerian Polity*; Lee Patterson's rereadings of "Theban repetition" in *Chaucer and the Subject of History*. Carolyn Dinshaw's *Chaucer's Sexual Poetics* opened up queer ways of reading Chaucerian criticism as well as Chaucer's poetry; Gayle Margherita challenged medieval studies' enchantment with the past in *The Romance of Origins*.²³

The relations between psychoanalytic and historicist approaches to medieval culture have, of course, often been strained. Psychoanalysis is sometimes regarded as ahistorical and exclusively focused on individual subjectivity, despite the fact that history is crucial to the thought of Freud and Lacan. Historicism's use of psychoanalytic concepts has, in turn, often been underappreciated by theorists who regard its understandings of change as facile. But many historicists today, even in Anglo-American medieval studies, appeal to psychoanalytic concepts of subjectivity, memory, image, narrative, body, and signification, in highly productive ways. Historicist approaches have engaged psychoanalytic ones, and vice versa, powerfully enough to produce Walter Benjamin, the Frankfurt School, Frantz Fanon, Susan Sontag, Sol Friedlander, Deleuze and Guattari, and Hortense Spillers. Judith Butler's *The Psychic Life of Power* and Robert Miklitsch's *Psycho-Marxism* indicate the continuing productivity of thinking the psyche through the social, and vice versa.²⁴ The use of psychoanalytic theory extends all the way across the human sciences, from political science (e.g., James Glass) to epidemiology (e.g., David Levine), as even a cursory glance at the *Journal of Culture and Psychology* would reveal.

Historicist medievalists who have done important work with psychoanalytic concepts include David Aers, Sarah Beckwith, Tony Spearing, Sarah Kay, Simon Gaunt, Sarah Stanbury, Larry Scanlon, Sheila Delany, Elizabeth Scala, Patricia Ingham, Jeffrey Cohen, and Michael Uebel. The cross-pollination of historicism and psychoanalysis remains vital within as well as without medieval studies. The future is bright; there remains much to learn about the history of the signifier from cognitive science.²⁵ (For example, Merlin Donald argues that acquiring the ability to imagine, narrate, and perform representations of the counterfactual was decisive for the invention of tools and fire.)²⁶ And much remains to be learned about historicism in general, and its medievalist versions in particular, from the perspective of the ethics of psychoanalysis. The idea that discipline is closely related to desire may help us address why and how, in literary and historical studies today, the discipline of medieval studies *stands for* discipline. If sacrifice serves enjoyment, what does this suggest about historicism's view of its ethical responsibility to the past—its obligation to put aside present interests? This question has been pursued by Charles Hûchet, María Rosa Menocal, and Kathleen Biddick, to name just a few.[27] Polemic, then, is only one way psychoanalysis and historicism have engaged each other in medieval studies, and itself bespeaks a certain mutual fascination. It is always worth remembering that Freud (who called transferences "new editions" and "facsimiles") and historicist philology were *both* part of the shifts in knowledge production that took shape in the later nineteenth century. A history of such exchanges lies behind this book, and I hope I have begun to indicate some of my debts.

Sentience and the Signifier: Techniques of Living and the History of Sensitivity

Considering in greater detail what is at stake in theorizing sacrifice as enjoyment will also help us with questions that have emerged about the role of the signifier in particular histories. The particular history I will be most concerned with here is the history of courtly love, including its history in theory. Both have something to say about the historicity of "sentience."

The relations between embodiment and signification have been powerfully analyzed by Elaine Scarry's *The Body in Pain*, especially the concept of "sentience." Sentience, according to the *Oxford English Dictionary*, is "consciousness, susceptibility to sensation"; something is sentient if it "feels or is capable of feeling," has "the power or function of sensation or of perception by the senses."[28] Sentience is awareness of aliveness, thus of sensuousness and embodiment. Techniques of living stylize this capacity for sense-feeling and awareness, and the functions and powers based thereon. Through various regimens, we rework our aliveness and extend its reach through prosthesis.[29] In doing so, we make tracks in the real, but we also can pleasurably imagine that we repair our faults, by trying to reduce the sphere of our nonknowledge, the group thought that thinks us, and the insentience of the very signifiers that give rise to subjectivity. The signifier, as Deleuze and Guattari put it, bears "witness to '*an inhumanity immediately experienced in the body as such.*'"[30]

Insentience is not necessarily the nonawareness of a dead thing. It is also the opacity, to us, of the inhuman structures that structure the human, and emerge in our artifacts. Paradoxically, the very regimens and artifacts we create to reduce our helplessness (which means also our non- or irresponsibility) reflect back to us the uncanny autonomy of all our objects, including those inside us. The signifier is alien to the realm of subjectivity. Signifiers do not know or think or desire anything. They are not present to themselves. Nor does the subject, group or individual, bring the signifier into being; it is shaped by subjectivity only insofar as it shapes subjectivity. We try all the time to supplement its opacity with the kinds of meanings that mean something to subjectivity, but in the end these are still just collocations of yet more signifiers. Insentience lives an uncanny life within or through us. But the effect of subjectivity is produced by the *interplay* of insentience with sentience.

The telescopes that help us see the stars, the buildings that house the shelters that are our bodies, are insentient; and yet we extend sentience through them. But the more we make the machines and products that extend subjectivity into the world, the more insentience is part of us, or we are part of it. Forces are at work within us that do not "mean" anything; parts of ourselves cannot account for themselves. The work cannot account for itself, or disclose anything about itself, or even be questioned. The problems it poses for us resemble those posed by the object, as analyzed by Georges Bataille: we can know the object because we can measure, describe, and test it, but only in the mode of its alterity or exteriority.[31] As extensions of sentience, our works participate in our aliveness, but only insentiently, and this is why work is alienating. Marx's theory of alienation as the result of our loss of intimacy with our works is a "political-economical" conceptualization of the interchange between sentience and insentience. Lacan asks, "man has the possibility of making his desires tradeable or salable in the form of products.... How is it possible?"[32] But however much alienation may be differently designed in different times and places, or by different modes of production, even the potter loses her work the moment she creates it, to alterity. According to the book of Genesis, even God had this problem.

The insentience of our works—including our techniques of living—is why we fear them. Though "ours," they turn a deaf ear to our invocations, like the idols we make out of "stocks and stones." Medieval literary theory often opposes the rhetorician's investment in technique to the struggle of a sincere subject aiming to express truth; the hope is that the latter will breathe life into the signifier, because the letter killeth. The problem of insentient matter was the focus of medieval Europe's most arduous philosophical project, the Christianizing of Aristotelian and Averroistic thought, and of the Manichaean dualism that almost kept Augustine, Christianity's reluctant rhetorician, from the bosom of the church, threatening again in the twelfth century to steal Languedoc, Provence, and other parts of Western and Central Europe wherever Cathars, Waldensians, and Bogomils were to be found. Cathar territory was also the territory of the poets of *fin 'amors,* whose sincerity was in question from the very beginning ("I'm the only one who means it when I say I love you"). As would again be the case in the fourteenth and fifteenth centuries, when Wycliffe queried the nature of transubstantiation, many of medieval Christianity's crises, including the "Reformation," consisted of stumbling over matter, hitting the wall of insentience, and hitting it again when language threatened to lose its power to convey spirit and become either overly material or not material enough.

The ethical problem of work derives from the insentient status of the work. Whatever artifact or technique we bring into being is always, immediately, exterior to us; by making our works, we lose them, which is why some artists cannot sell their sculptures. With them, we lose something of ourselves—at the very least, one more inscrutable object has been added to the world that, so far as communication is concerned, seems to turn its back on me. It is not hard to recuperate this as sacrifice, or to see why a certain consent to loss might seem to be a sine qua non of the will to make.

Exchange disseminates, but thereby can also groupify, the loss attendant on production; it provides time for objects to acquire the patina of value, being touched by many hands, "returning" with a (sublime) difference. Sublimation poses the question, indeed, of what compensates us, and the other, when we send one of our works out into the world.

Sacrifice defends us from the insentience of our works by suspending our relation to work. Derrida proposes that, for sacrifice to appear as such, it must take place during an atemporality that is also an *aneconomy,* an instant when actions cannot be referred to a future, products cannot be anticipated, and rewards cannot be calculated. It is the impossible time and timing of the gift. "Understanding...and reason cannot seize...it; neither can they negate [it]: in the act of *giving death,* sacrifice suspends both the work of negation and work itself, perhaps even the work of mourning."[33]

But, as Bataille also discovered, the violence and excess of sacrifice keeps close company with calculation. The impossible time of the gift does not so much suspend economy as time it. Sacrifice means to get back, with interest, whatever it renounces. Like apocalypse, the aneconomic moment suspends, even violates, time so that the time after will be different from the time before—more dignified, more sublime: excoriated. The tight bond between calculation and aneconomy is one of the organizing principles of the Christian testament, and of countless Christian discourses in the Middle Ages, but a literal reference to sacrifice in the Preamble to Frederick II's *Constitutions of Melfi* reveals the indivisibility of the material economy of work and the sublime economy of grace: "And so we...wish to render unto God a double payment for the talent granted us, out of devotion to Jesus Christ, who has given us all we possess. Therefore, we will sacrifice a young calf in honor of justice and law-making."[34] The exaltation of the law requires that the gift be returned with the difference of the signifier, the signifier as humiliator. A young calf returns the value of "all we possess" only as *marker* of how little we can really afford to give if we are to stay alive. But just there is where the facts of life reenter the picture, especially for the young calf who died on that occasion. The sacrificed "work" doubles the minimum and therefore can still be counted.

According to Scarry, the "vibrancy" and "certainty" of sentience, particularly in the exacerbated form of pain, can be used to "substantiate" (to confirm the substantiality of) abstractions and "cultural fictions" such as lordship or country.[35] This work of substantiation confers the value of sentience on insentient ideas. Insentient things are made to seem alive and to have the values of life: energy, awareness, sensitivity, appreciation of the divinity of aliveness, so much so that gratitude will seem a higher form of aliveness. Our philosophical traditions privilege sentient life—the more sensitive, the better—as though life were self-evidently a good, *the* Good, a gift for which we should be grateful. The subject's ability to be so aware that it can even be aware of itself is treated as godsend, something that falls from above.[36]

The privileging of awareness has a long political history, in the form of the sentient Law: "as the soul dwells in the heart of man, and gives life to the body, and supports it, so justice dwells in the king, who is the life and sustenance of his realm."[37] If the soul is to justice as the heart is to the king, then the Law (justice) is so far from insentience and arbitrariness as to be the very principle of the realm's animation, which is to say, the animation of matter. The discourse of justice, *sol iustitiae*, sublimes the Law by associating it with maximum sentience, that is, with the power to give the precious gift of life.

But sentience is a double-edged sword. If, as Scarry has suggested, "pain is the equivalent in felt-experience of what is unfeelable in death," this is so because pain is the form of sentience that registers the *trauma* of aliveness.[38] Pain reveals that the gift of life is *really* the gift of death— that life is aversive—startling, anxiogenic (it cannot be prepared for), and demanding (it requires constant vigilance). Nietzsche tells the story of one of King Midas's characteristically overreaching questions, What is the nature of man's greatest good? The satyr Silenus replies (under duress): "[w]hat would be best for you is quite beyond your reach: not to have been born, not to *be*, to be *nothing*. But the second best is to die soon."[39]

To desire is always to call into question the value of living (which is one reason why doing so can be so enjoyable). If our good were self-evident, if we had achieved satisfaction, we would not have to hunt down satyrs to ask them questions about it. Man can possess no form of the Good better than not being Man in the first place. Our good is not *a* good, not an object or service, but nothing at all: the nothing that preceded our work and works, our desires and curiosity. Our good is no thing and nothing; no good is any good to us or for us. Our mode of being is not possession or satisfaction, but desire. Perhaps, then, the biggest trouble we have with the good—with the object—is that we do not, in the first instance, want it, or want what it means for us. This is one reason why, once inserted into the order of the goods, we find the rewards so disappointing.[40]

The chief difference between Silenus's formulation and Innocent III's *On the Misery of the Human Condition* is that Innocent does not think life's aversiveness is such a big secret. *Contemptus mundi* does not depress the self-evident value of life so that we will turn to something apparently more precious; its enjoyment comes straight from the death drive, as its repetitive form confirms. *Contemptus mundi,* to be sure, joins in the opposition between enjoyment and *ascesis;* but what beats inside it may not be a heart. The death drive is formulated in Freud's *Beyond the Pleasure Principle* as the creature's urge to return to a state of inanimacy.[41] Why do we repeat unpleasurable, even traumatic, experiences? What economy of pleasures or goods, what conception of an organism (self-)regulated for maximum pleasure by means of access to the most reliable goods, can explain the spectacle of human (self-)destructivity?[42] The insentience that is within "me" but beyond me—that which is "in me more than myself"—drives me as well as frightens me, indeed frightens me *because* it drives me.[43]

The strength of the hold insentience has on the living is also the import of the birth trauma. Before choosing any object (itself the prototype of making one), we must choose sentience: to breathe, to live, to not be indifferent to life. This is why the moment before an infant begins to breathe is such a critical one, even if the baby is healthy, and some perfectly healthy babies never take the bait. The newborn who, upon learning that Hannibal had crossed the Alps, begged to return to his mother's womb, decided against "the traumatic state of helplessness which birth introduces" and the lifetime, however brief, of vigilant (self-)defense that must follow.[44] Our techniques of living must work as hard to interest us in life as they do to keep death—or the wrong kind of death—at bay. They overvalue the strength of the appetites and the irresistibility of their objects in order to *substantiate* them—to improve on their power to compel us. If *contemptus mundi* tells a lie, it is that we desire life too much. Maybe we can be persuaded that what we want is not just life, but life perfected by techniques of living. But we can be so lured because these techniques *enable* our enjoyment. They try to drive our drives by repetitions that call to the drives by promising endless beginnings *and* endings. We can desire the unpleasure of discipline because it substantiates the absence of our good.

But could the pleasures of aliveness really be so intermittently or imperfectly seductive as to require a *paideia* to keep them before our eyes? We spend so much time pursuing them; and the wish of every creature to keep its life was acknowledged even in the ascetic discourses of the Middle Ages. "I is an other."[45] Or, to go further, it is the ego that is other to everything else. When Freud reads the death drive as the organism's drive to die *in its own way*, "its own" refers not to the ego but to the organism as a whole. It is not that our desire to live and grieve over our losses are illusions; it is that they are only part of our story.

Techniques of living define the very desires and objects they seem to master. If intensified (almost) to the point of unpleasure, pleasure, now in the form of *jouissance*, shares pain's ability to focus subjectivity on the fact of its sentience and therefore on its embodiment. *Jouissance* is the point at which pleasure and pain crisscross, when there are no more objects, and the only thing left for desire to desire is the unknowable beyond of insentience. With the loss of its objects, the *I* also loses its self-presence—or, at least, the vulnerability of its self-presence becomes felt experience. Pleasure protects us from *jouissance* by delivering as much *jouissance* as the *I* can bear and still be there to bear it.

Techniques of living and dying have historically entailed changing notions of what makes life worth living, and what is worth dying for. In these annals, sentience acquires, by art, the value of the artful, that is to say, of work and the work. Sentience becomes an artifact: "sophisticated," "cultured," "refined," "polished." (Or otherwise: "crude," "rude," "dull.") The "gentil tercelet" says to the lower-ranking birds in Chaucer's *Parliament of Fowls*, "what love is, thow canst nouther seen ne gesse."[46] The lowborn have no "sentement," no gentility of heart, and therefore no sensitivity to pain and loss. "Sentement" belongs to the rhetoric of the sublime, the elevated, that which stands out and is set apart. The practices associated with "*courtoisie*," and later with "civility," "civilization," and "culture," promise to rarefy our aliveness, which also means to mortify it. "[I]n myn herte is korven every veyne," says Chaucer's royal eagle and aspiring *finamen*—another young creature in danger, but now proud of its anxiety (l. 425).

The most persistent and powerful narratives of European historiography concern the mannering of sentience. One is the "rise" of courtly love and the individual during the twelfth century's "revolution in sentiment" or "renascence."[47] Courtly love's emergence is linked to heightened sentience through the symbolics of (re)birth: Kristeva calls it "a miraculous creation of the twelfth century."[48] Indeed, courtly love designs the future of amorous European subjectivity by subliming sublimation. The technique of raising the object to the dignity of the Thing is itself exalted, as a consequence of which its object—the Lady—is doubly fascinating, as not only "she," but the artifice that makes her, now points us toward our *jouissance*. What, then, could be more courtly than European historiography's fascination with courtly love—with the topics of desire, spectacular language, and their interdependence in the history of styles of European feeling?[49]

The continuing power of courtly modes of enjoyment to organize desire is evidenced in the importance of the early lyric to the Romance philologies of the nineteenth century, when the nations of Europe took their historical-linguistic turn.[50] In the last century, theory's linguistic turns—both structuralist and poststructuralist—also turned toward desire. The escalating violence of the nation-state, the emergence of fascism, and the particular mystification of the object enabled by commodification all pointed to a *linkage* between fanaticism and rationalization that required distinctly post-Enlightenment techniques of knowledge production and analysis.

Courtly love has participated in these attempts to reformulate the political ethics of aesthetics, especially in connection with themes of historical change (rupture and renewal) and subjectivity (sadomasochism, acting "against interests," the sentimentality and connoisseurship of brutal-sophisticated men and women). For Kristeva, the joy *(joie, joio, jòia)* of the troubadour is in utterance, in *breaking into* song. It is an irrecoverable joy, but affects us still through the nostalgia provoked by its absence.[51] Menocal links the courtly lyric to the theme of rupture: the lyric breaks, vulgar, ebullient, with classical literary languages. But, for Menocal, the rebelliousness of the lyric links it to postmodernity, not to the lost medieval past.[52] Both associate the lyric with a special aliveness, the aliveness of lost beginnings or of fast-breaking contemporaneity, which is or has been in danger.

For Žižek, courtly love had to await "the emergence of masochism" in the later nineteenth century before we were able to grasp its "libidinal economy"; some of its most significant meanings could only be "read retroactively." The courtly letter insists in history, forging new signifying chains that discipline *jouissance,* whereby the "logic of courtly love continues to define the contours of the relation between the sexes."[53] But even in the eighteenth century, Swift's Celia poems—which, if I may say so, have the most remarkable effects on readers of any poetry written in that century—reprise the relation between the abject and the sublime that also fascinated Arnaut Daniel, William Dunbar, and eventually Lacan. Swift even accommodates the relation to the register of organic life; yellow tulips (courtly ladies, Celia) *grow* from dung ("A Lady's Dressing Room"). A century of gardeners indeed. Courtly love has not timed out. It is revocalized whenever the relationship between *jouissance* and submission to the signifier is historically repositioned. Deleuze and Guattari's comments on courtly love emphasize the power of sadomasochistic discipline to rupture the group and individual subjects, psyches, and histories (*"destroy the instinctive forces in order to replace them with transmitted forces"*).[54] The special aliveness of the languages of and about courtly love breaks through the boundaries of past and present, enabling the writing of new kinds of histories concomitant with transformations in the history of art.

The History of Art

Lacan's remarks on the history of art begin his discussion of courtly love in *The Ethics of Psychoanalysis*. Courtly love emerges ex nihilo; it is a breakaway moment in the history of the signifier, when changing forms renew the relation of the symbolic order to *jouissance*, or *"das Ding."*[55] Freud used the term *das Ding* to describe the subject's intuition of being inhabited by a Thing, something or someone unknown, a stranger, an uncanny "neighbor" *(Nebenmensch)*. Is this Thing inside us, or are we inside it? *Das Ding* is a not-quite reification or personification of those processes inaccessible to the subject, but on whose functioning (and breakdown) the subject nonetheless depends. Lacan's coinage *extimité* refers to the uncanny inside-outsideness of the signifiers (codes, markers, mnemonics, "-emes") whose movements structure, but are absent from, consciousness. *Das Ding* is an effect of signification, brought into being at the same time as the subject. It is a figure for that "Real" part of our being inaccessible to the subject it constitutes.[56] Our corporeal being—including and especially our *jouissance*—lives on regardless of the split that founds the subject (e.g., in the intricate but nonsubjective decision making of our nerves), as our living being knows, and is knowable, in ways that create but are also extrinsic to subjectivity and even sentience.

The figure of *das Ding* is central to Lacan's understanding of the history of the signifier. This history consists of the varied ways in which the subject, so to speak, tries to speak to the Thing, and the Thing tries to speak through the subject—not necessarily in the mode of communication or expressivity, but always in the mode of *effecting* activity by means of the marking function. The subject indicates the void place of the Thing by decorating that spectral absence with the signifier, as the Invisible Man's clothes make his invisibility visible. When an object is "raised to the dignity of the Thing," that is, given the function of standing in for the absent Thing, that object is rendered sublime. It will now have the function of marking the marking function itself, of making spectacular the effectivity of *showing*, of being able-to-be-seen, even of being able-to-see. The colorful patterns on a butterfly's wings do not so much "mean"—if they do, that function is secondary—as they mark the butterfly as able-to-be-seen, without need of any particular looking back.[57] It is, as the God of Love might say of Alceste in *The Legend of Good Women*, to show that one *is*.

The history of the signifier includes, but is not limited to, the making of meaning. Barbara Johnson explains that "signifiers can generate effects even when the signified is unknown"; because of this, "[when] one writes, one writes more than (or less than, or other than) one thinks." One may be trying to write a text, but instead one will be participating in "textuality," "the manifestation of an open-ended, heterogeneous, disruptive force of signification and erasure that transgresses all closure."[58] This open-ended process is the history of the signifier. It is a tangled, nonlinear history of diversions of previous arrangements of signifiers. "Signifying chains" can strike out in unprecedented directions or double back on themselves. Lacan's ex nihilo is a *function* of just such a rhizomatic web, and is foregrounded or sublimed whenever the mirror cracks and the domesticated, boustrophredonic fabric "floats wide," as it does for the Lady of Shalott the moment *jouissance* strikes. It is not so much, however, that the tapestry/text must be torn as that its inherent incapacity for perfect repetition makes its growth uncontrollable. This does not mean "chaotic," but rather the unpredictability characteristic even of systematic replication, like cells trying to follow blueprints for reproduction and *thereby* producing organic change.

Courtly love, in Lacan's account, raises the Lady to the dignity of the Thing. This is extraordinary, because medieval women are "nothing more than a correlative of the functions of social exchange" (*Ethics of Psychoanalysis*, 147). Can anything be made to count apart from exchange—including men—a question asked by both *The Knight's Tale* and *Troilus and*

Crisdeyde? Courtly writing also marks men as a correlative of the functions of social exchange; men are wards, bridegrooms, prisoners, and *vileins*. They can occupy the whole range of uncanny sentient objects that feature so largely in aristocratic economies. The *trobairitz*, the women troubadours, write to the *finamen* in a common idiom as if they saw that men and women were both used and sublimed by (sacrificial) exchange in alliance formation.[59]

The uncanniness of the lady, furthermore, is linked to her *access to jouissance*, not just to her status *as jouissance*. If the subliming of the Lady registers certain "discontents" of the age, it does so, in part, by affirming the *jouissance* of the woman. Her vulnerability to exchange cannot extinguish the possibility of her *jouissance* until she is driven out of life altogether, and not much more than this, perhaps, can be said of the masculine *finamen*, however differently privileged he may have been. It is true that Emelye's situation in The Knight's Tale differs unenviably from that of Palamon and Arcite, and also true that in the end (so to speak) each suffers from a certain positioning in the order of the signifier. The Lady is, qua Lady, an affirmation of the status of women as subjects, insofar as the subject *is* a certain organization of sentience that *is moved* through exchange, where exchange is not the operation of a purely rational systematicity, but is founded on the arbitrariness of the Law, and provides the routes along which *jouissance* rides. Paradoxically, if she is an "object" raised to the dignity of the Thing, she *must also be* the subject speaking to and from the standpoint of the Thing, because that is what the subject *is:* a signifier in the discourse of the Other. If she is the "inhuman partner," standing in the place of the Thing that inhabits the desiring male subject, she must also be the subject, because that is what the subject (also) is: a signifier (characterized by the alterity of the object) standing for or in the place of the Thing.[60] By extension, not contravention, of this logic, the "Lady" does not necessarily designate a "woman." Shifts in grammatical gender and terms for lordship in the troubadour lyric queer the sexual relation: Though, or even *because*, we are correlatives of the functions of social exchange, we are sublime.[61] This is more exciting than it sounds. A mortal discourse—courtly love— says that there is something valuable in "being-as-signifier": in being, as well as articulating, "the sign of a gap, *a beyond relative to every law of utility*" (*Ethics of Psychoanalysis*, 81; emphasis added).

The subject is a version of this gap: a signifier embedded in living being, a sign that living being is beyond utility. In figuring the Lady—or, indeed, the beloved *finamen*—the subject, and thereby living being, says that possessing the goods or the "good" is not how it will find satisfaction. It will find satisfaction in *not* fully possessing goods or the good; it will find satisfaction in having trouble with its objects. Courtly love shows that desire is in fact what we find most difficult to renounce.

Lacan suggests that we might view a given artistic practice—his example is cave painting—as an attempt to render an economy "from the perspective of the Thing" (ibid., 140). This formulation suggests that the Thing has a standpoint—not a conscious, self-present standpoint, but a standpoint nonetheless.[62] How do all the codes, switchpoints, and (neuro)transmitters that constitute the Real unconscious Thing from which the effect of subjectivity emerges "see" the economy that supports them? Objects of exchange in the Middle Ages were often seen as material signifiers—whether prisoners, children, spouses, serfs, booty, land, animals, or relics. Medieval economies exchange, and are preoccupied by the value of, objects characterized by aliveness or even sentience. These economies are not unable to imagine the calibration of exchange by means of abstract instruments; rather, the relation of abstract instruments to the living, which is to say dying, beings who create them is what is of interest. Courtly love discourse enacts the economy of "feudal" subsistence "seen from the perspective of the Thing"—meaning, among other things, seen as a matter of life and death, as counting absolutely. As a corollary it performs in the theaters of exchange the loss of the artifact that is interdependent with its creation, true whether the artifact in question is an abstract instrument (the euro) or the recollected subject. Courtly love sublimes the very *relationship* between *jouissance* and the movements of the signifier that generate kinship systems, economies, and desiring subjects.

Andreas Capellanus's *The Art of Courtly Love*—a "scholastics of unhappy love," in Lacan's phrase—works to a point of near exhaustion, and gives an effect of inexhaustibility to, the ranking arrangements central to exchange in the twelfth and thirteenth centuries. A treatise on how lovers should speak and behave, *The Art of Courtly Love* reveals that the signifier's power to rank is erogenic in this culture, and that dialogue between different positions in the symbolic (if the lover is of the lesser nobility and the beloved a commoner; if the lover is of the higher nobility and the beloved of the lesser) is a mode of enjoyment. The treatise delivers the pleasures of codification, debate, and verbal "showing," and indicates their productivity with respect to the (verbal) artifact or object of love—a plasticity finally sublimed by the rejection of earthly love at the end of the treatise. Like the feudal object of exchange whose many changes and exchanges it rings, this treatise foregrounds the plasticity of the borderline between the sentient and the insentient or hypersentient. *The Art of Courtly Love* illustrates that desire and its objects are never *not* effects of the signifier—desire can move among ladies, gentlemen, and disciplines, *because* the signifier is at stake in all cases; but it illustrates that the signifier is never not embedded in living being and its *jouissance*. The genealogical relationship between courtly love and (to twist Lacan's phrase) the Freudian "analytics of unhappy love" emerges most clearly on this score. Courtly love and psychoanalysis are different means of making spectacularly apparent the materiality and mobility of desire, its dependence on the signifier and the Law, and our constitutive vacillations between sentience and insentience, subjectivity and objectivity, exteriority and interiority, the orders of the corpus as text and as body.

The Nature of the Law and the Enjoyment of Submission

In Lacan's famous formulation, "*the unconscious is structured like a language*" (*Four Fundamental Concepts of Psychoanalysis*, 20). It is designed by the signifier—by the codes that make language possible. Long before the living being enters into language as such, it has had experience with marking activities—for example, with Kristeva's *chora,* a matrix of heat and light that provides the infant with a point of enjoyment around which she can organize space. The first signifiers we encounter do not "mean" in any conventional sense.

> Before any... individual deduction, even before those collective experiences that may be related only to social needs are inscribed in it, something organizes this field [of the unconscious], inscribes its initial lines of force.... Nature provides—I must use the word—signifiers, and these signifiers organize human re-

lations in a creative way, providing them with structures and shaping them.⁶³

Lacan's emphasis on the priority of the signifier to the construction of human community and subjectivity is the context for his understanding of libido as driven by the rule-bound activity of signifying chains. In Freud's conceptualization of the unconscious as structured activity, the "drive" (*Trieb*) is neither raw nor formless; "it is not simply instinct," as Lacan puts it, but "embodies a historical dimension" (*Ethics of Psychoanalysis*, 111). The drives impress and are impressed by the history of the subject, and therefore partake in the larger movements of the history of the signifier and its productions (ibid., 209).

Lacan derives his understanding of the signifier not only from Claude Lévi-Strauss's readings of the symbolic structuration of human groups, but also from Freud's work on the broken or patched-up connections, the eruptions of "other" signifiers into the "linguistic system," that characterize both the dream-work and parapraxis (*Four Fundamental Concepts of Psychoanalysis*, 25). Signifying chains—DNA, human language—are active and multiple; probabilistic rather than certain; open systems rather than closed ones. The rules that govern the interplay of the signifier constitute the Law and structure *jouissance*. But they also generate "impediment, failures, split" (ibid.). The difference between one signifier and another is necessary to the functioning of signifying chains.⁶⁴ "Discontinuity... is the essential form in which the unconscious first appears to us as a phenomenon... in which something is manifested as a vacillation." The unconscious irrupts/interrupts when desire tries to bring something forward which "demands to be realized," to come into being, "something which appears as intentional... but of a strange temporality." The disruption caused by this "something" is by definition traumatic, because, if nothing else, it demonstrates that the signifying system is neither seamless nor unified and *can* be disrupted. Furthermore, "what occurs, what is *produced*, in this gap, is presented as *the discovery*"; the unconscious is not a predetermined script, but rather an inventive process of divagation exploiting minimal differences (voiced [b] or unvoiced [p]) that can set off earthquakes.

The Law is neither completely determining nor determined. It is not substantive or positive. It means nothing in particular, but consists simply of the rules that enable the condensation and displacement of signifiers. Substantive law will attach itself to this formal Law, but only belatedly. The *nom du père*, the "name of the father," illustrates the point. It is assumed (wrongly, by the way) that the identity of the mother is self-evident, but the father must claim the child symbolically. Paternity depends on signification; the father is "him of whom we are never sure," or, to put it another way, your father is the man who says he is your father. The signifier "father" thus points to the formal, arbitrary character of the symbolic order. The biological father must, to be "father," signify as such. This is why, as Žižek puts it in *Enjoy Your Symptom!*, "there are always two fathers"—the "father" as guarantor of absolute, impartiality, of that aspect of the law that is "no respecter of persons," and the "father of enjoyment," who exercises power capriciously.[65]

Splitting the paternal imago defends against the fact that the impartiality of the law *means* indifference and even arbitrariness.[66] Today, Herod declares, the baby boys will die. The figure of Fortune ($\bar{O}$) exploits this plasticity: what could be more regularly irregular, more fairly unfair, more impartial *and* arbitrary, than Fortune? In Lady Philosophy's words: "Thou wenest that Fortune be chaunged ayens the; but thow wenest wrong *(yif thou that wene):* always tho ben hir maneres."[67] The medieval association of Fortune with the court figures the vulnerability of a courtier's life to the caprice of the lord. The court is driven by the royal will's "sudden change[s] of purpose" (Peter of Blois).[68] The manner of living of the court of Henry II of England is completely dependent on the king's movements: "courtiers as have let themselves be bled, or have taken some purgative, must yet follow their prince forthwith without regard to their own bodies"; "men rush forth like madmen," and "flock...to get tidings of the king's journey."[69]

This "Pandaemonium made visible" results from living the days of one's life in the form of obedience to (and as prosthetic body of) "the head of the kingdom. As the thoughts which come from the head direct all the body, so the commands which come from the king...direct the people, who must be ordered and guided by him" (*Those Who Fought*, 40–41). The head may (or may not) know its reasons; the body is not aware of them in the mode of subjectivity, but obeys and performs these reasons in the mode of exteriority. Obedience to the law depends on its opacity, and the opacity of the law produces the effect of chaos, revealing once again the intimacy between authority and arbitrariness.

INTRODUCTION

The protocols of state *show* (in the Lacanian sense) the enjoyment produced by submission to form. A companion of the King of Bohemia's German envoy to England in 1466 reported that the queen, Elizabeth Woodville, "sat alone at table in a costly golden chair. The queen's mother and the king's sister had to stand below. And if the queen talked with them, they had to kneel before her until she drank water."[70] A similar enjoyment of form and its power to coordinate bodies and the body is discernible in writing on the "just war." According to Stephen Langton, if a soldier were called to service by his lord in an unjust cause, probably no scandal would ensue if he withdrew "from service; but if everyone withdraws, it would cause a scandal and would thus publicize [the king's] guilt. Some of them are obligated to withdraw, since no one of them causes a scandal from his own withdrawal; therefore all are obligated to withdraw from him. But if all of them withdraw, they cause a scandal."[71] Like questions of love in courtly poetry, these paradoxes are "puzzles" in every sense: bewildering tangles that challenge us to find solutions or lose face (*OED*, s.v. "puzzle"). Reasonable demands are always putting reasonable men in impossible positions.

Certainty and uncertainty, the personal and the impersonal, are interdependent, not opposed, in the formative work of the signifier: the personal can only be generated by an impersonal structure of differences; the conditions of possibility of certainty depend on uncertainty. "I," precisely, is a word that *everyone* uses. Identification with the signifier is possible only because the particular referent of the signifier is impossible to fix.

In the mirror stage, the infant is able to take the mirror-image as "hers" because the image is suspended in exteriority and thus susceptible to appropriation. The image gives the nascent subject the idea of form and a specific form in which to see "herself." It promises thereby to fix her into a recognizable position, but the generality that enables this promise also makes it impossible to keep. The image is fascinating partly because it dangles the subject between the iterability of "her" identity and its particularity, the latter of which includes her living being. In a sense, the subject is the effect of this fascination by the signifier.

Lacan stresses that the subject's identification with the mirror-image yields a mixed experience of jubilation and alienation: joy because of the promise of a structured and gravity-free body; alienation because actual bodily experience remains so frustrating. The identification with the image is never complete. The image is "me," but "I" am somewhere in front of it. Hence the subject is founded on the image of the other, an image the subject must accept as "hers" *and* seek to adequate. The subject is the fascinated effect of a suspension between the lived experience of the body and its form, between alienation and identification, and between the certainty and uncertainty of the law (the law, in the form of form, structures "me," but incompletely). Henceforth the question of justice, of "an agency that rewards," will be inseparable from the question of the intelligibility of the body and the subject. The mirror stage constitutes the subject through her submission to a Law whose arbitrariness is the foundation of its power of general application. But because this law is insentient and senseless—because it has no purpose, no identifiable "good" in mind—submission to it is, as Žižek puts it, "obscene enjoyment."[72]

For Lacan, "*das Ding* presents itself at the level of unconscious experience as that which already makes the law.... It is a capricious and arbitrary law, the law of the oracle, the law of signs in which the subject receives no guarantee from anywhere" (*Ethics of Psychoanalysis*, 73). This law is, once again, not meaningful; as oracle, its messages are indecipherable; the reliability of its signs is not vouched for by any god, partly because no "person" speaks it; the person as such is spoken by it. The subject will seek to make sense of the law, to give it reasons and a "face"; indeed, this is one important function of group subjectivity, which relies on the senseless circulation of signifiers to construct the meaning-effects of allegiance. But nothing obviates the foundational senselessness of the Law, or the obscenity of submission to it. One submits for no good reason, and no "good" will come of it. The Law is inseparable from desire because it designs the drives, which is to say that submission to the Law is a form of obscene enjoyment.

Rescue, Help, Charity: Sacrifice and the Group

Courtly love dignifies the oscillation between sentience and insentience that fascinates and constructs the subject. Courtly culture exalts the erogenic and divisive power of the image, making spectacular arts out of sacrifice. The obscene *jouissance* of submission is central to chivalric culture's modes of enjoyment. Its techniques of living form, and form themselves around, this *jouissance*, a process reprised in its rescue fantasies—including fantasies of self-rescue. Heightening the fascination of un/certainty, the courtly warrior takes himself as "an object of knowledge and a field of action," so as to transform, correct, and purify [himself], and find salvation.[73] In chivalric ordinances and romances, this "subjectivation" works clearly on the level of the group as well as the individual subject. The nobleman is to re-create himself as a rescuer and defender of the faith, the Eucharist, his *patria,* his lord, widows, and orphans. As Foucault writes, "the work of oneself and communication with others were linked together."[74]

Freud and Lacan would agree: the Law of the group, the symbolic order, stylizes subjectivity. This is why rescue fantasy is such a powerful means of making sacrifice feel sublimely good. From the standpoint of psychoanalysis, the distinction between self-rescue and rescue of the other is impossible to sustain absolutely. A subject founded on the image of the other must always be other to itself, and the intuition of this split tells the subject there are limits to her agency: her ability to help or even to be helped is finite. But because the subject's desire is founded on that of the other, her enjoyment—which means also her trauma management—will readily take the form of helping or being helped. To sacrifice to the other on whom one's desire is founded is readily assimilated to helping oneself. The subject wants to redress the lack it fears in the other, and wants the other to redress the lack it fears in itself. The Ōther, the symbolic order, is "known" to be lacking, but the lack is disavowed, producing the fantasy of O, and sets in train the invention of apotropaic techniques and objects.

But nothing can change the fact that the other and the Other have limits (Lacan, *Ethics of Psychoanalysis,* 73, 304). The symbolic order does not guarantee meaning, redemption, or enjoyment; its import is the finitude of powers and of the subjects who take shape through their workings. The Ōther is limited because it too desires, and changes. And if the power of the Ōther is limited, then in relation to his finitude man "can expect help from no one"; nor can ultimate enjoyment be attained any more than absolute power (ibid., 293). Rescue and enjoyment are intertwined. We try to stop the gap of desire through fantasies of rescue, and to secure the infallibility of those who help us by giving them our *jouis-*

sance. But nothing can fill the gap desire leaves in the subject and the Other.

The subject is tempted to comfort herself vis-à-vis the waywardness of the Ōther by interpreting its desire as a demand addressed to her. She replaces the indifferent, roving gaze of the Ōther with a look intended for her or her group, alone. She even turns the Ōther's desire into the demand that she *become* a subject. Because she has fantasized this demand, however, there is something persistently inscrutable about it, and thus she cannot fix herself in the form of its addressee. Žižek would say that she "is incapable of translating this desire of the Other into a positive interpellation, into a mandate with which to identify."[75] If the Other's demand is difficult to read, it must be because the subject cannot read well; if the Other cannot get a bead on the subject, it must be because she is not in focus.

Perhaps, then, what the Other wants from her is more self-definition. The Other seems to "call" to the subject, and she is "interpellated" when she identifies with what she hears the Other call her. She will sacrifice her *jouissance* to live up to this nomination, to lead an exemplary life, and she will welcome techniques of living that excoriate her sentience. She wants to become the "purified remnant" of the living being that could not fix itself in the Other's gaze. The Other's fantasized ethical demand is the reflex of the lack she detects in it. In sacrificial enjoyment, the subject denies the contingent, indifferent process that gives her being, by turning her life into a gift of life from the Other. This gift of life is also a "gift of death": if she watches over herself, she will be able to give her life back to the Other, but burnished and perfected.[76]

Ascetic techniques of living reinforce the borderline between self and other, while exploiting its permeability. Vigilance seems to redeem the split in the subject: instead of being irremediably multiple, she takes one part of herself as an object to be watched over and sacrificed. The pain of one part must be transferable to the other's account, who acts for the Other who calculates. The sacrificial subject gets itself and the Other back, with the difference produced by exchanges of enjoyment that burnish the subject-object sufficiently for it to return as gift. The gift of death is a melancholic incorporation of loss and a bid for the surplus promised by the psychic exchanges enabled by extimacy.[77] In short, the subject refuses to mourn the impossibility of full *jouissance*; instead, she defers it, believing that *jouissance* will reward her for sacrificing *jouissance*. This, she tells herself, is why the Other does not really satisfy her: because she is busy preparing herself.

The promise that an other (part of herself) can die on her behalf obscures the fact that no one else can die her death for her.[78] Although I can end my life on someone's behalf, or spend my life serving another, I cannot give them my living substance or sentience directly; they cannot live *my* life, however much they might want to live their lives through me. But I can act out this impossible transfer within myself through the fantasy of group identification. If living and dying set the limits of exchange—or at least pose formidable obstacles to it—sacrifice dissimulates those limits, exchanging *jouissance* for the consolations of identification and "groupification."[79] By means of identification, sacrifice promises to relay suffering from subject to subject, and so readily becomes a group effort.

Charity also obscures and exploits the interdependence of sameness and difference in the subject. If the "*I is an other*," there is no pure self, no pure selflessness, no purely selfless love, and no pure love of self. The idea that self-sacrifice is indeterminate, moreover, is not a modern one. Ockham, Holkot, and other fourteenth-century English psychologists questioned whether enjoyment (*fruitio*, the act of inhering in love with something for its own sake) could be distinguished from the pleasure the self takes in enjoyment.[80] If God mandates what is good for us, then in what way does the assumption of that mandate involve sacrifice? In fourteenth-century psychology, distinctions between self-love and love of God, desire and the Law, subject and object, could not be taken as self-evident. They were, in the strict sense, puzzles.

In *Civilization and Its Discontents*, Freud writes that the greatest technique of living is "the way of life which makes love the centre of everything, which looks for all satisfaction in loving and being loved" (31). Love is "one of the foundations of civilization" because it produces collective as well as individual relations; the "oceanic feeling" of "oneness with the universe," for example, is caused by love's power to dissolve the "boundary between ego and object" (53, 13). As one fourteenth-century mystic put it: "Qwhat is lufe bott transfourmynge of desire In to pe pinge lufyd?"[81] Our vulnerability to transformation is, for Freud, the common ground of religious feeling and of love, and it is fundamental to sacrifice as it is to *jouissance*. Excess enjoyment shatters the subject; at the same time, the sense of risk that characterizes our approaches to *jouissance* honors the irreplaceability of the living being. Sacrifice and charity seem to diminish the risks of approaching *jouissance* by emphasizing the equivalence among subjects-objects of desire. This is why they are difficult to distinguish from the *asceses* that break apart one assemblage of "forces" so that another can take its place (by emphasizing equivalence, sacrifice also remakes identity), and this is why they are so seductive. But when sacrifice is *acknowledged* to be a mode of enjoyment, *jouissance*—that is, not purely for the (abstract) other—remains risky and is not easy to expropriate or appropriate.

Freud sees the negation of particularity characteristic of charity as a form of melancholy. Freud distinguishes between his view of love and that of Saint Paul on this score. The Christian object of love must be an object of identification (the "neighbor") (Freud, *Civilization and its Discontents*, 62–66; Rickels, *Case of California*, 55). This object is to be loved, furthermore, not for its own sake but for the sake of God's unselfish love for his creatures (an unselfishness attested by Christ's gift of his life and death on behalf of the fallen). The Christian must identify, as a loving being, with Christ as well as the neighbor. Group identification—which melancholically reworks the split in the subject by passing difference on to the other—is, in Christianity, the most sublime (and, in its later medieval forms, the most grotesque) of all techniques of living. As Rickels argues in *The Case of California*, "[t]he Christian church introduces modern group psychology by doubling group identity back onto its identifications" (73).

CHIVALRIC SACRIFICE IN THE MIDDLE AGES

The cross was premier signifier of sacrifice in the Middle Ages, and mediator of the interchange between the laicizing of sacrifice and the sacralizing of lay culture. Elaine Scarry writes that in the form of the cross "the weapon returns, more concrete and cruel than...ever....it becomes tangible, singular, and still."[82] The cross is an invincible sign and a sign of invincibility. It signifies the very power of the melancholic sign to turn suffering into militancy, isolation into inclusiveness, dreadful twist of fate into the acme of vigilance and preparedness *(felix culpa)* that is salvation history. The cross is a sign that "the world and the devil [are]...

completely conquered," a "means of demonstrating the Christian realization that...supernatural battles must and can be fought."[83] According to Rabanus Maurus,

> All things come together in this cross because on it suffered Christ, the creator of all things. For the Passion of Christ holds up the heavens, rules the world, and harrows hell. The angels are confirmed in their righteousness by it, the people are redeemed, the hostile are confounded. It secures the structure of the world, breathes life into the living, keeps feeling in the sentient, illumines the intelligent.[84]

As sign of (traumatic) conversion—when suffering mortality turns into the invincible group body (all things) that never mourns—the cross apotheosizes the gift of death. The stillness with which it sustains the memory of pain and fragmentation claims the triumph of preparedness, that is, the "living beyond" death that delivers the biggest all-time rush of aliveness (Rickels, *Case of California*, 73). The "way of the cross" could shift from martyrdom to monkish battles with invisible armies to the "kind of living death" of daily mortification: "that other type of sacrifice, short of death, which could allow those who made it also to follow the way of the cross, and so lay hold of the power it released."[85] The cross is apotropaic, the ultimate weapon, but also upholder of the integrity of space and awareness.

Later in the Middle Ages, the cross is palladium not only against the demonic armies that invade the air or the soul, but also against the infidel and the heretic. The militarization of the Christian church and the sanctification of warrior culture proceed interdependently, through practices that mortify, subjectivate, and "responsibilize" the laity. The gift of death keeps on giving us ever more reasons to count: the five wounds of Christ, the seven sorrows of Mary; itemized inventories of the defamations of Christ's name, the weapons used in the crucifixion, the affected organs. The church gave close attention to pogroms (often led by pilgrims), Franciscanism, self-mutilation, pus eating, mystical transportation. It is as though, with the vicissitudes of crusading history, the cross were to move and keep on turning, at one time "confounding the hostile" as it seeks to "secure" the Holy Land, at another confounding "the people" themselves. Or perhaps it is the people who turn it now one way and now another, oscillating between projection and introjection, sadism and masochism, mania and melancholy. It signifies the subject's loss and gain of the artifact—now I am paid up, now in debt again, now it is my rescuer, now my persecutor—which compels the attempt of pilgrimage to resecure all things and uphold the integrity of space: the relic, the holy missing thing.

The devotional arts of the later Middle Ages raise the penalized body to the dignity of the Thing. The unstable sentience of objects of exchange, hence of signifiers, is also seen from the standpoint of *das Ding*, of *jouissance*, in the form of the transubstantiating Eucharist (Fourth Lateran, 1215) and stigmata (first worn by Saint Francis). These corporealizing figures are signifiers of the submission of the flesh *to* the order of the signifier, the Law or system of exchange that makes persons interchangeable. By fixing the body in suspension between life and death, debt and payment, man and God, the sublime image of Christ in agony *shows* that sentience passes and is passed on by the signifier. The sacrificial body in pain captivates us because it gives us a fixed, constant image of sentience *in transference,* not only with respect to the passage from life to death, but also from one "neighbor" to another via the unconscious group on whose behalf sacrifice, the antidote for the group's lack of sentience, is putatively endured.[86]

The most captivating of all late-medieval devotional signifiers is, then, the very image *of* the potentially sacrificial impact of the signifier on living being. The role played by the "apotheosis of guilt" that was the cross in the history of the signifier was to *show* the sadomasochistic "excesses" of devotional signification that reform discourses in turn recognized as forms of *jouissance*. Chaucer's poetry focuses on the implications for artisanship of this overdetermined "Gothic" signifying of the *relation* between sacrifice and the signifier, wherein the lost artifact returns with a vengeance to inflict suffering, to reenact rather than simply recall sacrificial violence.

Freud's *Group Psychology* presents military brotherhood as an example of the "artificial group"—highly organized, built to stay, and more archaic than the Christian church.[87] In the Middle Ages, the mystique of military fraternity was exalted to an extraordinary degree by its borrowings from the mystique of religious fraternity, and vice versa. While the Christian church in Europe became militant and militarized, the military sublimed its life, suffering, and death, producing a flood of discourses on the relationships between sacrifice and brutality. The tight bond between desire and the law formed aristocratic as well as ecclesiastical techniques of living, and was shown, made spectacular, by them. Even the pleasures of court life were not a result of power indulging in raw instincts, but rather were part of the court's preoccupation with "manners" or the "civilizing process."[88]

Chivalric culture enhanced its sentience, subliming the military group by infusing its esprit de corps with the prestige of devotion. "As our Lord has chosen clerics to maintain the holy Catholic faith against unbelievers, using Scripture and reason, so our glorious God has chosen knights to vanquish those unbelievers who strive to destroy Holy Church by force of arms."[89] Both the militant Christian group and the individual knight are rendered sacrificially just as, in the devotional lyric, Christ is portrayed as our "Lover-Knight."[90] Saint Bernard of Clairvaux praises the "*nova militia*" who followed the "*vita perfecta*."[91] Although the aristocracy—not all of whom, in Bernard's view, were members of Christ's chivalry—fetishized rank, chivalry also upheld the principles of equivalence and substitutability through the military orders, indeed, through the very idea of the order of knighthood as offering techniques of living to all noblemen, regardless of rank.

According to the myth of the origins of knighthood presented by Ramón Lull in his *Book of the Order of Chivalry*, "[w]hen the world lapsed into wickedness, it was fear which restored justice. And so the people were divided into groups of a thousand, and from each group one man was chosen who was the most loyal, most brave, most knowledgeable and most courteous of them all" (in Speed, *Those Who Fought*, 89). The story assimilates distinction to equality—the "homogeneity" that enables identification, putting the group's relay power into play, to the "heterogeneity" that sublimes the group by means of what is withdrawn from it.[92] In pursuit of the enhanced sentience of the group, chivalry laicized techniques of self-rescue, paralleling the training of the knight's body with his ethical training: "And as a knight should exercise his body, so he should practice justice, wisdom, charity, loyalty, truth, humility and hope, so that he may perfect his soul" (in Speed, *Those Who Fought*, 93–94). The ceremony of initiation into knighthood described by Geoffrey de Charny in *The Book of Chivalry* is a (self-)purification ritual: the knight "must take a bath, and remain there a long time, *thinking* that he is washing his body clean of the grime of sin"; subsequently, he is "clad anew in what is white and pure, signifying that he should... keep himself pure and free from sin" (ibid., 90; emphasis added).

This gift of new life is also a gift of death: "Then the knights ought to clothe him in a red tunic, showing that he must shed blood to defend the faith of God and the Holy Church.... [He] must be ready for death at any time"; in this time of sacrifice, moreover, he must signify his withdrawal from the order of things: "since gold is the most coveted of metals, it is placed on his feet, because his heart has lost all desire for it" (ibid., 90–91). These showings of splendor help the knight recollect (himself), help him remember his excoriation and rebirth into an extraordinary state of vigilance over himself and preparedness for death through submission to the law of his order: "Then the knights should slap him on the cheek, as a sign that he must always remember that he has received the order of chivalry, and act as that order requires" (ibid., 91). Pain substantiates/impresses the knight's rebirth into the order of the signifier itself, the only order in which a splendid showing can be taken to mean that by putting on such a showing one has given up the living being. The ponderous explicitness of this allegory further displays the centrality of the signifier to sacrificial preparedness for death: the chivalric exegesis of the signifier is another sign that sacrifice demands submission to *an order of signs*.[93]

Not only was Christ identified with chivalry through the figure of the lover-knight, but the chivalrous subject was also to bear the cross on militant pilgrimages to reclaim the Holy Land, and identify with Christ's passion. In Philippe de Mézières's *A Tragedic or Declamatory Prayer on the Passion of Our Lord*, the crusader is subject of a tragedy that should be "humbly 'sung' before the crucified Christ." Mézières hopes that his work will "[s]uffice for the obtaining of tears, so that... sweet Jesus, who makes the mournful happy... may in His clemency deign to prepare us for this table of tears[.]" This relay of identification turns tears into an effect of the signifier that serves as gift in exchange for consolation that consists of preparation for (more) tears. Christ's clemency is addressed by Mézières's own capacity for "compunction and tears," which both generates and is induced by his *"hystoria lugubris et lacrimabilis."* Devotional exercise is entirely compatible with chivalric chronicle; the poem also memorializes the "tearful and most bitter tragedy" of "the new militia of Christ's Passion that was not brought to pass" when Alexandria was lost as soon as it was won by Peter of Lusignan, the "foremost crusader of the [fourteenth] century."⁹⁴ The crusader keeps vigil over himself through identification with the crucified Christ, taking himself *and* the "militia" as "object[s] of knowledge and ... field[s] of action, so as to transform, correct, and purify [themselves], and find salvation," and even the failures of crusaders can be assimilated to the tragedy of Christ's passion.⁹⁵

As a function of the "imaginary"—the mode of subjectivity that fills out lack by constructing imaginary identifications—the figure of the group (body), like the image of the crucified Christ, "captures" enjoyment. The group enhances sentience through the power of relay, or passing *it* on. Interchangeability of persons lets the group stylize and idealize loss. What is suffered by one member can be disseminated throughout the group body; one never dies alone (Jonestown, Heaven's Gate), and the group never mourns except on solemn occasions that spectacularly show the action of relay (the king is dead; long live the king). The mourning "obtained" by passional devotion enables identification with the lost object as *living on*, rather than separation from, the lost object as dead. The relay power of the mystical body of Christ is greatly enhanced by the imaginary neighbor ("imaginary" because the neighbor bears "my" image). Divinized for Christianity by the figure of Jesus Christ, the neighbor figures the "equality and interchangeability of all group members" (Rickels, *Case of California,* 73). The Crucifixion, which Lacan calls the "apotheosis" of sadism, shows a proximate, humanized God, God as neighbor, who feeds us with his lifeblood while divinizing in his own person "the limit in which a being remains in a state of suffering," and thereby taking on all the evil that lies within the hearts of all the neighbors.⁹⁶

By identifying with the neighbor—by referring the question of her satisfaction to her neighbor—the subject circulates her desire. Note that she cannot be sure it will not, like the *daimons* in Pandora's box, come back to haunt her. The group manages the destructivity of *jouissance,* and the *jouissance* of destructivity, by sacrificing enjoyment, guaranteeing "that the pleasure to be had will be enjoyed only by the Other" (ibid., 56, 73). This sacrificial relay produces enjoyment: by loving like and what the Other loves for the sake of the Other, "every body... is at everybody's disposal," rewired for sadomasochism (55–56). The group body is "an indestructible support." Like the crucified Christ, the group body is a "double" of the object-subject "made inaccessible to destruction." As the "signifier of a limit," it has the same "power to support a form of suffering" that Lacan attributes to the object of Sadean torture; "[s]uffering is conceived of as a stasis which affirms that that which is," *because it bears the signifier,* "cannot return to the void from which it emerged" (Lacan, *Ethics of Psychoanalysis,* 261). The pain of the tortured object-subject phantasmatically substantiates interchangeability and the endurance also referred to the body of the group. Once again, the image of the crucified Christ images the very power of the sentient signifier to endure the vulnerability of living tissue to pain and interchangeability.

If identification refers my enjoyment to the other and circles back through the compensatory structure of sacrifice, it also makes me feel I know my neighbor all too well. The group can effect a traumatic overfamiliarity despite its powers of mobilization. Lacan's reading of *Civilization and Its Discontents* argues that the subject recoils from the obligation to love her neighbor because of the "evil" that dwells within him, that is, the *jouissance* the subject does not dare go near, but which she intuits *because some form of "fundamental evil... also dwells within [her]"* (*Ethics of Psychoanalysis,* 186). Because I cannot love either my own *jouissance* or my neighbor's, I have to try to get rid of it; I can only identify with *and* love my neighbor if I can get rid of my neighbor's *jouissance,* which means that I have to do something about my own. The part of me that is terrified by every body's *jouissance* will be relieved by the hope of doing away with the evil that lies in the heart of my neighbor; the part of me that doesn't want to "give way" on my own *jouissance* will recoil from such a voluntary loss.

So, instead of a love that would acknowledge *jouissance,* in my neighbor and in myself, I offer my neighbor the helping hand, re-creating her according to the "reassuring image of my own narcissism." My rescue of her is inextricably linked, via identification, to my own experience of the gift of death. Altruism secures the apotropaic image; through it "I can avoid taking up the problem of the evil I desire, and that my neighbor desires also.... What I want is the good of others provided that it remain in the image of my own.... the whole thing deteriorates so rapidly that it becomes: provided that it depend on my efforts" (ibid., 187). It must depend on my efforts because my sacrifice is essential to the conversion of the trauma of identification (e.g., I am unhappily reminded that "I" is an other) into (self-)rescue. Charity is a showing that "I am," even if I am showing this only to my own vigilance (an act that can easily make matters worse, because in the end a split is a split is a split). In truth, charity is, like many forms of trauma management, directly anxiogenic.

The idea that "I" have a neighbor who is just like me and to whom I must give will inevitably recast "me" into symbolic interchange (being a signifier), and undermine that aspect of giving that depends on belief in the difference between donor and recipient. "I" projects the self-rescuing structure of subjectivity outward only to find that its vicissitudes with respect to the neighbor (who is so difficult to improve) do not improve on its vicissitudes with respect to care for the "I." Anxiety over the life-and-death significance of sacrificial identification as warranty of triumphant submission to the signifier reached a peak in the later Middle Ages, when salvation seemed to depend more than ever on the ability to discriminate between the deserving and undeserving poor.[97]

The apotropaic promise of identification—the promise that its dangers can be converted into safety—helps to explain why pity is a structure of enjoyment. We retreat from "assaulting the image of the other, because it was the image on which we were formed as an ego" (ibid., 195). The wish to refrain from harming the other is a concomitant of identification. "Here we find the convincing power of altruism," writes Lacan; here (in the subjective space where our destructivity is made to vanish, with mirrors) we also find "the leveling power of a certain law of equality—that which is formulated in the notion of the general will" (ibid.). The desire for "an agency that rewards" equitably derives from the same structures of identification that support pity as a form of enjoyment.

This imaginary rendering of exchange—that is, "the leveling power of a certain law of equality"—makes submission to the signifier rewarding. The one who is justly rewarded has fulfilled the expectations of the Other—the only agency capable of calculating each distinctive contribution to all the exchanges of all the neighbors. This kind of distinctiveness is conferred only by group membership (identification and interchangeability). I can only be calculated with respect to others when we have all been reduced to equivalent calculable units. So "I spend my life, by cashing in my time in a dollar zone . . . in my neighbor's time, where all the neighbors are maintained equally at the marginal level of reality of my own existence."[98] Through the kind of obsessional timing and counting that makes every thing comparable, I save myself from being overwhelmed by the desire for anything so particular as to be irreplaceable. Living in the time of the other defends me against the potentially shattering effects of loss and hence *jouissance*.

The discourse of Death-as-Leveler so important in the later Middle Ages was terrorizing, but also a response to terror. The hate and fear that break out after the Pardoner's performance in Chaucer's *Canterbury Tales* register this doubleness clearly. The injustice of not being rewarded according to deserts could perhaps, however, be consoled by a justice that was at least fair, and treated everyone just like everyone else. Everyone has to submit to a final reckoning. One's reward was the kind of distinction that can produce the paradox of a purified totality. When the apocalypse comes, the undeserving will go for good, and the burnished remainder will contemplate the Good (and the Bad, pitilessly) for all eternity. "The other is always the first to go" readily takes the form of "come one, come all." The redeemed group is identified, all for one and one for all, once and for all, and given the values of identity. The role of repetition in trauma management is legible here; rather than dying alone, my image is put into massive circulation. But it is well to remember how many accounts of the plague testified that it was the poor who died en masse, not the rich, and that part of the crisis was the breakdown of charity.

The relation between helping and the signifier is emphasized by Aquinas in *De regimine principum*. Helping, like communication, is itself a sign, in this case, of the individual's dependence on others. Indeed, the circularity of Aquinas's logic formalizes the enjoyment of identification: because "a man cannot adequately provide for his life by himself," "it is natural for man to live in association with his fellows."[99] Helping is not just natural, but "necessary," because of our dependence on the other, the neighbor. Helping has foundational value—the value of something that "must be" if other things are to come into being. The signifier has the power to form the group, because it is in turn essential to helping; it enables transmission, and on top of that signifies its own significance as token of our participation in the symbolic order. The signifier of community shows the role of any and all signifiers in relaying group desire. We join in multitudes for the sake of our living, and "[t]his is most clearly demonstrated by the fact that man uses words to communicate his thoughts fully to others."[100] Once again, the chief sign of our dependence on the other is the signifier itself.

At least from the twelfth century onward, amorous suffering is rendered consequential for groups and forms their techniques of living. Lacan links the "apotheosis of the neighbor" in Christianity to the *bon vezi*, the "good neighbor," in courtly love (*Ethics of Psychoanalysis*, 151–52). Courtly love identifies the group of fine lovers, those who know what love *is*, by their devotion to the figure of the Lady/*finamen*, and the Law that s/he embodies. The "Lady" is the neighbor seen as sublime object, who screens—hides *and* shows—the Thing: the neighbor in the form of the object who lives right next door to one's own *jouissance*. The "Lady" differs from the crucified Christ not because she is less exacting (she is not), but because she beckons us to pursue our *jouissance*; her import is that *jouissance* is the Law, is what rules us, artifices us, and emerges in our artifacts, including herself. The proper ways of speaking to him or her, detailed so carefully in Capellanus's *The Art of Courtly Love*, are a technique of living for a group, gathered together—in fact or in fiction—as courts of love, cults of the marguerite, flowers or leaves. In the later Middle Ages, chivalric culture stages spectacles that show this version of the neighbor to be judge of, and reward for, tourneying knights. Discourses that groupify chivalry proliferate: biographies, chivalric ordinances, heraldic descriptions of solemn events, rolls of honor, the Orders of the Garter and the Star, the Court of Chivalry. Monasticism was regrouped through Cistercianism (from there into the Crusades and the monastic orders of the Templars and their ilk) and Franciscanism (from there into evangelism, preaching, and enhanced attention to the poor). Extraordinary fervency was displayed by laicized and spectacled devotional practices (flagellants, Corpus Christi drama), and the proliferation of lay orders (Beguines) and guilds. The formalization of *ascesis* as group experience is the wider historical context for the emphasis on sacrifice in representations of the signifier in the later Middle Ages. Showing the signifier as the means to sacrificial *jouissance* is the "cause" of Chaucer's poetry, of its desire to speak. But before we listen to what it has to say, the next chapter will discuss contemporary historicism and psychoanalytic theory, so we can gain a better sense of how and why Chaucer has been situated in his time, and what that situating has said about the role of enjoyment in his work.

1

BECOMING MEDIEVAL

PSYCHOANALYSIS AND HISTORICISM

*Donc si je suis théologien, je suis un
théologien de la mort de Dieu.*
—Alexandre Leupin

Gerald of Wales, famously put off by Geoffrey of Monmouth's *History of the Kings of Britain*, tells the story of a prophet named Meilyr, who "was immediately aware" if "anyone told a lie in his presence," because "he saw a demon dancing and exulting on the liar's tongue." He could also put his finger on the "offending passage" of any book that contained inaccuracies or deceptions.

> When he was harassed beyond endurance by... unclean spirits, St. John's Gospel was placed on his lap, and then they all vanished immediately, flying away like so many birds. If the Gospel were afterwards removed and the *History of the Kings of Britain* by Geoffrey of Monmouth put there in its place, just to see what would happen, the demons would alight all over his body, and on the book too, staying there longer than usual and being even more demanding.[1]

It is a fabulous story, indeed. Unclean demons are powerfully drawn to error in general and to the *History of the Kings of Britain* in particular. Not just deception, but scholarly inaccuracy, are part of the field of unclean desires, demonic temptation, and wishful thinking that lead people to consult oracles like Meilyr in the first place.

Meilyr is being punished for transgressive desire. If, on a certain Palm Sunday, he had not "happened to meet" a girl he loved on the way home from church, and had not tried to "taste [her] delights," she would not have turned into a monster "repulsive beyond words," he would not have lost his wits, and he would not have acquired the familiarity with unclean spirits that enabled him to prophesy the future even after he was healed of his madness by the good men of St. David's.[2] Meilyr's story is phobic; it posits oracular truth telling as the equivocal aftereffect of too much erotic familiarity, not just with girls, but with the hairy devil himself. The narrative reverses the charges of Christ's journey into Jerusalem on Palm Sunday, turning the intentionality of salvation history into "chance" encounter, sacrificial pain into carnal delight. Could the truths of historical and prophetic discourse, and the restorative powers of "saintly men," be any more embedded in desire and destructivity than this—in a story that points to the terrifying nature of our desire, but retains its aftereffects nonetheless as the shaky ground of historical knowledge, forward and backward?[3]

On one level, the tale Gerald tells earns its points with respect to truth by managing enjoyment; it relays the perils of (homo)eroticism and other forms of forbidden or risky knowledge (divination and mnemonics) into the relieved, if still demonically pestered, body fostered by the monastic group. Gerald's narration of this tale may, of course, be tongue-in-cheek. He seems to enjoy pestering Geoffrey of Monmouth himself, and marvelously. Could Gerald have been amused by the dependence of many medieval styles of truth telling on extraordinary transgressions, penitential suffering, or supernatural intervention? The Meilyr incident shows that history makes its truths in accordance with desire and its defenses—in this case, phobic language and its attempts to counter trauma.[4] Historical narration cannot get free of enjoyment. History is, and has always been, an erogenous zone. Gerald's fabulous remake of scholarly debates declares a certain affinity, if only as a companion piece in enjoyment, with the *History* of that egregious liar Geoffrey of Monmouth.

Techniques of knowledge production do not negate, but are forms of, desire. For many historicists today, giving truthful accounts of the past is an ethical imperative (so that we do not repeat what we ought to remember). Increasingly, however, historians agree that producing an objectively truthful account of the past is impossible, though even these routinely write *"as if"* the objectivity they relinquish were possible.[5] The historicisms of our time remain largely committed to the alterity of the past. We also know that historians are as bound by place and time as historical periods. How can we know an "other" past if we ourselves are bound by the terms of our present? And, why have we been unable to resolve this quandary? Are we simply giving ourselves an excuse to conduct business as usual?

There is never anything simple about the desire to conduct business as usual. For one thing, the impasse of alteritism permits us to reiterate indefinitely the split between passion and scholarly integrity. We *enjoy* the rigor of discipline, but for some of us this enjoyment would be spoiled if we acknowledged it. Further: in the humanities today, academic medievalism often *stands for* discipline and the sacrifices it requires. Medieval studies is charged with more than its share of the ethical burden of contemporary historicism: to put aside our modernity, especially the preferences it might imply, for the sake of truth.

At least two appeals to newness have turned on this historiographical form of sacrificial enjoyment: the nauseating excitement of the revolutionary break with the past that ushered in the ambivalences of nineteenth-century historical alteritism; and the twentieth-century *renovatio* of National Socialism, which was followed by intense reinvestment in radical historical difference. Alteritism is in part a means of rationalizing unbearable newness or difference. But forms of knowledge production that respond to trauma are not thereby valueless. If the history of desire is tightly bound to that of knowledge, perhaps the conclusion we should draw is that responses to trauma can produce truth. The Holocaust, Hiroshima, Nagasaki, Dresden, the trenches of World War I, to say nothing of the massive losses inflicted by slavery and colonialism, have already formed the knowledges they serve, belatedly, as limit cases.

If what we know about the past is always a function of desire, from what position can we say that Holocaust denial is a crime, or even inaccurate? How could any historian committed to the authority of testimony feel anything but malaise at the prospect of thirteen ways of looking at the Middle Passage? Holocaust denial, while illustrating the role of desire in history writing, does so in such a disreputable way that it keeps vigilance in good repute. I would rather believe in an agency that judges than accept Holocaust denial as historically responsible. Holocaust denial is as posttraumatic as is the distrust of totality in recent academic historicism. But this does not, in my view, mean that academic historicism and Holocaust denial are, at bottom, the "same thing."

On April 12, 2000, the *Los Angeles Times* reported that "Britain's High Court called Hitler biographer David Irving 'anti-Semitic and racist' in a scathing ruling...that rejected the libel charges he had brought over claims that he is a Holocaust denier." The ruling was based on belief in a certain version of history. "The defense brought in some of the top experts on World War II to prove not that the Holocaust took place—that was a given in the case—but that Irving had willfully distorted facts." Important new historical sources emerged: "The Israeli government had released the 1,300-page prison memoirs of Nazi war criminal Adolf Eichmann for use by [defendant] Lipstadt's legal team." Judge Gray concluded that Irving misinterpreted, mistranslated, and omitted documents so as to present Hitler in "an unwarrantedly favorable light." No doubt we should be disturbed by the idea of taking anything as a historical given. But for now I am interested in Judge Gray's consideration of the kinds of texts that count as evidence, and the kinds of techniques that count as acceptable method, for the discipline of history today.

Gray's decision epitomizes Michel de Certeau's argument in *The Writing of History* that disciplines make knowledge through the co-construction of the law of a group and the law of a specific technique: "each 'discipline' maintains its ambivalence of being at once the law of a group and the law of a field of scientific research."[6] Not only is procedure of great importance, but judgment must proceed by evaluating many kinds of knowledge and their implications for truthful narrative. The fallibility of judgment is no secret, but it is also unavoidable. In fact, it is the uncertain ground on which knowledge making must take place. This should inspire us to work within our limits instead of wishing for impossible certainties. Knowledge is a real thing, made by a collective process of adjudication over time, from place to place, planned and practiced. Real knowledge is also made by trial and error, drift, unforeseen byproducts, crazy inventions, play, and frivolous speculation.[7] Groups can make knowledge unknowingly: rigorous technique can result from faffing around. The productions of group knowledge can be as intricate as the Taj Mahal and as simple as a teaspoon. Some knowledges will be "marginalized," and some of those will, in turn, displace dominant forms of knowledge, or remain fiercely resistant. Others will collapse if their appeal to the group is so toxic or avoidant of reality that it cannot be heard unless the group is along for the death drive, heading straight (back) toward the trauma it has not been able to mourn.

How can psychoanalysis address the desire of historicism for knowledge? Psychoanalytic hermeneutics are based on the productivity of desire for understanding. It is not, for psychoanalysis, simply a matter of recognizing that the position of the observer will change the object of observation, though some historicists have still not caught up to this early-twentieth-century contribution to scientific method (Is light a wave or a particle? Depends on how you look at it). Psychoanalysis contends that the un/conscious desire of the observer changes the object of observation, and that *analysis of this desire can produce knowledge about the object,* insofar as such analysis tries to speak and hear language that produces a significant relationship between the psychic and material experience of subject and object.

We are not faced with a choice between objectivity and relativism. Our alternative is to make the desire of the knower the basis of a process of interpretation and knowledge making that requires and depends on intersubjectivity. In "Psychoanalysis and the Polis," Julia Kristeva argues that the truth of psychoanalytic interpretation "is demonstrable only by its effects in the present," that is, in the transferential relationship between analyst and analysand.[8] But "the efficacy of interpretation...[as] a function of its transferential truth...is what political man learns from the analyst, or in any case shares with him" (1081). When a political discourse—the "three estates," for example—becomes hegemonic, it is because that discourse has interpreted the "utopian desires," not the "needs" or "exigencies," that structure the group's modes of enjoyment. An interpretation is truthful if, moreover, it expands "the boundaries of the analyzable" (1079).

"Freudianism"—meaning not only the psychoanalytic theory, practice, and institutional and economic structures that followed from Freud's work, but also its many adaptations, from Nazi psychoanalysis to FBI profiling, war games, the advertising industry, and more—has been enormously successful. Does this mean that it has been true, in the sense of "having read rightly the utopian desires" of its own history? Could it be said that Freud must have been truthful about our utopian desires to have had such profound effects on the production and dissemination of the knowledges we created in the twentieth century? Of one thing there can be no doubt: Freud insisted that we were creatures not only of our time, but also of our highly particular histories—our families, their families, the other families they knew, and our phantasmic transformations of them into memories, ideals, expectations, disappointments, responsibilities, and utopian desires. And it is strange when historicists who believe that there is significant interchange between people and their time, but that this interchange is not transparent, break out in hives at the possibility that they might have had significant interchange with their particular histories that are not fully transparent or known to them. Why should this (as one sometimes feels is the fear) be shaming to the individual when it is not considered to be shaming for groups?

The idea that an interpretation (of the past) must be true because of its effects in the present might seem deracinating or irresponsible to some historicists. To be responsible, we must be historical; To be historical, we must be responsible. But what if, as Derrida writes, "the classic concept of decision and responsibility" were "to exclude from the essence, heart, or proper moment of responsible *decision* all historical connections"?[9] But if we were to be responsible to ourselves, that is, truthful about and to ourselves, we could not simply ignore the fact that we have grown up in a post-Freudian world in which self-care books based, however reluctantly, on Freudian concepts, make the best-seller lists, and corporations have turned in large numbers to organizational psychologists for help in sorting out the desires of working groups. Historicist ethics nonetheless obliges us to analyze history by rising above any claims that our specific, local histories might make on us. We avoid this impasse by identifying the histories that particularize us as desires in need of discipline, or (the same thing) as erroneous superstitions that, despite their awesome success in re-creating our culture, can simply be disposed of as wanting. This seems to produce a strangely naive sense of history—as if, post-Darwin, we could somehow not be affected by the cultural effects of Darwinism, of which creationism is surely a prime example.

The alterity of the past, privileged in historicism since the early nineteenth century, creates a borderline that enables crossover as well as containment of the dead and the living, the nocent and the innocent.[10] This is a borderline traditionally fraught with responsibility. The concept of responsibility, like that of consent, entails the idea of freedom, of freely choosing to be responsible. It thus requires a subject capable of choice, reliable enough to remember its commitments, or to remember that "it" is what made those commitments. It is not odd that the debt historicism believes it owes is expressed by reverence for techniques of evidence gathering that promise recovery of the past as other. But when academic discipline is marshaled to dig through the rubble, the rescue operation is put into the hands of a rather dubious Red Cross: the post-Freudian, post-Einsteinian, post–Betty Friedanian subjects of the twenty-first century.

On the one hand, historicists seem to have little confidence that, as Alexandre Leupin puts it, "the other of the text, the remains of the text and the text as remains will always return."[11] On the other hand, we proceed confidently *as if* our historical writing could bring about this most unlikely of developments. Once again, to what extent does alteritism work simply to protect business—or "practice"—as usual? Does our skepticism about the signifier's ability to return simply enable a certain overconfidence in *our* power to obliterate strangeness? Surely it is not *possible* for us utterly to obscure the past. Alteritism denies the power of medieval texts to speak unless spoken to, by *us*. If we are the only people who can provide the answers—but must give ourselves up, become other to ourselves, in order to do so—then sacrifice will be the act that makes possible responsible historical analysis. But who is the "we" that gives itself up, and what does it become afterwards?

At least since the Enlightenment, the valorizing of archival sources has driven wedges between popular and academic history—between the histories we "love" (dashing pirates, Roman love-slaves) and what Norman Macdougall calls "true historical scholarship."[12] It has driven wedges between medieval historiography (chronicle, local legend) and "true historical scholarship." Academic medievalism in fact abjected *both* medieval and contemporary popular historiography. Chronicles are too dramatic, partisan, or fantastic to be responsible (e.g., Geoffrey of Monmouth's *History*), and so are speculative popular histories (e.g., William Godwin's *Life of Chaucer*). Never mind that history can sometimes be rather dramatic, especially for those to whom it is happening, or that Godwin's habit of suggesting that Chaucer may have been quite affected by thus and such because thus and such happened in the fourteenth century remains the basic method of Chaucer's recent scholarly biographers, however improved their reference apparatus. Popular culture's current fascination with the Middle Ages registers their common repudiation by true historical scholarship.

The remains of the medieval text, and this text as remains, require but do not address our critical methods. The medieval text is in-nocent. The kinds of "innocence" attributed to the Middle Ages extend practically across the word's semantic range: ignorance, blindness, self-deception, deception of the ignorant, all the way to corruption; or from unknowingness to purity, inviolacy, safety, and thus the capacity to enjoy the body without guilt or self-consciousness. In Foucault's *The History of Sexuality*, volume 1, we gain access to the truth of premodern sex through the figure of the village fool, both being simple compared with the constant excitation/management of latter-day organizations of sexuality.[13] The medieval love of bodies and pleasures may have overcome Foucault's critical capacities on this occasion, but at least it can be said that Foucault enjoyed breaking up the history of *la France* by finding *liberté* on the wrong side of the Revolution. Throughout his œuvre, in fact, Foucault called for constant rethinking of historical categories (period, source, etc.) *as* we used them—not a strong feature of American Foucauldian historicism, which has tended rather to the reification of most such categories while betting the ranch on voiding the distinction between ordinary and literary language. The utopian desires or modes of enjoyment that history tries to explain include desires *for* history—for *a* history, and for ways of purveying historical knowledge. The persistence of modes of historical representation *(Shakespeare in Love, Elizabeth)* out of favor with the academy is itself a sign of the remains of the medieval text and their power to disturb the scene of academic knowledge making.

De Certeau reminds us that historiographical terms such as *archaism* or *survival* represent as lost in time what might just as easily be described as "still vital" or "of continuing importance." He criticizes the habit of applying "the notion of 'pre-Reformation'" to the early sixteenth century, when instead we should examine "scholastic currents however dominant or equal in importance. . . . [T]heological or exegetical writings have been virtually erased from the works of the great 'savants' of the sixteenth and seventeenth centuries as vestiges of epochs long since over, esteemed as unworthy of interest to a progressive society."[14] Raymond Williams's distinctions between "emergent," "dominant," and "residual" cultural strains point out how many epochs people might, at the "same" time, be living in. But how do we know what is dominant and what is residual, especially if the signifier can always return?¹⁵ Is the residual simply the oldest? What if it comes back, even in the form of farce? How old is it then? Were Roger Bacon's anticipations of flying machines emergent, or (only) Leonardo's? Retrospection is intrinsic to historical understanding; it opens up meanings hitherto unthinkable, or at least inexplicit. We did not know the meaning of courtly love, Žižek argues, until the emergence of masochism in the later nineteenth century. Perhaps even more important, retrospection is intrinsic to historical understanding because without it, we cannot see how signifiers work over time—when, if ever, they become sublime, after having humble beginnings; when, if ever, like the Roman signifiers Walter Benjamin pondered in *Theses on the Philosophy of History,* they return on behalf of a utopian desire to break with the past, for example, by rewriting the calender of the new French Republic. But retrospection itself is only one standpoint among many at work in the production of historical knowledge.

According to John Guillory, "the study of historical works need not be justified as an apotropaic exercise—because these works are supposed to embody hegemonic values—but because they *are* historical works."¹⁶ The question is then shifted to the value of studying historical works. Is that good for us *infra se*? What hegemonic (or other) values are embodied in such an assumption? History does have an apotropaic function. To a large extent, history remains *pietas*. It reminds us of our mortality; we are no better than the dead, we do not know any more than they do, we know less about them (and therefore ourselves) than they do, we are as limited in our point of view as they were, what we want is not important. But, paradoxically, we also are obligated to remember the dead correctly; we rescue the dead from oblivion. (For one thing, that is the only way to certify their deadness.)

This yoking together of humility with redemptive power (or, latterly, of can-do *as if* with either manly skepticism or heroic willingness to exercise authority in our sheepishly p.c. world) forms the death wish de Certeau spotted in the work of Jules Michelet. The wish that the dead stay dead, and the fear that they will not, is converted into a wish to understand and honor what is hopelessly lost to us. To construct knowledge about a time is to make that time past, to put it behind us; and/or we can only construct the past as our object of knowledge when it is ready to exit, stage left. Given how often wounds bleed, in de Certeau's history, it is not always easy to know whether he connects his own uneasy oscillations with Michelet, or begs to differ. As Cleanth Brooks might have put it, the paradox resolves into a certain irony when the irreplaceability of the lost object serves to deny the irreplaceability of the lost object, which means *me*, quite as much as any of my forebears. For the crime of still being alive (which part of me is happy about, despite my inevitable death, in which I cannot believe, however), I turn my desire for knowledge back onto myself, which puts me in the same position as the past. I develop a technique of living and knowledge, which restores my relation to the law and prepares me for joining the dead, so I am at once prospectively dead and obsolescently alive. But everything is okay since neither am I really *dead* nor do I want forbidden knowledge of the dead, since it is only me. My scrutiny of the obstacles posed by my desire to my knowing is the philosophical reflex of my desire to know, of "knowledge-desire" or curiosity.

If historicism has figured desire as a problem for understanding because doing so reverses the charge of the dependence of knowledge on curiosity, it has done so despite leads not only from psychoanalysis, but also from the history of science and cognitive science, which often recognize the "chaotic" nature of the history of invention, and the crucial roles played by pleasure and fiction in the making of new technologies. We have not wanted to acknowledge in full de Certeau's point that the group norms of our technique (kinds of evidence and evidence gathering, proper argumentation, plausible interpretation) both structure our desire and produce what counts as knowledge, as well as providing the seedbeds for change. But *there is no other kind of knowledge than this; this is what knowledge is, and we make it.*

Ambivalence about the past and anxiety over the future feed our need for an "agency that rewards" (that can tell us what is true). Medieval studies does not on the whole have strong positions pro or con about many critiques of knowledge (theoretical physics, philosophies of language, anthropology, etc.). When a historicist in medieval studies attacks critiques of truthful historiography, she or he is more likely to pick on psychoanalysis than on Edwin Hutchins or Michel Serres. Is this because "only one theoretical breakthrough seems consistently to *mobilize* resistances, rejections, and deafness: psychoanalysis"?[17] Psychoanalysis has served medieval studies as a whipping boy—or girl—for the convulsion in theories of knowledge that shocked every discipline in the twentieth century. What does it mean that historicist resistance to psychoanalysis takes the form of whipping boys and girls? We have not wanted to reconfigure our discipline's enjoyment of discipline because *ascesis* is foundational to it. The discipline itself is a symptom of our ambivalence toward the past, as is our willingness to whip into shape the girls and boys who seem to just want to have fun. This is a more enjoyably risky way to correct than it might seem initially. As noted earlier, for many humanists, medieval studies stands for the discipline in discipline, which means that when we want to free the curriculum, medieval requirements will be the first to go (and when they come back, as has been the more recent trend, they do so in the name of rigor). Poor us, since we cannot guarantee by withdrawing that the academy will be more free, nor can we guarantee by our presence that our students will be able once again to read, write, and speak. Scapegoats have ever generated more scapegoating, however, so perhaps we should be the less surprised by our compulsion to repeat the exclusion/recursion, with vengeance.

We are in trouble, though, if we cannot find alternatives to serving as the archaic irrelevance (which by its very irrelevance exposes the arbitrariness) of the law for the rest of the humanities. In part this is because the humanities are in trouble and we know this probably will not be good for medieval studies. Neither will it be good for either the humanities or medieval studies for us to accept the terms of a naive scientism and try to show that we, too, are plenty technological, informational, and testable. Part of our work is, indeed, to break down the assumption that language is not a tool, that its dissemination has not driven and transformed technology, and so on. But we have more to do than that.

First, neither medieval studies nor the humanities should be made to function as spectacular examples for larger anxieties about the nature of knowledge. Early in the twentieth century, scientists—way ahead of postmodernists—thought up relativity, uncertainty principles, and probability theory. (Roughly contemporary forays into hermeneutics, like Wimsatt's critique of the "intentional fallacy" and Empson's study of ambiguity, seem tame by comparison.) Now we have chaos theory, which, insofar as it has migrated into the humanities, has not stopped many humanists from thinking about history in fairly traditional ways. Biologists frankly acknowledge that they cannot define "life," a puzzlement made even richer by the possibility of "virtual life," and the study of light long ago produced a now-proverbial example of the role played in constructing his or her observations: is light a wave or a particle? It depends on how you look at it. One almost feels that the humanities, far from being responsible for the erosion of our belief in "truth," have been rather stodgy and behindhand in questioning verities like the "author" or indeed the "text." Can the idea that there is no single text, but only freeze-framed moments of intertextuality, really be powerful enough to undermine Western civilization by comparison with the somewhat similar idea that the sine qua non of the living "organism" is a vesicle? Despite the very real differences between the scientific commitment to testability and "verifiable result," on the one hand, and, on the other, the humanistic curiosity about the very elements of virtuosity, social variation, or historical context that have always hampered the quantitative and experimental (that is, repeatable) production of verifiable results, it behooves us to remember that the sciences and quantitative social sciences have often been way ahead of the humanities in emphasizing the role of the interpreter in interpretation and even, in some cases, the *productivity* of ambiguity. Most humanists today would agree that experimentation with models, fictions, and even "metaphors" (all terms used by scientists) is a form of action on the world rather than a failure to know its truth. Anthropologists have pointed out repeatedly that they create artifacts rather than factual accounts, because their presence transforms the very cultures they mean to record dispassionately. But they have wisely stressed that these interpretations are still adjudicable.

The "difference" made by the humanities—for example, its supposedly exclusive postmodernist role in the erosion of credence and credibility—is prone to regard theoretical physicists as delusional; theoretical physicists often see experimental physics as mere gadget-love. Frank Gehry remembers that when he was training to become an architect, his peers avoided art students like the plague because the latter always seemed to want to make some kind of "statement" and therefore were not "objective." Sociologists still fight over whether quantification or interpretation is the essence of their discipline(s). Throughout the twentieth century, linguists debated whether *langue* or *parole*, "competence" or "performance," was the right or most important level at which to study the phenomenon of language. Historians cannot decide whether they gather and present facts from the archives or tell stories. Are stories themselves counterfactual statements or meaningful constructs whose validity (elegance of argument, use of evidence, knowledge of similar objects, and so on) can be judged by comparison with others? And what is history good for anyway? Does study of the history of cinema have any actual value to the study of film production? If even educators ignore the *power* of invention and interpretation in the production of knowledge, why even bother? But if medievalists are going to continue bothering, let us at least refuse to serve as the (arbitrary) law that will save us from poststructuralism, and/or restore positivist vigor, and/or, once *purged*, will free us to make choices about what "we" want to learn and teach. None of these stratagems has had the slightest success in restoring either funding or prestige. Possibly this is because they do not work.

Because we have wanted to represent the desire to forget as the desire we need to correct, we do not often ask why we sometimes *want* to remember. Is remembering always something we have to force ourselves to do? Certainly, not all pasts, not all the time; we repress, we flatter ourselves; we refuse to pay. But we do not always have to force ourselves to look at "sad chapters." The title of Barbara Tuchman's popular book *A Distant Mirror: The Calamitous Fourteenth Century* promises something quite lugubrious.[18] We take great pleasure—disciplinary or otherwise—in seeing the past as our loss, our loss as the past. If the past is to some degree, at least as de Certeau would mean it, our creation, and therefore our lost object and persecutor, it is also a work that reworks us. The history of our understanding of history suggests that we enjoy being instructed by it. This is nowhere more evident than in contemporary medievalist fantasy, which entails work: collection (first editions of the Oz books, comic books such as *Camelot 3000*); love of code (Elvish language and script), new technologies (Ultima), geography (maps of Middle Earth are posted on the Web), knowledge (archives of the monastery's collections in *Baldur's Gate*, a Dungeons and Dragons game), and lore (understanding how to use the sword Glamdring's powers of illumination depends on knowledge of the old wars between the dwarves and the orcs). The "curious oscillation between fantastic neomedievalism and responsible philological examination" attributed by Umberto Eco to our "period of renewed interest in the Middle Ages" not only has echoes in earlier periods—in the Middle Ages itself, if Gerald of Wales's annoyance with Geoffrey of Monmouth is any indication—but is also an oscillation among friends. If popular medievalism is fantasy, the love of knowledge is part of that fantasy from the very beginning.[19] The transition from popular to scholastic medievalism takes work, but it is not the work of acquiring a taste for the work involved in producing knowledge.

Apotropaic identifications with the dead, and their management via techniques of living, are at work in both contemporary and medieval understandings of the ethics of historiography. Identification does not usually function now as it did then—for one thing, medieval attitudes toward history were themselves quite varied, as Lee Patterson points out in *Negotiating the Past*.[20] But the ambivalence of identification, mourning, and melancholy are points of convergence between some of the signifying effects of medieval historical literature and (popular *and* academic) medievalism today. In these convergences, different structures of enjoyment intersect, a consequence of the insistence of the memorial function of marking as developed in the later Middle Ages—"remember *me*"—and the desire to find new channels of communication with the (powers of the) missing so characteristic of technological and historiological production in the nineteenth and twentieth centuries: Michelet speaking to the dead; the Grimm brothers listening to the *Volksgeist* marching toward freedom to the sound of the Germanic consonant shift; Alexander Graham Bell still hoping his deaf mother would listen to him; elegizing in a language that had to be invented for the purpose—*a elbereth gilthoniel*—the sacrifice of the past, in Tolkien's ring trilogy; the Internet, postapocalyptic insistence of the signifier and home to a record of the past after the sack of Rome, the loss of Constantinople, and the burning of the monasteries in the ninth century, only to have its painstaking copies of the remains of the text put to the torch by a newly burnished remnant of "Reformation" types and their enlightened relatives, who felt—and still feel, if current views of the humanities expressed by the Christian right and those scientists whose passion for Reason is unabated are any indication—that they could use the power of the dead and the dying to blast themselves to heaven by exploding all the signifiers of the past. Is it any wonder, after Kristallnacht, Hiroshima, and the lesser light of Lon Cheney (as I like to think of her), after so many attempts to give the second death to get the second life, that our children wish they knew what it felt like to be a medieval monk? The nostalgia for the Middle Ages so ubiquitously thematized in cyberculture is nostalgia for a culture that tried desperately to write it all down before the "future" showed up again—and again, and again—and of course could not keep up with the so many times that ambivalence about past cultures and cultural pasts blew up into a killing rage against the irrational-arbitrary-corrupt old law. What, so to speak, remains uncanny, and has to be blasted out into the open time and again, is the insentience of the very signifier that records our remains. But there is, by that very token, something else, another way of insisting, which, if we cannot easily understand what it "means"—what it meant by that, what it means to do—because it makes meanings happen rather than having this or that one for all time, nonetheless addresses us from within and from without our works: the signifier. Provided, at least, that it remains, glossolaling on despite the best efforts of the dealers of second deaths, who want not only to use the bodies of the dead as fuel for their ovens, but also to obliterate the fact that these bodies ever bore, or made culture with, the signifier. The signifier may be weird and only half-intelligible; it is all we have left, and as Lacan would say, it is not nothing. When the signifier allows different historical structures of enjoyment to intersect, they create something new, quite without reasons or Reason, by the very act of yoking the remains of the past and the hopeful transmissions of the present. These convergences account not only for the overdetermined intensity of our current medievalist fascinations, but also for the new "lines of flight" they inevitably set off.[21]

In the Middle Ages, the past seemed difficult both to avoid *and* to preserve. Memory required intensive training, which was even more explicitly moralized than classical mnemotechnique. But *auctoritas*, the illustrious example that comes before (and in a sense "stands for" the enormous weight of all the lost remains), weighed heavily on the present. Both the weight of the past and its fragility amount to the same thing: the symbolic debt to its having been, irreversibly, in the order of the signifier, which is to say that I know it insists inside me/my group/work/culture even if I try to blast it to smithereens, or especially then. Medieval historiography sublimed the power of the signifier (omens, genealogies) over the time of the group, and everything, life, the fate of the soul, the well-being of Christendom, depended on how the living-on of the past was treated. The potentially inimical effects of the dead on the living, as well as blessing, were transmitted by signifiers that, so to speak, did not mean, but *be:* the not intelligible things that channeled magical power from the dead to the living—talismans, the Eucharist—as well as

> the christianization of memory and of mnemotechnology, the division of collective memory between a circular liturgical memory and a lay memory little influenced by chronology, the development of the memory of the dead and especially of dead saints, the importance of memory in an educational system depending on both the oral and the written, and finally the appearance of treatises on memory *(artes memoriae)*.[22]

The ethical handling of the signifier by the living could rescue the living from wrongful enjoyment. *Pietas* was made a question of piety, of interior mnemonic and affective events, in the form of the pity (etymologically related to *pietas*) solicited by devotional practice. *Pietas* becomes the center of cult activity, but deterritorialized, tied to the ancestral gods of neither the family nor the state, and thus (through Christianity's mobilization of the general equivalent, the equivalence among Christians) divinizing, extending beyond all limit, sacrificial memory.

The powerful effect of texts on later readers was an axiom of medieval literary and historiographical theory; then, no one needed to prove that texts shaped, as well as reflected, "life," to say nothing of death.[23] The effects of the past on the present could perhaps be disciplined, through proper ethical and signifying techniques, to the profit of the living. Modes of enjoyment of the past were matters of practice and preparedness. The emphasis on anxiety management and preparedness is one signifying resource for the embrace of medievalism in contemporary children's entertainment. Making history live well is "care of the self," for the individual and for the group. The care for transmission of the remains of the past on behalf of an always-threatened future, the care for the scene of youth's education not just by teachers, but by *age,* oddly but explicably positioned history writing for commodification when communications technology began to shift between the monastic scriptorium (copying is sacrificial labor, monastic discipline), the lay scriptorium (servants produce records of, in all senses, aristocratic "expenditure" for patrons), and print.

The "Prohemye" of William Caxton's 1482 edition of the *Policronicon* praises the benefits and pleasures of knowing the past:

> For certayne [history]... is a greete beneurte vnto a man that can be reformed by other and straunge mennes hurtes and scathes / And by the same to knowe / what is requysyte and prouffytable for hys lyf.... Therfore the counseylles of auncyent & whyte heeryd men / in whome olde age hath engendryd wysedom / ben gretely preysed of yonger men / And yet hystoryes soo moche more excelle them / As the dyuturnyte or length of tyme Includeth moo ensamples of thynges & laudable actes than thage of one man may suffyse to see.[24]

The value of history lies in its power to relay "ensamples" "prouffytable" for "oure mortal lyf." It is a technique of transmission that magnifies sentience. Hearing about the "hurts and injuries *[scathes]*" of others will illuminate the most difficult of question, What is it that is "requisite and profitable for life"? The scene of counsel reverses the charges of the *Phaedrus*; writing on stone tablets deals death to the spirit of the community, whose justice can only be preserved by inscription in the fleshly tablets of the heart; for Caxton, histories excel word of mouth, while nonetheless preserving the fantasy of living, speaking "ensamples," dead or alive, and with the power to keep us alive. Some Thing inside Caxton the technologist, the publisher, the editor, proposes to him the value of alterity; his writing sounds almost wondering when it introduces the ability of men to be "reformed by *other* and *straunge* mennes hurtes and scathes" (emphasis added). And history writing transmits even further this power of the other, the very outsider distrusted in the *Phaedrus*, to enhance the life of the young men of the group. But why "hurtes and scathes"? Something has shifted in the history of the signifier on this point also; the very "unwar strokes" that carry off great men enable their return via the signifier. Suffering is the foundation of history's power of rescue; history is always a cautionary tale, because it remembers (as mnemonics teaches) what is striking, in all senses: cover a mnemonic image with blood, and you will never forget it.[25]

History is a means of knowledge production, and the knowledge it produces is a matter of life and death. It can confer "blessing" *(beneurte)* (or not) because its signifiers transmit between the dead and the living, thus multiplying possibilities for identification with "straunge" men. The structure of enjoyment of identification is in the register of the "imaginary"; multiplication can intensify identification or threaten it.[26] Enhanced identification in turn enhances the possibility of disaster, but also of rescue and redemption. "Ancient and white-haired men" benefit from time by accumulating knowledge and experience; therefore, their "counsels" will be "greatly praised by young men." History then magnifies the power of identification (and hence the signifier) to transfer knowledge by turning alterity into identity.[27] History is a communicative technology; and printing is a historiographical project because of its power to repeat the signifiers of the other. Advertising, at this moment in history, takes the risk of trafficking with the dead in order to enlarge the sentience of the living.

One of the salvific virtues of history is its incitement to the glory of sacrifice, *pro patria mori*.[28] The "Prohemye" states that history is more able, by many magnitudes, than good counsel to "move" "ryght noble Knyghtes" to put themselves in jeopardy on behalf of the "country and public weal" (histories move noble knights "more valyantly to entre in Ieopardyes of batayles for the defence & tuicion of their countrey and publyke wele" [65]). Through the records history keeps of the wounds of others, young men will be more likely to risk their lives for the common good. Turning the classical scene of ethical training toward preparedness for war, the "Proheyme" suggests that we learn from records of the wounds of others a readiness to wound and be wounded.[29] The historically close link between war and technology emerges here in its melancholic reformulation (as sacrifice and as group mobilization) of the dependence of sentience on prosthetic powers of extension. Alterity (scathes) is recuperated in the name of "tuicion" of entire countries. The recording techniques of historical transmission promise not only to take care of the group and the territory, but also to relay sacrifice to all corners of the land and the ends of time.

Caxton's writing often explores relationships between different kinds of "enterprise," and participates in the interchange between the laicizing of sacrifice and the sacralizing of lay practice in the later Middle Ages. Chivalric writing drew on legal discourse to resignify military enterprise (e.g., regulating the ransom market).[30] The legists and canonists were among the most important sources for the sentiment of "*pugna pro pa-*

tria," a maxim drawn from "the moral *Distichs* attributed to Cato and read by school boys throughout the Middle Ages."[31] The Prologue of Caxton's edition of *Caton (Cato)*, dedicated to the City of London, laments the diminution of London's prosperity,

> the cause [of which] is that ther is almost none / that entendeth to the comyn wele but only euery man for his singuler prouffyte / O whan I remember the noble Romayns / that for the comyn wele of the Cyte of Rome / they spente not only theyr moeuable goodes / but they put theyr bodyes & lyues in Ieopardy to the deth.[32]

Sacrificing one's goods for the common weal is not as valuable as sacrificing one's body in its defense, but it is not too far off. One's "goodes" are *defined* as sacrifice-worthy by exploiting the unstable relationship between the subject and the desires it translates into products and objects of exchange, that is, into alienable signifiers that act out in markets the unaccountable accountability of being-as-signifier.

History according to Caxton suggests that particulars and universals are constructs that mutually define each other and shift over time and place. Countries are generated through the perpetual transformation of and identification with otherness—"other and strange men's hurts." Sameness between men is taken for granted here; it is created out of men's strangeness to each other. Trying to enhance our power to record particulars of the lost past, history already makes a difference: the new prosthesis of print. Nothing, it seems, gets us off this hook: our most inspired attempts to replicate the past cannot help but change the world. We change the world when we put the past back into it. The ethical challenge of historiography is aversion of our trouble with the signifer. It is not simply that we fear we distort the past, and therefore the work is bad, or even à la de Certeau, that we kill off presumably obsolescent parts of ourselves when we define a past to write about (the death wish), but that *any* of our works, once made, changes the world—the signifying order—it enters. Our works create the openness to change that we also hope they might capture in the form of a showing. The Middle Ages was never the same after John Kemble's work on the Anglo-Saxon laws, or Carlo Ginzburg's *The Cheese and the Worms,* nor is it the same now after Carolyn Dinshaw's *Getting Medieval.* Our fear of the power of the work to change the signifying order it works in or on can be replayed as fear of distortion of an unchanging object, but this will indeed prove to be a dead end in working through historical responsibility. The "Prohemye"'s wishful image of receptive young men indicates that knowledge of what happens in time helps us pursue our desires, and therefore does not "fix" anything because it is always changing the future.

For example, the discovery of sacrifice as a means of disseminating/diluting the losses inherent in cultural preservation offers history to us as a gallantly self-exiled time. As noted earlier, popular culture today is fueled by an extraordinary association of childhood and maturation with the signifiers of medieval military culture. What the sword lacks in relevance to contemporary weapons of mass destruction or international corporate competition, it makes up for in the seductiveness of its promise to give a total form to maturation, as practice and preparedness.

A recent television ad for the Marine Corps features a young man, stripped to the waist, fighting a fiery dragon with a sword. The image derives from the visual culture of video-gaming. It implies that today's military activities are as ennobling as those in medieval romance, and that the skills acquired through video warfare can ready young men for further training in the armed services. The neomedievalism of our period often takes the form of a phantasmic relocation of chivalric risk taking into the future. This once-and-future timing skips over the traumatic Real of the present. It is as if the blankness of the present marked the place of our Thing: the threat of nuclear/chemical/biological warfare and the hatred of (other) cultures—not so much of specific nations or tribes or even religions, though these are ever-present, but of entire "ways of life" (modes of enjoyment, in Žižek's terms)—that distinguishes the practices of envy after the turn into the twenty-first century. The survivalist fantasy of postapocalyptic culture (the practice of culture as cult of preparedness) is not confined to wackos but can be seen everywhere in our productions of enjoyment for children.[33] The place of mnemotechnique in these explosions of *jouissance*, whether neomedieval plastique or fantasy, reveals the place of philology in popular culture's dreams about the life and death, salvation and extinction, of the group.

The power of *jouissance* to make itself felt—if we push it back in one place, it is going to come back in another—is not only why we should, but also why we *do*, keep on asking why we love the past, and how our love for it can make us better readers of history. Just as contemporary popular medievalism's focus on military preparedness and cultural preservation intersects with chivalric culture's use of history to make subjects desire "more valyantly to entre in Ieopardyes of batayles," so its reprise of courtly love in romance novels and innumerable toys, games, and videos addressed to girls intersects with courtly literature's recognition of the Thing inside the lady. Contemporary popular medievalism knows a lot about the queerness of medieval love lyric, the writings of the *trobairitz,* and the use of sexual difference in courtly love genres to multiply rather than reduce modes of enjoyment. Medievalism is an important part of modern sexual practice. Many people love historical "costume" not only on parade (dress uniform), but also in the bedroom. Medievalism is almost as important in contemporary pornography as it is in the toy/games industries.[34] *Pulp Fiction*'s use of the phrase "get medieval" is not the only popular association of the Middle Ages with sadomasochism; the latter is usually to be found in the "dungeon" of pornography sites on the Web. The symbolics of blood is central to contemporary fantasy: the loss of blood as the condition of possibility for engagement with the Other, now plugged into and recalled on behalf of the prosthetic body of the Internet.[35] The sword, the whip, and the swoon substantiate "characters" in games such as Ultima through a process of reassemblage of parts, functions, matter, and gaps between material events, showing that the body extends its *jouissance* in time as well as in space. And why not? Like Deleuze and Guattari's schizo, though (it is to be hoped) less shatteringly, we live, even just as individuals, through many different historical positions and identities.[36] My mother uses the signifier to dedicate my life to filling the gap left behind by my grandmother, who died at Auschwitz. Regardless of my resistance, I will nonetheless have been shaped in relation to this gap and the invitation to enter it. Our *jouissance* extends itself by means of the signifier's power to (re)distribute life and death. Post-Holocaust, we can try to rewrite the order of the signifier. Many of these survivalist uses of the signifier converge in today's rites of passage from girlhood into womanhood: as I write this, I hold in my hand an invitation, passed on to me by a colleague, to a bas mitzvah that summons guests to "participate in the festivities at Balmoral Castle." The font is Gothic, the girl's name has a crown above it, the borders are reminiscent of those used in medieval manuscripts, and the whole is embossed in gilt on paper made to look like vellum.

Rather than relying on an uncritical alterIt is m to stabilize temporal identities, then, we can see the past itself as fractured, desiring, layered with the possibilities of its futures as well as its memories: a "history that will be," in Jonathan Goldberg's memorable phrase.[37] Past times do not know themselves, or their pasts or their futures, in fullness, free of desire. Nothing can account for itself in fullness, because desire is unaccountable; it is always on the move, rephrasing itself, relocating itself. The "Prohemye" in Caxton's *Policronicon* suggests that the love of men inspires, and is enhanced by, technologies of replication. According to Earl Jackson, the desire to recover the lost body of the past fueled humanist philology.[38] These understandings of premodern recording techniques have been inspired by present interests, but they have also asked questions that have produced brilliant results in terms of new scholarship, building a broader understanding of earlier thinking about the role of enjoyment in techniques of preservation and dissemination, and also showing that some aspects of the writing of "techniques of living" in the past could not materialize or enter into certain assemblages until the present moment.[39] The past is not the present, but it is in the present, "participating unnaturally" in our techniques of living.[40] What has medieval studies contributed to our understanding of this unnatural participation?

In my view, responsible medievalism requires exploration of the enjoyment at stake in methods as well as objects of study (for one thing, the two are always related), and psychoanalysis still provides us with some of the most detailed and provocative language about enjoyment now available. That it may design us even as we use it to design our questions is true of every method of study, not just of psychoanalysis. The question for the moment is, How can we make these imbrications enabling, rather than disabling, for our work? Foucault's *The History of Sexuality* places psychoanalysis in a long history of "subjectivation"; the history of psychoanalysis includes, according to Eugene Vance, the "theological discourse[s] that emerged in the fourth century."[41] Contemporary historicism, which has surfed many of the same intellectual currents as psychoanalysis, depends altogether on an idea of the subject as shaped and limited by experience, but also (by that same token) capable of change. But how do we decide which of the limits that provide shape to the subject are most significant? On what bases would we privilege some limits over others?

In his *Littérature médiévale et psychanalyse,* Jean-Charles Hûchet asks whether historical alterity is the most important alterity at stake in reading medieval culture. And in a 1983 review of Roger Dragonetti's work,

Alexandre Leupin wrote: "can we assume... that the reader... more easily identifies with texts out of the present than those of the past? Or... that readers distance themselves from past works in such a way as to make them ipso facto 'other' for the sole reason that they are inscribed in a different historical context?"[42] Does historical difference exhaust the category of "difference"? If the cultures of the past "are as other to all of us as minority cultures are to some of us," are we speaking of the same sorts of otherness?[43] At minimum, what seems significantly marked by "alterity" to one person may not be so for another. If time is experienced differently in a different culture, what becomes of our sensitivity to difference when we analyze that culture exclusively in our own alteritist terms? Again, the Middle Ages had many different ways of thinking about history, but despite medieval interest in the form of time we call crisis, radical alteritism was, to say the least, not hegemonic. In fact the interpenetration of times (different kinds of time, different moments in time) was unavoidable, axiomatic, and desirable in ecclesiastical understandings of salvation history as well as aristocratic understandings of genealogy. Neither liturgical nor seasonal time stressed unrepeatability; on the contrary. What respect do we show the Middle Ages when we say that responsibility involves understanding the Middle Ages exclusively in its own terms, and then insist—in effect, if not explicitly—that only postmedieval alteritist views of time and methods of knowledge production are capable of the attempt? Religious alterity has been far more significant for many of the peoples of the world than historical alterity. For peoples suffering from repeated persecution, alterity needs to prove that it has more to offer than categorical nostalgia or reassertions that specific ideological fantasies—which are always material—are equivalent to realness.[44]

Hûchet also suggests that we problematize the relations between psychoanalysis (we could extend this to historicism, Marxism, etc.) and *all* literature, not just that written during the centuries that have come to be known as the Middle Ages.[45] Psychoanalysis has no more inalienable right to address silent film, just because both were around in the early twentieth century, than it does to address Guibert of Nogent's maternal imaginary or late-medieval psychology's fascination with enjoyment.[46] On the other hand, distaste for psychoanalysis and distaste for "theory" provide alibis for each other *throughout* literary and cultural studies, not just in medieval studies. But forgetting this helps us forget the medievalism of such theorists as Marx, Bataille, Kristeva, Lacan, and Jameson, as also the theoretical contributions of medievalists such as Dinshaw, whose performative understanding of identity appeared in *Chaucer's Sexual Poetics* a year before Judith Butler's *Gender Trouble* came out.[47]

In turn, Anne Middleton's knowing allusions to "master narratives" and "imported critical paradigms" would sound odd to the many medieval philosophers—Duns Scotus, Aquinas, Ockham—who were enchanted with high theory and eagerly read the work of their counterparts in other countries, at a time when Paris was one of the most influential, if not *the* most influential, intellectual sites in Europe. Even David Wallace compares "adherents of more recent critical movements" to Petrarch's followers, "content... to bask in the reflected glory of their distant master."[48] There is plenty of discipleship, however, in historicism; in the twentieth century, many torches were handed on from one generation of "auncyent & whyte heeryd" historians to the next, as is attested by *Medievalism and the Modern Temper* and its evil twin *Inventing the Middle Ages*.[49] These transferences and transmissions may be problematic for many different reasons (exclusion, inclusion, perpetuation, denial, exploitation), but they are *not* problematic simply because they involve "overvaluation" of objects, that is, love, and the faith that usually accompanies it. Love does not necessarily disable knowledge production, or at least does not self-evidently do so any more than any other form of allegiance. Which simply brings us back up against the question of whether historical responsibility requires the sacrifice of allegiances— but in the name of what? Would we ever sacrifice our allegiances for anything other than another allegiance?

In *Shards of Love*, María Rosa Menocal asks why we should not want to write accounts of the Middle Ages that inspire us in the present moment.[50] Could we want more from our experience of time than true testimony about the past? If we did, would we inevitably compromise the project of testimony? Does the circulation of desire implicit in the idea of inspiration make or break our ability to be responsible to those who precede and follow us? Can language (about history) do anything besides trying, and failing, to refer? At times in the Middle Ages language could be fallen (hence, fail to refer truthfully), but it could also be a means to *renovatio*. Discussing the "modernity" of Geoffrey de Vinsauf's *Poetria Nova*, a "new poetics" that celebrates the rejuvenating powers of *transump-*

tio (in the twelfth century "la langue rajeunie est fontaine de jouvence et ivresse amoreuse revivifiant le corps et l'âme"), Charles Méla asks:

> quel est en effet le lieu où prend forme par l'opération spirituelle la manifestation textuelle? C'est un lieu d'amour et virginal, à l'opposé d'Ève gonflee d'orgeuil ("tumefacta") face au serpent dressé ("erectus"). Marie représente l'aula... la cour ou l'enceinte aux portes closes et qui le resteront.⁵¹

> what is, in effect, the place wherein textual manifestations take shape through a spiritual operation? It is a place of love, a virginal place, as opposed to Eve, puffed up with pride, and [thus mirroring] the erect serpent she stands before. Mary represents the hall [in which one finds safety], the court or enclosure whose gates are closed, and within which [we] will stay.

Doesn't this writing—and de Vinsauf's—help us remember that loving and loving the signifier are but one thing? When is philology not also logophilia? Hûchet's *Littérature médiévale et psychanalyse* notes the zeal of nineteenth-century philologists in editing out of existence textual vagaries interesting to, and readable by, psychoanalysis, so as to produce properly sifted canons of the fathers of national literatures. Leupin heralds Dragonetti's embrace of a "new philo-logia" that moves beyond melancholic reparations of the past: "what constitutes the limits of a work, a genre, a writing at a time when... the so-called 'copyist' has the exorbitant privilege to create by the same right as what we are calling the 'author'?"⁵² Leupin's *Barbarolexis* tries to remind us of the exuberance of medieval textuality, its playful rhetoricity, its awareness that the enjoyment of the signifier as such is intricately linked to the desires of mortal bodies and the designs of material books.⁵³ When we try to work out our truths about medieval textuality's thoroughgoing fascination with parapraxes of every kind, would our accounts be irresponsible if, as Menocal suggests, they might also enjoy "destinerrings"?⁵⁴

Play, however, precisely does not mean "no history." The destinerrings of the signifier, it should be emphasized, depend on and enact the historicity of the signifier and its material embodiments.⁵⁵ Leupin rightly asserts that for the Middle Ages the "Real" is not so much "historical" as it is God.⁵⁶ For some psychoanalytic theorists today, the "Real" is not history either. But that does not mean that history is insignificant. Again, far from it. In my view, the term *history* usually describes the activities of the symbolic order, if we are thinking of changes over time in kinship practices, architecture, cosmetics, taxation. History is not other to the signifier; history consists of the history of the signifier, in *all* its forms—mathematical, visual, literary, technological. History concerns what the signifier does, and what happens to it.[57] Moreover, while the symbolic order is systematic, its fixity, as I noted in the introduction, can be greatly exaggerated. The symbolic order is an open system: it destineers, its destinations are pointless, its effects arbitrary, "its" consistency merely one of its arbitrary effects, because "it" is always changing. When we imagine this directionless activity as a meaningful structure, and act (do science, buy stocks, make friends) according to this image, we are participating in ideological fantasy, which is not "unreal," but rather responsible for the arrangements of the buildings and industries and institutions that surround us: "[i]llusion is not on the side of knowledge, it is already on the side of reality itself, of what the people are doing.... The fundamental level of ideology... is not of an illusion masking the real state of things but that of an (unconscious) fantasy structuring our social reality itself."[58]

Not only is it the case that "ideological" reality is continuous with the order of the signifier; it is also true that the drive "embodies a historical dimension" (Lacan, *Ethics of Psychoanalysis*, 209). One can need food. But, as Marx points out, as soon as one tries to satisfy such a need, nothing is simple. With what does one satisfy oneself, when, and how?[59] Desire plays a fundamental role in economic activity. According to Jane Jacobs, impractical objects (ornaments, toys) are commonly developed before their practical applications: "pigments (which were... the first known uses of iron ore), porcelain,... glass and the practice of welding all started with luxury or decorative goods. Possibly even wheels were at first frivolities; the most ancient known to us are parts of toys"; in the twentieth century, "computer games preceded personal computers for workaday use."[60] By contrast, John Guillory's *Culture and Capital* seems to argue for the autonomy of literary and economic spheres. It is undeniably important for us to understand the salience (historical and otherwise) of the different forms production can take. But imaginative activity never tends to do very well in formulations that emphasize the autonomy of "spheres"; it rarely emerges, that is, as a sphere that has far-reaching effects on our daily lives. New Critical emphasis on the autonomy of literature sublimed its object of study, but did little to persuade the general public (or the academy, for that matter) that study and practice of the arts and humanities are techniques of living as potentially important for our well-being as economics or engineering. But there are other reasons to eschew a discourse of "autonomy." Things can differ from one another and still engage in important, productive relationships. Indeed, relationships can only transpire between things that are not identical. There is no reason, theoretically or otherwise, to assume that developments in literary activity could not be influenced by developments in economic activity, or vice versa; in fact, there are good reasons to assume that ornamental or ludic creativity *lead* changes in other spheres of production. The most important reason of all, however, is, in my view, the principle that human activity always seeks to materialize desire and works by means of the apparently endless and variable resources of the signifier, from string theory to traffic lights to charters.

World-making, "making things happen," is one of the things our species *does,* and *enjoys doing.* We also enjoy (in the strong sense) bringing the past along with us, an effort that also requires imaginative activity. Rather than polarizing (or autonomizing!) fantasy and history, what, in the register of the signifier, links them together? The movements of the drive are paradoxically inspired by the impulse to return to a former state or position of satisfaction, which, in its absolute form, would be the ground zero from which sentience takes off. In doing so, the drive relies on the signifier's marking function: the drive impels itself toward signifiers that mark places or positions that promise to lead back to ground zero (e.g., the Danish coast in *Beowulf,* the lamppost in *Narnia*). The drive, of course, can never really return to ground zero; ground zero will not be the same after the drive's destinerrings. But to whom or what will it not be "the same"? What cannot be absolutely satisfied will insist, it will return to its lack and try to fill it, over and over; this is the Lacanian view. But whether the problem is "the same" once the drive has returned to it is not possible to determine absolutely. Indeed, everything points to the likelihood that the drive is never very sure about this either. Nonetheless, the drive, writes Lacan, "refers back to something memorable," "because it was remembered. Remembering, 'historicizing,' is coextensive with the functioning of the drive in what we call the human psyche" (*Ethics of Psychoanalysis,* 209). The signifiers that design the drive are memory traces. In Freudolacanian psychoanalysis, *nothing is registered in the unconscious except as a memory*. The markers that guide the drive are experienced as mnemonic in psychic reality; we cannot desire without having a memorable experience. We may not remember when we first learned about griffins (this is one kind of personal memory), but what we know about griffins is also memory. These understandings of memory and inscription do not polarize repetition and change, history and fantasy, but rather show that they are formed out of similar signifying activities.

Kristeva argues that psychoanalysis is one of the "rare discourses" that refuses either to glorify or to hate origins; it "invites us to come back constantly to our origins [childhood memories, family] in order better to transcend them."[61] Psychoanalytic narratives—at least, the really interesting ones—imagine a return to origins that *enables* change. There is, of course, no "real" origin to which we can return, if only because "we" change. But by this token, the point of origin is always a point of starting *over*, never purely past or purely new. Instead of the melancholic narratives that structure certain accounts of history and, indeed, mourning, psychoanalysis offers narratives that demand neither *pietas* nor a complete break with the past in order for the subject to move forward. Kristeva asks: "What if Freud alone allowed us to come close to carrying out that biblical and evangelical exhortation [to leave father and mother]?"[62] I would ask a slightly different question: What if Freud allowed us to renegotiate our origins without having to sacrifice them? If home always has something *unheimlich* about it, how does revisiting it differ from being there in the first place? Do we always have to give it up to get on with it? In 1929, Freud writes to Ludwig Binswanger on the subject of mourning:

> Although we know that after such a loss the acute state of mourning will subside, we also know we shall remain inconsolable and will never find a substitute. No matter what may fill the gap, even if it be filled completely, it nevertheless remains something else. And, actually, this is how it should be, it is the only way of perpetuating that love which we do not want to relinquish.[63]

Our fixations try to refind the objects that have *changed* us most profoundly. Freud offers the suffering—those lost in space, tied up in knots, at loose ends, or out of time—the idea of a transformation that depends on reworking rather than renouncing their histories. And because every inscription of the drives in the Freudian unconscious goes down as a memory, reworking memory always has the potential to remake *jouissance*, for the subject and whatever she is in the process of becoming.⁶⁴ One advantage of such a conception of narrative is that it allows us to imagine group subjectivity as potentially a process of reworking the past, neither determined by it nor radically other to it—though group subjectivity is also perfectly capable, in its melancholic forms, of repudiating history (Heaven's Gate) or encrypting it (Disneyland's Fantasyland) or both (National Socialism).

The claims of religion are embedded in medieval studies and affect every discussion of historicism and psychoanalysis. Lacan argues that "religion in all its forms consists of avoiding [the]...emptiness" of the Thing (*Ethics of Psychoanalysis*, 130). At the same time, nothing in Lacan's or Freud's writing suggests that the question of religion is something we can simply waive, even or especially if we are atheists, because its phantasmic power is deeply embedded in our supposedly secular age. Do Freud's and Lacan's views on the imaginary functions of religion impair or further the ability of psychoanalysis to address the Christocentric cultures of the later European Middle Ages? The short answer is that their work enjoins that we take utterly seriously the workings of group fantasy and religious subjectivity in the Middle Ages, but do so in order to analyze how religious desire works as a form of enjoyment, not in order to conduct philological worship services, as seems to be the case in the "return to religion" in Renaissance studies.

The ginger reception of psychoanalysis by medieval studies has as much to do with the religious commitments of many members of that discipline as it does with the putative transhistoricality of psychoanalysis. Complaints about "transhistoricism" sometimes screen arguably transhistorical complaints about impiety; medievalists who revere the Virgin's purity, for example, are not likely to like some of Kristeva's analyses of maternal *jouissance* in *Desire in Language*.⁶⁵ It is ironic that the injunction to understand the medieval past as it understood itself should serve as an alibi for preserving Christian idealism, an impulse based more on identification than on appreciation of alterity. This alibi is, however, not exclusive to Catholic medievalists, many of whom, it should be added, care deeply about history. (My late colleague Frank Gardiner remarked to me once that the only church we had much chance of understanding was the incarnate and historical one.)[66] Medievalists of other faiths, perhaps because they have the habit of reverence, can also find some kinds of critical and cultural analysis of religious icons offensive. And many medievalists who do not *believe* at all, in the psychological sense of the term, act (or write) *"as if"* they did, polemically and otherwise, whether because doing so appeals to their political conservatism, or their longing for sublimity, or their fascination with the experience of faith as such, or their desire to advance in a field of study that made "sympathy" for its object normative for most of the last century.

One of the central functions performed for contemporary religion by post-Enlightenment medieval scholarship, then, devout or not, is the conversion of religious belief into philological modes of truth. From the standpoint of cultural studies—indeed, increasingly from the standpoint of religious studies—religion is a historical phenomenon. Indeed, religious studies has turned increasingly to the work of theorists such as Foucault and Bourdieu to analyze belief as cultural activity and ritual as subjective structuration.[67] But when scholarship is motivated by religious commitment, it does not see religion as (just) a historical phenomenon. When Christian scholars write *as if* it were, however, this enables Christianity to preserve a hold on various cultural enterprises to which it could not otherwise lay claim. Medieval studies, in (re)turn, gets to borrow the sublimity of its objects of study. I remember it being said of a certain charismatic medievalist who taught at my graduate school that "you always feel like you've been in church after listening to him." And I remember learning to ventriloquize devotion: how to write about Marian drama in a voice full of admiration for the power of her consent to make the world young again.

Perhaps one of the reasons that religion still embeds itself in our secular world is that even if we have lost it, or never had it, we mourn it, restoring its absent presence melancholically by means of authoritative technique (e.g., philology). Perhaps, as Lacan suggests, it is because the death of god is interior to Christianity, which links the function of guilt in Christianity to its conceptualization in psychoanalysis: breaking with the past is only going to bring the past back, now in the form of remorse (*Ethics of Psychoanalysis*, 177–78). Kristeva writes that "there is always a moment in history when [certain] discourses ... obtain a general consensus ... because they correspond to the essentially utopian desires of [the] majority. Such political interpretation interprets *desires*; even if it lacks reality, it contains the truth of desires."[68] Religion interprets desires; so does psychoanalysis. Both address grief and consolation; both address the question of how to move on in hope of a better future. Kristeva recalls that "... a man must leave father and mother": the Pauline *ecclesia* enables, through the suffering of "uprooted wanderers, identification with the passion and resurrection of Christ."[69] The idea, developed further by Augustine, of "tearing oneself away from *any* identity (including one's own) in order to accomplish subjective fulfillment in the boundlessness of *caritas*" is part of a "dynamic process" that leads to the Freudian "discovery" whereby we come to "know ourselves as unconscious, altered, other"; and "only strangeness is universal."[70]

But genealogical links between Judaeo-Christian and psychoanalytic thought should not obscure their differences, which are salient for how people think about their suffering, their enjoyment, and the suffering at stake in enjoyment. If Pauline writing addresses the suffering of the homeless by—as Deleuze and Guattari would put it—"deterritorializing" *dignitas*, it is precisely the *suffering* of the uprooted wanderer that leads to redemption.[71] Augustine envisions the dissolution of the agony of desire into the boundlessness of *caritas*, but only on condition of the sacrifice of the broken heart. Psychoanalysis does not posit suffering as necessary to enlightenment. It asks us to recognize in renunciation the very lineaments of desire, and to use it on behalf of our access to *jouissance*, in which our truth lies. The appreciation of universal strangeness, and of the desire of exiled creatures for a future, in my view depends on such a recognition.

The distinctions I make here between Christian and psychoanalytic views of suffering can clarify some important problems in current knowledge making about the Middle Ages. Devotional modes of enjoyment in the later Middle Ages have been the focus of a recent body of work, often nuanced by psychoanalysis if not always psychoanalytic in overall approach, that sometimes conflates different styles of enjoyment too easily. Sarah Stanbury argues that the cross was the intersection of *multiple* sightlines of power; Kathleen Biddick argues that the host was "haunted" by "hybridity" and bled to boundary-transgressing excess; Karma Lochrie argues that devotional practices wrought havoc with categories of gender and subjectivity ("Qwhat is lufe bott transfourmynge of desire In to þe þinge lufyd?"), so that women mystics turned the permeability of female flesh into a means of transgressive signification, and undid the binary of victim/victimizer.⁷² These authors pursue goals I admire: critiquing the pathologizing of female mysticism, to which psychoanalysis has contributed all too much; broadening the scope of women's agency; rethinking the heteronormativity of earlier accounts of gender and mysticism.⁷³ But if we learn to see female mysticism as potentially multiply empowering performance, not as vulgarly transgressive of post-Reformation religious decorum, does this mean that we have *averted* the impulse "to judge [the]...performances" of women artists and medieval mystics, as Biddick suggests? Do we believe that Biddick has not arrived at her own judgments? And why shouldn't she?

If we cannot ask for value-free scholarship, we can ask the historian to understand her stakes in the enjoyment she analyzes and to use this understanding for insight. Possibly the experiences of some feminist medievalists with Catholicism might have given them reasons to ask good questions about medieval devotional practice that were not asked before feminist medievalists began writing. This is perhaps the simplest way in which historians' histories of enjoyment contribute to knowledge rather than obstructing it. The intimacy feminist Christians or ex-Christians might have with women's varied responses to Christian structures of feeling and belief can lead them to ask *more* specific questions, and more *specific* questions, than other analysts might, even if some of the answers to the questions turn out to be unhelpful. Bynum's relationship to Catholicism undoubtedly helped to inspire her powerful development of topics of incorporation—fasting, feasting, hunger—even though it probably also contributed to her far less interesting isolation of sexuality from other drives and desires.⁷⁴ What I am calling for is not confessional self-situating (which usually just gets on with business as usual anyway) but a working awareness of how one's relation to history could help one to design important new questions that could change what counts as knowledge about the Middle Ages or how such knowledge is made. This is crucial because the multiplicities, intersections, and hybridities we find in medieval devotional practices do not necessarily work the same way as they do now, or even the same way they do in Geoffrey de Vinsauf's *Poetria Nova*.

It is true that "acting out" in the name of Jesus and his mother is much more improvisational than celebrating the Mass, and Margery Kempe's version thereof resembles contemporary performance art in its use of disorientation to put sentience under extreme pressure. But

Margery's acting out is not *the same* as acting out in the pursuit of enjoyment. We need to know whether the performance in question disturbs the logic of sacrifice, or not.[75] Enjoyment does not have to be acknowledged for mystical performance to be fascinating, innovative, transformative. But it matters whether and how enjoyment is acknowledged before an all-seeing God—not only because I wish those mystical girls could have had fun piercing their bodies for different reasons, but also because the analysis of devotional practice must include discussion of *the fantasy of an agency that rewards*. Otherwise that devotional practice will not be grasped as abjection performed for a certain all-too-indifferent Gaze.

Moreover, multiplicity as such guarantees nothing with respect to progressive politics or historical change. First of all, multiplicity is unavoidable. Second, it is as helpful to strategies of domination as it is to strategies of resistance. In and of itself, it does nothing to disturb the logic of sacrifice, which is directed to an Other capable of estimating as well as enjoying excess, multitudinousness, and difference (God's absurd love for his people, beyond merit; the Father's many mansions).[76] So much depends on whether multiplicity tries to repair lack in the Other or registers the open-endedness of the symbolic order. The former uses, of course, cannot succeed in stopping change or restoring the Other *sans faute*. But they can oppress. When sovereignty deploys multiplicity and difference, it does not necessarily dispel fascination; it can also compel multiple desires to gather round its splendor. An intersection of libidinal forces is an extraordinary place. When it is a sovereign intersection, as Lacan points out in relation to the Passion, it can work us up *and* poison us with the guilt we naturally prefer to our mortality (*Ethics of Psychoanalysis*, 262). Still, despite power's power to confuse us about our *jouissance*, we can try to discriminate between political/libidinal strategies that rely on the fantasy of agencies that reward, and those that do not. If we do not, not only will we be unable to discriminate between different ideological realities, but we will also learn nothing about the *enabling* power of a symbolic order that lacks. Instead of the lifetime warranty given by the agency that rewards, we discover that we are already part of an open-ended and far-flung process of *(re)making* meaning and knowledge.

How does the view of enjoyment pursued in this book change the way we read, rather than simply revealing something hidden? Let's take, as an example, subversion and containment, the famous duo that has become something of an analytical cul-de-sac for Foucauldian new historicism. I think it is probably true that no subversion, no introduction of the heterogeneous, can be fully contained, and no containment fully subverted.[77] But that is not the claim I want to make. The claim I want to make is that *containment is a mode of enjoyment,* just like subversion. Moreover, subversion *requires* the law that seeks to contain it; the law calls it into being. This may make subversion seem less exciting to some, but I do not think it should; it is just what subversion *is,* and the fact that it is thrilling and needs the law for its thrills does not make it bad politics. Why not be thrilled? Neither does the fact that containment is also a mode of enjoyment (which requires something to contain, by the way) make it "good." Enjoyment is what it is, and it can entail suffering for the other. We can pretend to ourselves that the "good" is really the same thing as *jouissance,* but it is precisely this formulation that has always boded the most ill for the wretched of the earth.

Only if we recognize the communal nature of desire (the role of individual fantasy is sometimes to obscure the group fantasy in which it participates, and vice versa) can psychoanalysis break free of philosophical idealism's privileging of subjective interiority as the only part of the mortal creature worth fixing—an idealism that tends to leave the group in the realm of exteriority, insentient, requiring *objective* study, posing ethical and epistemological problems quite different from those that interest psychoanalysis. Of course, many social scientists do not take this view, but the association of history with the study of collectivities (often assumed to be insentient as such), and psychoanalysis with the study of the interiority that is the subject, is implicit in much medievalist scholarship.[78] Even where the individual subject (in its non-Enlightenment uses) is concerned, however, the subject is only one part of my being, and need not be the standpoint from which psychoanalysis begins, or history ends. In the end, our ethical problem is not "how can we develop relations with the other?" but "how can and should we intervene in our endless *transformations* into otherness?"—into what Deleuze and Guattari call "becoming," the activity of turning into machines, organs, functions, or other beings.[79] And despite Deleuze and Guattari's differences with Freud, the force of transference across time and space emerges as one of Freud's most important ethical perceptions. In *Civilization and Its Discontents,* the greatest of the techniques of living, Freud says, is love; the "oceanic feeling" of "oneness with the universe" is really the result of love's power to dissolve and transform the "boundary between ego and object" (13). "Qwhat is lufe bott transfourmynge of desire / In to þe þinge lufyd?" Our openness to transformation is, for Freud, the common ground both of religious feeling and of love.[80]

The body's multiple conjunctions/disjunctions with parts, groups, and territories are material and productive. "Becoming," in Deleuze and Guattari's sense, does not cultivate the self for self-possession; it cultivates ongoing metamorphoses that even cross the border between sentience and insentience. Is a prosthetic arm really not part of my body? What about the organ transplanted into me? Were medieval soldiers wrong to feel they were part of a unit, the "horsman"? Desire makes the world by following and firing up new lines of force and flight; the subjective "interior" and the Other, the inside and the outside, the inside that lacks the world and the outside that lacks sentience, are already stabilizations of becoming, or, to put it another way, the subjective interior is really just another form of the activity of becoming. The signifier bears "witness to '*an inhumanity immediately experienced in the body as such.*'"[81] It is a bit of code enabling a particle to pace itself alongside another so that "unnatural nuptials" can take place.[82] Why else would we dignify this inhumanity in the form of the Law ("common sense," "the way things are")?

In conclusion, we should try to avoid repeating the hidden homogeneity of historicist practice: namely, that while positing the alterity of the past, we must alter our point of view in order to be as much *like* the past as possible. Even some of the most radical alteritist positions assume that only identity can make a knowledge; only if we suspend our difference can we approach the other. But if there were competing versions of reality in the Middle Ages, how do we choose which version to adopt as our standpoint? And how are we to mark for analysis the oneiric or fantastic qualities of medieval standpoints or ideological realities? "Becoming medieval" does not require complete identification with the past; for one thing, that is impossible, and for another thing, even if we could do it, we would not be "becoming." Sometimes we should approach medieval texts with critical languages that differ from those their authors, even their audiences, might have approved. We cannot confine the work of knowing the Middle Ages to replicating, however hopelessly and/or heroically, medieval cultures' self-understandings. We also should explore how medieval cultures, like all others, may have misunderstood themselves. As D. Vance Smith puts it, we need "new kinds of history [that] can be written by looking at the edges of memory, by examining what traces are left of events that the Middle Ages did not choose to regard as memorable."[83] Steven Justice has argued this of "antiquarian" practice itself:

> If we allow ourselves the antiquarian privilege of seeing representation as mistake, we can see it also as parapraxis: the slip of the tongue or of the pen that betrays not only the fact of repression (in both senses), and not only its incompleteness, and not only the anxieties that caused it... but also, to a degree, its content, the repressed matter itself.[84]

If medieval cultures, like all others, are "sites of contestation," then different critical strategies will help the force of emergent medieval questions to become clearer. Books as challenging and transformative as *Writing and Rebellion*, *Social Chaucer*, *Chaucerian Polity*, and *Chaucer and the Social Contest* could never have been written otherwise. Even as we still desire to "become" medieval, to "extract particles between which one establishes the relations of movement and rest... that are *closest* to what one is becoming," we also find that *not* entering "into composition with other affects" is part of becoming. Without both, how else can we aim for "criticism," for "the critical difference," in Barbara Johnson's term?[85] If we let ourselves become enthusiastic over it, psychoanalytic work can help contemporary medieval studies to an ethics that does not bind, nor bind itself to, the past as dead weight, but lets it loose in the historical signifiers that still trace their way through our passions.

> We know nothing about a body until we know what it can do... what its affects are, how they can or cannot enter into composition with other affects, with the affects of another body, either to destroy that body or to be destroyed by it, either to exchange actions and passions with it or to join with it in composing a more powerful body.[86]

2

"My Worldes Blisse"

COURTLY INTERIORITY IN *THE BOOK OF THE DUCHESS*

Understanding Chaucer's poetics depends on understanding his edgy experiments in tragedy—*The Monk's Tale* and *Troilus and Criseyde,* but also poems with particularly rich links to these experiments and their intertexts, such as *The Book of the Duchess* and *The Legend of Good Women.*[1] Particularly since the early nineteenth century, critics have tended to distinguish these poems from *The Canterbury Tales,* a collection that has often seemed more "social," more "various," more "lively," and exemplary—indeed, constitutive—of the tradition of "English" writing. Although I believe that certain features of Chaucer's poetics emerge with especially painful clarity in such poems as *The Book of the Duchess* and *Troilus and Criseyde,* I hope to attenuate and complicate considerably the borderlines that have been drawn between *The Canterbury Tales* and so much of Chaucer's "other" poetry. The first and last poetic fictions in *The Canterbury Tales, The Knight's Tale,* and *The Manciple's Tale* provide, after all, a kind of interior frame for Chaucer's collection, one that edges the collection's opening and closing collections with poems about helplessness. And the premier example of tale collection that Chaucer includes in *The Canterbury Tales* is *The Monk's Tale.* Chaucer's poetic encounters with irreparability and its designs on *jouissance* cannot be safely attributed to a certain period in his career, to continental influences, to the tastes of aristocratic patrons. Critical attempts to split the melancholy or courtly or conventional Chaucer off from the lively or middle-class or individual Chaucer symptomatize the very extent to which a certain defense of life has defined, and still defines, the writing of

English literary history. What can Chaucer's poetry be doing, in the way of scariness or seductiveness, vitalization or mortification, to produce such a simultaneously apotropaic and ambitious reception? What might have been at stake in Chaucer's attempts to reframe the sublime?

Chaucer used courtly love and the figure of Fortune to develop a poetics of tragic interiority that was decisive for the artificing of "life" in subsequent periods.[2] Classical and medieval literary theory commonly associates love laments with elegy rather than with tragedy.[3] Love seemed insufficiently a group matter for its miseries to qualify as tragedy. There were exceptions: Ovid's *Tristia* linked love to tragedy, and some medieval commentators followed suit. But increasingly from the twelfth century onward, amorous suffering was, to use Laurence Rickels's term, "groupified," that is, rendered consequential for groups and used intensively to form them.[4] The secular discourse of courtly love, central to which was the capacity of the "gentil herte" to feel pity, began to formalize and groupify an amorous experience that would dignify aristocratic subjectivity. Putting amorous suffering and consolation into discourse involved the development of laws, taxonomies, scenarios for public debate and entertainment. In the "cadre" of the court, one was in or out, one fell or ascended, according to one's ability to speak of love.

As we have seen, courtly love insisted on the court's special claim to *jouissance*—its pursuit, its travail, even its passionate self-extinction.[5] The delectation *and* leveling of difference between courtiers was one of its powerful fantasies, a way of artificing the life and death of rank as a principle of group organization.[6] This emphasis on leveling as well as distinction is one reason for the linking of courtly *jouissance* and its vicissitudes to the figures of the desirable "neighbor" *(bon vezi)* and the jealous, spiteful one *(lauzengier).*[7] But because this fantasy made the rise and fall of rank its central mystery, it also distinguished the aristocracy from the (unrankable) commons. Especially in the form of pity, courtly love was a "sentement" only the aristocracy could feel. As the "gentil tercelet" insultingly remarks to the lowly birds in Chaucer's *Parliament of Fowls,* "Thy kynde is of so lowe a wrechednesse / That what love is, thow canst nouther seen ne gesse" (601–2).[8] Courtly love artificed a specifically aristocratic *jouissance* of rank. Moreover, because it did so by designing the interiority of the courtly subject in ways that seemed vitally to link "heterogeneity" to "homogeneity," courtly love became a promising resource for later redefinitions of the social meanings of loss. Courtly tragedy was not so much displaced by the category of class as instructive to it.[9] *The Book of the Duchess* will help us understand why this might have been so. I begin with some theoretical discussion of tragic discourse, and then read what *The Book of the Duchess* has to say on the subject.

Tragic discourse focuses relentlessly on the relations between physical and metaphysical, social and ethical movement: on rising and falling. On chance and "the issue of the downward movement," Jacques Derrida writes:

> One can fall well or badly, have a lucky or unlucky break—but always by dint of not having foreseen—of not having seen in advance and ahead of oneself. In such a case, when man or the subject falls, the fall affects his upright stance and vertical position by engraving in him the detour of a *clinamen* [deviation], whose effects are sometimes inescapable.[10]

A failure of vision is at stake in falling. What "happens" to us is that which we cannot see in advance and ahead of ourselves. Falling involves an idea of exteriority, of encountering that which by definition cannot be anticipated.

The Middle Ages imagines Fortune turning her wheel, arbitrarily and unpredictably, because alterity befalls us in an instant, and the instant is a vertiginous one. Prosthesis is often recommended as defense against the uncertainty of Fortune. Can we redress sudden changes of position by refining our techniques of living, our ways of extending and improving sentience? How can we see and foresee better, so that unimaginable events might not subject us to their motions? How can we stand upright and free, so that our vision is unimpeded? Can we make ourselves a little like the angels—Gabriel, the angel of prophecy; Michael, "protector of warriors from shrines high upon mountains," the apotheosis of strength?[11]

Despite our efforts, we are more moved than moving. Events befall us, and we swerve to avoid them. When we swerve, we are engraved by a downward trajectory. The engraving is inside the subject; it marks the subject's "lapse" into sentience, repeating the helplessness of the human body absolutely to master space, and informing all other such engravings. In some rhetorics of falling, if we can be moved, this means that we do not last, and we can be moved to end our desire: "one senses the enemy inside oneself... one senses the end, the transience from which one in vain would wish to flee into some unknown distance. Is that all? One would like to ask. Is that the highpoint, the climax, and nothing more beyond that?"[12]

To swerve is to fold in upon oneself, to become other to oneself. Now part of me can try to correct my vision and position in the world by taking my own helplessness as an object of concern. I can develop "preparedness," a state of watchfulness that protects me from indifference to what the world has to offer, when all it seems to offer are states of emergency.[13] Not only do I fall; I am thrown helplessly and unwillingly into life, and I am tempted to cast myself out of the aversiveness of living mortally—or to cast out the aversive life that inhabits me, the life that terrifies me precisely because, though unbidden, it seeks my protection. H. Ansgar Kelly notes that "a general moral has been seen in the... phrase, *fugienda vita:* namely, 'the lesson expressed in tragedy is the rejection of life.'"[14] Our helplessness—which includes the problem of our having had no willed relation to our own inception—is the reason why the defense of life and the rejection of life are so terribly interdependent. Tragedy bewails not only the loss of life and fortune but the fortune, the unchosenness or befallenness, of sentient life itself: as Albertino Mussato puts it, "the struggles of uncertain life which contain every kind of cruelty" ("que species omnis crudelitatis habent").[15] In psychoanalytic terms, tragic discourse might be said to consist of the death drive bewailing the awakening to life and the resulting burden of lifelong vigilance. Bewailing is nonetheless preparedness, if for no other reason than that we do it instead of dying.

Derrida remarks that "the same semantic register" at stake in considerations of chance and luck also "supposes the idea of whatever falls... to someone's lot—that lottery said to be attributed, distributed, dispensed, and sent... by the gods or destiny...—as if this gift and these givens obeyed, for better or for worse, the order of a throw coming down from above" ("My Chances/*Mes chances*," 7). In a more recent work, *The Gift of Death*, Derrida shows how the figure of the gift of life also implies "the gift of death."[16] If life is a gift from the Other, it can perhaps be taken away. To awaken into life is already to be lost and at a loss. Lest this not seem much of a gift, the finitude that estranges us from our inception and makes us, qua our aliveness, unintelligible to ourselves (we cannot have been "there" to choose and know our beginning) is turned into a trouble spot we must watch over, thus attaining the triumph of preparedness entailed in correct vision. This gift of death, this knowledge of our finitude, remains part of the gift of life, because only if we know that we will die can we reconceive our lives on this basis, and prepare toward death. The attempt to become "sovereignly mortal" preserves the death drive by protecting us from it.[17]

Signification is a fundamental defense against life. Signification *forms* sentience, partly so that sentience can defend itself better against its emergencies. In this way, signification is on the side, so to speak, of preparedness, helping to keep us alive by making life less traumatic, more negotiable. But signification also preserves the death drive. By making representations of a self that can endure and even outlast its own finitude, signification lets preparedness take shelter *in* inanimacy. If one seeks eternal life through, but fears the deadness of, the signifier, one also seeks repose in its inanimacy—in the image we make of the lost object during mourning, in the mirror image through which we (mis)recognize ourselves.[18] The "work" is ethically troubling because we enjoy the deadness of the artifact (and our own role in making it) just as much as we wish to enliven it, or ourselves through it. My sentience is designed by the inanimate signifier, by something "other" to the aliveness that is already only problematically "mine." This is not all bad, however, because the very insentience of this signifier that is other to my aliveness makes it attractive as a means of designing images that will defend against my aliveness and the world into which it throws me. The signifier, image, and incorporated/projected object defend against life by preparing me, by putting me in the position of having already been through death.

One defends against life and its objects by replacing them—for example, giving oneself the option of getting rid of them, including oneself, by incorporating them. Even though, however, we ourselves construct "the object" and its power over us, the particularity we grant to it poses a problem for living. Insofar as the object *is* something designed to appear to us as distinctively desirable (to be introjected) or undesirable (to be projected), the difficulty of finding substitutions for it makes us liable to mourning. A way to defend against this power of the object is to universalize or multiply objects, an apotropaic activity that makes use of indifference but rescues us from the outrage we would have to commit to achieve it. The phantasmic ability of the object to endure suffering, to be suspended in the limit between life and death, accomplishes a similar negotiation, as does the anxiety management central to Chaucerian tragedy (its emphasis on the power of the unexpected and on the need for preparedness or "caution").[19]

Taking things into ourselves, pushing things out of ourselves: even in breathing, Rickels argues, we are always deciding whether to live or not (*Case of California*, xx). Making things internal, making things external: these are our earliest techniques for crafting desire and our desire to end desire. We make the "arts" to enhance our failing vision. We remedy the limits to our vision by means of, in Foucault's phrase, "techniques of existence," which allow us to keep vigil over ourselves—to "take care of," "rescue," "reunite with" ourselves by replacing ourselves. These techniques tell of "the subject's mode of being"; they teach the subject how to mourn in advance, prepare for suffering to come, take herself "as an object of knowledge and a field of action, so as to transform, correct, and purify oneself, and find salvation."[20] When the subject designs her interior, she takes herself as the pattern of the recalcitrant object, the object that could give her grief, and the way she treats herself as an object will forever be a resource for and an indication of how she will treat others or other things as objects. The "development of the art of living under the theme of the care of oneself" sought to link the design of one's interior with the question of one's fortune and one's position in the world. Tragedies of fortune concern themselves with the resistance to life that paradoxically necessitates these elaborations of it.

In *Civilization and Its Discontents*, Freud also wrote about the "techniques of living" that helped mortal creatures endure the life they also craved. One of these, he argued, is love. In his view, however, Christian love negates particularity; it is a love in which the object of love is also an object of identification (the "neighbor").[21] The neighbor, moreover, is to be loved not for his "own sake" but for the sake of God's unselfish love for his creatures, an unselfishness attested by Christ's gift of (his) life and death on behalf of the fallen. To be fallen is to be undeserving; and because everyone is fallen, to love the undeserving is to love universally, not particularly. The fallenness of the object thus opens up the space of sacrifice and *imitatio Christi*. Never mind, or all the better, that the neighbor you must love has evil in his heart. You are already alike because neither of you merits love; you can be even more alike by nonetheless loving each other. And in loving each other despite the fact that you are undeserving, you are not only doubly like each other, you are also like Christ. Rickels argues that "[t]he Christian church introduces modern group psychology by doubling group identity back onto its identifications" (*Case of California*, 55). The group never mourns. It gets rid of loss because of the equality and interchangeability of all members of the group, recovering destructivity by sacrificing particularity and by guaranteeing "that the pleasure to be had will be enjoyed only by the Other"; through the endless *différance* of loving like and what the Other loves for the sake of the Other, "every body...[is] at everybody's disposal" (56). "Only sadomasochism realizes the pleasure principle which, with Christianity, became the rule...[in part] because Christian eschatology keeps everyone in suspense; in turn waiting around is the essence and holding power of mass masochism" (185). The militant Christian group is rendered sacrificially, in tandem with the identificatory doubling of the figure of "Christ as Lover-Knight," and with the obligation of Christ's knight to passional devotion.[22]

As was discussed in the introduction, Lacan's reading of *Civilization and Its Discontents* argues that we recoil from the obligation to love our neighbor because of the "evil" that dwells within the neighbor, the *jouissance* we do not dare go near, but which we intuit because some form of unspeakable evil dwells also within us.[23] Instead of love, we offer our neighbor the helping hand, re-creating her according to the reassuring image of our own narcissism. Altruism secures the ideal image, the insentient signifier in which we can take refuge; through it "I can avoid taking up the problem of the evil I desire, and that my neighbor desires also.... What I want is the good of others provided that it remain in the image of my own.... the whole thing deteriorates so rapidly that it becomes: provided that it depend on my efforts" (*Ethics of Psychoanalysis*, 187). Moreover, we retreat "from assaulting the image of the other, because it was the image on which we were formed as an ego." The desire to refrain from harming the other, and even the desire to rescue the other, do not result from "civilization," but are inevitable concomitants of the construction of subjectivity, just like aggressivity. "Here we find the convincing power of altruism," the "natural basis of pity," and "the leveling power of a certain law of equality—that which is formulated in the notion of the general will" (ibid., 195). Living in the time of the other under the "law of equality" defends me against the exacerbation of sentience, the destructivity, of *jouissance*. The insentient image on which the ego is founded, the image that is "other" to the living subject not least *because* of its inanimacy, supports the operations of abstraction and generalization that produce the law of the signifier within the subject and the group.

The transitivism of pity both manages and exposes the finitude implied by the founding of the subject on the image/desire of the other. Although pity is not exclusively the inhabitant of the cultivated heart, it is also not simply a "sentiment" that has nothing to do with sociality. It has an insistent relation to the constitutively senseless law and the processes of subjectivation and group identification.[24] It signifies the feeling of being bound to the other, as its derivation from *pietas* suggests. *Pietas* is "dutiful conduct toward the gods, one's parents, relatives, benefactors, country, etc., *sense of duty*," "love"; in later Latin, "gentleness, kindness, tenderness, pity, compassion."[25] Crossing the line between subject and other, pity—*pite* in Middle English—is an important term in the specular construction of goodness and identity, the linking of identity to the gift: to open oneself up or pour oneself out is to show what one is and that one is.[26] Hence the "apotheosis of the neighbor" (and of sadism) in courtly love, in the form of the lovely *bon vezi*, the "good neighbor," and also in Christianity in the form of a proximate, humanized God, who takes on all the evil that lies within the hearts of all the neighbors (*Ethics of Psychoanalysis*, 151–52, 262). Pity offers the gift of death. One who pities is already a survivor of the misfortune that has befallen, or is about to befall, the other who is also the similar.

Saint Augustine, in his *Confessions,* identifies pity as transitivist, a form of suffering that comes through the defile of the other. Augustine is troubled by tragedy because it "shows that sorrow and tears can be enjoyable." The pity of mortal creatures can never be free of desire for the suffering of the other: "a man whose sense of pity was true and sincere might want others to suffer so that he could pity them." Our enjoyment of pity, marked out by the fact that we *choose* occasions and *stage* events that will make us feel it, suggests to Augustine the difficulty of distinguishing between "friendly feelings" and "lust." Tragic pity is a way of loving through which one survives oneself, "freed" from the tyranny of the object, from the isolation of loving particular others. It is one way of turning back toward life for the sake of the Other—"toward the witness, neighbor, or friend one likes to be like," and likes to help.[27]

Moreover, despite the reservations about pity expressed by writers such as Augustine and Aelred of Rievaulx, the laicization and massification of passional devotion in the later Middle Ages intensely valorized pity and the "tragedy" of the Crucifixion.[28] The period's groupifications of military culture were no exception: Philippe de Mézières's *A Tragedic or Declamatory Prayer on the Passion of Our Lord* proposes the crusader as subject of a tragedy that should be "humbly 'sung' before the crucified Christ"; he hopes that his work will

> Suffice for the obtaining of tears, so that my soul, enticed by this multifariously ventilated tragedy to compunction and tears, in my often repeated prayer, you may be moved more devoutly than grace, so that sweet Jesus, who makes the mournful happy... may in His clemency deign to prepare us for this table of tears, and finally, in affirming my declamatory little petition, grant it.

The doubling of identification back on itself means that Christ's clemency will depend on Mézières's capacity for "compunction and tears" as induced by his own "*hystoria lugubris et lacrimabilis.*" Mézières's poem also memorializes the "tearful and most bitter tragedy" of "the new militia of Christ's Passion that was not brought to pass," when Alexandria was lost as soon as it was won by Peter of Lusignan, the "foremost crusader of the century," followed by the "holy death of the disappointed supporter of the campaign, Peter Thomas, patriarch of Constantinople."[29]

Mézières's work exemplifies how pity as aide-mémoire opens up immensity within the devotional subject. In Bachelard's terms, it gives immensity through the form of intimacy.[30] The deviation traced by the helpless body becomes not only an "engraving" but a memory image. It founds an interiority by representing the traumatic experience of the body's entry into space. This inscribes dimensionality within the subject. Moreover, to remember is to carry within oneself the trace of something that has "already" happened. This founds a temporality, a "before-me," in the subject, which forms the basis for vigilance and preparedness: one has fallen, but one has also endured. Both in antiquity and in the Middle Ages, the discourses that taught the "techniques of living"—for example, the dream treatise by Artemidorus studied in the first chapter of Foucault's *The Care of the Self*—are preoccupied with vigilance as a means of averting tragedy.[31] The arts of living link the interpretation of an interior form of "life," the awakening of the interior that is a dream, to the question of one's fortune and one's position in the world (ultimately, too, in the afterworld).³¹ Psychic interiority is cultivated as prosthesis and miniaturization of exteriority.

The experience of immensity thus depends on the development of an interiority enhanced, even constituted, by prosthetic images. This produces a "consciousness of enlargement" wherein "we feel that we have been promoted to the dignity of the admiring being" (184). Expression has magnifying properties, if only because it makes more than one (version of a) thing. This applies even to the expressiveness of the intensive miniature, the "intimate immensity"; any kind of "[p]oetic space, because it is expressed, assumes values of expansion" (201). Tragedy, in particular, is for many centuries strongly associated with *clamor* and stylistic magnification. Boethius's Lady Philosophy, whose formulation of the tragedy of fortune was decisive for Chaucer, speaks of the "clamor of tragedies." Tragedy is associated not only with the startling power of noise but also with deformity and an excess of form. An excess of the signifier that has the power to deform, the power of noise to shock, the power to "magnify" and thereby induce "wonder," measures the immensity of the fall into life. Horace associates "raising of the voice," "bloated mouth," and "overgrown words" with tragedy; Placidus (sixth century) associates tragedy with the *stilus altus*, "high-sounding words"; Aquinas uses the word *tragedia* "to signify bombastic style or loudness of speech," used when "one intends to excite wonder by the magnification of words," "*ad admirationem movendam*."³²

We can, of course, be held as well as excited by wonder. The vulnerability of the subject to inscription means that she can be overtaken: enchanted, captivated, possessed.³³ This vulnerability is formulated by psychoanalysis in terms of the return of the death wish. One seeks—for example, through the "industry" of mnemonic technique—to enhance prosthetically one's power to communicate with what is lost.³⁴ But the lost seems so often to return with a vengeance, because the subject reproaches herself for its disappearance. Those who mourn remain as convinced of the omnipotence of their thoughts as any helpless baby hallucinating her satisfactions.³⁵

The death wish is linked to the fantasy of the insentient "work." The power of images to "magnify" is also a power of in-differentiation; it pushes the image toward universality and the refusal of all particular objects enjoined by the defense against life. The death wish can be indifferent. We can wish for the disappearance of this or that object; we can also wish for the disappearance of the object as such—of anything that cannot be replaced if lost. The love of beauty is powered by the death wish: lost in fascination with the image of the object, the subject can become indifferent to the object in any way that goes beyond the *jouissance* of seeing it.[36] And this dissimulates time and space. In the wonder that is oneiric experience, Bachelard writes, "both time and space are under the domination of the image" (208). Oneiric experience "flees the object nearby and right away it is far off, *elsewhere*, in the space of *elsewhere*" (184). The refusal of life and of our helplessness in space and time is recoded by the oneiric image as accession to immensity in the form of the apparently unlimited space of the psychic interior. Wonder gives us awareness, but in the form of captivation, the state of envisioning proper to the death drive. We address the question of our aliveness to the object of fascination because contemplating such an object allows us to suspend our aliveness without suffering from it: in reverie, in gazing, we are undead.

Rickels remarks: "that the eternal is . . . the internal follows from a fact of life: the other is always the first to go" (*Case of California*, 23). The subject knows of her finitude from the beginning; but to know that she can fall is not the same thing as knowing she will die. We learn of death only by means of seeing the other die. That death belongs to the other is the very limit that the gift of death tries to supplement by structuring a subject who can prepare for and oversee its own dying. All too often we believe the other has died because we wished it would. But this other who is always the first to go is also the other on whom we are founded. Hence the gift of death is also caught up with the death wish: preparedness is also involved in the rescue of the other. No wonder we believe profoundly in our hostility to our creators, and theirs toward us. We cannot, in our psychic negotiations with life and death, escape the ethical ambiguity of creation and its works.

This is why the self's *re*-creation of itself through techniques of living was so strongly ethicized in antiquity and the Middle Ages.[37] When Simonides invents the art of memory by remembering the places where his unfortunate fellow dinner guests, crushed by a falling roof, once sat, he can do so because of a godsend. Simonides had delivered a panegyric on Castor and Pollux at this banquet, and the ill-fated diners mocked his long-winded devotion. Simonides is spared because of the quality of his devotional attention, the sacrifice of his "work." His legend locates the art of memory not simply in violence, but in sacrifice: a scenario of triumphant survival that complexly interweaves the divine "throw" of destiny with the subject's ability to remember that he can indeed be thrown. Moreover, Simonides develops the art of memory because the kin of the crushed guests wish to show *pietas* and bury their fallen ones in proper form. To do so they require the recovery of the signifier: in broader terms, the development of the ability to artifice, interpret, and properly locate images within the psyche. To unmourn trauma, to restore the connection between the dead and the living, one technologizes the psyche itself. One does so by associating particular images with experiences of wonder, enjoyment, horror that can "move the soul . . . and therefore better help the memory."[38] The art of memory is itself *ascesis*, a technical development of *jouissance*. Part of what Simonides retrieves from the wreckage of his dining pleasure is disciplinary: "Be war." Increasingly throughout the Middle Ages, memory is ethicized as "virtuous activity," ever more linked, through the virtue of Prudence, not only to the preservation of the past, but also to right action in the present and retrieval of the future.[39] The art of memory pushes back the borders of our befallenness; it trains interior space to preserve repetitions that enable the subject to "live past" trauma—to "be mortal twice over: sovereignly, extremely mortal" (Blanchot, *The Space of Literature*, 96). What befalls us can be submitted to what scholasticism called "judgment." We can correct our vision of whatever lies beyond us or behind us—but only through the gift of death.

The arts of divination sought nonetheless to supplement the dependence of human foresight on the internal activities of memory and judgment. Origen understood divination to be consolatory in function and to spring from man's insatiable desire to know the future.[40] Farsighted angels could inspire images "of things which it is useful to know, for this is a gift of God."[41] The gift of angelic foresight promises an intended magnification of life, a chosen cast into the future. Demonic dreams, on the other hand, are often lies; they make us fall again by making us not ourselves, persuading men "in marvelous and unseen ways, . . . mingling themselves with men's thoughts."[42] For Gregory the Great, even these trials are a gift: God's "loving-kindness" allows this "lest in the souls of the elect their mere sleep, though nothing else, should go without the meed of sufffering."[43] The frustration of demonic purpose, and the demonic attempt to frustrate men's purposiveness, are the terrorized and terrorizing "opposites" of angelic foresight and the gift of divine knowledge, of "images of unknown places and likenesses of men both living and dead."[44]

Increasingly throughout the Middle Ages, the dream became valuable as a source of psychological and medico-ethical knowledge. Like memory images, oneiric images are understood to form when we yearn for what is absent, or are full of anxiety: "there are [dreams] that, as though the mind has been gravely struck and beaten by the deeply imprinted vestiges of pain, revive in sleep images of a past consternation."[45] The way one slept was morally significant. Too much sleep could figure poor vision. But one could, as Blanchot puts it, sleep too little, "make night present," "be unable to find one's position" (*The Space of Literature*, 265). The disorder of insomnia was even groupified for the court in the later Middle Ages, in the form of *amor hereos*, love-melancholy.[46] But sleep could free us from our daily cares, and permit heightened attention to matters of life and death. Pascalis Romanus, a dream theorist of the later Middle Ages, writes: "when the senses have been lulled and all external cares and occupations put aside, ... [reason,] free and mindful of its divine origin, then better recognizes future things."[47] By taking us elsewhere, sleep negates the world but also fixes it (Blanchot, *The Space of Literature*, 266). It is a way of having already not been, and of being resurrected from that condition into a newly intense living. Hence sleep is not opposed to awakening: "vigilance ... consists in not always keeping watch, for it seeks *awakening* as its essence," transforming "myriad possibilities into a single stopping point upon which I ... reestablish myself" (ibid.). Through the production of interior images, sleep, dream, enchantment, and memory work all hold out the lure of indifference, of a state in which one will not suffer from one's aliveness. They also preserve us, however, from what is frightening about becoming insentient: the shattering of sentience involved in dying. Living on in an afterlife that has nonetheless not put an end to the subject, so that the subject can imagine itself to "know" its death and therefore to "possess" it, is the goal of preparedness. Whether in the form of knowledge of the dead, the future, or one's own proper regimen, forms of preparedness deliver the *jouissance* of the death drive, even as they protect against it.

Expressive technologies promise to save me and my others from death and my own death wishes. This is a promise doomed to failure. It is not possible for expressive technologies to rescue us from befallenness, however brilliantly they can work to enhance our sentience. This is why I have, in the past, critiqued the tendency of critics of Chaucer's *Book of the Duchess* to read the poem, approvingly, as a "work" that gets us out of the isolation of mourning through the sacrificial power of language.[48] I want to explore anew how our readings of *The Book of the Duchess* might change when we consider language as imbricated in, rather than transcendent of, loss. The movements of desire between the desire to desire and the desire to end desire structure Chaucer's *Book of the Duchess*, which embeds within a courtly dream vision the kind of story Chaucer would later, in *Troilus and Criseyde*, explicitly call "tragedye."

The Book of the Duchess was probably written for John of Gaunt, considered by many scholars to have been Chaucer's patron, as a memorial of the death (from plague) of Gaunt's duchess Blanche. Because of its fairly clear association with Blanche's death in 1368 or 1369, the poem is generally regarded as an early one, composed when Chaucer's relations with John of Gaunt must have seemed well fortuned, and when Gaunt's prominence in national and international affairs was reaching a certain zenith. This was the time of Gaunt's and Chaucer's adventures in Spain: Chaucer traveled there in 1366, possibly as an ambassador to the court of Pedro of Spain, and Gaunt's next duchess (in 1371) would be Constance, Pedro's daughter, through whom Gaunt claimed the title of King of Castile and León. Chaucer's wife Philippa de Roet was likely part of Constance's first household.[49] Chaucer regarded Pedro as of sufficient importance to be included in *The Monk's Tale*; the tragedy of Pedro of Spain, *De Petro Rege Ispannie*, is one of the four "no-fault" "modern" tragedies Chaucer wrote for the Monk: "'O noble, O worthy Petro, glorie of Spayne, / Whom Fortune heeld so hye in magestee, / Wel oghten men thy pitous deeth complayne!" (2375–77). Situated after the first devastating outbreaks of the century's agonizing form of group death, but at a time of survival when Fortune had nonetheless only just begun to pull away the bright feathers of England, Edward III's sons, and those favored by them, the poem presents us with a courtier's gift in the guise of the gift of death. The poem requests, and promises, vigilance, in the form of attention: attending on and to, paying and getting attention. The tragic story of the Man in Black's loss of White (the Man in Black and his lady White are generally taken as stand-ins for Gaunt and Blanche, and/or aspects of the dreamer's interiority) is embedded in the development of a "transference"—a moment of heightened awareness and communication.[50]

The poem's narrator begins in a state of wonder; he is astonished that he still lives, he has slept so little.[51] He is himself a wonder; he ought to be dead, because it is against nature ("agaynes kynde" [16]) to live this way. He has survived beyond a certain limit of nature and is still around, ghostly, to ponder the prodigy of his own continuing sentience. This "living on" in the form of insomniac vigil seems less miraculous than uncanny, however. The narrator personifies the haunting return of fear and aggressivity through the very circuits and images that are supposed to put life in touch with death for the sake of preparedness. Afflicted with "melancolye," the very aliveness of his spirit has been slain ("Defaute of slep... / Hath sleyn my spirit of quyknesse"), yet he fears the coming of death (25–26). This ghost suffers from vigil gone bad, a life lived past all attachment to life. Instead of taking the care prescribed by the scene of vigil, he takes no heed of anything and feels neither desire nor loathing ("I take nor kep / Of nothing... / Ne me nys nothyng leef nor looth" [6–8]). Desire is dead in him; he is in a state of indifference to objects, but not a pleasantly enchanted one. The narrator's situation becomes even stranger when he refers mysteriously to a physician who could heal him, "but that is don" (40). Wonder multiplies: the narrator wonders, he is himself a wonder, and now we wonder even more intensely why he crossed the line into ghostliness in the first place.

These enervated wonders sublime the state of indifference. They solemnize not only the limits to vision and desire, the objects of which are such a problem, but anticlimax itself: one's objects, one's desire, is that all? Would it be more scandalous to be presumptuously curious about wonders, or to care less? Although we are not meant to find the narrator comforting, his very emptiness gives him the dignity of immensity, the immensity of "nothyng." The courtly attitude of yearning to the point of senselessness is given tragic magnitude through the interminability of mourning and the immensity of the interior that lacks. The very intangibility of interior space becomes a prosthetic replacement for the finitude of one's position in exterior space.

The narrator is rescued from the vertiginous aspects of this attenuation of space when he picks up a romance to drive the night away. He is inspired by it to pray for sleep, and gets his wish. Ovid's story of Ceyx and Alcyone, from the *Metamorphoses*, saves him. Alcyone mourns her husband Ceyx, who has been lost at sea. She gets "news" of his death after she prays to Juno and Juno commands the gods of sleep to enlighten her. One of these gods appears in the image of Ceyx's body and asks for the proper burial rites. At the end of the story, Alcyone miraculously encounters Ceyx's body near the shore, swims out to greet him, and is rewarded for her fidelity when the gods turn them both into halcyon birds: symbols of good fortune and safety at sea.

Chaucer modifies the story significantly. His Alcyone dies of sorrow. The heterosexual couple comes to a dead end. Hopefulness emerges not in anticipation of enduring hetero coupledom or reproductivity, but in anticipation of the male-male couple formed later by the narrator and the Man in Black. Still, the narrator presents Ovid's tale as "a wonder thing" that can put "in minde" the fables of old poets (61, 55). Something old, like Seys, is being reawakened, through the power of language to extend sentience over time. The poetry channel opens up also along the lines of similarity, old poets speaking to new ones. Transmission is a group effort, involving the clearing away of sexual "difference" (the status of which, of course, is not exactly "real").

The transferential power of images is central to Chaucer's revisions of Ovid. In his version, Morpheus actually creeps into Seys's corpse when he goes to enlighten Alcyone, whereas in Ovid's one of the gods of sleep simply assumes Ceyx's shape. The image presented to Alcyone is made up of the corpse inhabited by a "daemon" delivering the gift of true knowledge about the past and counsel for the future. Chaucer's point seems to be that dazzling technologies of transmission are always going to bring back the corpse they are supposed to talk our way out of. The death drive comes through loud and clear when we are chatting across distances of time and space. The vicissitudes of technological and rhetorical prosthesis are often a concern in tragedy: *Lear* is definitely an exercise in getting around the kingdom.

Morpheus's appearance in Seys's dead body yokes vigilance to awakening. It looks as though Alcyone is being sent back to life, the border between the living and the dead will be reasserted, the power of the death wish and its cruel returns will be laid to rest, when Alcyone "lets be" her sorrowful life. But even this call to life has a deadly core. The command of the corpse-image to Alcyone, "let be your sorwful lyf," invites either a turning back toward life or a letting be of life, a refusal of life and its sorrows. This corpse-image that images the insensibility of the image gives no more clearly the gift of life than the gift of death—though critics have sometimes blamed Alcyone for failing to live up to this call to life, this godsend.

Chaucer wants to go one better than Ovid by appealing to the appeal of death itself. So he speeds things up, cutting off the elaborate complaint Alcyone is given in the *Metamorphoses*, because it would take too long to tell and he needs to get back to what he was saying. In short, why wait? Why sit through Alcyone's complaint? Is it that the narrator wants to underscore the dead end of the couple? Or is it that Alcyone's tiring of life is *mirrored* in the narrator's rush to closure—a closing down of sentience and transmission adumbrated by the failure of Alcyone's vision ("hir eyen up she casteth / And saw noght" [212–13; she cast up her eyes and saw nothing]—and finished even before Alcyone is finished ("But what she sayede more in that swow / I may not telle yow as now; / Hyt were to longe for to dwelle" [215–17; what more she saw in her swoon / I cannot tell you right now; / it would take too long])? The image, which begs for animation but which thereby offers the lure of insentience, mediates the narrator's hectic liveliness, which is also a rush to death. Getting busy, paying attention, taking care, are all ways of getting to the end of the story. Of course, one can get so excited about the feeling of moving on that one cannot finish—Alcyone's complaint, for instance. Yet all this excitement is linked to anticlimax. "To lytel while oure blysse lasteth" (211; our bliss lasts for too little a while) is the last thing Seys-Morpheus says to Alcyone before she disappears from life and the narrator disappears her complaint. The image speaks, proverbially, for the law of the group, the inevitable limits that characterize "us." Why dwell on that? Surely that is not all there is?

The narrative is structured as a series of survivals: the narrator wondrously survives his own melancholy; Alcyone survives Seys; the narrator survives Alcyone, at a moment when the narrative pace gets seriously manic. Now *jouissance* moves things along. The sole survivor of (the) death (of the other), restored by the magnifying power of poetic transmission, can now turn to the friend he wants to be like. The "first matter" *(first matere)* of the poem will be relayed not by a solitary narrator reporting on a text in which he does not himself appear but by a narrator who makes a friend for whom he acts as witness. The hetero couple, along with its sentient/transient products and modes of reproduction, dies off but is introjected, sheltered by the power of replication sometimes thought to be characteristic of the male-male bond. This preserves the lady as a memory and as the matrix of remembering.

Sameness is also enhanced by the poem's shift from a text and its powers of transmission to the interiority of dream. Yet the movement into greater intimacy also brings on contestation. "Me mette so ynly swete a sweven, / So wonderful that never yit / Y trowe no man had the wyt / To konne wel my sweven rede; / No, not Joseph..." (276–80). Wonderfulness, as oneiric unintelligibility, is now a means to defeat the best dream readers in Scripture and classical literature. The narrator's interiority achieves immensity through its own mystery; but now the dreme is "swete" rather than ghostly.

The survivals that take wonder from creepy revenant insomnia to the sweetness of renewed inner life gradually overlay the deadness of the corpse-image. The narrator promises a richly decorated bedchamber to any god that can make him sleep; this promise of a redecorated interior, uncannily anticipated in the haunting of Seys's body by Morpheus, is fulfilled by the dream chamber into which the narrator awakens. Inside the dreaming subject, where, Freud argues, the unconscious knows nothing of death, the fatal potential of exteriority can be circumvented. The narrator is "affrayed" out of his sleep by "a gret hep" of songbirds (295–96; startled). Part of the rich semantic registry of "unexpectedness" in *The Book of the Duchess*, the word *affrayed* points to an experience startling enough to be unpleasurable, but also beautiful and *swete*. The springtime opening conventional in the courtly poem is used here to mark the way artifacts make sentient territories, in this case giving space extension and quality through audio transmission.[52] More specifically, we are reminded that the power of sound to design space and make it tangible, or at least audible, is not inherently benevolent. We are startled into life; we can only hope that someone will start singing. The decoration of the narrator's chamber makes a similar point. The paintings of *The Romance of the Rose* on the walls, and the window engravings of the terrible stories of Troy and of Medea and Jason, do not "affray" the narrator's eyes. And yet their topics are linked with tragedy in medieval understandings of the genre.[53] The beauty of etchings that never seem to mourn is a power of horror. But one can simply be fascinated by them.

Once outside the bedchamber, the narrator discovers a sentient environment of phenomenal sweetness: the air is bright, blue and clear, neither too hot nor too cold—as though one could be startled into life and even go through memory images of the tragic past and still discover that life intends nothing startling to one's aliveness. Psychic space becomes more and more of a refuge in which sentience can complicate and extend itself without encountering limits and falling to earth: virtual. This prosthetic interior space appears vulnerable to nothing but the limitless wonder of its own capacity to unfold itself. The upcoming encounter with the Man in Black is given the value of a pleasurable curiosity because it is set up as a chance meeting that is nonetheless consistent in its mode of being with that which surrounds and precedes it.

But in this paradise, hunting is allowed, and the "hert" (hart, deer) is in peril. "Octovyen's" hunt, which the narrator briefly joins, reminds us that if encounters can be salvific, they can also be fatal—and it is not always so easy to tell the difference between the two, as critical commentary on the hunt suggests.[54] The ambiguous value of the hunt derives partly from the fact that it stages befallenness; as encounter, it is a setup. The chase artifices desire by subliming its targets; not just any "herte" will do. There are "many an hert and many an hynde" in the forest (427); but, for arbitrary and mysterious reasons, the object of the hunt must be *this* one.

And when this hart "rused and staal way, / Fro alle the houndes a privy way" (381–82), a lost whelp, who "koude no good" (390), leads the narrator toward a space of even greater enchantment, deeper into the heart of the forest. Something has escaped; an animal has survived. We are no more the wiser, but our uncertainty is increasingly inflected with wonder, and in its more disarming aspect. The whelp's value is also ambiguous in his critical tradition, which makes a certain sense since he companionates as well as exemplifies the passage from risk and its delectations to even more charming pleasures. The whelp makes the transition from hound of the hunt to the animated animal whose cuteness contains, posttrauma, the scariness of the death wish.[55] The figure of the whelp promises that "passage," transition, even when futures and purposes are indecipherable, can make safe and be made safe. As "transitional object," the whelp can transmit and be transmitted to but seems not to be haunted by the death wishes of transmission (and indeed of reproduction). This uncanny little figure who is also harmless, suasive, and perhaps fearful of, but not finally subject to, care is a lot like the narrator of *The Book of the Duchess*, and like the images Chaucer creates of "himself" elsewhere in his poetry. The whelp unknowingly and therefore innocently transfers the narrator to his new status as friendly witness and companion to the Man in Black, whose relation to suffering is mediated by the image of the other. The whelp-narrator is part and subject of a relay whereby his own wondrous insentience, lostness, being-at-a-lossness, will be refound in the image of the other body that, except for his high (human or aristocratic) estate, is like, but not, his own.

The gradual specification of this series, in which figures saturated with immense, because unfathomable, meanings emerge from the crowd, implies that sublimely safe territory can be rendered through figures of number and variety as well as indifference. Paradise is a miniaturization: *heimlich,* but infinite in its riches. There are many varieties of birdsong in an exquisitely sentient territory; there are "many grene greves" in the interior forest. As Bachelard notes, the forest has so many different kinds of life in it as to be unaccountable: both incalculable and impenetrable (*The Poetics of Space,* 185–89). Its infinite secret lives make endless surprises; variety wondrously refracts the specificity of the living creature. The forest is "so ful of bestes" that even Argus would "fayle to rekene even / The wondres me mette in my sweven" (434, 441). But even though the wonders of this dream are incalculable, it gives itself also the deep pleasure of distinctiveness: "every tree stood by hymselve/Fro other wel ten foot or twelve— / So grete trees, so huge of strengthe, / Of fourty or fifty fadme lengthe" (419–22). What can and cannot be counted intertwine to produce something sublime; and there is no loss.

Deep within this place of many secret lives, where difference seems suspended in, but not dissolved by, indifference, the narrator finds the Man in Black. Perhaps because the forest softens the clamor of its own multifarious sentience, it can shelter an image of the other body whose suffering is, or can become, similar: recognizable, communicable.[56] In this "poetic space" the Man in Black will give expression to another version of a life lived beyond the attachment to life. Like the narrator, the Man in Black is a maker of verses that make "deadly, sorrowful sounds." Like the narrator, he is a "wonder"; he too has gone beyond the limit of Nature: "Hyt was gret wonder that Nature / Myght suffre any creature / To have such sorwe and be not ded" (467–69). Furthermore, this wondrousness is piteous; the Man in Black's "complaint to himself" evokes for the narrator "the most pitee, the moste rowthe, / That ever I herde" (465–66). This is not a transition to symbolicity as such, but rather a new use of the groupifying power of the image. On this score it matters little whether the Man in Black is John of Gaunt, or the melancholic aspect of the narrator's psyche, or both. What counts is that they are enough alike that that they can perform for each other the role of the other through whom one can recognize oneself.

The complaint and its reception by the narrator show how courtly love develops group prestige by cultivating the life lived beyond all attachment to life, and, through pity, its sufferings. The complaint's topics are conventionally oxymoronic: abundance of sorrow, privation of joy, the visibility of an invisibility ("my lady bryght... Is fro me ded and ys agoon" [477, 479]). Aristocratic sorrow confers the magical ability to see what has disappeared and have plenty of lack. Oxymoronic rhetoric works to extend the courtly interior through the very unintelligibility of its contradictions. This announcement of the vastness of the Man in Black's possession and vision of nothing calls attention to the negative ambitions of the courtly vigil. The courtly vigil extends the sentience intensified by loss so that it can take as its object of perception the very thing it cannot, but desires to, see. This is indeed an indifferentiating of the grievous particularity of the object of desire. The life lived beyond all attachment to life is that of the survivor who lives on to solemnize the lack that gives psychic space immensity. The death drive might like to go this way, by converting the objects of the waking world into memory images and "places" that design the courtly interior, expanding the terrain over which the courtier has some clout.

When the survivor's heightened capacity for vigil intersects with the death drive's wish to abandon vigilance and its objects, the rhetoric of the lady's goodness and vitality makes its appearance. The appearance of the lady raises the question of the courtly lover's loving, and how that loving marks *his* aliveness, more precisely his survival of her death. One can only love if one lives, but one can love something dead; indeed, one must and will: that is the very quality of love, to survive the death of the beloved and testify to its endurance.[57] The knight explains that Death has taken his "lady swete... Of al goodnesse she had no mete!" (483, 486). The courtly—and sovereign—trope of matchlessness images a realization of a quality intense enough to negate all similarity. The aggressivity of this mode of idealizing particularity isolates the object from all objects of like quality. But it does not end there. The ideal object is a "group of one," a figure of distinction that contains the groupifying power of the ideal. Her gender and her status as *objet a*, as phantasmic particular, set her apart from the *finamen*, and this distinctiveness, strangely, can make her all the more secure a shelter for the group. But in this poem she is replaced by the greater alikeness and likeability of the friend who manages to make mourning a sociable activity.

The first encounter between the narrator and the Man in Black illustrates this point. The Man in Black has swooned; "his spirites wexen dede" (489); all his blood has fled to his heart, the principal member of the body, because it "sees" that the heart had harm (492). His very body is groupified, and its multiplicity associated with a power of rescue. Moreover, as the hetero couple gives way to friendship, relations of reproduction and substitution give way to replication. The Man in Black imitates Blanche's deadliness; the narrator imitates the Man in Black's very blood, by seeing suffering and intervening, "going to" the right place ("Anoon therwith whan I sawgh this . . . / I went and stood ryght at his fet" [500, 502]). Courtly love has been displaced by courtier love, which stylizes the court through the vigilant and equalizing mannering of the group body always aware of and anticipating its own destructivity: "at the last . . . / He was war of me, how y stood / Before hym and did of myn hood" (514–16); "Loo, how goodly spak thys knyght, / As hit had be another wyght; / He made hyt nouther towgh ne queynte" (529–31). The mannered body and voice equalizes, but does not dissolve, rank; it deflects, but registers, danger. Rank permits special gifts of friendship, because a great man risks a little prestige when he condescends to courtly friendship with a lesser man, and a lesser man risks what rank he has by approaching a greater man. Courtesy is an economy of sacrifice as well as prosthesis, a mannering and extension of sentience that elaborates the form of *the* group, so that no one goes alone and the endlessly deferred other always goes first: says the narrator, "by my trouthe, To make you hool / I wol do al my power hool. / And telleth me of your sorwes smerte; / Paraunter hyt may ese youre herte" (553–56). The potential loss of distinction risked by courtly culture is apparently redressed: one survives loss by risking it through the *depense* ("expenditure") of courtly manners.[58]

The Man in Black intensifies the stakes of this consolatory exchange. He thanks his "goode frend" (560) but explains that nothing can make his sorrows disappear—not all the remedies of Ovid, nor of Orpheus, the god of melody, nor of Dedalus with his clever devices, nor any physician, neither Hippocrates or Galen, could help him (567–73). The techniques of living are useless to a creature who regrets falling into life in the first place ("wo that I was born!"), whom sorrow has made into the epitome of the liminal time between life and death: "My lyf, my lustes, be me loothe, / For al welfare and I be wroothe" (581–82). But because he inhabits the zone of an exacerbated sensibility, he epitomizes the courtly art of mourning-until-death. Through the living-on of his fidelity to Blanche, the identification with whose deadness attests his devotion, the Man in Black is thrown toward death, and made to share the exemplary status of his lost object: "For y am sorwe, and sorwe ys y" (597).

The "I" coincides with a form of suffering. "I" is pure symptom, "lapse," and pain finds being through personification. This condition, like Blanche's exemplifying of goodness, is a set-apartness that makes the "I" a group of one. Now that it "safely" interiorizes Blanche, Black's exemplarity can be enjoyed as well as subsequently restyled. It is here that Black announces his tragic status, through the rivalrous catalog that is his narrative signature and desire. The Man in Black, who is always dying and yet not dead, has more sorrow than Sisyphus, who lies in hell (588–90). The narrator will meet the challenge of assuaging a Sisyphean sorrow beyond the arts of healing (Galen) and machining (Daedalus). The transitivist structure of friendship helps to turn even consolation of the inconsolable into triumph. In the Aristotelian-Ciceronian tradition, the way of loving proper to friendship is benevolent: "to love *before* being loved."[59] But the purity of benevolence has constantly to be tested. Benevolence, fidelity, *pietas* are closely coordinated forms of enjoyment that impel the friend toward the testimonials only death can offer.

The narrator must pass the test of pity: says the Man in Black, "But whoso wol assay hymselve / Whether his hert kan have pitee / Of any sorwe, lat hym see me" (574–76). Indeed, someone who is not able to pity the Man in Black's sorrows has "a fendly herte" (594). To be a courtly friend, one undertakes an *ascesis* of rivalry; one must be able to feel inside oneself, inside one's heart, a suffering for the other that resembles the other's suffering. "Provided the whole thing depend on my efforts": courtly friendship has the lineaments of a rescue fantasy. The courtly one imagines that he can save the life of the other on whom his "own" life depends, a way of coming "before" the other who is the first to go.

Rivalry is thus in fact not so much renounced as it is refigured. And my reward for my sacrifice is the triumph of a heart careful enough of itself to "assay" itself.

Now the Man in Black presents himself as victim of the scourging power of alteration known as Fortune. The death wishes of courtesy rebound, after the technological advance on epitome, in the form of the figure who epitomizes happening. Black portrays Fortune as elaborately malign. She refracts the power of alteration of the subject's own (death) wishes: to have any object, to have no objects, to disappear the particularity of objects.[60] She does so by beating the Man in Black at chess. The reappearance of contest, this time with fatal consequences, casts something of a shadow on the just-preceding test of pity. Fortune turns out to be similar to the Man in Black in at least one particular: for both of them, contest is a structure of enjoyment, as is suggested by the digressive technical detail and valorization of skill in the Man in Black's description of the chess game's end point: "Therwith Fortune seyde 'Chek her! / And mat in the myd poynt of the chekker, / With a poun errant!' Allas, / Ful craftier to pley she was / Than Athalus, that made the game / First of the ches, so was hys name" (659–64). To be superlatively crafty is one aspect of Fortune's power; her technical know-how is matchless. And the Man in Black also knows the rules. The poem adds Fortune to its tableaux of technicians of foresight and outcome—Daedalus, Argus, Joseph—whose arts promise to avert disaster. Thus the poem develops a series of (con)tests of skill in the arts that promise to repair befallenness, a series over which Fortune appears to reign supreme, through her unbeatable power of sheer preference: she takes the best (684).

Moreover, as the test of pity shows, the transitivist and probative quality of these catalogs links them to the testing of the courtly friend's preparedness toward death. The friend who loves lives; true friendship is tested and attested by the living on of its love after death. The cultivation of life—its transformation into art—thus seems, in *The Book of the Duchess*, to make life probative. To fall into life is to engage in a test of skill, and one either stands or falls. Our time would then always be in relation to the test of skill, preparing for it or beyond it, thrown toward it or having survived it. The test of skill repeats the fall and its unexpectedness, but in the context of the law of the group. The fall is repeated as intended; helplessness is refigured as helpfulness, painful surprise as the planning of risky encounter. Fortune represents Black's desire to will the disappearance of his objects. Thus his narration of Fortune ends in an unabashed (and somewhat anticlimactic) admission of their similarity. Instead of projecting his wishes onto her, he says that he would have done the same thing Fortune did, if he had been what Fortune was; and "She oghte the more excused be" (678). Really, it is almost as though they were friends.

Previous to this final assertion of empathy, the Man in Black's projections reveal a lot about his Fortune-like desire to possess the "best." Fortune is "an ydole of fals portrayture" (626), an image whose aliveness is not to be trusted. She represents the allure of the work's insentience, the way we allow our works to enchant us into believing their aliveness, but also the helplessness of sentience to help itself absolutely through its own works. We are creatures whose *jouissance* is caught up in artificing life and death, one aspect of which is the very limit placed on our works by our befallenness. The figure of the idol consoles by reminding us of its opposite: proper objects of devotion who live intensely enough that their vision can see into the future, and help us live by sharing their vision with us.[61] But the figure also makes clear why we find Fortune—who *is* after all one of our works—irresistible.

Fortune is also "th'envyouse charite / That ys ay fals and semeth wel" (642–43). This figure consoles by suggesting that someone enough like me to want what I want, so badly that she is willing to pretend a generosity she does not feel in order to get it, is responsible for my vulnerability to falling. I do not have to confront my inability to possess objects (let alone the "best") absolutely. I am reassured that I have things valuable enough to be coveted, and to make my sacrifices meaningful. Fortune figures our trouble with objects, but she also figures how *we* get our objects into trouble. For the sake of the test, the contest, the prize, we are always willing to make our objects into counters.

Idolatry and envious charity are both forms of image making and gift giving that take advantage of the befallenness of creatures who mourn. Our "works"—charitable and otherwise—are riddled with *jouissance,* the evil that lies in the heart of the neighbor, but is a lot like the evil in our own hearts. Fortune—whom the Man in Black will ultimately find so neighborly as to be just like him—is the very "pley of enchauntement, / That semeth oon and ys not soo" (648–49). The seductiveness of enchantment lies in the the appearance of oneness. I fascinate the other by appearing to be "one"; the other can see a wholeness in me, and need not look elsewhere. But "I" am founded on the image of the other. And the stranger, the *jouissance*, inside me is also inside the other. It is no wonder we cannot tell ourselves apart; yet the image has sufficient power of generalization to suspend that confusion in a solution of oneness. This is exactly the enchantment being played out between Black and the narrator.

In *The Book of the Duchess*, Fortune poses the question of how one pays attention, of when and where attention should begin and end. How should the subject attend to the image of the (lost) object? Through a fascination whereby the object and therefore its lostness can be treated to a suspended animation, its status as object temporarily dissolved and its transience, its "is that all" given the possibility of revenance because, in a state of suspended life, it might return and undo finitude and guilt? As if turning back to life, the poem now gives its attention to suicide. The narrator wants to be the one who fascinates, who gives the gift of life/death to the Man in Black; like many before and after him, he insists that life and death be in the hands of the Other. He tells Black that if Black murdered himself, he would be damned as rightfully as was Medea (724–26). He goes rapidly through a catalog of grisly stories, most of which Chaucer would later retell as tragic, but which are here treated with dislike—or at least with a brevity that goes beyond anything the Monk will attempt in the way of tragic miniaturization.[62] The *Duchess*-narrator's *jouissance* with respect to love stories that come to dead ends differs, however, from the Monk's enjoyment of pure form, insofar as it is yet another instance of the poem's fascination with contest. Specifically, the narrator wants these dead loves to back off because he does not want the dead end of the couple: the terrible mourning that results from attachment to the kind of object of which one can have only one. The friend offers something more consoling: the group of two that makes consolation its business.[63] The poem moves from the abbreviated exteriority of competing, but losing, tragedies, to interiority and groupification.

On the way, Blanche will make a comeback for a valediction. The danger of her return will, however, already have been treated apotropaically, because the moment when Black will begin to speak of this loss beyond friendly comprehension is also a moment when Black and the narrator dedicate themselves to heightened attentiveness. By such means is Blanche channeled "safely," that is, without the revenance of destructivity. Black promises to tell the narrator everything he wants to know on the condition that the narrator will dedicate himself to "herkene hit. / Swere thy trouthe therto!" (752–53). The pact that makes the group of two and redeems credibility is a dedication to heightened sentience, which can deliver the living object and its frightening exteriority to the relative safety of the survivor's story and the more malleable interiority of the memory image.

As Freud notes, mourning re-places the lost object in an interior terrain whose laws of operation do not recognize death.[64] As a devotional process, the work of memory redeems guilt over one's death wishes. These death wishes come alive, if for no other reason, because of our fear of any particular object—fear of its power to make us mourn, fear of its power to make us mourn desire when its "is-that-all" emerges. The subliming of the dead object is a devotional offering—depense, a concentration of prosthesis into *ascesis:* the vigil, redeeming guilt, restoring the "is-that-all" to tragic "greatness."

The turn toward interiority through devotional *ascesis* is announced through the story of a submission to "Love," to whom (through "plesance") Black becomes thrall. This submission to Love comes to Black "kyndely," by nature, prior to knowledge and to particular objects: "And ful devoutly I prayed hym to / He shulde besette myn herte so / That hyt plesance to hym were" (771–73). When "plesance" is conceived as lordship, lordship is interiorized as the joy of sentience. Submission indicates both the presence and the "plesance" of the law. The interiority of courtly sensibility is developed through its allegorization (hence the linking of *The Romance of the Rose* to the tragic matter of Troy in the decor of the narrator's dream chamber); it has characters, manners, rank, rule, history. Once inside, one can perhaps enjoy surprise visits, the way the Arthurian court of medieval romance will look forward to the arrival of "marvels" on feast days. But even better, "Love" comes to one as godsend and as god; one's love is divinized. The object's power over us is subordinated to the relative in-difference of Love as an affect waiting to happen. If he is not altogether in repose—his psyche is on the move—the baby courtier is at least full of Love and belongs fully to Love before he loves this or that lady, a situation treated with considerable comic pleasure in *The Tale of Sir Thopas.*

The figure of a Love that comes to the courtly subject before the love of his life reworks indifference into preparedness for the future enhancement of one's interior *through* the prosthetic attachment of objects.

The difference implied by the lord-vassal relation is also evened out as a writing on the "whit wall" that once was Black. Black understands himself as a work of portraiture, a white wall "redy to cacche and take / Al that men wil theryn make" (781–82). The memory imprinted most strongly on this wall is love: "But for love cam first in my thoght, / Therfore I forgat hyt noght; / I ches love to my firste crafte" (789–91). Black's explanation of why he remembers Love is sophisticated, recalling Aquinas's remark that we remember best the experiences of our childhood because then the world was so new to us and so provocative of wonder.[65] The world is also implied by Black's psychobiography because Love's "making" on the white wall of his interior is later remade into a figure of exteriority, the long castle with white walls toward which Black rides "homwarde" at the end of the poem (1215). Black begins as a white wall that will be crafted by the art of Love, and heads for a *heimlich* castle where the wall of wonder becomes a defensive wall, a material sign of seigneurial power.

The receptivity of the subject to inscription by befallenness is valorized through a psycho-autobiography of the courtly interior. Its purpose is to produce greatness through intimacy with the friend but also with one's "self," above all through the communication of the self to the friend; as Foucault explains, the arts that care for the self always enjoin confidence, a sociality.[66] The cultivation of "me" and of the way "I" live prepares me toward death, but doubly so through the figure of the friend to whom I describe my interiority. The hopefulness of transference registers this throwing of oneself toward survival "after" death, by extending one's channels of communication through the testing of attention. For *The Book of the Duchess,* this is the structure of enjoyment proper to the genre of tragedy, that is, to tragedy as "craft," as "work" made for the other. It is also an ideological fantasy that inscribes and supports the power of a group life and law (in this case, of courtliness) *to* cultivate one's life so that one can live on. Insofar as the Man in Black triumphs over Fortune, it is through the ideology of courtliness, which enjoins stylized friendship with the rival, the patron, the supplicant: the neighbor who would steal my fortune, the lord who can give me the gift of fortune, the client who petitions me in seeking his fortune. Larry Scanlon has argued that the figure of Fortune hides the destructivity of courtly culture; when the wheel of fortune descends for me, the chances are that one of my "friends" has given it a push.[67] But it is also true that courtliness masks a contingency beyond the reach of either its elegance or its aggressivity.

Premodern exemplarity attempts to make heterogeneity and homogeneity coincide as a means of ameliorating finitude for the group and for the subject within the group. Allegory is particularly expressive of this art of rule: the group of one, the sovereign or the universal, offers a "unique" figure that can link the distinctiveness of objects to the *jouissance* of insentient generality. In Chaucer's *Boece*, the "stature" of Lady Philosophy—a figure of redeemed figuration, that is, of the capacity of the mind to know universals via images—

> was of a doutous jugement, for somtyme sche ... schronk hirselven lik to the comune mesure of men, and somtyme it semede that sche touchede the hevene with the heghte of here heved ... [and] percede the selve hevene so that the sighte of men lokynge was in ydel. (*Boece,* I, prosa. 1)

We know that something like this exemplarity *is*—or was—Blanche. Black's first sight of her is of "oon / That was lyk noon of the route" (818–19). She drains the group of distinction, she is alone "ryght as hirselve" (832). As illustration, she has the power to out-illumine as well as to share, to pour her "self" out to and for the other and the group. If White appears both as a figure for the receptivity to engraving that gives the subject its interior life, and for the triumphant technological relay of that intimate impressionability (Black's castle), then "White" must be a fantasy of a matrix of aliveness, of its sentient subjectivity and its technological self-extensions into (and out of) the world. White is the personified, feminized, humanized figure of the capacity of sentience to "receive" or be structured by the signifier and to reproduce that receptivity in its works. Making her dead, feminine, and human helps to make this capacity for engraving less fearful: safely in the past, not as powerful as the masculine subject, but recognizably human. The "prosthetic maternity" of the courtier-friend recalls her, but from the standpoint of the "larger" sociality of the group, which lives on.[68]

The outpouring of splendid and artful illustriousness that is White is central to the presentation in the later Middle Ages of female sovereignty as set-apartness that negotiates difference and indifference by linking charity to beauty as premier modes of manifestation. White is the capacity of whatever "is," but may be hidden, to appear or to be given—to become available to sentience and group communication. She has the brilliance of the courtly arts of living; she is the most eloquent, the best at conversation, and so on. She also harbors reposefulness, drawing back into safety whatever is precious.[69] "Trouthe hymself over al and al / Had chose hys maner principal / In hir that was his restyng place" (1003–5).

As the reversed image of Fortune's deceptiveness and thievery, Blanche manifests goodness and being, becoming distinctively what she is by being wholly lovable, the epitome of the *objet a*—the object of love so powerful that it can rival and replace the love of the self or the group (1035–36). As the epitome of sentience, moreover, Blanche *is* the Man in Black's fortune: "For certes she was, that swete wif, / . . . Myn hap, myn hele, and al my blesse, / My worldes welfare, and my goddesse" (1037–40): "yif that she / Had among ten thousand be, / She wolde have be, at the leste, / A chef myrour of al the feste" (971–74).

The urgency of distinguishing her as uniquely lovable is one of the reasons why the Man in Black's blazon of her beauties and virtues is so lengthy and obsessively detailed. As particular object, as the most distinctive object that ever was, White can be lost irreplaceably. This gives her the value of extreme rarity, but poses a problem for that aspect of desire that seeks its own dissolution in indifference. And in fact, as I have been suggesting, Blanche must be "made" according to the law of the group if she is to achieve sublime specificity, that is, the value of the object raised to the dignity of the Thing not only by one lover but by a community, representationally, so to speak: in such a way that she represents the very value of specificity made sublime. Thus Blanche looks like all beautifully courtly ladies, the very pattern of beauty and model of Nature's works. But Black renders her, with an overdetermined and excessive specificity. Not only, for example, is her neck smooth and white, but we are told that it had no holes in it and no nasty, visibly jutting-out collarbone (943). The intimacy of examining "every heer on hir hed" (855) turns Blanche into a world. But the way that world-class aliveness begins to shade back ever so slightly into the corpse—Blanche's description verges, deliberately, I think, on the grotesque—reminds us of the embodied status of particular objects, and of what is at stake in Black's ability so to describe her. Black lives on through the privation that now defines his mode of being and expressivity. The duration of his complaint, moveover, marks the survivor's bid for a life that continues, postcatastrophe, by calculating its losses. Black not only lives on through his ability to attend to Blanche; he also lives on through the attention he can command from his consolers. Indeed, one's ability to listen carefully is sometimes tested by the gambit of Black's long-winded responses to the narrator; but consolation demands that the consoler's attentiveness be complete, whether or not it takes the form of complete understanding. The extent to which the *objet a* can be attended to as sublime, as that paradoxical fantasy of distinctiveness which gathers the group together, is the warrant of survival and its rights of attention, and it is what Chaucerian tragedy will repeatedly test.

The value of female sovereignty as, so to speak, a means of getting attention was immense in the later Middle Ages. As aristocratic communities valorized ever more intensely the riskiness of the prestige union, the consort bore ever more clearly the value of distinctiveness, of difference from the community over which she was to reign. And yet what was at stake was precisely the conversion of her heterogeneity into an asset for homogeneity. At a time when political communities were groupifying—one might say "nationalizing"—queens, as "outsiders," could represent unities transcending the realm's internal divisions. Love for that she who, *because* of her differences, could both represent the nation's status as sublime object, and be the sublime object *for* the nation, was developed partly through pageants of mourning like *The Book of the Duchess*. In 1446 at Saumur, René d'Anjou came to his Emprise de la Gueule du Dragon "arme d'armes toutes noires" "because of his country's misfortunes" and the "recent death of his queen."[70] The nation's love of the queen was to be sublime, making the nation tragic subject, but also survivor. Although *The Book of the Duchess* makes ample use of this collocation of intimacy and immensity, it does so to establish the greatness of the loss to which the courtier will offer himself as enlivening alternative. The narrator answers Black's equation of his "hap" with Blanche by chipping away at the tragic status and miniaturizing power of the consort: "I leve you wel, that trewely / Yow thoghte that she was the beste / And to beholde the alderfayreste, / Whoso had loked hir with your eyen" (1048–51). Black's response is a catalog of the virtues of past heroes, which, had the Man in Black possessed them (Alcibiades' beauty, Hercules' strength), would not have kept him from seeing Blanche as the best! Symptomatically, this catalog digresses into the telling of tragic stories that have no immediate relevance to the Man in Black's point: "And therto also hardy be / As was Ector, so have I joye, / That Achilles slough at Troye—/ And therfore was he slayn alsoo / In a temple, for bothe twoo / Were slayne, he and Antylegyus, / (And so seyth Dares Frygius), / For love of Polixena" (1064–71). A Monkish interest in tragic stories *as stories* emerges here, along with a certain pleasure in erudition. Tragic anticlimax is seeping in. That aspect of tragedy that brings out the insensible law of group communication in the form of the law of the genre makes its appearance. That this happens just when the courtier is "arriving" with his rhetorical gifts and hopes of good fortune identifies the court with the law that promises the *jouissance* of submission to indifference.

My point is not that the counseling and consoling courtier historically supplants the lady, or the sovereign group of one characteristic of allegory and heroic exemplum, but rather that these figures all circulate in court culture, sometimes competing with and sometimes mutually supporting each other, offering crucial resources for the crafting of political and tragic subjects. Crossover between them is evidenced when, shortly after his catalog of tragic greats, Black defends himself against the slenderest of implications that he might stray from devotion to Blanche's memory: "Nay, certes, than were I wel / Wers than was Achitofel, / Or Anthenor, so have I joye, / The traytor that betraysed Troye, / Or the fals Genelloun, / He that purchased the tresoun / Of Rowland and of Olyver. / Nay, while I am alyve her, / I nyl foryete hir never moo" (1117–25). Remembering as devotional practice is defended through another testy and testing catalog that conflates the hetero with the male couple: to betray Blanche's memory would be worse than the worst ever betrayals of false counselors and brothers-in-arms. The equivalence between Black and the narrator intensifies, as Black responds to the latter's request to be told about the first time he spoke to Blanche by describing his "life" as a poet: "I dide my besynesse / To make songes" (1156–57).

Resemblance is also associated with enhanced powers of communication (and the reclamation of tragic sublimity) when Black remembers the first time he spoke to Blanche, who rebuffed him: "trewly Cassandra, that soo / Bewayled the destruccioun / Of Troye and of Ilyoun, / Had never swich sorwe as I thoo" (1246–49). It is the fate of the oracle to be misunderstood or unheard, just as it is the fate of petitioners to have difficulty interpreting it. Blanche cares "nat a stree / Of al my tale" (1237–38). But the desperately unheard Cassandra, like Blanche herself, is "just" a memory for Black, whose story will have a different outcome. Blanche eventually comes to "understonde / My woo" (1260), a triumph of transmission and confidence that anticipates Black's attempt to communicate with the narrator—doubly so in that when Blanche finally understands, she rescues Black, feeling that it would be a pity if he were to die (1265–66). *The Book of the Duchess* takes pains to purify transference of the death wish, to imagine a transmission and a bond free of guilt and anticlimax: "is that all?" "oh no! not this again!" The replication of Blanche's moment of understanding in the narrator—when he learns she is dead, his immediate response is pity—offers the melancholic lure of the new work, which seeks to reanimate the lost object without fear of reprisal.

The ending of *The Book of the Duchess* is full of life. The "king" journeys rapidly homeward toward a place suddenly "ther besyde," "from us but a lyte." This part of the poem has the fast pace of awakening into a world in which dreams can appear simply to be "queynte"—curious, but not horrifyingly Real. The new time of transference between prince and courtier is "beyond" death, engraved by the fall of loss but awakened by it, ready now to engrave (write poetry) rather than be engraved.

Still, this awakened world (as always) seems not to know the dreamworld, and vice versa; they are as incommunicado as the oracle and its auditors. This anamorphosis flickers throughout the poem's ending.[71] With all the promise of the new time of transference, the ending of the poem can feel unsettling because of the unexpected speed with which things, and viewing points, change. The tolling of the castle bell reintroduces the vigilance of timekeeping after the enchanted leisure of the interior; and rapidity produces anticlimax: "She ys ded!" "This was my sweven; now hit ys doon." Looked at one way, all is cozy: nothing much has really happened, what a funny dream, here I am still with my book in my hand, think I'll write it down. The apotropaic cuteness and comedy of the Chaucerian narrator seeks to deliver the death drive tax-free. But maybe that is why he needs to get out of there so fast.

The rendering of courtly love as tragedy, and vice versa, gave medieval aristocratic culture powerful—indeed, fascinating—ways of defining subjectivity, sociality, and their interdependence. Courtly culture experimented with the codification and groupification of sensibility, with structures of enjoyment that could link heterogeneity to homogeneity, the intimate to the "great." The fall of greatness, and the tragedifying of falling in love, once made conducive to wonder and consequential for the group, could magnify the importance of the interior experiences of grief and pity to the point of catastrophe. Courtly love enabled an intensified psychology of falling. Interiority could now, like history, become the terrain of life-and-death matters, on which one's position in life would be lost or recovered. But interiority also promised the re(turn) to sociality. The role of courtly discourse in the mannering, magnification, and transmission of desire was explored and heightened through the figure of the friend-as-interlocutor, whose presence in the text invited attention to the arts of attentiveness. The witness in turn magnified the importance of grief by promoting it to the dignity of something worthy of witness. These steps were decisive for the ways in which subsequent transformations of tragedy's sociality and class effects were enabled, because they offered techniques for displacing sublimity and for the transformation of sensibility into a virtual world. Tragedy as a matter of sensibility—"sentement" was Chaucer's term—is prepared for by the courtly tragedy of the later Middle Ages, which already links a special group body to a special psychic interiority that can, through this linkage, be codified, analyzed, discussed. When domestic tragedy arrives in the eighteenth century, it has at its disposal a generic interdependence of psychic intimacy and exterior immensity, a power of miniaturization to express group concepts, that was the result of courtly love's intersection with tragedy in the later Middle Ages.

3

The Ninety-six Tears of Chaucer's Monk

Life, as we find it, is too hard for us; it brings us too many pains, disappointments, and impossible tasks.
—Sigmund Freud

Unlike death or the dead, catastrophe befalls everyone at the same time and thus gets absorbed by its product: the group, which never mourns.
—Laurence A. Rickels

[At] the level of the signifier every cycle of being may be called into question, including life in its movement of loss and return.
—Jacques Lacan

The Book of the Duchess works hard to construct a rich interior that will give depth to the white-walled surface of the nascent *finamen*'s subjectivity and his courtly world. The poem also works to overcome the figure of dead exteriority with which it begins: a narrator so lost as to have no inner life, "felynge in nothyng" (11).[1] But traces of insentience reappear throughout the poem, most startlingly at its end, in its moments of "anticlimax": "She ys ded!" (1309), "hit ys doon" (1334). The poem's critics have been prone to ask, "Is that all?"[2] Although critics have appreciated how powerfully (and suddenly) Chaucer can make us feel "nothing," some have felt the poem's abrupt shifts from the humorous to the sublime, the hyperbolic to the mute, to be awkward evidences of "early" work. But in these moments of often-comic vertigo, the smile meets the "grimace" and we just about die laughing.[3] Such shifts in tone betray the close relationship between the cuteness of Chaucerian caricature and the phenomenon of abruptness, when bodies fall, thoughts rise, ground shifts, and moods change.

Moments of transience and deadness, of the "is that all" linking vertigo and blankness, are often stretched out in Chaucer's poetry. If critical responses to *The Legend of Good Women* and *The Monk's Tale* are any indication, Chaucerian *brevitas* often evokes the muteness of the grave. Countering, but also accompanying, this muteness is "transference": the hope of refinding the dead in the living through enhanced techniques of attention; the endless deferral of disappointment from one transferential object, communicative situation, or technology to another. The dissipation of disappointment—that is, of nascent indifference—through deferral runs the economy of the gift, or the "pact" sealed by laughter. As Derrida remarks, what befalls or descends on us, even as it comes from above, always disappoints our expectations.[4] But we can always try to give it to somebody else.

The figure of the disappointing gift is thus linked to the rhetorical complex of the engraved subject's befallenness. The intrication of the "mark" with movement, "hap," and gift is sublimed in the figure of the angelic messenger, bringer of the gift of divine information. Good fortune is promised by all emissaries, by all who oversee the transmission of the mark. The fall into life is chancy—at least, the subject seems to feel she was not there when what she was to become began—partly because we do not know what might be coming down the pike, or what the good word is. Thus the projectile of chance "is a matter not only of projection, the throw and the send-off *(le lancer)*, but of the missive or dispatch *(l'envoi)* as well.... In addition to the dispatch we have the sending back or adverting to *(renvoi)* and, indeed, the boost *(relance)*," that is, the raising of the stakes in chance: "One raises or *relances* when one knows how to play with what falls" (Derrida, "My Chances/*Mes Chances*," 14). As I argue in chapter 2, in *The Book of the Duchess* the gift of death involves the cultivation of attention.[5] Both dreamer and mourner need rhetoric: techniques of petition, confession, apology. And in order to succeed at the courtly game, one must learn to play with whatever falls to us from the master, either by passing it on or by turning it to good use. This is one reason why risk was so intensely sublimed in aristocratic culture. And the "higher" the stakes, the greater the need for prosthesis: divination, good counsel, chivalric "ordinances." Or so it would seem in tragic discourse, which pertains to "regnes," and in which the stakes are so high as to require the sovereign's own mastery of risk.

In the Middle Ages, an image could only grant petitions if it was sentient. The idol was by definition dead and helpless to help.[6] The anxieties that propel animation also run between these poles, even though this kind of animation, especially in its early stages *(Tom and Jerry)*, prefers endless repetition of the body's death and resurrection to the search for the Other in its "imaginary" form, full of grace. When the status of aliveness is addressed in the form of the dead image, the central question becomes: what is the status of the sentience to which petition might be addressed? If not "alive," what is the nature of its capacity to take "pity" on human desires? *The Book of the Duchess* sets in train Chaucer's lifelong fondness for making regular, and comical, appearances in his work. He always seems to be in need of attention: "like" us, or even like his puppy, he "koude no good" (390). Despite the fact that he has trouble asking for things for himself—he seems to know that the gift of knowledge is no joke—he usually appears in a petitionary context: he would like to get some "tydinges," as in *The House of Fame*, though preferably not aerially; in *The Book of the Duchess*, he has given up on remedy, which is of course implied by its absence. But he moves on to a "positive" rendering of petition, in his retelling of Ovid's story of Ceyx and Alcyone (*Metamorphoses*, book 11).

When Alcyone prays to Juno for news of her husband, this particular "idol" is sufficiently alive to hear Alcyone's prayer. Juno "ryght anon / Called thus hir messager / To doo hir erande, and he com ner" (132–34). Ovid's Alcyone burns incense

> to all the gods; but most of all she worships at Juno's shrine, praying for the man who is no more, that her husband may be kept safe from harm, that he may return once more, loving no other woman more than her. And only this of all her prayers could be granted her.

> But the goddess could no longer endure these entreaties for the dead. And that she might free her altar from the touch of the hands of mourning, she said: "Iris, most faithful messenger of mine, go quickly to the house of sleep." (79–87)[7]

Alcyone's petitions illustrate the frailty of human communication. We appeal to those we cannot see and who perhaps will not hear us on behalf of those who may already be beyond help. Appeal may even be "aporetic," insofar as it tries to convey the wishes of the living to the indifferent undead. If one loves, one is alive; if one desires, one must *be* alive, and both Alcyone's aliveness and the desires dependent on it are a matter of indifference to Juno—and to Ceyx, who will never love another. Hence Juno replies only because she wants to *break* the connection between the living and the dead, those who care and those who must be persuaded to care, those who ask and those who answer. The speed and immediacy of her own response, and then of her messenger to her call, are a fantasy of preparedness, imagined (in Chaucer's case) at a time when the court's use of prosthetic administrative apparatuses was both intensifying and troubling. Could redress be accomplished by proxy? Could the sovereign show *cura*, care, for his beloved subjects, when he or she is far away? Moreover, the extension of courtly communication was accomplished partly through the efforts of messengers just like Chaucer, who frequently traveled and spoke for his prince.[8] The circuits that link the living to the dead are also the circuits of rule.

In order to break the importunate connection, Juno must, paradoxically, speak. In fact she goes so far as to activate an elaborate relay of messengers. In Ovid, Juno's messenger must go to Morpheus and in turn bid Morpheus to send a message to Alcyone. The god of sleep chooses Morpheus, one of his thousand sons and "a cunning imitator of the human form" ("artificem simulatoremque figurae"; 164–65, line 634) to appear to Alcyone in the guise of Ceyx, and tell her that "he" is dead. Why does this message go through so many different hands? Prosthesis—in Ovid, the deferral/dissemination of finitude by handing it on—appears, phantasmatically, to bridge the gap between sublime indifference and mortal desire. The poem fascinates us by stirring up superreal (in)sentience: the divine hauteur, *noli me tangere*; and the response of the image that lives beyond desire is indeed a "sending back." But fascination modulates into consolation when divine hauteur is groupified. By the time Alcyone gets the bad news, transmission itself is bearing a certain charge of enjoyment.

Group talk—for example, tragedies about "the realmes of greet nobleye"—sublimes anxiety by giving it an object: a matter that touches us all.[9] Chaucer's Juno does not state a distaste for more particular touches of desire/mourning; her distance registers through her power of "dispatch," the speed with which she means to make things clear, in contrast to the obsessive time of Alcyone's waiting. "Goo now faste, and hye the blyve!" Juno tells "hir messager" (152, 133). She gives directions, reminds, warns, because she knows that circuits can get backed up if people do not prepare. "Go bet... to Morpheus—/ Thou knowest hym wel, the god of slep. / Now understond wel and tak kep!"(136–38). The "mission" demands vigilance and a heightened motility: deliberate comings and goings, taking heed of how things come and go. All this is beyond the powers of the melancholy narrator of the beginning of the poem: "I take no kep / Of nothing, how hyt cometh or gooth" (6–7). It is almost as though the narrator were a masterless man, or, what amounts to the same thing, a man in need of a "sign." What is called up at the moment of emergency preparedness in the story of Seys and Alcyone is the uncanny image of Seys-Morpheus. The groupifying power of transmission (and vice versa) is expressed as the power of the image to compel attention.

When, in Ovid's version, Morpheus puts on the image of Ceyx, he cannot resist asking Alcyone if she recognizes him or if death has changed him very much: "Do you recognize your Ceyx, O most wretched wife, or is my face changed in death? Look on me!" ("agnosers Ceyca, miserimma coniunx, / an mea mutata est facies nece? respice"; 166–67, lines 658–59). Chaucer's version makes things—and their transmission—even stranger. Juno asks her messenger to tell Morpheus, now the god of sleep, to

>   take up Seys body the kyng,
>   [And] Bid him crepe into the body
>   And doo hit goon to Alcione
>   The quene, ther she lyeth allone,
>   And shewe hir shortly, hit ys no nay,
>   How hit was dreynt thys other day;
>   And do the body speke ryght soo,
>   Ryght as hyt was woned to doo
>   The whiles that hit was alyve. (142–51)

Now it is not enough to send a cunning imitator of the human form to impersonate Seys. Now it is necessary that the god of sleep actually creep into the body of Seys and make it go to Alcyone, show her how it was drowned, and speak as "it" did formerly. Chaucer's image of Seys is made up of a corpse inhabited by a "daemon" delivering the gift of true knowledge. The channels of emergency transmission start going "now faste," and call up a corpse: as Rickels puts it, "the body that has been lost can only be reanimated" (*Case of California*, 63). Technologies of transmission and rule, however dazzling, bring back the corpse that lies beneath the group talk of the group body, especially since it is so hard to forgive the departed for leaving. It is clear that the deaths of kings had seemed particularly insulting for many centuries before Chaucer wrote—one reason for their sacrificial interpretation.

Where do the death wishes lie that bring back the corpses in *The Book of the Duchess*? It looks like Alcyone is going to take the rap. The abandoned Alcyone wants to know (much more strongly in Chaucer's version than in Ovid's) whether Seys still lives or not. As Blanchot might have put it, "it does not suffice for [her]... that he is mortal... he must be mortal twice over: sovereignly, extremely mortal."[10] Perhaps the desire for "news" or "tidings," which so often afflicts the Chaucerian narrator, serves the death drive as well as desire: at least we always seem to believe that when we "know" we can "put the past behind" us.[11] The knowledge provided by communications is the warranty of our indifference; channeling through to the secrets of the otherworld can be a way of making sure of the objects over there. In effect, this is the gift of death: preparedness, in the form of the appeal for "news." But how can the subject prepare for the death of the other?

According to Rickels, the structure of enjoyment that is sadomasochism is the "law of transformation of 'nerve energy,'... [which] dispenses and disperses the gadget-love bond with one's own technologization and reversibility" (*Case of California*, 18). The subject who would master the unexpected takes herself as an object that, through redesign, can live beyond the limit of life, even and especially through the endurance of a chosen suffering. Unexpectedly, the world turns out to be a dicey place because it is where death is *not*. In the *Metamorphoses*, death is *not* even where there seems to be sure knowledge of it: Juno does not want her altar touched by mourning hands. As Blanchot puts it, "[w]hat makes me disappear from the world cannot find its guarantee there; and thus... having no guarantee, it is not certain" (*The Space of Literature*, 95). Although we are perfectly capable of dissembling or complicating our idea of death as absolute limit, it is nonetheless our own idea. This is because we want to know death, to make "'death understood'...[the] only content" of our lives (100); and "[i]t is when [we concentrate] exclusively upon [ourselves] in the certainty of [our] mortal condition that [our] concern is to make death possible" (96). But because the death drive has a habit of sending the death wish back after us, these attempts to certify death often turn into nasty surprises. Chaucer's poem projects onto Alcyone a desire for a knowledge that would end desire, and that obligingly ends by ending her. Insofar as this is a "fall," it is, so to speak, the primal scene of petition.

"That the eternal is...the internal follows from a fact of life: the other is always the first to go" (Rickels, *Case of California*, 23). Although death's absence from the unconscious can be very consoling, it nonetheless multiplies the uncertainty produced by death's absence from the world. When destructivity makes the other endure past the limit of life, it wants to get rid of death by getting to know it. It wants to make death visible, to make the dead come before it in review—like the dead in *La Divina Commedia*, or in Boccaccio's *De casibus*, who, "with the signs of their earthly misery about them...tell their story or demand that Boccaccio tell it."[12] The subject who prepares for death is always a necromancer—a point made in reverse by Chaucer's Knight when, on the occasion of Arcite's death, he declines to know Arcite's ultimate destiny: "I nam no divinistre" (*The Knight's Tale*, 2811). The gift of death claims to distinguish the subject of responsibility by granting her a particular death: only she can die her death, even though she may do so on behalf of others. Indeed, the economy of sacrifice depends on this distribution.[13] To determine the knowledge of death's secrets/the secrets of the dead is the acme of preparedness; but if one has converted one's life such that "making 'death understood' [becomes] its only content," the death drive has, after all, achieved indifference to anything else. The gift of death dignifies the isolation it invites not so much by asking the subject to renounce all objects as by offering it an opportunity to do so. One becomes uniquely responsible when one's death is given a kind of group power—a power to fascinate that is, at minimum, equal to that of the *temporalia*.

What is wanted both by dominance and by submission is a "law" that will arrange the drives, and therefore their objects, in relation to one another. What is wanted is a law that can dispense, transform, and disperse "the gadget-love bond with one's own technologization and reversibility." In this, the sadomasochistic subject is already rewiring the law on which she is founded. "One" is always already systematic: the law of the signifier structures the unconscious, and it enables the production of artifacts, of prosthetic selves.[14] The law enables further recodings of the subject, wherein gadget-love becomes, in the register of technology, how we make "death understood" the content of our effort. The death of the other is produced as successful death wish through the "omnipotence of thoughts" that for Freud "underlies every detour taken by narcissism via yet another extension of the senses, ranging from belief in magic to media technology" (Rickels, *Case of California*, 24). And if "one" is always already systematic, one is always already many. The miraculous group body—the codified sensorium of the courtly lover, or the exemplary suffering of the tragic "hero"—extends narcissism through its magical-technological magnification and rewiring of the sensorium.

The legalism of courtly love—its "scholastics of unhappy love," its "very precise poetic craft"—is striking (Lacan, *Ethics of Psychoanalysis*, 145–46). Through group activities of codification and debate, courtly love enacted itself as the law of the "fine" lovers, set apart by the delicate complications of their knowledge and practice of "sentement." Courtly love was love put into discourse, ruled expensively, luxuriously, by the signifier; law was lavished on "feeling." Courtly love developed an explicitly groupified rhetoric, and thereby policed and enhanced the identities of those who could use it well: for example, Gawain's reputation for courtly speech in *Sir Gawain and the Green Knight;* also, Andreas Capellanus's systematic treatment of rank in *The Art of Courtly Love*. This legalism marks the intimacy of *jouissance* with the law of the signifier, and thereby with the generalizing power of language to adequate love and myth by "restaging the individual present impression," "render[ing] generic the personalized labels of individual experience" (Rickels, *Case of California*, 142).

Nonetheless, the group discursivity of courtly love, though fascinating, also veils itself to some extent. This dissimulation is produced through the ethical "problem" of how the courtly lover, the *finamen,* can claim authenticity for his love when the forms of his expressivity are so widely shared. Sincerity is the "problem" that structures Chaucer's *Parliament of Fowls*. It also informs *The Book of the Duchess*, through the motif of testimony, in turn shadowed by the figure of the flattering/backbiting *lauzengier*.[15] What is at stake in veiling the intrication of *jouissance* and the law? Lacan writes: "*Das Ding* [the Thing] presents itself at the level of unconscious experience as that which already makes the law.... It is a capricious and arbitrary law, the law of the oracle, the law of signs in which the subject receives no guarantee from anywhere" (*Ethics of Psychoanalysis*, 73). "*Das Ding*" is the *jouissance* made inaccessible to the subject when she is designed by the signifier; the place of the "Real" made inaccessible to the subject when she is so designed; and that blank spot or emptiness which nonetheless resonates with the unspeakable promise of a *jouissance* that cannot be reached (again). For Freud, Lacan suggests, the term *das Ding* is apposite to the unconscious-as-*Nebenmensch*, neighbor, the stranger within who is not, but is nonetheless within, the subject. *Das Ding* is "the central place, . . . intimate exteriority or extimacy"— a concept that, while relying on the "metaphysical" opposition of inside versus outside for its element of surprise, nonetheless clarifies the dialectical nature of that opposition, as also of law versus desire, system versus chaos, and subject versus other.

Securing these very oppositions enables medieval psychology to place Reason "above," closer to heaven, and the appetites "below," further recessed into the corporeal structure of the subject; or, sometimes, to place "judgment" between "imagination" and "memory" as the evaluator of their truth. These formulations allow the law to be sublimed as (relatively) free of befallenness. The consequences for ethics are immense. The "problem" of sincerity, the "difficulty" of heaving one's heart into one's mouth, supports the ideological fantasy that the law of the signifier and *jouissance* are not only distinct but often opposed: estranged by the "fall," only "grace" can reunite them. As Žižek suggests, this fantasy hardly does away with *jouissance*; on the contrary, it supports a *jouissance* of form, Žižek's "*plus-de-jouir*," and of the commission of or submission to its dictates.[16] It is in relation to the *jouissance* of form that we can locate the coincidence of desire with technologization. As we shall see, it is also here that we can locate the designs of *genre*, of "groupified" signifiers, on enjoyment.

Once we are *as* signifiers, even the death drive can only go forward; hence its investment in the very preparedness mounted to guard against it. If we cannot go back, we will already have begun to move inexorably, we will already have acquired directionality, before we will have acquired intention: fated. At the same time, Derrida notes, "In the destination *[Bestimmung]* there is ... a principle of indetermination, chance, luck, or of destinerring"; the "capacity for diversion" is imprinted within the "very movement" of the "iterability" of the mark ("My Chances/*Mes Chances*," 16). Fate begins, so to speak, as form; but although form designs, it does not necessarily do so intentionally, let alone with anything "particular" in mind. "A certain interfacing of necessity and chance, of significant and insignificant chance," emerges precisely in the context of the resistance to life (6).

Fortune, who figures that resistance (she wants "objects" only indifferently), is thus both inexorable but dicey, cruel but obedient, illusory but necessary to human instruction, of the utmost significance but meaning and meant to mean "nothing," the negation of the (value of the) thing. Fortune's actions participate in what Derrida calls "insignificance": they "enter into the play of the destination," they engrave "the possible detour of a *clinamen*"; they establish "that a mark in itself is not necessarily linked, even in the form of the reference *(renvoi)*, to a meaning or to a thing" (15). The mark is not primarily bound to reference; it is first and foremost something designed for repetition. "To be a mark and to mark its marking effect, a mark must be capable of being *identified*, recognized as the same, being precisely *re-markable* from one context to another" (16). This "stereotypy" of the mark rules the plotting of caricature from life to death and back again, as well as the somewhat misleading irreality that attends the transferential object. It rules also the allegorical figure, whose stereotypy is itself what Fortune marks or "indicates," insofar as it is she who acts out stereotypy, whose arbitrariness is revealed by the endless repetition of the "same" motions: striking, turning, fleeing.

In his *Policraticus*, John of Salisbury represented Fortune as a tragedian, and the world as "the scene in which [she] ... enacts her plays."[17] Fortune's status as the stereotype of stereotypy is linked to her status as tragedian. Tragedy marks aliveness as insignificant in ways that seem catastrophically significant. "What other thynge bywaylen the cryinges of tragedyes but oonly the dedes of Fortune, that with an unwar strook overturneth the realmes of greet nobleye?" (*Boece* II, prosa 2). *Only* the deeds of Fortune? Overturning realms of great nobility: "Is that all?" The abbreviation of tragic catastrophe, and its manic reversal into the catastrophizing of merely particular fears, are central to the poetics of

The Nun's Priest's Tale, in which the rise and fall of significance strongly "mark" the tragicomic swerves of the (animal's) body. Lady Philosophy's goal in abbreviating catastrophe is metaphysical: to serve the Other in its "imaginary" form, full of grace, superreal, beyond aliveness; to teach mortals how to "work" and "do" "byforn the eyen of the juge that seeth and demeth alle thinges" (*Boece* V, prosa 6). Fortune's aporetic condensation of chance and necessity, significance and insignificance, figures a long-standing difficulty in the history of responsibility and therefore of tragedy. Like many critics of medieval tragedy, Lady Philosophy wants to disperse this condensation, or turn it into something altogether different, a "unity." This is why, in Book IV, she ethicizes Fortune as an instrument of divine "purveiaunce" and its gifts of death:

> So as al fortune, whethir so it be joyeful fortune or aspre fortune, is yeven eyther by cause of gerdonynge or elles of exercisynge of good folk or elles by cause to punysschen or elles chastisen schrewes; thanne is alle fortune good. (IV, prosa 7)

All differences of Fortune—the joyful, the bitter—resolve into the image of "alle fortune"; the *jouissance* of her cruel indifference, and thus of her variability, turns simply into "good."

Moreover, just as Fortune, Blanche, and Black begin to converge on one another in *The Book of the Duchess,* so in *Boece* do Fortune, the Muses, "purveaunce," and Lady Philosophy, who cares for the self by inspiring and confirming virtue, and who intentionally targets those in need of her attention. In a narrative movement reversed in *The House of Fame's* up/downward spiral from pedagogy to fame to rumor, by the end of *Boece* Fortune no longer affects everyone arbitrarily. She succors the good folk, strikes down "schrewes," and *means* to school the impatient in patience. And Lady Philosophy can define "hap" as follows:

> hap is an unwar betydinge of causes assembled in thingis that ben doon for som oothir thing; but thilke ordre, procedinge by an uneschuable byndinge togidre, whiche that descendeth fro the welle of purveaunce that ordeyneth alle thingis in hir places and in hir tymes, makith that the causes rennen and assemblen togidre. (V, prosa 1)

It is not that the law is open and arbitrary; on the contrary, it is that even "hap" only *seems* like an arbitrary concatenation of unrelated causes. Really, their concatenation is "bound" by providence.

Boece's repudiation of indifference culminates in Book V, in its subliming of prosthesis and "omnipotence of thoughts" in the form of "purveaunce." Symptomatic of this—the internal is always the eternal—is *Boece* V's concern with interiority and its dependence on exteriority. Boethius worries that the soul is insignificant: if prosthetic of *"withoute,"* only because it begins as a mere engraving of befallenness. As old "Stoicyen" philosophers believed,

> *the sowle had ben nakid of itself, as a mirour or a clene parchemyn, so that al figures most first comen fro thinges fro withoute into soules, and ben emprientid into soules* [which] ... suffrith and lith subgit to the figures ... of bodies withoute-forth, and yeldith ymages ydel and vein in the manere of a mirour.... whennes comith thilke knowynge in our soule, that discernith and byholdith alle thinges? (V, metrum 4)

The subliming of the eternal-internal requires a disquisition on faculty psychology, which leads in turn to affirmation of the wonderful interiority of providence, on which depends its secret power to concatenate causes. Divine interiority itself is like the "[o] strook of thought" by which intelligence "byholdeth alle thingis" (V, prosa 4). But "strook" is, for Chaucer, also a tragic word; it is Fortune's weapon, and its semantic range also includes the "mark." A "strook" is a "throw" that has the power to divide; it is a mark whose ability to re-mark paradoxically depends on its ability to redistribute "alle thingis," suddenly and completely, ex nihilo.[18] As Lady Philosophy puts it: "What other thynge bywaylen the cryinges of tragedyes but oonly the dedes of Fortune, that with an unwar strook overturneth the realmes of greet nobleye?" (*Boece* II, prosa 2). Kelly notes that "Chaucer's choice of the word 'unwar' to translate Boethius' *indiscretus* gives both the active and the passive sense of the term. Fortune's blow is both undiscerning (it comes for no logical or just reason) and undiscerned (no one can predict it)."[19] Fortune, once again, conflates without "resolving," let alone "discerning," the contraries of activity and passivity. Divine interiority also discerns by one stroke; its omniscience consists in fact of one eternal stroke of discernment. The

"Eternal-Internal Now" seeks to redeem the alterity of the mark, stroke, happening by making the stroke into the very "character" of divine sentience. Instead of being "subgit to the *figures*...of bodies withouteforth," and yielding "ymages ydel and vein," divine sentience makes bodies by marking. The divine stroke is, again, an apotheosis of prosthetic signification: its mark is, far from being undiscerning—careless of reference, for example—the acme of discernment; its character is not primarily to be re-markable, but to make. And yet its semantic link to Fortune's stroke, indifferent (undiscerning) and inscrutable (undiscerned), is unmistakable.

Through the figure of the stroke, *Boece*'s recuperation of intentionality and intelligibility redelivers destructivity, including the destructivity of the mark. One hears loud and clear in *Boece* the feedback of the death wish over the channels of a sensorium enhanced to the point of superreality. The delicious cruelty of Fortune's carelessness reappears as preparedness, in the form of the philosophical care for the self. Lady Philosophy's hyperattentiveness or *cura* ("with the lappe of hir garnement... sche dryede myn eien," "to myn eien repeyred ayen hir firste strengthe" [I, metrum 3]) is one of philosophy's gifts of death, which oblige us to "reunite with" ourselves: "Art nat thou he?" (I, prosa 2).[20]

But so is Lady Philosophy's militant (and militantly sentient) power of correction, first revealed when she throws the "poetical muses," busy "enditynge wordes to my wepynges," out of Boethius's cell of woe: "sche...glowede with cruel eighen. 'Who,' quat sche, 'hath suffered aprochen to this sike man thise comune strompettis of...the theatre?'" (I, prosa 1). These Muses are "enditynge" *daimons* of an orgiastic, rather than rational, power of inspiration. Like idols, they have "none remedies"; instead of healing the sick and consoling the sorrowful, as does Lady Philosophy, they "fedyn and noryssen hym with sweete venym" (I, prosa 1). Their difference from Lady Philosophy is meant to keep her free of the taint of tragic enjoyment, that is, the death wish; like Augustine in the *Confessions*, Lady Philosophy would repudiate the desire *for* suffering exposed by tragic "enditynge."[21] *Boece*'s invocation of the *pharmakon*— "But tyme is now...of medicyne more than of compleynte" (I, prosa 2)— asserts the alterity of poison to cure, poetry to philosophy. But Boethius's early, uninstructed image of Fortune nonetheless resembles Lady Philosophy, with her "cruel eighen," and her ability to cast down and expel from joy ("this companye of muses, iblamed, casten wrothly the chere dounward to the erthe, and, schewynge by rednesse hir schame, thei passeden sorwfully the thresschefold" [I, prosa 1]). She also, in her fondness for poetry, resembles these very same Muses.[22] Her status as figure of a redeemed figuration, that is, of the capacity of the intelligence to know universals through particular images, precisely re-marks her as stereotypic. *Boece* does not escape—nor is it clear that it wants to—the ethical ambiguity of the mark.

The fantasy of Fortune's malevolence—recuperated but repeated in Lady Philosophy's determination to fix *this* man—marks her as a figure of the death wish, an impresario of the spectacle of cruelty.[23] She poses, by deflecting, the Nietzschean question: "how can the infliction of pain provide satisfaction?"[24] But it is also an Augustinian question: "why it is that men enjoy feeling sad at the sight of tragedy and suffering on the stage, although they would be most unhappy if they had to endure the same fate themselves?"[25] Modern writers on tragedy have also found this a difficult question. In *The Medieval Heritage of Elizabethan Tragedy*, Willard Farnham wrote that

> artistic tragedy...does not begin until man brings...creative pleasure to the dramatic imitation of life's destructive forces....
> [T]his pleasure is mysterious...since to take pleasure in the contemplation of pain may seem either perverse or morbid, and yet is actually neither when the contemplation is of the most profound tragedy.[26]

What a relief. One might have been worried there for a minute.

Farnham redeems the queerness of enjoying the contemplation of pain by appealing to the artistry of tragedy, though the link between the genre's "creative pleasures" and its more destructive ones remains "mysterious." Farnham seems to reverse the ethical charges of Augustine's view of artistry; for Augustine, as also for Nietzsche, the determination of culture's "works" to turn suffering into tragic spectacle exposes our desire to witness the pain of the other. But can we distinguish art from suffering, even if only for so long as to make one explain the other? Doesn't the "stroke," the "mark" of which form consists, have within itself the power to "divide" and cast down?

In what way does our habit of repeating, in the "work," the trauma of befallenness redound to our credit? The destructivity of the *jouissance* of form—if nothing else, the ex nihilo changes everything, by throwing something into the world that was not there before—at least clarifies why we so readily sacrifice our desire. One way or another, *jouissance* "is suffering because it involves suffering for my neighbor."[27] Farnham will dissipate the problem of our queer taste for suffering by subliming the arts that, for Augustine, reveal the problem in the first place. But don't we have to take responsibility in either case, precisely in relation to *jouissance*? Does it help Oedipus that he did not know who his father was? Mightn't he regardless have considered what killing strangers at crossroads implied about the situation of our *jouissance*?

In the context of the trauma of awakening into life, we ask a melancholic question of our *jouissance* when we try to determine whether the particular shape life will take is our own responsibility or the other's (and the Other's). The question dissimulates the fact that responsibility is undecidable in these terms, despite their authority in philosophy, partly because the particularity of persons is never secure from indifference. Tragedy can sometimes be rigorously indifferent to the alibi of the distinct difference between fate and fault, chance and providence, self and Other. *Oedipus* certainly insists that responsibility is always already inscribed in the befallen relation between the one and the other who comes after him. On the level of the subject's experience, no father chooses *this* "son," no son *this* "father." Reproduction can be quite indifferent. For Antigone too only the mark can make a responsibility. The mark is what makes me responsible to *this* "sister," who now will never stop being my sister. But the re-markability of the mark, the stereotypy on which the "never stop" depends, reminds us that, after all, almost anyone could have shown up as *this* sister and made her claim on me. This is part of the point of Polynices' criminality, that one does not choose in any obvious sense to whom one will be responsible, even though, at the same time, responsibility requires a kind of adoption (Lacan, *Ethics of Psychoanalysis*, 255). Apparently, we cannot avoid choosing.

But tragic discourse is also perfectly capable of trying to distinguish properly between fault and fate—for example, by distributing them differently in the history of the genre. Kelly notes that although many medieval writers on tragedy thought of the genre as retributive, "this was not the usual view." The more usual view, which was also Chaucer's, was that tragedy often pictured "undeserved suffering" as well as punishment for crimes. Eschewing "the narrow moralizing tragedy of the theorists," Chaucer introduced the "open-ended view of tragedy" "to the modern world."[28] For Farnham, however, the most problematic thing about medieval understandings of suffering was not the fondness for retributive justice, but rather the refusal of life—*contemptus mundi,* for example, which found the misery of the human condition undiscernible and undiscerned. The world had to become significant again before it would see "Shakespeare's profound analysis of the lines of tragedy in responsible human action."[29]

For Farnham, Fortune figured the medieval refusal of life; she was "a convenient image of all those ways of God which were past finding out." And she too needed to be "subdued" before Shakespeare could arrive.[30] But precisely because she personifies the coincidence of arbitrariness and the inexorability of the law, Fortune is the ghost in *Hamlet*'s machine. In horror at the spectacle of Pyrrhus's "bleeding sword" falling on Priam, Hamlet's "Player" cries out, in the voice of Lady Philosophy, "Out, out, thou strumpet Fortune! All you gods, / In general synod take away her power, / Break all the spokes and fellies from her wheel, / And bowl the round nave down the hill of heaven, / As low as to the fiends" (II, ii). Polonius helpfully remarks, "This is too long." He gets into trouble with Hamlet for saying so, and will soon die "accidentally," but only after he tells Hamlet that he once enacted Julius Caesar: "I was killed i' th' Capitol; Brutus killed me" (III, ii). After Hamlet kills the man he took for his "better," he tells him, "take thy fortune; / Thou find'st to be too busy is some danger" (III, iv). Never mind that Polonius is now beyond hearing, let alone advice as to conduct. Why does it become so hard to tell these two moralists apart just when their lines of communication get broken? And just when Hamlet is determined to wring his mother's heart? One had better listen to the death wish, and remember its capacity to be indifferent as to persons, in the company of those whose words like daggers enter into people's ears. Hamlet is in no mood for pity.

Augustine doubts whether tragic pity leads to responsible action: "the audience is not called upon to offer help, but only to feel sorrow."[31] This concern has motivated several new-historicist discussions of tragedy's mystifications, as has the question of whether the fantasy of a pitiless Fortune is meant to conceal human responsibility for suffering. In his classic cultural-materialist critique of pity, Jonathan Dollimore argues that *King Lear* shows how "in a world where pity is the prerequisite for compassionate action...the majority will remain poor, naked and wretched."[32] In "Sweet Persuasion," Scanlon argues that Fortune was wildly popular with medieval aristocrats because she displaced the arbitrariness and cruel competitiveness of courtly culture.[33] Private ambitions and vicious rivalries regroup under the universalizing sign of Fortune's wheel. In Rickels's terms, we could say that the figure of Fortune's leveling power helped medieval aristocrats to exchange the mortal, particular body "for the corpus which comes in the one size or age that fits all" (*Case of California*, 61). For Dollimore, too, the complexities of history—particular social distributions of power and helplessness—are elided by readings of *Lear* that posit "man" as a universal subject, who recollects himself when he learns that he can both suffer and pity.

Dollimore reads pity as screening the indifference of the wealthy to the poor. He reads universal "man" as screening particular class interests. In either case, affect is split off, either disguised or disguising. Neither universality nor pity has purchase on sociality except for the negative power to dissipate agency. For Scanlon too, Fortune's universal arbitrariness screens the class-specific destructivity of the aristocracy. Both readings rely on, and have helped to develop, the interrogative power of historical "specificities" with respect to totalizing strategies of domination. We cannot do without this interrogative power, if we wish, among other possible goals, to understand how art participates in sociality rather than "rising above" it.

But we also cannot do without the interrogative power of totalizing constructs with respect to isolating strategies of domination. Recent historicists are sometimes ontologists for the "specific" or the "local" just as much as patristic historicists were ontologists for the "types" used by providence to work its way through time. But specifics and universals are interdependent and shifting constructs. They cannot be collapsed into one another because they mutually define one another; by the same token, they cannot be separated. Also, they are not illusions, but "works" that change the world into which they are thrown. They gain their purchase on ideological fantasies in part because they style, and are stylized by, desire. Such a perspective makes it easier to see that universality and pity are embedded in subject-formation, in particular of the stereotypy that makes the subject a re-mark of the other, recognizable to and even prosthetic for the other.

To the extent that, as Lacan puts it, "the subject's experience of satisfaction is entirely dependent on the other, ... the *Nebenmensch*," how could we ever be absolutely particular? (*Ethics of Psychoanalysis*, 39). Can I be absolutely particular if I am in any case inhabited by the desires of a stranger I can never fully know? But this does not contradict "the deep finality of that really remarkable diversity" of desire (5). Transferences enact the convergence of diversity and stereotypy in the construction of the subject; they "cause one sign rather than another to be valorized for [the subject] ... to the extent that this sign may be substituted for the earlier sign or, on the contrary, have transferred to it the affective charge attached to a first experience" (33). To valorize a sign, to desire the *objet a*, these are achievements, so to speak. As we have seen, nothing guarantees that we will desire to desire, or that we will desire particular objects, let alone this or that particular one; we might instead remain indifferent, though "we" would not exactly be a "we" if we managed to do so. The dreamer "does not have a simple and unambiguous relationship to his wish. He rejects it, he censures it, he doesn't want it" (14). "We" come into being through our relation to desire, in other words, through the stereotypy *and* historicity on which the valorizing of signs, indeed, on which the sign itself, depends. Yet when we have valorized a sign, or, to put it another way, when we have cathected an object, we do so in the name of its particularity; and although "desire is change," its reluctance to give up its attachment to the particular objects it has constructed for itself is quite notorious. The role of the group in mourning—which is to disperse the power of the particular through the relays of the group body—can scarcely be thought outside this perspective. Neither can the idea of responsibility, because its problematic has typically been conceived in terms of particular bonds and the stereotypies that enable their intelligibility and iterability.

The association of tragedy with critical moments in the history of responsibility was not unknown in the Middle Ages. Walsingham referred to his accounts of the Peasants' Revolt of 1381 as tragedies.[34] The fallen emperor Henry IV described his life as a tragedy.[35] The four "no-fault" tragedies (tragedies involving no concept of retribution) added by Chaucer to *The Monk's Tale* were all fourteenth-century instances with important links to Chaucer's literary and official life. One of these "modern instances," as they are known to Chaucerians, laments the assassination of King Pedro of Castile and León by his illegitimate half brother, Don

Enrique of Trastamare: "O noble, O worthy Petro, glorie of Spayne, / Whom Fortune heeld so hye in magestee, / Wel oghten men thy pitous deeth complayne!" (2375–77).³⁶ In the 1360s, Chaucer visited Spain to pursue the interests of the Black Prince and John of Gaunt. In 1378, he also visited another of his soon-to-be tragic subjects, Bernabo Visconti, lord of Milan. Bernabo's niece married Chaucer's first patron, Lionel, duke of Clarence, and offered his daughter Caterina in marriage to Richard II. The tragedy of Ugolino of Pisa is probably based on Dante's account in the *Inferno,* and thus also results from the visits to Italy that seemed to have interested Chaucer deeply in Italian literature and politics. Finally, *De Petro Rege de Cipro* laments the assassination of Peter I (Lusignan) of Cyprus in 1369, treated as a martyr by Machaut in the *Prise d'Alexandrie* and by Philippe de Mézières in his *Tragedic Prayer on the Passion of Our Lord.* The "modern instances" were, in one way or another, part of Chaucer's own experience of the chances, changes, and cruelties of "princely" courts, and indeed were for all fourteenth-century European courts spectacularly "disappointing" instances of insecurity.

According to Chaucer's Monk, if tragedy is to do the work of memory, it must itself be remembered, through "olde bookes."

> Tragedie is to seyn a certeyn storie,
> As olde bookes maken us memorie,
> Of hym that stood in greet prosperitee,
> And is yfallen out of heigh degree
> Into myserie, and endith wrecchedly. (1973–77)

The renewal of old books through memory is a perennial Chaucerian concern, but the Monk's version is distinctive in emphasizing the recovery of a genre. We are to appreciate that our understanding of tragedy depends on techniques of storage and transmission; without such techniques, the Monk could not "declare" to us the features of the genre. Tragedy is precarious, perhaps as vulnerable as he "that stood in greet prosperitee, / And is yfallen out of heigh degree / Into myserie, and endeth wrecchedly." *The Monk's Tale* memorializes knowledge of and writing about tragedy just as much as it memorializes the falls of unfortunate men. An instance of the "processes of representation in the work of mourning which have ever extended living to the dead," *The Monk's Tale* reserves "a place for a double invention: technology and the unconscious"

(Rickels, *Case of California*, 14). The Monk further raises the stakes by magnifying these representative processes through metalanguage. But "With every emergency measure taken to ... traverse distance and death, the ... tele-touch with the nearest and dearest only retrieves in their absence the death wishes (and ghosts) jamming the circuits" (196). I have argued that the question of whether interiors contain anything but the ghosts of their own death wishes is posed by the mood swings of the cute but melancholy narrator in *The Book of the Duchess*. The question is also posed by *The Monk's Tale*, but in relation to the stereotypy of genre. The Monk seems (some critics find this tasteless) more fascinated by the ways tragedy is marked as such than by its particular instances.

Ghostliness haunts *The Monk's Tale* in the form of an excision. Boccaccio wants to reanimate his dead victims; in the *De casibus* they appear before him in review like *imagines agentes*—the striking, sometimes horrible images used in the arts of memory "to give an emotional impetus to memory by their personal idiosyncrasy or their strangeness."[37] In Chaucer's poem, the Monk is summoned to tell his tale by the "Host" of the pilgrimage, Harry Bailey. The Host seems impressed by the Monk's vigor and know-how, traits that he might seem, in his own way, to share, were it not that, like Boccaccio's dead, he has his own complaints to make about the vulnerability of sentience. He praises the Monk: "Thou art a maister whan thou art at hoom" (1938); "Thow woldest han been a tredefowel aright" (1945); "Thou art nat lyk a penant or a goost" (1934). But is the death wish at work in the Host's summoning of the Monk?

Probably, if the Host's not-ghost is an instance of negation—"not just any old no," but "the manner in which what is simultaneously actualized and denied comes to be avowed," the form in which the unconscious "essentially presents itself" (Lacan, *Ethics of Psychoanalysis*, 64–65). In the Host's fantasy, the Monk, unlike Boccaccio's ghosts, needs *nothing*. He makes *no* appeal. So far from being a ghost, in fact, the Monk is—or might have been—an inseminator for the species. But the Host admires the Monk's "tredyng" potential through a charmingly invidious comparison with lay "shrympes," who, because the religious have stolen their virility, make "heires ... so sklendre / And feble that they may nat wel engendre" (1955, 1957–58). Religious enjoyment of "tredyng" turns out to be something of a torment after all, for monastics who are supposed to renounce it but do not, and for the reproductive lay body, which is now in a state of emergency, its continued life menaced by the theft of its enjoyment. Whereas Boccaccio enthuses, in the *De casibus*, over the invigorating powers of discipline, the Host feels that asceticism enervates reproduction's powers of transmission. Even as he admires the Monk, his rhetoric associates the latter with the vampiric potential *of* aliveness—its capacity to drain the life of its neighbor. Harry Bailey curses those who first brought men such as the Monk "unto religioun!" (1944). The ghost missing in the "wel farynge" Monk has been refound.

But the ghost is also missed in the Monk's portrait in the *General Prologue*, where the narrator of *The Canterbury Tales* closely anticipates Harry Bailey's phrasing: the Monk "was nat pale as a forpyned goost" (205). In the narrator's fantasy, the Monk rejects the "old and somdel streit" rules of monastic asceticism (174)—seclusion, working with the hands, study—and chooses instead the rich, active life out in the world. No indifference to life for the Monk; he craves it. He desires to be new, and busy with his aliveness: "This ilke Monk leet olde thynges pace, / And heeld after the newe world the space" (175–76).

The portrait emphasizes the Monk's prosperity and enhanced sentience. He possesses and consumes fine objects: supple boots, a beautifully tended horse, warm furs, fat swans. He tends his own and his mount's bodies beautifully, and Chaucer's language emphasizes the identification: the Monk "was a lord ful fat and in good poynt"; "His bootes souple, his hors in greet estaat" (200, 203). The Monk makes sure that the body, corporeal and prosthetic, is groomed, polished, well fed, cozy, pleased, and well equipped. He takes care to take care; if he rejects monastic preparedness, he undertakes his own kind of vigil. Does this begin to suggest that he might be a little bit ghostly after all?

His devotion to the chase might say so: "Of prikyng and of huntyng for the hare / Was al his lust, for no cost wolde he spare" (191–92). This mighty hunter must always be on the move, after something. As we saw in chapter 2, hunting constructs particular objects by staging its intention to destroy them. Perhaps the taste for the object on which he has designs impels the Monk's twin obsessions with the chase and with prosthetic things. The object, for the Monk, is both that which can be singled out for deliberate destruction and that which can be cultivated to enhance sentience. Both of these object-states enable the Monk to re-mark falling in the guise of flight: something is fleeing; something else is equally fleet, but purposive, trained, coordinated, vigilant: the group body of the hunt, the group of two, the hunter and the hunted.

That something else also wants to be "sovereignly mortal," to *know* death. He wants the hunted object to stake its life, to know that it is mortal, but wants the knowledge of that extreme mortality to be completed in himself. He wants to be in the position of the one who knows how it all ended. To wish, for the Monk, is to wish to "live on" past the limit at which life becomes a life-and-death matter. But this is no simple dream of mastery. All wishes wish to live on; all wishes do live on, in the sense that they "go beyond" the limits of the life that is at that moment wishing them. The interior space they occupy is thus not unlike the space of the vigil, a fact registered by the tendency of faculty psychology to reembroil the imagination with memory just as soon as it gets them separated out. Everything about the Monk's portrait—its reversals of freedom into befallenness, flight into chase, taking care into taking life— suggests that our attention is being drawn to the very structure and effectivity of the wish. Wishing is not only bringing something out of nothing or trying to send something back into the indifference from which it emerges; it is always and at the same time wishing the subject into an interiority of altered sentience. The Monk's loving/deadly care for objects is itself a form of indifference; whatever he wishes for them will not involve the preservation of their distinctiveness, because what he wishes is to transform "everything," but through an interior state that can witness this apocalyptic transformation as spectacle. The term *death wish* would thus, for the Monk, be redundant, as might "omnipotence of thoughts."

The Monk's portrait therefore includes a powerful sign of an aggressive interior. We perhaps wouldn't even need to know the Monk loves the chase to know he loves to kill; we could tell just by looking at him. "He was a lord ful fat and in good poynt"; but "His eyen stepe, and rollynge in his heed, / . . . stemed as a forneys of a leed" (201–2).[38] It is a stark contrast, one that recalls in an uncanny way the shape-shifting of Lady Philosophy, who "glowede with cruel eighen" (I, prosa 1). The Monk is a connoisseur: he wants to miss nothing, to have the best of everything, to be "sovereignly" sentient. But the power of some terrible changefulness threatens to escape his cultivated frame, and it is not naively conceived of as something "raw," but rather as something that is preparing, forging, altering: already technologized. Ramazani calls the Monk "the death's head of the *Canterbury Tales*."[39] Indeed, he is an anamorphosis, and not the kind that reminds one just of any old death.[40] He reminds one of something murderous as a wish. He reminds one of something "extimate," and it is up to something: it is cooking. The Monk's anamorphic body reveals that the signifier boils and bubbles—it does not just try to restrain or "sublimate" death wishes. This suggests that insofar as we try to solve the problem of loss or destructivity through liberal applications of the signifier, we are missing a certain point: the signifier is what terrifies, opens up the cauldron, makes even the strongest stuff melt and drift away.

But the Monk is doubly anamorphic, even more anamorphic than this view of him permits. "This view," after all, consists of a reading of the projections of the narrator of *The Canterbury Tales* and of Harry Bailey. Their projections in fact jam the circuits so badly that the most important message has a hard time getting through. Perhaps when the Host blames religion for stealing the laity's reproductive power, he feels on his neck the breath of something unspeakable. Maybe he is on to something when he (mis)recognizes the evil that lies in the heart of the Monk as the genocidal drive of monasticism. The Host's manner is, however, typically *sportif*. Apocalyptic as his prophetic group talk about the enervation of the lay body might be, he may, once again, still be missing that frightening Thing, that "forpyned ghost," seething inside the Monk. But Bailey's high spirits remind us again of the intimacy of laughter, trauma, and the caricature of the body—in this case, the shrimpy little group body of the laity. This posttraumatic laughter wants to get there before things really fall apart, and still be around to make cracks about it afterwards; hence the Host's fun borrows from the power of prophecies of doom to reassure, to promise a certain triumph.[41]

Discourses of catastrophe, including tragedy, produce the group body—a body made by (anticipation of) a common, "indifferent" trauma. Speaking "before" with a knowledge of "after," the group body offers a melancholy alternative to the reproductive body, vulnerable to disruption. Putting catastrophe into discourse gives reason to hope, to anticipate a reborn order of things, to reorder the transmission of things according to relations of transference—replication, identification, relay. Groupification rescues us from the death wish by turning it into sacrifice.[42] To destroy the world would involve sacrificing one's wishes with respect to particular objects; it therefore presents itself as an act of supreme indifference *and* a triumphant exercise of decision making. Acceptations of death that choose on behalf of the group seem to give sacrifice an aura of choice, and sanctify wishing by giving it the form of responsibility.

When Augustine criticizes tragedy because, as work, it reworks the befallenness of suffering into intended spectacle, he points to the ethical vulnerability of sacrificial celebration of the transformation of cruel necessity into choice. What makes the difference between cruelty (or masochism) and sacrifice is the appeal to the "good," which is always already an appeal to the group: the "something beyond" particular preference on whose behalf this appeal is made emerges from the group's power of relay.

Traumatic figuration is embroiled in the ethical difficulties of the work because it artifices, and because it posits the wish as the means to rescue the helpless body from enervation. The gift of death obliges us to choose death rather than letting it choose us. But because it is also a gift of triumph, it is ethically vulnerable. As Blanchot puts it, the man who chooses death hopes to become "master... of that omnipotence which makes itself felt by us through death, and he will reduce it to a dead omnipotence.... Hence his strange conviction that his suicide will inaugurate a new era" (*The Space of Literature*, 97). Mastering death masters the helplessness vis-à-vis exteriority that denies our wishes magical power and sets in train the forging of prosthesis. Hence the intimacy of suicide with the group: the one appeals to the other because both involve prosthetic reparation. If we can hand mastery on to and through the group, we give the gift of the future, of preparedness, and thus become responsible.

The relay system of the group, with its power to produce the effect of the "good," of "something beyond" preference, works to set sacrifice apart from suicidal grandiosity and other enjoyable forms of submission to the arbitrary law. It also produces the effect of the witness. When the group dies, perhaps someone will be left alive, whose mission will be to transmit the meaning of this spectacular death to the future. Or, no one will be left, but until the last minute someone of the group will watch the death of the group unfold, stretching out the moment of dying by relaying it from one body to another, and no one will be able to steal that knowledge of death because it will die with the group. Alive or dead, the group will know more about death than anybody else.

Anamorphosis reverses the transformation of the unexpected into the expected, expectancy into certainty, and this is why it structures our encounter with the Monk. In keeping with Chaucer's interest in the "unwar strook," the Monk's second anamorphosis, in the Prologue to his tale, reveals something even more unexpected than does his portrait. And we might be doubly surprised if we thought that the revelation of his destructivity was a scandal to end all scandals, shocking enough to put an end to any future anamorphoses. True, the Monk's hatred of what is "old and ... streit" seems clear enough from the curse attributed to him in his portrait: "Lat Austyn have his swynk to hym reserved!" (188). But this is, after all, an attribution. When the time comes for the Monk to tell his tale, and the Host is cheerfully cursing religion, the Monk "took al in pacience, / And seyde, 'I wol doon al my diligence, / As fer as sowneth into honestee, / To telle yow a tale, or two, or three'" (1965–68).

The Monk submits himself readily to the law—to the old and "streit." He promises the very labor ("diligence") that his portrait imagines him refusing. Although his memory is not sufficiently trained for him to be able to present his tragedies in good order, he nonetheless has read very many tragedies, answering in the affirmative the bullying question he is said, in his portrait, to have posed: "What sholde he studie and make hymselven wood, / Upon a book in cloystre alwey to poure ... ?" (184–85). In the Prologue to his tale, he exhibits the virtue of patience in adversity, when, despite his rank and evident power, he takes the Host's ribbing without "making it tough." As soon as the Monk opens his mouth, he suddenly seems *already,* long ago, to have embraced the vigilant imitation of corporeal death that was monastic asceticism. Thus one crucial thing we may have missed about the Monk is the engraving that tells us that the aliveness of which he is such a splendid example comes *after* a fall. Sentience *is* a tragedy.

Thus it would appear that the scandal of ethics, the *ascesis* of will and wish at the extreme of responsibility—that is, put up with what your lord tells you or does to you, regardless of whether it makes sense but especially because and when it does not—generates the *jouissance* of submission to the empty form of the law, even more powerfully than when that law masquerades as reason. Why should he study, and make himself crazy? It is not at all clear that he has an answer to this question, but apparently he has done it anyway. The Monk's cathexis of form and rule explains his commitment to the memory of an old genre.

The Monk is a narrator who treats harrowing matters mechanically. Ramazani suggests that the Monk's "narrative method is circular: he defines his genre, and then demonstrates that his tales bear out his definition."[43] This indeed would seem to dispose of the unexpected. But what the Monk has to say in his strangely mechanical way is quite dreadful.

And this does not simply prove his insensitivity to dreadfulness. He emphasizes that it is the business of tragedy to "bewail." He raises the stakes of tragedy, catastrophizes it further; tragedy is not just about an "overturning" or an unhappy end, but about falling to an end utterly without resources: "the harm of hem that stoode in heigh degree, / And fillen so that ther nas no remedie/ To brynge hem out of hir adversitee" (1992–94). It is about fallenness as complete dispossession and helplessness, the absolute absence of "remedie" for unfortunate men of high estate who end "wrecchedly," like the "wrecched ympes" (1956) born to Harry Bailey's shrimp-men. When Fortune wishes to flee, no man can "withholde" her course. Tragedy invokes the limit beyond which action, technology, enhancements of sentience are relevant; but one is still alive; it is life beyond the limit of attachment to life.

The vigilant preparedness advocated by the Monk offers the hardbitten allure of the postapocalyptic state: "Lat no man truste on blynd prosperitee; / Be war by thise ensamples trewe and *olde*" (1997–98; emphasis added). He advocates preparedness and nothing but preparedness. Possession will never be secure; Fortune can make away with the goods whenever she wants. The Monk links helplessness and poor eyesight to the figure of Fortune's unstoppable flight. She cannot be chased successfully; all pursuit of her is hopeless. Helplessness has to do with an inability to hold on, to retain, to keep possession of objects. It is as if the Monk knew that the enjoyment of objects attributed to him in his portrait *already* puts the object under erasure. His dispassionate treatment of this version of fear of falling suggests that helplessness is precisely that which lets go of the passion for life. The flight of Fortune is a trajectory that desire might want to pursue, all the way to indifference.

Fortune figures the radical insecurity of our hold, not just on life, but also on our wish to live. At the end of the Monk's tale, he remarks that "Tragediës noon oother maner thyng ... biwaille / But that Fortune alwey wol assaille / With unwar strook the regnes that been proude. / For whan men trusteth hire, thanne wol she faille, / And covere hire brighte face with a clowde" (2761–66). The fall into helplessness and refusal of life is rendered as the suffering of the "unwar strook" central to Chaucerian tragedy. Fortune is indifferent to objects and to the enjoyment she menaces, and her indifference is a projection of our own. Not only what we have or that we can have, but also that we would even want to have, is in question. This deflating of desire is aptly rendered by another of the Monk's images: Fortune covers her "brighte face" with a cloud: the beautiful object, specifically the beautiful sight, turns into an occlusive nothingness, a just-visible invisibility indifferent (and therefore fascinating) to the gaze of desire—as if she, turning into a barely visible non-Thing, led straight to the empty place of *das Ding,* where desire finds its limit. This is, again, a trajectory ruled by the insensible, arbitrary law, which admits chance as the closest possible companion to direction.

As Ramazani has pointed out, the Monk is, among other things, a collector; his performance displays a kind of obsessional gathering wherein what counts as much as anything else is number: how many tragedies he has in his "celle" ("an hundred"), how quickly he moves from promising to tell the audience "a tale, or two, or three," to the seventeen he does manage to get in before he is silenced by the Knight and the Host. Ramazani associates this love of number and groupification with a failure of communication: "To tell tales is less a matter of communicating than of displaying a mass of things."[44] Indeed, the Monk displays the apotropaic retentiveness of the arts of memory, as expressed in the legend of Simonides, which extols the conservation of the image. So powerful, however, is the Monk's interest in accumulation that even mnemonic principles of temporal or spatial ordering take a back seat to number. He apologizes, as does the narrator of *The Canterbury Tales* in the *General Prologue,* for not telling "thise thynges" "by ordre ... / Be it of popes, emperours, or kynges, / After hir ages, as men writen fynde, / But tellen hem som bifore and som bihynde, / As it now comth unto my remembraunce, / Have me excused of myn ignoraunce" (1985–90). Above all, the Monk's desire is to collect a group of many members. The "thynges" themselves—the tales—are secondary to this defensive amassing "as it comes." The Monk defends against the precariousness of desire by privileging the groupification of possible objects of beauty or value rather than the objects themselves.

But the fact that the Monk wants to *display* the many tales he has gathered together remains salient. It is not clear how securely we could, even if we wanted to, distinguish between display and a naively ethicized "communication." Ramazani's argument exemplifies a strong tendency in the Monk's critical tradition to associate the Monk's formalism with a failed sociality or failed participation in the spiritual body. Yet, as Ramazani's own phrasing makes clear, it is through quantification that the Monk constructs a formal body he is willing to share with the pilgrims.

Quantification, which preoccupies not only the Monk but his century, is a use, not a disuse, of the signifier. The elaboration of theories of signification and logical predication, the development of logic in the direction of what would become propositional calculus, the reinterpretation of metaphysical questions in psychological and epistemological terms, and the radical positivism of Ockhamist ethics were all characteristic of the intellectual culture of fourteenth-century England, whose curiosity about the signifier on all fronts of learning was both intense and extensive. Ockhamist ethics argued that an action could be understood as "good or moral, not because it is in conformity with an eternal law which exists of itself... but simply because it is ordained and commanded by the will of God, who 'can command anything He pleases. For God is nobody's debtor.'"[45] The analysis is, finally, rhetorical: when God uses the imperative mood, he is to be obeyed irrespective of the "positive" qualities of his command. His communications are instructions, with immediate binding power; they do not necessarily appear to be rational; we interpret them not so that we can understand the "something beyond," the Good, but so that we can do what we are told.

Increasingly, the analysis of "signification" reformulated referential understandings of how the signifier could make "true" statements and what that kind of "truth" entailed.[46] Although Ockhamist logic retained notions of reference through "absolute" terms, that is, terms resulting from "an immediate intellectual contact with objects and... acts of abstraction based on this," "connotative" terms were "susceptible only of a nominal definition, answering the question 'What is meant by this term?'" and indicating "the elements which enter into the composition of a term." By such means, "quantity" in Ockhamist philosophy not only "directly signifies a body or colour, but connotes that these subjects have parts distant from other parts."[47] "Quantity" is not simply the quality of an Ockhamist "subject" (i.e., object), but a description of an object's calculable structure, its constitution by parts that can be isolated, analyzed, and numbered. The object that "has" quantity is one whose structure can be described by mathematical or logical statements. Alfred Crosby, in *The Measure of Reality*, insists on the historicity of "what can be measured in terms of quanta": "when in the fourteenth century the scholars of Oxford's Merton College began to think about the benefits of measuring not only size, but also... motion, light, heat, and color, they forged right on... and talked about quantifying certitude, virtue, and grace."[48]

To regard these developments as an attempt, foreign to Chaucer's sensibility, to "reduce" the incalculable to calculation, would be to miss the passional nature of calculation. It would also be to further the ideological-fantastical split between calculation and *jouissance,* a split that disavows, and therefore fuels, the destructivity of the mathematical signifier (Lacan, *Ethics of Psychoanalysis,* 314, 324–25).

Moreover, the few facts we have about Chaucer's life suggest that he might have had intimate appreciation of the *jouissance* of calculation. He dedicated his "litel tragedye," *Troilus and Criseyde,* to Ralph Strode, a logician at Merton College, Oxford, as well as to John Gower. Crossover between the *jouissance* of sex and that of "reckoning" structures *The Shipman's Tale*; Chaucer's merchant is so obsessed with counting that he neglects his marriage debt.[49] Chaucer also achieved, according to some enthusiasts, "astonishing astronomical and astrological facility," acquiring a "level of skill equal to that of any academic astronomer"; he fondly dedicated to his son Lewis a treatise on the astrolabe.[50] The astrolabe was an important instrument in the new lay culture of quantification, and was still associated with the glamour and danger of occult knowledge.[51] Chaucer's mastery of the astrolabe would have been notable also because of the fascination with astrology, magic, and technological know-how in late-medieval court society, where one could rise or fall on the basis of one's power to "arouse wonder."[52] Chaucer's interest in the technology of the "marvel" was distinctive among fourteenth-century English poets. *The Squire's Tale* and *The Franklin's Tale* include unusually detailed descriptions of the "mechanical wonders" and illusionism in vogue at the time in courtly entertainment. These tales also explore the power of such devices to enchant and rewire desire—a fascination that, Kieckhefer remarks, we need to appreciate in the context of the "major advances that were occurring in mechanics and engineering in and around the thirteenth century."[53] Hilary Carey also notes, regarding "Chaucer's brilliant and informed references to the occult sciences," that Chaucer "introduced into English poetry the Italian habit of using astrological allusions to refer to time or anticipate events or describe character."[54] Chaucer both explores and participates in his century's subliming of technology, which can so compellingly be raised to the dignity of *das Ding* because *das Ding* "already makes the law." The Monk's desire to display impressive numbers is, in short, also, at some level, a Chaucerian desire, if not precisely a desire of Chaucer's.

So is the Monk's desire to get the group identity right. As noted earlier, his concern to introduce and "declare" the genre of his tale is unusual among the Canterbury pilgrims. He begins with some points of genre criticism, and returns to this theme just before the Knight and the Host prevent him from finishing his tale: "Tragediës noon oother maner thyng / Ne kan in syngyng crie ne biwaille / But that Fortune alwey wol assaille" (2761–63). Tragedy consists of the compulsion to repeat and thereby to defend against the trauma of desire. Tragedy is able only to do this, and this alone: cry and bewail, in song, that Fortune will always assail us. The tragedian is like a recording, "mechanically" repeating the crying and bewailing of helplessness that is her only office. Tragedy has just one kind of thing to say; but it insists, it persists, it "re-marks" itself in and through saying so. This is what it has to "communicate": the signifier will not tire of iteration, but this tirelessness generates befallenness (stereotypy's unavoidable *clinamen*, or swerve) even as it eternalizes (Derrida, "My Chances/Mes Chances," 28). Lamentation, for the Monk, translates into the verbal and musical signifier what is being "said" by the repetitiveness on which quantification relies.

Crosby remarks that quantification requires the identification of "a category of things... sufficiently uniform to justify our measuring them."[55] Quantification is a way of groupifying objects. One *identifies* "particulars" or "parts of things"; one identifies the links that enable propositions to be made about them; one quantifies them. The passion for number, as one form of the death drive, frees desire from partiality, from the inherence of quantity in the particular object, from its imbrication in the qualities of that object, delivering whatever *jouissance* lies along the approach to indifference.

The identification of repetition in exteriority is an analogue to foresight; if nothing else, it makes rhythmic the space into which we emerge. Befallenness emerges from the incalculable exteriority of space through the rhetoric of "the innumerability of the reasons or the causes... that are in nature."[56] This incalculability pushes Nature in the direction of arbitrariness and "chance"; her "countless experiments" in aliveness, moreover, are indeterminate not only because they cannot be counted, but also because "a mistake always remains possible" (Derrida, "My Chances/*Mes Chances*," 31). And yet this incalculability also pushes the "countless experiments... that force their way into experience," including "every one of us human beings," in the direction of an inexorable law, through the figure of the secret and of "filiation": "There are more things in heaven and earth, Horatio, / Than are dreamt of in your philosophy" (28; *Hamlet*, I, v)—namely, the ghost of the dead father, who seems to be asking for a tragedy, and who certainly jams the circuits of Hamlet's newly educated mind. One of the places in which chance and inexorability converge is that of reproduction, where, again, quantity and repeatability senselessly produce the possibility of the *clinamen:* the Host's "ympes," sons who do not listen obediently to the paternal ghost, and so on.

Unlike most of the other Canterbury tale-tellers, the Monk is interested in number in the form of prosody. In the Prologue to his tale, just after he notes tragedy's concern with ending "wrecchedly," he explains that tragedies

> ben versified communely
> Of six feet, which men clepen *exametron*.
> In prose eek been endited many oon,
> And eek in meetre in many a sondry wyse.
> Lo, this declaryng oghte ynogh suffise. (1978–82)

As is true of the Monk's overall presentation of his tragedies by row (but not "by ordre" [1985]), this passage combines the impulse to conserve—"this declaryng oghte ynogh suffise"—with an apparently gratuitous display, in this case of the Monk's knowledge of the numbers and form of his *kind*. The mechanical quality of tragic lamentation is also emphasized in the first line of his tale: "I wol biwaille in manere of tragedie" (1991). It is a bewailing according to the form of the Monk's literary kind: a bewailing, a heartfelt outcry, and a meeting of the demands of group form. The helplessness of the engraved body that haunts the tragedy of Fortune is transformed into the mass of regulated signifiers that constitutes the genre. As genre, tragedy, for the Monk, is "a category of things . . . sufficiently uniform to justify our measuring them." Tragedy signifies what this uniformity implies for subjectivity; it signifies "the tight bond between desire and the Law," the bond that constitutes our being as signifier, which is susceptible to groupification because created by iteration.[57]

Groupification wants to "pass on" the unexpectedness of the deviation that will inevitably emerge in a stereotypic or reproductive chain. But the Monk's performance consoles us with nothing. We will have to see that aliveness is resurrected neither by the eternalizing effect of the mark's iteration nor by its curves, because both are already part of "the conflict at the level of the living structure from the very beginning" (Lacan, *Ethics of Psychoanalysis*, 212). Otherwise we will miss the anamorphosis; we will find, in *The Monk's Tale*, nothing but an exteriority (bad), a surface (without depth), or perhaps just any old nothing. The ending of *The Monk's Tale*, when the somnolent Host and the melancholy Knight prevent the Monk from continuing, has sometimes been read as evidence for the Monk's aesthetic and/or spiritual failure. Peggy Knapp thinks that *The Monk's Tale* is "bad philosophizing"; she notes that it "calls up" and perhaps challenges "a position the Knight himself respects": "The Monk misses his chance to teach a moral lesson as well as his chance to offer consolation for the reversals of this fickle world. His performance is, in that sense, more pagan than the Knight's."[58] Although I value differently the Monk's challenge to the Knight, I think that Knapp is on to something. The Monk's performance brings out the intrication of chance and inexorability, stereotypy and variation, as a problem of hearing and reception within and without the pilgrim community.

The Monk's Tale does not in fact get as much critical attention as it should, even in studies whose particular concerns would seem to make it relevant. Lee Patterson writes a chapter called "From Tragedy to Comedy through the *Legend of Good Women*," but the Monk is only cited for his definition of tragedy, taken by Patterson as evidence for the historicity of the genre, that is, its concern with "the world of public events."[59] Critics whose projects are centrally preoccupied with issues of genre, interpretation, and language can also miss the Monk almost entirely. Perhaps because she did not find *The Monk's Tale* enough of a mess, F. Anne Payne's *Chaucer and Menippean Satire* remarks only that it is a "relentless satire" of "Fortune's shallow echo of Aristotle's definition [of tragedy] in the *Consolation [of Philosophy]*."[60] Dolores Frese mysteriously argues that "the Monk means to denigrate literacy itself."[61]

Nonetheless, several critics have developed wonderful readings—or at least the beginnings of wonderful readings—out of the tale's putative lack of interest. Donald Howard contends that Chaucer "didn't have to rewrite his 'tragedies' to suit the Monk; they suit him for their cheerlessness." The Monk's interest in tragedy is simply, but tellingly, predictable: he "has never left behind the nobleman's interests," and "for the scholarly work a monk must do he collects stories about the rich and powerful."⁶² More recently, Wallace has argued that the tale is "energized chiefly by pressures external to its own formal constitution," namely, the changeful histories of contemporary "myghty men"; read in Ricardian England, the falls of tyrants could never have a single or simple meaning.⁶³ H. Marshall Leicester's interpretation redeems discourse analysis somewhat: the "quasi-citational character" of the Monk's portrait in the *General Prologue* "introduces a measure of uncertainty as to who is speaking," and suggests that both narrator and Monk are "aware of the discrepancy between the impression [the Monk] makes and the ideals of his estate."⁶⁴ Michaela Grudin, in stark contrast to Ramazani, argues for the remarkable *diversity* of the Monk's tragedies, a diversity that "demonstrate[s] the difficulty, in practice, of the general and explicit command, 'Be war by these ensamples trewe and olde.' Is it possible, even in a genre so overtly aimed at moral improvement, to penetrate the guard of the listener?"⁶⁵ Grudin is right; in fact, it is no laughing matter. If tragedy is meant to give us the gift of preparedness, this is, after all, not a simply pleasurable thing to receive. *Jouissance* rarely looks like fun. Tragedy, it seems, can either stupefy or horrify, put us on guard or put us off guard, make us watch or make us sleep—extreme and paradoxical effects well registered, for example, in *Hamlet*. At the end of *The Monk's Tale*, the Knight commands the Monk to stop: "good sire, namoore of this! / That ye han seyd is right ynough, ywis, / And muchel moore; for litel hevynesse / Is right ynough to muche folk, I gesse" (2767–70). By contrast, Harry Bailey commands the Monk to stop because "ther [is] no desport ne game" in his tale (2791). Had it not been for the clinking of the Monk's bridle bells, "I sholde er this han fallen doun for sleep, / Althogh the slough had never been so deep" (2797–98). Partly because the clinking of the bridle bells recalls the *General Prologue,* when the Host begins the "game" and when the Monk is revealed to be steaming, I think it unwise to treat the Host's reactions as exemplary. And, as Grudin points out, the Knight's desire for "a genre that records the rise to 'properitee' ... would mirror and validate his own situation and suggest its continuance. If there is any genre that by definition cannot do this it is tragedy."⁶⁶ Why would we allow the Knight's and the Host's responses to guide critical reaction, when we do not follow Gertrude's and Claudius's responses to the players' "tragedy"—for which, it will be remembered, the players "beg your hearing patiently" (III, ii)? Claudius also likes happy endings, and Gertrude does not want Hamlet to be so dark all the time.

What interests me is the question of how it is possible that the Monk could be both terrorizing and stupefyingly boring. Well, why not? If so, he would simply be the reverse of the contradictory pair of qualities that have characterized characterizations of Chaucer at least since the late eighteenth century: safe, *and* lively. As a way of understanding the apparent breakdown in communications at the end of the Monk's performance—though really the point is that too much has gotten through—I want to explore further why Chaucer pairs the Knight's inability to bear the "disese" of tragedy with the Host's inability to stay vigilant when listening to it, or, as Wallace so beautifully puts it, why Chaucer pairs "the potential of the [tragic] genre's affective power" with "its remorseless monotony."[67] Which ghosts jam the circuits of the Monk's performance, and why?

For the Knight, "it is a greet disese, / Whereas men han been in greet welthe and ese, / To heeren of hire sodeyn fal, allas!" (2771–73). The Knight emphasizes the falling action of tragedy, its suddenness, and "ese" versus "disese," that is, the disruption of a pleasing, homeostatic relation to one's world and its gifts. Tragedy asks us to hear about sudden falls, vertiginous missteps, sentience alarmed and transformed. The hearing of it seems to involve just as much "disese" as experiencing it, almost as though it were pouring "leperous distilments" into the porches of the Knight's ears; falling and hearing about falling are both "diseses" of and to sentience. The Knight's high estate (compared to the other pilgrims, at least), and the association thereof with tragedy, obviously make him particularly vulnerable to vertigo and to the genre's ability to dis-ease through the ears, as the "modern instances" and their connections to the Knight's own campaigns might suggest. Getting on with his death drive, he reacts to *The Monk's Tale* not with pity, but with the refusal of life's befallenness. At a certain point, Gertrude too cannot bear being admonished further: "O, speak to me no more! / These words like daggers enter in my ears; / No more, sweet Hamlet" (III, iv). The only motion the Knight can bear to hear much about is one in which men "wexeth fortunat, / And there abideth in prosperitee" (2776–77). To reverse the falling motion; to grow, and then to retain position and abide in enjoyment of the godsend—these alliances between extension and retention, rising and abiding, are powerfully at work in the Monk's critical tradition.

The Host has not been able to follow what the Monk has been going on about, except that there was something about Fortune and tragedy ("I noot nevere what" [2783]), but he is prepared to say that "no remedie / It is for to biwaille ne compleyne / That that is doon, and als it is a peyne, / As ye han seyd, to heere of hevynesse" (2784–87). Listening to the Monk makes the Host into the sleepy, "unwar" man tragedies of fortune ostensibly seek to awaken and animate.[68] Perhaps it will be useful to remember here the link between preparedness or vigilance on the one hand, and "sleep" on the other: as we have argued, preparedness actually keeps indifference safe by guarding against (too much of) it. Has the Host simply been had by the down side of enchantment? Is his stupefaction a caricature of tragedy's power to evoke wonder—a posttraumatic grin/grimace that reminds us of the body's liability to falling into a "slough"? The nightmare of trying to keep one's seat when one has lost one's head is treated with cruel jocularity in the Prologue to *The Manciple's Tale*, when the Manciple will not even let the Cook *start* talking.

Would this mean a joke on Harry Bailey? Ramazani does not think so; he reads *The Nun's Priest's Tale* as commenting retroactively on this aspect of the Monk's performance: "telling the stories of Croesus, Hector, and others permits Chauntecleer to master his fear so thoroughly that he is tranquilized.... [The effect of] [t]he Monk's *de casibus* formula is not to make one 'Be war' but its opposite, to make one be somnolent." Indeed, critical affection for *The Nun's Priest's Tale* is as strong as its disaffection with *The Monk's Tale*. Comparisons between the two often trace the same "rising" narrative—tragedy to comedy, loss to recovery—that has mastered Chaucer criticism since the nineteenth century: writes Ramazani, "we certainly experience the [Nun's] Priest's tale as a deliverance from the Monk's closed world." This rising narrative—from the "closed world" to the open horizon—has been seen to structure *The Book of the Duchess*, the relation between *Troilus and Criseyde* and *The Canterbury Tales*, and, last but not least, Chaucer's entire career.[69] No wonder it is harder to see the problem with the Host and the Knight than it is to see the problem with Gertrude and Claudius. But the Monk may, as it were, see Chaucer differently. Wallace has argued that the Host is disappointed in the Monk because he has not delivered enough of what is now called "action"; the Host asks for a tale about hunting, and the Monk responds that he has no more "lust to pleye" (Prologue to *The Nun's*

Priest's Tale, 2805–6). Here it is as though the Monk himself has "fallen" in Bailey's eyes, and as though, even if Harry Bailey has been dozing, the Monk has not; he knows the import of his own stories, and at this point he does not feel like playing another man's games. Perhaps he knows that what befalls or descends on us is always destined either to disappoint or to exceed our expectations (Derrida, "My Chances/*Mes Chances*," 5).

The implication of Ramazani's argument is that preparedness is possible and desirable. The implication of Wallace's argument is that when we are trying to love a "myghty man," it is his strength that interests us, not his weakness. Either way, the Monk is either too masterful or not masterful enough. These approaches put asunder modes of enjoyment that are in fact interdependent. And it is possible that they do so— Ramazani more clearly than Wallace—to separate the Monk from Chaucer. Here is more of Ramazani:

> the open and expansive scope of the *Canterbury Tales* dwarfs the Monk and his dry poetics of limitation and abbreviation.
>
> The Monk's tales ... are a negative or inverse image of Chaucer's, a disturbing and crowded miniaturization of the tales of which they form a part.
>
> The Monk's formalism ... prevents him from seeing that the basis of tragedy is not an "objective" structure but an affective and hermeneutic program, carrying us from comic hope to tragic grief.[70]

The Monk is deadly: dessicated, and dessicating in his use of *abbrevatio*; closed where Chaucer is open; flattening and limiting rather than expansive; "merciless" rather than, as is Chaucer, interested in "the pathos of the tragic victim."

Of the story of Dido in *The Legend of Good Women*, Ramazani writes that "Chaucer allows us to participate in her sense of betrayal and anguish. He gives ample space to her lament and doesn't describe her bodily death, whereas the Monk would have excluded the lament and hoisted her immediately onto her funeral pyre."[71] Ramazani finds the Monk pitiless. He ascribes to the figure of Fortune-as-Monk that emptying out of interiority, of "character" or feeling, which some historians of tragedy ascribe to medieval tragedies of Fortune. The Monk, like the tragedy of

Fortune, is indifferent to the particular feelings of particular tragic "victims"; he does not get attached to them. By contrast, the kind of tragedy "Chaucer" wrote (as opposed to the "Monk") cares about the interior state of the victim, her feelings, and the way her feelings make us feel. Not for him the sadistic exteriority of the Monk: Chaucer "doesn't describe her bodily death," whereas the Monk "*would have* excluded her lament and hoisted her immediately onto her funeral pyre" (emphasis added). (Never mind that Chaucer, or at least his narrator, excludes Alcyone's complaint in *The Book of the Duchess,* substituting lightsome offerings of feather beds and gorgeous cushions to the gods of sleep.) But even if Chaucer created the Monk as an illustration of what he did *not* want to be, such a projection is always an intimate portrait nonetheless, and it is helpful to remember that Chaucer's treatments of pathos are among his most equivocal works. Ramazani seems to think that pity is free of aggressivity; its channels are clear; and they lead to "us," the auditor who lives on.

Although Augustine would not like it, this approach at least has the advantage of clarifying the nature of certain investments in tragic interiority, as that space in which suffering is redeemable in the currency of exchanged feelings. The body is finite; though I may sacrifice my life for others, I cannot die their death for them. This is part of my befallenness. But in the prosthetic space of my overseen and vigilant interior, I can introject, I can identify, I can (be made to) feel what others feel, I can even be groupified, spared the isolation of what I can suffer only by myself.

Wallace's reading of *The Monk's Tale* focuses not on a putatively Chaucerian maximization of discourse or celebration of the open-endedness of human life, but rather on the historical danger *to* human life and community, in particular to associational polity, posed in the later fourteenth century by Italian and potentially English despotism. The Monk's formulaic handling of tragedy, "the stabilized repetitions of oft-told tales," is, for Wallace, broken up by this highly particular historicity, which suggests that "renarration is always imminent...it may already be in progress."[72] The values of openness and unfinishedness located by Ramazani outside *The Monk's Tale* are found by Wallace to be part of the tale's own meanings. Not altogether unexpectedly, then, Wallace agrees to some extent with previous critics who associate the Monk with sterile artistry and failed sociability. Despite the open-endedness of the tale's political message, and despite the apparent inexhaustibility of the Monk's "seed, his supply of new *vires*," "his narrating proves barren: its substance cannot take root because...[it] makes no concessions to group pleasure." Moreover, "the Monk (unlike Chaucer the pilgrim) refuses the offer of a second chance at narrating," "remains strangely detached from the 'compaignye' he rides with," and, "in telling of the fall of *viri illustres*," "reenacts their isolation from human 'compaignye' through the monotony of his narrating.... He is finally brought down by an alliance of burgess and knight (a classic revolutionary combination). He will not speak again."[73]

But few, if any, of the pilgrims in *The Canterbury Tales* make friends along the way, and hardly any speak at all after their tales have been told. "Chaucer the pilgrim" is precisely an exception. Moreover, Wallace's view reinstates the rising action of Chaucerian critical narrative: forward historical movement versus the sterility of repetition.[74] By contrast, alliances between Hosts and Knights anticipate the revolutionary future. But given his stated preference for, purely and simply, "a genre that records the rise [of *vires illustres*] to 'prosperitee,'" the Knight could anticipate such a future only unknowingly.

For Wallace, the sterility and monotony of repetition is inimical to pleasure as well as the forward movement of history. Solitude is also inimical to pleasure conceived as a group phenomenon. The Monk seems to lack popularity. He does not like people. He is unlikable. He is unlike Chaucer and the other pilgrims, and he does not succeed in getting them to like his tale. But I think we should consider the possibility that the Monk's performance exposes enjoyment we like to deny. The pleasures of liking and of being like have the power to produce the group body, and thus to *preserve* our most dangerous drives. Wallace's argument participates to some degree in the logic of pity: the enjoyment of likeness, the valorization of its "communication," the power of such communication to exclude and isolate whatever does not fit the "general will." And, paradoxically, what might most menace the "general will" is coming face to face with its own empty but exigent formality. The borderline between heterogeneous association and mass groupification haunts not only the Monk's performance but *The Canterbury Tales* as a whole.

In a sense, then, I agree with Ramazani that *The Monk's Tale* is a "disturbing and crowded miniaturization" of Chaucer's artistry. But I like the way it is disturbing. I find it interesting that the example of collection inside Chaucer's collection should relentlessly focus on the fear of falling entailed in loss; on the engraving of the subject by a narrative image of the subject's helplessness to master space; on the seductiveness of falling out of aliveness altogether; and on the seductiveness also of grouping our fears together in the form of the body that cannot mourn. If *The Monk's Tale* is stupefying, that is partly because it is sentimental about nothing. It seeks neither to ennoble nor to defame the human "spirit" and its experience of misfortune. It shows that the tragedy of Fortune exhibits the workings of the law. It shows the arbitrariness of that law, the law of our befallenness—we can be taken from without—and its inessential relation, its exteriority, to human "character." It shows, indeed, the inessential relation of human "character" to tragedy. It shows that submitting to the law can be a structure of enjoyment, rather than an "ascetic" renunciation of enjoyment. And it shows that the deadness of the law (its inanimacy, insensibility, mechanicity) informs signifying forms, like the tragedy of fortune, that refuse life and maintain what they can of indifference by constructing groupified (generalized, codified, uniformed, but also groupified temporally, that is, repeated) representations in which the death drive can seek refuge from the torments of aliveness and desire.

That the forms of these representations have a murderous quality about them, which indeed imitates the destructivity pictured in the Monk's tragedies, is, after all, the point. The Monk's tragedies of Fortune show us that we are susceptible to making universalizing forms and codes as much to shelter ourselves from our own sentience as to enhance it, and that the enjoyment structured by such groupifications, codifications, and uniformities is or can be destructive. It can show us all this because its representation of the process of groupification and its kinship with artifice are pitiless rather than sentimental. *The Monk's Tale* strips the group down to the bare bones of the law that structures it, and shows us that the law is arbitrary and inanimate. The effects of this handling of tragedy are undoubtedly unpleasant, partly because it is about something unrelenting inside of us: the desire to get to the end of our own story.

Rather than thinking of *The Canterbury Tales* as a judgment on the Monk's collection, then, I prefer to think of *The Monk's Tale* as a warning to the reader: "Be war!"; treat all of Chaucer's poetry with due caution. Chaucer may not be as cute as we think; or, more precisely, cuteness may be scarier than we think, and no less enjoyable for that. If nothing else, *The Canterbury Tales* and *The Monk's Tale* have this much in common: both are "works"—insentient artifacts whose deadness we enjoy. But I think they also share a desire to reflect on the ethical complications of putting new signifiers into the world.

The Monk's Tale addresses everyone at once (1997) and universalizes Fortune. To be sure, this does not accomplish everything one might wish from an analysis of suffering. But I think *The Monk's Tale* shows that the potential for destructivity is everywhere and at all times, and that this will never go away, even if histories can always be renarrated. Pity, empathy, and other forms of "being like" will not change that, especially because pity is a way of "being like" that tries to conserve the insentient image by giving the gift of fellow feeling. Pity, indeed, will not save the suffering, but not because it is powerless or superficial; pity is absent from the Monk's performance because its primary function is to defend, by defending against, the subject's extimate deadliness.

The dislike of the Monk that sometimes appears in his critical tradition indicates, on the other hand, that we can "other" the Monk. We can shrink from recognizing "ourselves" in the Monk's deathly form, and look anywhere else for a more charitable image of literature. Insofar as *The Monk's Tale* offers to break down the force of negative projection by insisting on a certain commonality, it is totalizing; in this the Monk resembles the Pardoner, who, having long ago lost patience with being picked on, likes to remind his audience that *everyone* is going to be judged, and how. But at least this totalization has the force to interrogate both isolating and utopian strategies of domination. Derrida's insistence on the variability inherent in iteration troubles Žižek because Žižek fears that "the aspiration to abolish [the traumatic kernel, the radical antagonism through which man cuts his umbilical cord with nature], is precisely the source of totalitarian temptation."[75] History is open, but by that very token, *never* finished with the conflicts of living structures. This is the field of operation taken up by psychoanalysis, through transference.

In a historical *lapsus* Žižek himself would particularly appreciate, Freud, Lacan, Klein, Kristeva, and Žižek all take up the critical force of the anamorphic memento mori through the analytical encounter with finitude, in many forms: "the omnipresence of a sense of guilt"; the "Will for an Other-thing"; "a subject who doesn't know in a point of extreme...ignorance"; "the 'I' which asks itself what it wants"; "the demand not to suffer, at least without understanding why?"[76]—or, as Derrida puts it, psychoanalysis as obtaining from metaphysics the concepts it will interrogate in its own "operation—notably, the oppositional limits between the psychic and the physical, the inside and the outside, not to mention all those that depend on them" ("My Chances/*Mes Chances*," 27). By reworking these oppositional limits, Freud conceives of the lapse, the symptom, the error, as offering precisely "the chance for the truth to reveal itself": "A *lapsus*...gives another truth its chance. The limit between...the unconscious 'I' and the other of consciousness, is perhaps this possibility for my fortune *(mes chances)* to be misfortune *(malchance)* and for my misfortune to be in truth fortunate *(une chance)*" (ibid., 21).

To posit befallenness is not to posit it as closed to history. If nothing else, because of the uncertainty that death's otherness to the living subject paradoxically produces, perhaps even the story of death is never over. Instead of turning back, as the *ars moriendi* commonly did, to the divine Other we know in our hearts we must already have done in—why else would we owe it our lives—we now have the possibility of accepting a little bit of help from our friends instead of falling for the cruel hoax of absolute rescue. We have the possibility still of encountering in all its aversiveness the problem of the object, but now, of valuing the *temporalia* despite, or even because, they are finite, constructed. The transience that is in the object and emerges in us as what is in us more than ourselves, "is that all?" But isn't it also too much, and, in any case, doesn't this give us the chance "to come to terms with [the 'death drive,' this dimension of radical negativity], to learn to recognize it in its terrifying dimension and then, on the basis of this fundamental recognition, to try to articulate a *modus vivendi* with it"?[77] Is it possible that we only "get somewhere" when we know that some things never end? "Now" may not be so different from "then" as all that. As noted earlier, critics such as Knapp have felt that "the Monk misses his chance to teach a moral lesson as well as his chance to offer consolation for the reversals of this fickle world." But perhaps the Monk does not think consolation is moral. "When one approaches that central emptiness, which up to now has been the form in which access to *jouissance* has presented itself to us," and which "religion in all its forms consists of avoiding," "my neighbor's body breaks into pieces" (Lacan, *Ethics of Psychoanalysis*, 202, 130). The

Canterbury Tales seem to anticipate the Last Judgment by hanging the scales of Justice in the sky while the Parson is repetitively and formulaically describing sin. But doesn't this point in the direction of a spot of silence *The Canterbury Tales* might be trying hard to hear? An emptiness that tries, by not answering our desire for a mirroring recognition, to tell us something true about the difficulty of loving our neighbor? "Henceforth, we know that we are foreigners to ourselves, and it is with the help of that sole support that we can attempt to live with others."[78]

4

SACRIFICIAL DESIRE IN CHAUCER'S *KNIGHT'S TALE*

> *The justice which began with the maxim,
> "Everything can be paid off, everything
> must be paid off," ends with connivance...
> at the escape of those who cannot pay to
> escape—it ends, like every good thing on
> earth, by destroying itself.... The self-
> destruction of Justice...! we know the
> pretty name it calls itself—Grace!... it
> remains, as is obvious, the privilege... of the
> strongest, better still, their super-law.*
> —Friedrich Nietzsche

> *Sacrifice the sacrifice...*
> —Slavoj Žižek

The discourses of charity that proliferated in medieval culture sought to determine what it meant to be "poor in spirit" and gave to the powerful a remarkable ally and model in the figure of the poor. The practice and casuistry of charity offered multiple points of crossover between poverty and power—between, as Nietzsche puts it, "those who cannot pay to escape" and those determined not to.[1] The "super-law" of grace; the hypereconomy of sacrifice that seeks, as in mourning, to keep that which it gives up; the absurd and infinite love of a God who plays "scape-goat for his debtor"—these concepts, as Derrida has argued, accredit the believer who must believe in the unbelievable, who must give credence to that which is beyond instruments of credit, submit to an incomprehensible law.[2] We know who is left out of, indeed, who is corrected by, the hypereconomy of sacrifice, except of course insofar as they subsidize it: those who *can* or *must* pay—the Jew, the sodomite, the usurer, the infidel, the heretic, those figures whose sacrifices Christian culture did not want to pay for, and who disturbed for centuries Christian calculations of forgiveness, of the love of the neighbor that refuses requital.[3]

The logic of sacrifice structures the militant European Christian subject (Derrida, *Gift of Death*, 29–33). This logic, the function of which is to recuperate aggressivity and loss, includes the infinite compassion that requites and corrects, and the renunciation of life, for example, the penitential subject's gift, without hope of reward, of one "broken heart" (far more satisfying to God than the rectitude of many just men), as a gift submitted to an inscrutable and incalculable divinity, whose response (the gift of ultimate enjoyment) is assured in the apparent indeterminacy and infinity of the hypercontract of mercy. The logic of sacrifice must be taken into account if one wishes to consider the history of European militancy, of the knights of faith; and it lies at the heart of Chaucer's *Knight's Tale*.

As we have seen, the psychoanalytic notion of the dependence of "the subject's experience of satisfaction... on the other suggests why desire and sacrifice are tightly bound together.[4] Lacan's "mirror stage" imagines the infant taking on "her" image through the mediation of an "other" image, the image in the mirror or the face of the mother. A subject founded on the image of an other will never be full, or fully be; it is and will always be other to itself. And because of this, its ability to help or to be helped is finite, as is its access to enjoyment.[5] The Ōther that structures the subject also has its limits. The symbolic order is open to change, it offers no absolute guarantee of meaning or redemption or enjoyment, and its import is the finitude of powers and of the subjects who take shape through their workings. And if the power of the Ōther is limited, then nothing can help human beings rid themselves of finitude; nor can ultimate enjoyment be attained any more than absolute power, because desire *is* "change as such" (Lacan, *Ethics of Psychoanalysis*, 293). We need, *for the sake of* our *jouissance, which also* means for the sake of the other within and without us, to break the lethal promise of ultimate rescue. No other, divinized or abjected, can make us whole.

The logic of sacrifice seeks to occlude that the O̅ther *itself* lacks, desires, and is transitory.

Let us recall that when the subject posits the demand of the Other, she cannot translate this demand into a positive or specific mandate, a clear mission, a signifier that would be her "own."[6] In place of this impossibility she puts the demand of the Other, through the figure of sacrifice, the "gift of death," which condenses the O̅ther's multiple desires (including the O̅ther's indifference) into the Other's desire for the subject herself, for the subject *as such*. The Other is seen to desire the subject to *be subject*—to be interpellated as a subject, to subject itself to interpellation. Thus, in the logic of sacrifice, in the gift of death, the subject denies the decentered, contingent, and ultimately indifferent process through which she has come into being, by refiguring her own role in that process (her attempt to locate and assume "her" signifier) as a gift—a gift of life from the Other, and, to the extent that her own activity is acknowledged, a gift that gives back her life *to* the Other, imagined as her creator. The subject enters into this phantasmic exchange of gifts in the hope that the Other desires her, and in the hope that such an exchange will reward and thus perpetuate that desire, despite its inscrutability, which is an effect of its phantasmic status. (How can we know, reward, and rekindle a desire that does not exist?) Thus the subject tries to secure her belief in the power, indeed, in the subjective status, of the Other as that which can recognize her and thereby give her life as a subject, through the specularity of the gift.[7]

Because the signifier that constitutes the subject is arbitrary, she cannot know exactly what the Other really desires with regard to her; hence the inscrutability of that father who sees in secret, whose reasons are his own, but who knows and can calculate what the subject has given, suffered, loved (Derrida, *Gift of Death*, 56–57). In truth, the O̅ther does not know what it wants from her either, because it is barred, unconscious, shot through with the remnants of the very *jouissance* it carves up with its significations. The flawed sentience of the barred O̅ther—the inability of the *alta mente* to see all things—is masked by the fantasy of the omniscient big Other. This secret must be guarded, as Theseus seeks to do, because the contingency of the symbolic order means that it is open to our intervention.

The elaboration of a subjective identity through the philosophical or religious "taking on" of death must always be a melancholic incorporation of death, (ibid., 16). By entombing/keeping death inside oneself as stand-in for the incorrigible thing, the knight of faith triumphs over the flesh, thereby acquiring the excoriated militant angelic body, shining, super-existent, completely imbued with—one might almost say, made of—the power to rescue and to "correct" (itself), and to transmit God's signifiers to other sublunary missionaries.[8] Because *jouissance* is not full and absolute enjoyment, it must always be deferred, bought and paid for with the sacrifice *of* enjoyment—thus we explain to ourselves why the Other is not making us perfectly happy: because we are waiting, disciplining, readying ourselves. We betray our *jouissance*, as if to say, neither I nor the other is important enough to justify *these* kinds of risks; but sacrifice ennobles my cowardice and treachery. The sacrifice of the subject-and-object enjoined by charity is hypereconomic because it rewards us (phantasmatically) for cheating. Grace never fails to promise us our reward; that reward is "beyond exchange"; what we cheat ourselves/the other out of turns into our "debt," which we are rewarded for paying. This is, indeed, to get away with something. Sacrifice and responsibility give us access to an obscene enjoyment (Žižek, *Sublime Object of Ideology*, 43, 81); the discourse of charity obscures this by driving its absolute wedge between selfless love and love of self. In truth, there is no pure self, no pure selflessness, as late-medieval English psychology makes perfectly evident.[9] That theology is, in its own way, as open to the difficulty of distinguishing between desire and the law as is psychoanalysis, which locates "the genesis of the moral dimension ... nowhere else than in desire itself" (Lacan, *Ethics of Psychoanalysis*, 3).

The embrace of the subject's strangeness to itself involves not the philosophical "vigil" over death that has for so long promised to give the subject to itself (Derrida, *Gift of Death*, 13), but rather an openness to *jouissance*, and a knowledge of the risks entailed therein: death of the self-identical subject, death period. That this involves a knowledge of the "evil" or *jouissance* that we might pursue, as well therefore as of the evil or *jouissance* that lies likewise in the heart of our neighbor (Lacan, *Ethics of Psychoanalysis*, 186), is the ethical challenge posed by desire, a challenge that Lacan addresses by invoking the "value of prudence" (3): know what you risk, for yourself as well as for the other; neither of you will be able to keep what you have given away. At best there will be something different. Our loves live on in us, but not the way they lived before. As Elaine Scarry has so beautifully pointed out, in the losing time of emergency, we count.¹⁰ Exchange, then, breaks with itself; it needs no hypereconomy. What we return is never the same as what we have been given, and what we receive is never the same as what we have given up. The openness of exchange to change, without benefit of transcendence, may of course be dissimulated by oppositions of gift to fixed, vulgar, "selfish" commercial transactions. Shylock wants his pound of flesh, but, after all, he is right. We *will* have to pay; we are kidding ourselves to think we are going to get it for free. But in what coin? Even the pound of flesh we get back is not the one we give up, which is what makes the matter interesting. To insist on the letter of the law is, paradoxically, always already a disturbance, an eruption of the Real. To avoid this Thing, Christian hypereconomy devalues the calculation of the old law, the Jew, while of course retaining the power of calculation to count its inestimable gains. But all calculations are passional.

The critical tradition on *The Knight's Tale* oscillates between certain disputed points: whether the chivalric culture for which the Knight stands, and which he represents in his tale, is or is not obsolescent; whether *The Knight's Tale* represents chivalric culture as the source of order or disorder; whether the tale is or is not fraught with contradictions; whether the Knight is or is not blind to those contradictions; whether Chaucer is or is not similarly blind.¹¹ Though much of the criticism produced through these disputations has been brilliant, the alternatives outlined earlier are caught up in a certain imaginary characteristic of historical writing on chivalry; and because of this captation, criticism on *The Knight's Tale* has done insufficient justice to the vile enjoyment and identificatory power of this tale. Catherine La Farge puts the problem well:

> Theseus is like a god and like God. The tale lets us read this the other way around: God is like Theseus. Chaucer's Providence has too long been granted amnesty on the grounds of its Boethian affinities.... In so far as Providence may be responsible for the apparent arbitrariness of the plot, its methods are more than odd: the death of Arcite is a circuitous route to the happy marriage of Palamon and Emelye.¹²

There is indeed something "odd," something irresolvable, about *The Knight's Tale*. But I think it seems odd to many of its readers because it cannot be confined to the categories of order versus disorder when conceived oppositionally. In the imaginary that guides so much writing on chivalry and on *The Knight's Tale*, the idealism of chivalric culture—its commitment to heroic sacrifice—is understood to be in oppositional relation to the aggressivity of war, to the *jouissance* of war, the horrors of which become a touchstone for the "reality" that is contrasted with the illusory status of the chivalric ideal of sacrificial rescue.[13] The opposition insists on the difference between the *jouissance* of aggressivity and noble sacrifice—thus preserving the integrity of the latter even while pointing to the improbability of its having ever been a reality. Critiques of late-medieval chivalric culture too often preserve that culture's own fantasies: the notion that the knight of faith's "gift of death" would, if it were (or regardless of whether it were) ever indeed offered, be charitable rather than concupiscent; the notion that the knight of faith, if he ever existed, would perform "correction" out of infinite love of the enemy, and not for the concupiscent motives of glory or terrestrial lucre or the malice that demands requital.[14] Hence the endless preoccupation, in medieval writing on war, with the "heart" of the knight of faith; with the calculation of wartime profit, of when and under what circumstances plunder can be retained, ransom demanded, pillage permitted; with the identification, as noted earlier, of those enemies to whom the other cheek must be turned, and of those who may be persecuted.[15]

The fantasy of chivalry is a sublime economy that powerfully recuperates the *jouissance* of aggressivity by rewriting it as incalculable, inscrutable love; it is a structure through which a certain obscene destructivity may be glimpsed and enjoyed, but only to the extent that the gift of death is offered in payment thereof. Military discipline and its breakdown are not opposing forces, as a traditional ethics would have it; they are hand in glove, as is exemplified by the stunning beauty of the angelic hosts (if, with Lacan, we read beauty as the sign that points us *toward*, as well as away from, our *jouissance*), and by the uncanny power of the theme of "Christ the Lover-Knight."[16] The "mourning for the front," for pure confrontation with one's "proper" enemy, that characterizes histories of chivalry and of atonement is driven by an unacknowledged acknowledgment of the phantasmic nature of absolute rescue, paired by the manic triumph of superexistence.[17]

European military culture has been an eminent cultural site for submission to an arbitrary and exacting law. The production of both obedience and transgression is central to military culture. The logic of sacrifice, far from being in an obsolescent relation to the economies of its culture, helped to produce them, through its occlusion of the mutual intrication of sacrifice and aggressivity—as is attested by the unhappy deployment of the casuistry of charity in connection with the harassment of vagabonds in both France and England and the concomitant elaboration of an ethics of labor.[18] The cultural power of sacrifice is and has always been enormous.[19] It mobilizes subjects for loss and destructivity: the "deterritorializations" of crusade and pogrom and flagellation, massive redeployments of bodies that Lacan would read as the tragic return of the Real when it is foreclosed by the image of sacrifice.[20] In the Middle Ages, spectacular charity monumentalizes itself in stone, in the glorious architecture of surplus value, the architectural "actualization of pain" (Lacan, *Ethics of Psychoanalysis*, 60), built to house spiritual paupers and broken penitential hearts. And there are also the "everyday" forms of medieval life, for example, the hypereconomizing of kinship and marriage, the sacrifice *of* the household economy, of the *oikos*, in favor of the sublime capital of the sublime body of Christ—a sacrifice that produces, among other things, an endless series of monastic "reforms" throughout the Middle Ages.[21] Or one might think of statist conceptions of community, such as Aquinas's magisterial reconstruction of Aristotelian notions of the need to discipline private desires on behalf of the common good, on which ground Aquinas stands when retheorizing the just war and the enemy on behalf of the newly consolidated states of the thirteenth century.[22]

In commenting on the Sermon on the Mount, Derrida notes that "the opposition between the mediocre wages of retribution or exchange and the noble salary that is obtained through disinterested sacrifice... points to an opposition between two peoples, ours, to whom Christ is speaking, and the others" (the others are *ethnici* or *ethnikoi*, translated variously as *goyim, pagans, publicans*; *Gift of Death*, 105–6). In Lacan too we find sacrifice at the heart of "everything that depends on the image of the other as our fellow man" (*Ethics of Psychoanalysis*, 196), which we might broaden to "fellow creature"; it is at the heart of everything at stake in the definition of "fellow," indeed, of "creature," of everything at stake in the harrowing complex of strangeness and intimacy through which subjectivation, always preoccupied with creation and creatureliness, takes place.

The subject does not cease to be inhabited by that extimate Thing, that *jouissance* which suffers from the signifier but does not cease to mobilize it, to put it through its paces. Lacan's formulation, it will be recalled, is as follows: "*Das Ding* presents itself at the level of unconscious experience as that which already makes the law.... It is a capricious and arbitrary law, the law of the oracle, the law of signs *in which the subject receives no guarantee from anywhere*" (*Ethics of Psychoanalysis*, 73).[23] At this level of experience of the law, the rules that enable the very waywardness of the signifying chain carve up or design *jouissance*, thus producing the subject and her "surplus enjoyment"—that portion or stylization of *jouissance* resulting from the operations of the signifier. The law of the signifier conveys its "mandate" to the subject, but unintelligibly, leaving to the subject the attempt to scrutinize it, to confer upon it the enjoyment-in-sense proper to ideology, to "identify" with it as "hers." What clear demand attends the signifier that is one's name, what does one's name guarantee, other than the inscription of the subject into an endless chain of relations with other signifiers, whose import can never be grasped in full?

It is on this level of the law that Lacan locates the radical dimension of courtly love, in the form of the lady as sublime object, who, standing in the place of but also pointing in the direction of *jouissance*, of the Thing, appears as an "inhuman partner," a traumatic object with whom no relation is possible, an apathetic void exacting senseless ordeals.[24] It is also on this level that Žižek locates the obscene enjoyment at stake in submission to the law. Emphasizing the Lacanian definition of the unconscious as, like the courtly lady in her more rigorous forms, an "automaton," a dead, senseless letter that leads the mind unconsciously with it, Žižek proceeds to the notion of the "constitutively senseless character of the law" (*Sublime Object of Ideology*, 37). We obey the law not because of its positive qualities, not because it is just, good, or beneficial, but because it is the law. True obedience involves obedience to the command as such, that is, not just whether or not, but insofar as, the command is incomprehensible, traumatic, irrational.

The subject's attempt to internalize, and to give positive meaning to, the senseless injunction never fully succeeds:

> there is always a residue, a leftover, a stain of traumatic irrationality and senselessness sticking to it, and ... *this leftover, far from hindering the full submission of the subject to the ideological command, is the very condition of it*: it is precisely this non-integrated

surplus of senseless traumatism which confers on the Law its unconditional authority: in other words, which—in so far as it escapes ideological sense—sustains... the ideological *jouis-sense,* enjoyment-in-sense (enjoy-meant), proper to ideology. (Ibid., 43–44)

The enjoyment at stake in how we give credence to the law is, for Žižek, supported precisely by that senseless enjoyment which escapes the law; the enjoyment of our credence takes shape through our experience of the arbitrariness of the law at the level of the Thing, which accounts for how, in theorizations of belief, the notion of our accountability to belief so often takes precedence over its positive qualities. During the Middle Ages, obedience was uncoupled from the positive qualities of law through a number of discourses that privileged correction for correction's sake, often in the company of figures of secrecy: the analysis of tyranny; the rigorous treatment given to the question of military obedience in writing on the just war, whereby, particularly in the later Middle Ages, the conscience of the individual soldier was so often effaced, or, more properly, kept confined to the heart; and of course the inscrutability of providence.[25]

Insofar as we experience the law through its senseless structuration of the unconscious, the law points inevitably to *jouissance*. The scandal involved is partly that the law to which we submit has no foundational claim on us, no ethical content, no rationality; hence allegiance to it cannot produce free and responsible ethical subjectivity, unless we transform it through the sense-making operations of ideology. But the scandal is also that the law, because it stylizes our *jouissance,* is inextricable from it. What makes the hypereconomy of sacrifice so effective is that it not only infuses obedience to the command with positivity, it even more radically rationalizes the irrationality of submission and our desire for it through the figure of secrecy: that we cannot know the mysterious reasons of Providence or of the prince is an ideological form of nonknowledge, an *ascesis* of knowledge, a sacrifice of knowledge, that stands in the place of the impossibility of knowing what the law means, and in the place of the *jouissance* signposted by that impossibility. The asymmetry of creature and Creator, of what the creature's gaze can see and what the Creator's gaze can see, the taboo on divine knowledge, puts a prohibition on creaturely presumption in the place of an impossibility that has to do with our finitude, with the extimacy—the dead, senseless exteriority—of the law of the signifier that inhabits us, and therefore with our *jouissance*. The subject's strangeness to itself, that about itself which it cannot know, but which is also its desire, is refigured, through a form of mourning, as that which the Other knows in secret, into what Derrida describes as the "witness that others cannot see, and who is therefore *at the same time other than me and more intimate with me than myself*" (*Gift of Death*, 109).

Because the law governs the operations of the signifier, it is, Žižek argues, the *form* and only the form of the law, not its positive ethical content, that is interlinked with our desire, and drives us to accept its command, a formality related also to the way in which the beauty of the image, the image of beauty, commands the knight of faith in courtly love (*Sublime Object of Ideology*, 81). And our renunciation in relation to this law produces the *plus-de-jouir*, the leftover enjoyment that sustains our obedience (and *also* can become the basis for our refusal of obedience). Hence the obscenity of fascism, the "utterly void, formal character of its appeal, ... the fact that it demands obedience and sacrifice for their own sake" (82). The true value of sacrifice "lies in its very meaninglessness," and its enjoyment is the enjoyment of renunciation itself, that is, the enjoyment of the law's designation of desire; the renunciation of *jouissance so as to produce* the *plus-de-jouir*, the surplus enjoyment that will be embodied in the *objet a*, that fascinating but arbitrary object that fills out the void (of sense) in the Ōther (ibid.). This is in part the import of the beautiful captive Amazon Emelye's appearance to the imprisoned Theban knights, Palamon and Arcite, as a captivating image of freedom; as always already subdued, but as offering an image of the enjoyment at stake in the taking on of submission. And it is not only Emelye who functions as *objet a* in *The Knight's Tale*, but also Palamon and Arcite themselves. They, as subjects, make themselves into the *objet a* for the commanding and inscrutably desirous gaze of the law.

The logic of sacrificial subjectivation is at work in Lacan's notion of courtly love as a "mourning until death" that can be understood with reference to the structure of sadism; it is at work also in the melancholic mania of triumph produced through war, or through the vigil over death, the "care for the self" enjoined by philosophy, or through the transformation of necessity into choice analyzed by Freud in his essay "The Theme of the Three Caskets."[26] (Beware of unwar strookes.) It is a logic that transforms finitude into creative power, into the power to make a representation of one's finitude, a beautiful signifier of the absence of plenitude (which is one reason why *The Knight's Tale* closes with such elaborate speechifying).

To accept the gift of death from the Other, to choose it, as in the examples of Socrates and Christ, means also to interpret death, to give oneself a representation of death, to give oneself (by accepting from the Other) a *destination*. Thus, at the moment of this assumption of responsibility for one's own death, one *foresees*, keeps vigil; one also falls back upon oneself, recollects oneself, identifies with oneself in relation to one's own particular death (Derrida, *Gift of Death*, 10–13). The true philosopher looks death in the face; the concern for death becomes the concern for life. A vigilant superexistence is born from the event of looking death in the face, from the triumph over death, which, like all triumphs, retains the traces of the struggle from which it emerges—preserves "the memory of war" (ibid., 16).

The mania of triumph, of superexistence and of superknowledge (of that which cannot be known, i.e., death), which follows upon one's self-sacrifice, one's acceptation of death, is the melancholic *"jouis-sense,"* the form of enjoyment proper to the ideology of death, incorporating the memory of what one had to lose in order to get (back) one's superexistence. This melancholic *jouis-sense* domesticates the stranger within. It is named by the word *win*, which appears in the triumphant opening lines of *The Knight's Tale*, when the narrator says of Theseus that "Ful many a riche contree hadde he wonne" (864).

The cognates of *win*, and its senses in Middle English, link together the notions of obtaining, tilling the ground, exerting oneself, gaining by labor or exertion, suffering; striving, conquering, taking possession of, making profit; above all, for my purposes, "To regain, recover (something lost); hence, to make up for (loss, waste); to rescue, deliver; in religious use, to redeem: often with *again*."[27] *Win* is indeed a word that retains the traces of struggle, preserves, in triumph, the memory of war; and Theseus is indeed the winner in *The Knight's Tale*, as that sovereign subject from whom one must receive and to whom one must yield in order to be recognized as subject. Thus he is accompanied in his triumph not only by his Amazonian captives but by "al his hoost in armes hym bisyde" (874), by an image of community as sublime military body. *Host* is itself a word whose history tracks the path of triumph, from estrangement to the mania of superexistence and redemption: from Latin *hostem (hostis)*, meaning "stranger, enemy," come the medieval senses of "warlike gathering," "a great company," an etymology that marks the power of melancholic incorporation to domesticate the other.[28]

Moreover, to say that Theseus is the winner in *The Knight's Tale* is also to say that he is its most successful philosopher. The logic of sacrificial subjectivation allows us to understand why this tale tracks a path from war to philosophical discourse; it allows us to decipher the intimacy between war and the consolation of philosophy.

The Knight's Tale generates a *jouis-sense* of thoughtful puzzlement (which indeed is displayed by a number of its characters) over a very long series of riddles. These are: the foundations of Theseus's authority; the apparent arbitrariness of Palamon and Arcite's submission (why don't they do this or that?—the question they of course ask of themselves; why do they simply confess to Theseus in the woods and put themselves under his law? and so on); the apparent arbitrariness of Palamon and Arcite's identity (that is, do they deserve their "destinations," or not?); the apparently unmotivated pageant of intercession on behalf of Palamon and Arcite played out by Hippolyta and Emelye; the mystery, made more baffling in Chaucer's text than in Boccaccio's, of Emelye's unrecorded acceptance of Arcite and then Palamon after the brief glimpse Chaucer is careful to give us, during Emelye's sacrificial rites, of her protest; the awkward, flat, medicalized, almost comic (to some readers, at any rate) tone of the presentation of Arcite's death, followed by outbursts of communal mourning; the long delay that follows, in Chaucer though not in Boccaccio, which puts in question the meaningfulness of Theseus's elaborate creation, the amphitheater and the tournament, as means of resolution; Chaucer's linkage of the marriage between Palamon and Emelye with reasons of state, which has the same effect; the squabble among the gods, and the perplexing relation between Saturn's arrangements and Theseus's final speech.

Most of these riddles derive from moments when reasons and intentions are inscrutable, interiorities veiled. These critical cruxes have arisen when, precisely, what cannot be read in the tale is what is in the heart, whether of Jupiter or Providence or Emelye. The marked, insistent illegibility of subjectivity at the tale's critical moments of questioning, assent, submission, appeal, and sacrifice—Mars and Venus seem to promise what happens, but things take a further turn; Diana gives a sign, but we cannot understand it—actually supports the powerful movement of subjectivation in this tale, by making it clear that we become subject only through these performances for the oracular Other, that the law that will say yes or no to us in fact promises nothing, because the signifier is unstable. The law constitutes us only through our submission to it, at the oracular level of the emergence of the Thing, when our *jouissance* is designed and our fate decided, through our subjection to the signifier, to words we cannot understand but can only interpret.

The Knight's Tale is preoccupied with hiding, constraining, burying, and removing the things that emerge or become manifest inside it—things that embody that "fundamental dimension of the unknown in desire, of something that doesn't resemble me." The tale begins with an appeal to Theseus to bury the rotting corpses of Thebes, and there follows the creation of another pile of dead bodies, out of which Palamon and Arcite are taken and put into prison. Arcite of course dies and is given a spectacular funeral. After he is wounded, "[a]s blak he lay as any cole or crowe" (2692). The crow is a carrion eater and harbinger of trouble, marking the fact that Arcite now is fully *destined*, in between deaths, living only his dying. Coal is "[a] piece of burnt wood . . . that still retains sufficient carbon to be capable of further combustion without flame; a charred remnant, a cinder," "sometimes defined as *dead, cold, black, quenched* coal," which is the definition associated by the *OED* with the phrase "*as black as a coal*" (2a). Arcite is indeed this remnant that can still burn but is already no longer what it once was, a remnant, again, in between deaths, in radical anticipation of death.

What interests me here is in part how drawn out is the depiction of Arcite's dying, of his state as remnant; our attention is asked to linger upon his wound, and specifically upon the excess of stuff, of corrupted flesh, that is opened up to our vision through that wound. What emerges in and through Arcite is the Thing, that inert stuff of the real, the "clothered blood" (2745), the massified liquid that cannot circulate, cannot be emptied or moved; it is that which is in him more than himself; and the tale wants us to participate in this "traumatic eruption." This is, so to say, the most carnal moment in the tale, the moment when there emerges that strangeness within us that is not responsible to, does not respond to, the other; and that strangeness within us is what the law seeks out, insofar as that strangeness is what resists interpellation and must be offered up in sacrifice, as Arcite does here, the sacrifice of his spectacularly broken heart ("tobrosten" [2691]), the culmination of the mourning until death that is courtly love: "Allas, the peynes stronge, /

That I for yow have suffred, and so longe!" (2771–72); "And if that evere ye shul ben a wyf, / Foryet nat Palamon, the gentil man" (2796–97).

The consternation this scene has evoked in readers of *The Knight's Tale* (or numbness—Robertson remarks that "Arcite has very little dignity even in death"), points to the way this scene brings out a certain vile enjoyment, the obscenity of sacrifice: its meaningless, or perhaps we might say auto-significant (in the sense that, as Žižek puts it, ideology serves nothing, it serves only itself) fascination with opening the subject's wounds, opening the subject to the shameful remnant of *jouissance* that lies within, the "stuff" that the signifier designs but from which it also estranges us.[29] The desire of this tale is the desire of the sadist who does not acknowledge his own Thing, who does not acknowledge the way his desire is at stake in his subjection of the body of his victim to the trappings of the law.

What this sadist finds unbearable in the object of his attentions is, according to Lacan, the way that the subject "suffers from" the signifier, is absent to itself, inhabited by nonknowledge, by the remnant of *jouissance* that is not the subject. This sadist confronts the other with the truth of the subject's nonknowledge, by suspending the other in an impossible knowledge of the imminence of its death—a carnalization, indeed, of the anticipatory vigil over death sublimed by philosophy—and claiming total mastery over the signifier that is the other. The sadist re-creates the subject as perdurable, sublime object, filling the lack in the other by deferring, extending the period between the two deaths, the knowing of what cannot be known (one's own death, one's estimate nonself), suspending the victim in a radical interrogation, finally and phantasmatically filling the lack in the other by annihilating the other, so that the other finally coincides with its own absence, an inverted restoration of presence (Lacan, *Ethics of Psychoanalysis*, 202, 261). By transforming the other into the signifier, into his signifier, the sadist gains access to the *jouissance* residing in the fact that one creates a signifier as such, a form; the fantasy scenario of this sadist is an inverted fantasy of rescue, of re-creation of the other, through the gift of death, into an enduring signifier.

This is one way of accounting for how *The Knight's Tale* exacerbates the problem of meaning that attends Arcite's sacrifice at the moment of his dying, an effect that is produced partly through the disjunction between two different rhetorics of loss. The first is the dispassionate, knowledgeable, medicalizing gaze that presents to us in considerable detail the wound in Arcite's dying body.[30] The second is the passionate lamentation that suspends Arcite in the form of the question: he asks, "What is this world? What asketh men to have?" (2777), and gives no answer, nor is any given to him—certainly not by the narrator, who, in another passage that has seemed troubling to readers of the tale, suspends judgment as to Arcite's final judgment:

> His spirit chaunged hous and wente ther,
> As I cam nevere, I kan nat tellen wher.
> Therfore I stynte; I nam no divinistre;
> Of soules fynde I nat in this registre ... (2809–12)

Thus the destination of this by now thoroughly destined Arcite—in the sense that for many lines now he has been nothing but his anticipation of death—is ensealed, made secret. The narrator's knowledge, unlike that of the narrator of the *Teseida,* does not penetrate so far.

Whether this figure of the secret that is death is meant to evoke doubt, and therefore the meaninglessness of the subject's gift of death, or whether it is meant to evoke the absolute secrecy that is absolute knowledge of the universe, is not easy to determine. I would suggest that both are at stake: the text announces here that the meaninglessness of sacrifice will ultimately be referred to another kind of inaccessibility of meaning, not that of finitude, but of the father who knows in secret. The meanings of "divinen," from which "divinistre" (a theologian or a prophet) derives, track the ease with which the figure of doubt can be transmuted into the figure of absolute secret knowledge: "divinen" means to foretell future events, to predict, to prophesy, but can also mean to "engage in speculation or guessing"; "to be suspicious"; "to be in doubt about."[31] The narrator cannot know, he cannot find souls named in "this registre" (2812); the *OED* gives the medieval meanings of "register" as "[a] book or volume in which regular entry is made of particulars or details of any kind which are considered of sufficient importance to be exactly and formally recorded." No such exteriorized, accessible, written record can tell us Arcite's fate; for that, again, we would need to penetrate a secret that lies beyond codified knowledge, for that we will need a superknowledge. But the narrator knows what he does not know, which is more than Arcite knows, and is, it turns out, also more than the mourning women of the community know.

As discourses of consolation begin to find their way into *The Knight's Tale*, so do discourses of knowledge, of meaning. Arcite is joined in the form of the question by the mourning women of the community: "'Why woldestow be deed,' thise wommen crye, / 'And haddest gold ynough, and Emelye?'" (2835–36). This lamentation is followed by the first assertion of philosophical consolation in the tale, offered not by an undifferentiated mass of women or by the corrupt mass of dying flesh that is Arcite, but by Egeus, Theseus's father, the only man who can "gladen" the distraught duke (2837): "'Right as ther dyed nevere man,' quod he, 'That he ne lyvede in erthe in some degree, / Right so ther lyvede never man,' he seyde, / 'In al this world, that som tyme he ne deyde'" (2843–46).

Egeus's knowledge of "this worldes transmutacioun"—he has seen the world "chaunge bothe up and doun" (2839, 2840)—is a dispassionate assertion of superknowledge and of superexistence, the (impossible) knowledge about death which, in their different ways, the sadist, the medicine man, and the philosopher seek to construct—a seminal knowledge, finally a triumphant knowledge of and a care for life, passed on from father to son, intensified through a figure of genealogical survival of wisdom and of "gladness," of enjoyment.[32] But if the melancholic recovery of enjoyment is already under way here, in the form of a simple incorporation of loss through the masculine philosophical subject's knowledge of its facticity, there are, again, limits to what Egeus knows; "Deeth is an ende" of his knowledge as well as "of every worldly soore" (2849).

As noted earlier, Derrida emphasizes that the vigil over death, the philosophical anticipation of death through which the subject triumphs over that which she does not know, and chooses what she cannot avoid, involves the fashioning of a representation of death, a representation that incorporates the secret of "that which is in the subject more than itself" *into* the subject, or that, more properly, fashions the subject—and her community and history—through the incorporation of that secret, the corrupt bodily remnant (*Gift of Death*, 9). As with Lacan's sadist, the process of melancholic incorporation *is* the production of surplus enjoyment, a re-narcissizing of the subject's obscene submission to the law of the signifier. This is why melancholic triumph involves not just the power to represent, to make the image, but the power to *rescue* the decomposing image, the image that threatens to collapse into the corrupt stuff of the Thing that is in the subject more than herself. And because the image of the subject is founded on the image of the other, this triumphant rescue of the image of the subject will involve the triumphant rescue of the image of the other, and vice versa—a transitivism that Lacan names "the natural basis of pity" (*Ethics of Psychoanalysis*, 196), which founds the capacity to identify with the enemy, to attain the superexistence of that form of brotherly love so familiar in war and in charity, which is neither purely a selflessness nor a love of self, but a transitivist celebration of the triumphant reconstitution of signifiers of absent plenitude.

"[T]he soore" that, as he lays dying, "[e]ncreesseth" at Arcite's heart "moore and moore" is refigured in Egeus's speech in the form of knowledge that "every worldly soore" must end; but this sore has not yet been re-created into something beautiful, into that beauty that is the mark of the signifier itself, of its formal power and its power to form the *jouissance* of the subject. Arcite's "soore" has been turned into a fact of life and death, but the aestheticization of his image, and the secret incorporation of his corrupt stuff, is subject to a delay—a delay that is the time of mourning: "By processe and by lengthe of certeyn yeres, / Al stynted is the moornynge and the teres / Of Grekes, by oon general assent" (2967–69).

The end of mourning is, then, a figure for the unanimity of community and *assent*, that is, both concurrence and submission, a "compliance" *and* a willing that Theseus will mirror in line 3075 ("this is my fulle assent").[33] The time of deferral, which is the time of mourning, is crowned by that figure of chosen constraint which characterizes the gift of death and the economy of sacrifice, and which domesticates the stranger within, the *jouissance* that "must" be renounced because it was never securely "ours" to begin with. Insofar as the gift of death is a *gift*, its exchange will feature the delay that Marcel Mauss has identified as essential to the gift, to forms of aristocratic exchange that appear to break with the immediate reciprocity of commerce, that transform the stuff of what is exchanged into the sublime materiality of the gift.[34] This delay is also the time it takes to enact the melancholic economy of sacrifice, which seeks to retain what it gives up, but in the form of superexistence. That it is Theseus rather than Egeus who articulates the result of this sacrificial deferral, this period of "incommunication" that establishes the gift as such, its "break" with exchange, is a genealogical figure for the production of sublime and salvific speech, of the signifier that can be transmitted from father to son.

Theseus's speech is marked at the outset by its performativity, by its status as an artful production of signifiers: "And Theseus abiden hadde a space / Er any word cam fram his wise brest, / His eyen sette he ther as was his lest. / And with a sad visage he siked stile, / And after that right thus he seyde his wille" (2982–86). In the midst of parliamentary speech, of the passive voice ("Among the whiche pointz yspoken was" [2972]), of "oon general assent" (2969), the heterogeneity of the sovereign asserts itself as that sublime subject, that sublime point of communal subjectivation, whose gaze and speech are his will and his "pleasure," whose gaze and will emanate from an interiority that precedes them and is unaccountable even in the midst of the communal accountability that gives it its ethical force. The ethics of the community are absolutized through a figure of subjective interiority, of a sublime ethical unaccountability. This assertion of the interiority of the will correlates with the deferral that marks the gift, insofar as the spatial difference between the interiority of the sovereign subject and the exteriorized locus of the law is what makes the will sublime, a melancholic figure of recuperated absence, difference, foreign "stuff."

Theseus now introduces the Prime Mover as that absolutely creative subject responsible for the facticity of creaturely death because it is his law: the Prime Mover "Hath stablissed in this wrecched world adoun / Certeyne dayes and duracioun / To al that is engendred in this place" (2995–97). This figure of a law legible to creatures is, moreover, reconciled with the figure of inscrutable and secret interior reasons: the creature cannot know why, but only that it is so, which makes its submission at once obscene and perfect (perfect because to submit only for a good or positive reason is not absolute credence): "The Firste Moevere of the cause above, / Whan he first made the faire cheyne of love, / Greet was th'effect, and heigh was his entente. / Wel wiste he why, and what thereof he mente" (2987–90).[35] Hence also the way in which this speech itself, through its emphasis on performativity, problematizes its credibility; the gamble is that by positing Theseus's discourse as emanating from a sublimely recessed sovereign interior whose link to Jupiter is, precisely, unknowable, we cannot *know* its status; we can only believe, submit, assent, or not. But if we do believe, we will have, at once, the obscene surplus enjoyment of submission to that which can make no positive claim on us, as well as the absolute attitude of pure belief, the "ideological attitude" par excellence. What is asked for here is a boundless credence, a credence beyond the bounds of the law, which can only be produced through the arbitrariness of the law and the *jouissance* of the law's absurdity. Not all readers will take up this invitation to sacrificial enjoyment, to the sacrifice of knowledge; but we will not be able to sacrifice this sacrifice only by noticing that Theseus's authority is strangely evanescent.

Theseus then asks us "To maken vertu of necessitee, / And take it weel that we may nat eschue, / And namely that to us alle is due. / And whoso gruccheth ought, he dooth folye, / And rebel is to hym that al may gye" (3042–46). "[T]hat [which] to us alle is due" is death, submission to the law of which is correlated here with submission to authority. *Due* is a transitivist word, linking together the notion of that which "is owing or payable, as an *enforceable* obligation or debt" (emphasis added), with the notion of "[b]elonging or falling *to* by right," [o]wing by right of circumstances or condition;" it brings together the notion of that which we must pay to the other and that which the other renders to us "by right."[36] Someone who "gruccheth" what is due is someone who murmurs or complains, who makes the "jarring or grating sound" of rebellion, but is also someone who is "reluctant to give or allow (something)," who "begrudge[s]."[37]

Someone who makes such noises does not sing the "melodye" Robertson identifies with the New Law, with the hypereconomy of Christianity, a "melodye" that appears in the company of "alle blisse" when the bond of matrimony is made between Palamon and Emelye (3094–97), as also in the triumphal opening of *The Knight's Tale,* in the company of "victorie" (872), when Theseus is riding into Athens with his "hoost." Someone who is reluctant to give or to allow something does not join into the sacrificial economy of the community, where, as Theseus puts it, "gentil mercy oghte to passen right" (3089). Despite the fact that the community is of "oon general assent," the specter of the stranger who refuses the gift of death haunts Theseus's speech, as does the corrupt terrestrial economy, the corrupt bodily mass, associated here with those who will not cease to mourn the "foule prisoun of this lyf" ("foule" is strongly associated with putrefaction and corruption in its Middle English meanings).[38] Difficult though it may be to define Theseus's faith, to know what Chaucer thought of his "paganism," the emergence of the Christian hypereconomy is unmistakable at the end of *The Knight's Tale,* as the narrator prays to God on Palamon's behalf: "And thus with alle blisse and melodye / Hath Palamon ywedded Emelye. / And God, that al this wyde world hath wroght, / Sende hym his love that hath it deere aboght" (3097–3100).

But again, the emergence of this hypereconomy is accompanied by the shadow of a vaguely localized grudge (the community has indeed been mourning, but is not excoriated *while* it is in mourning). "[H]evynesse" must be transformed; this word for those afflicted with what is "[h]ard to bear" has a corporeal weight that must be exchanged for the weightless voice of "melodye," and for the "heele" (3102) of the sublime body.[39] And it is in the context of this transformation that Arcite's name is freed from the last shreds of that which was in him more than himself, from the grudgingly mournful "lustes" attributed to, though again not at this point displayed by, Palamon and Emelye (3066). There is in the closing movement of *The Knight's Tale* an apotheosis of honor, of the knight of faith's absolute coincidence with the signifier: "And certeinly a man hath moost honour / To dyen in his excellence and flour"; "To dyen whan that he is best of name" (3047–48, 3056).

At this moment of Arcite's "second death"—"second death" in the sense of that moment when the subject's being *as* signifier, the subject's constitutive absence, is most fully registered—Chaucer's knightly narrator interlinks chivalric sacrifice on behalf of the signifier of subjectivity itself, the name, with the hypereconomy of "mercy." In doing so, *The Knight's Tale* sees more than many critiques of chivalry saw even during the Middle Ages;[40] it sees that the sacrificial economy of honor, the apotheosis of name and fame, is a mode of subjectivation capable of richly supporting the gift of death in all its forms, including its Christian ones, insofar as it is the name that confers upon the subject that distinctiveness from other subjects without which the subject's death could not be sacrificially meaningful, could not witness to the scandalous price of absolute credence. In the name of the Lord, Amen: in the name of the Lord, we believe what has been said.[41]

La Farge reminds us of the sacrificial link between the death of Arcite and the marriage of Palamon and Emelye; but whether the marriage of Palamon and Arcite can be termed a "happy" one is another question.[42] The belatedness of the marriage, and Theseus's decision to marry Palamon and Emelye because of his desire to subject Thebes through alliance with Athens, is not a revelation, intended or unintended, of the harsh "realities" lurking behind the fantasy of chivalric benevolence, but another instance of the social productivity of those fantasies: it is yet another sacrifice, insofar as marriage, in D. W. Robertson's terms, is offered "as a solution to the problems raised by the misdirected concupiscent... and irascible passions."[43] Derrida's reading, in *The Gift of Death*, of Jan Patocka's *Heretical Essays on the Philosphy of History* reminds us of how often the history of the responsible European subject has been conceived as a history of sexuality, of the incorporation and "enslavement" of orgiastic irresponsibility.[44] The *ascesis* of eroticism that takes place at the end of *The Knight's Tale* can make sense only in this context; it is a "fulfillment" that enslaves "*jouissance*" to "justice," one that propels us into the future trailing intimations not so much of plenitude as of the endlessness of the sacrificial demand. But *The Knight's Tale* knows that this very effacement of *jouissance* has plenty of power to enthrall us.

5

LOVING THY NEIGHBOR

THE LEGEND OF GOOD WOMEN

*By means of sublimation specific to art,
poetic creation consists in positing an object
I can only describe as terrifying, an
inhuman partner.*
— Jacques Lacan

In *A Preface to Chaucer,* D. W. Robertson Jr. cites Saint Augustine's "classic Christian" definition of "the two loves," charity and concupiscence: charity is "the motion of the soul toward the enjoyment of God for His own sake, and the enjoyment of one's self and of one's neighbor for the sake of God"; cupidity "is a motion of the soul toward the enjoyment of one's self, one's neighbor, or any corporal thing for the sake of something other than God."[1] As is well known to students of medieval literature, Robertson's inference that "charity is the basic lesson of Christianity" becomes in turn the basis for his exegesis of medieval culture and literature.

The purpose of this chapter is to take further steps toward a psychoanalytic and culturalist rereading of charity and its implications for the study of medieval literature and sexuality, in order to analyze, rather than replicate, the vicissitudes of medieval bodies and pleasures. Several related figures of benevolence and self-abnegation will be discussed: chivalric fantasies of rescue; the "gentil herte" and its capacity for "pity"; woman as "helper" in the work of generation; the queen as "intercessor" and epitome of charity. Ethical discourse will likewise be an important concern because of the way it proposes to repair the fault in man's being through acts of (self-)rescue ("subjectivation") in which "one is called upon to take oneself as an object of knowledge and a field of action, so as to transform, correct, and purify oneself, and find salvation."[2]

Creationist formulations of sexual difference are central to the ethical deliberations on pleasure explored here. Their common project is thinking (and ennobling) an identity whose access to pleasure and to the Good, and therefore to fullness of Being, is ensured by its informed capacity to choose right action, and thus to re-create and rescue itself.[3] Saint Thomas Aquinas writes about the sexing of ethical generativity in the *Summa Theologica* and *Commentary on the Nicomachean Ethics*; Chaucer's F-Prologue to *The Legend of Good Women* teaches us what "Etik seith."[4] Freud's analysis of Daniel Paul Schreber's *Denkwürdigkeiten eines Nervenkranken* studies the ethical and sexual outrage creationist ethics can occasion in the hearts of obedient subjects.

Aquinas's *Commentary on the Nicomachean Ethics* considers how ethical judgments can be made about women and about men with bad habits. The problem posed by men who "take pleasure in pulling out their hair, biting their nails, eating coal and earth, and having sexual intercourse with males" is that one can only speak of continence and incontinence without qualification when the person being judged has sufficient power of reason to exercise "universal judgment," a power impaired in men with bad habits because of their "psychological sickness."[5] Women, "because of the imperfect nature of their body," do not govern their emotions in the majority of cases by reason but rather are governed by their emotions. Hence wise and brave women are rarely found, and so women cannot be called continent and incontinent without qualification.[6] People who have bad habits or imperfect bodies are unable to rule and rescue themselves or others: they rarely attain full ethical subjectivity, conceptive power, or the sacrificial generativity of heroism ("wise and brave women are rarely found").

Although Aquinas distinguishes men with good habits from women and imperfect men, these categories are not secure. Women are not the same as men, but they resemble some men (the kind with bad habits) closely; as ethical subjects their resemblance to perfect men is flawed ("qualified"), but unmistakable. This figure of flawed but evident similarity formulates an intimate or proximate other, a distanced but still recognizable (self-)image, an imaginary support for the perfect ethical subject.[7]

It is therefore not surprising that one of Aquinas's most significant deliberations on generativity and sexual difference concerns the ethical power of the flawed similar: that is, the question of how a female, a *"misbegotten male"* (in Aristotle's terms), can possibly be a *"helper"* to man.[8] Woman is only helpful in the "work of generation," "since man can be more efficently helped by another man in other works" (*Summa Theologica*, 466). But generation is not to be scorned; as a form of "active power," generation is, in plants, the "noblest vital function," and among human beings the "active power of generation belongs to the male sex" (ibid.). Woman's status as helper, then, resolves a problem about the Creator's own reasonableness, that is, the question that Aquinas's theodicy seeks at this point to answer: "It would seem that the woman should not have been made in the first production of things" (ibid.). Aquinas's argument, formally and substantively, seeks to secure the reasonableness of man and of man's Creator: man, helped by woman in the work of generation, helps himself better than she can, has a nobler power of life; moreover, "man is yet further ordered to a still nobler vital action, and that is intellectual operation" (ibid.).

One further possible problem with the reasonableness of creation is that if "subjection and limitation were a result of sin," but "woman is naturally of less strength and dignity than man," then "woman should not have been made in the first production of things before sin" (ibid.). But, besides "servile" subjection, "by virtue of which a superior makes use of a subject for his own benefit"—that is, the kind of subjection that is self-interested, which began after sin—there is another, charitable kind, "called economic or civil, whereby the superior makes use of his subjects for their own benefit and good; and this kind of subjection existed even before sin" (ibid.). Moreover, the reason why woman is subject to man, which is also the reason why he helps her more than she helps him, is that "in man the discretion of reason predominates" (ibid., 467). Fundamental, then, to Aquinas's mapping of gender and class onto conceptive power and charitable benevolence is the distinction between self and other—a distinction of intense interest not only to Augustine but also to Ockham and Bradwardine, to the psychologists of enjoyment, the casuists of charity, writers of mirrors for princes and princesses, theorists of the "common good."[9]

Thus Aquinas's answer to the third reason why women should never have been made ("occasions of sin should be cut off") is that it would not have been "fitting for the common good to be destroyed in order that individual evil might be avoided; especially as God is so powerful that He can direct any evil to a good end"; moreover, "if God had deprived the world of all those things which proved an occasion of sin, the universe would have been imperfect" (ibid., 466–67). The full perfection of the created universe, its reasonableness and its lack of any significant lack, is linked here to the "common good" and its precedence over "individual evil"; the common good acquires a creationist status, as product and sign of absolute conceptive power, of the ability to think universals that transcend change, loss, destructivity.

Although itself a bravura display of conceptive power, scholastic philosophy's structure of ceaseless question and answer opens up certain fissures in the seamless rationality of creation. The voice of the creature who discovers that it is mortally wounded, which means also and inevitably wounded in its perceptivity, that is, in the way in which reality is affirmed for it, has a way of raising itself, in inquiry if not in reproach. Aquinas's work indicates for us one mode of rescue available to such a creature: the profoundly ethical project of ennobling subjectivity by justifying its relation to its Creator. Ethics, that is, tracks a path that emerges in its psychoticized form as the "redeemer fantasy," wherein the help the subject can give, to himself or to others, desperately affirms the very principle of rescue—the phantasmic notion that absolute help might be on the way, that one's faults might be stably and lastingly supplemented by a subject-other mutual aid society.

The inability of fantasies of rescue to recuperate fully the fault in Being—for example, the empty or imponderable (non)origin that an encounter with shame might expose—is evident in the case of Schreber, who writes late in his struggle with his "illness" that "I have now long been aware that the persons I see about me are not 'cursorily improvised men' but real people, and that I must behave towards them as a reasonable man is used to behave toward his fellows."[10] Freud's observations on "megalomania" clarify the role, in redeemer fantasies, of the fragility of the subject's relation to the other, of the destabilization of the subject's ability to believe in the reality of a supplement or object invested with the power to rescue the subject.

This deficit in reality, however, can be refound and phantasmically repaired within the megalomaniacal subject only because the subject, in psychoanalysis, is always already modeled on the other. Megalomania reveals the ease with which the subject "becomes" the other in love or in mourning; it reveals also the difficulty of distinguishing categorically between injury to the subject's ideal image and injury to the image of the other. Thus, if a subject's (self-)love is too lost, perhaps because it loves in a way that reasonable reality finds shameful (a man with bad habits), or because it has an imperfect body and can neither remain constant nor judge constants (a woman), the subject may decide "*'I do not love at all—I do not love anyone'*... I love only myself." The resulting "megalomania" resembles the "overvaluation of the love object" that takes place in mourning; its purposive grandiosity, that is, is commensurate with the impossibility of the desire the subject cannot address.[11]

Schreber's *Denkwürdigkeiten eines Nervenkranken* demonstrates the shattering cost of theodicy when the creature in question has become unintelligible to himself. Schreber's metamorphosis is an almost parodic carnalization of ethical subjectivation. He dates his illness from a time when it occurred to him that "it really must be very nice to be a woman submitting to the act of copulation" (36; Freud, "Psycho-analytic Notes," 13). After this he begins to develop his rescue fantasy. It turns out that God wants Schreber to become a woman; slowly and painfully (because God is not very good at miracles), Schreber's body is changed into the body of a woman, impregnated by divine rays in order to redeem the world. His transformation reveals the workings of sexual difference and proscribed desire in the wish to become a redeemer—in the wish for a certain power of alteration, figured so often not only by the transfigured body (whether crucified or beatified into a phantasmic image of the power to endure), but by the subject as object of its own ethical powers of self-re-creation.[12]

But the kind of redeemer Schreber wants to become is more like the "immaculate virgin" than the son of God. His rescue fantasy reheroizes a mortified subject who wishes to "become" a "woman" (Schreber associates women with voluptuousness and silliness) and who wishes at the same time to possess unassailable honor and wisdom.[13] This is an exacting process: bird-souls with girls' names inject "corpse-poison" into Schreber's body, he is mockingly called "Miss Schreber," his organs are shattered, he dies and decomposes. Schreber's ordeal redeems femaleness—or at least his desire with respect to it—by turning it into an *ascesis* that will demonstrate the indestructibility of the messianic self Schreber adopts as the object of his love and the touchstone of his certainty.[14]

And one aspect of this messianic self is its triumphant remasculation. Schreber writes:

> every attempt at murdering my soul, or at emasculating me for purposes *contrary to the Order of Things* (that is, for the gratification of the sexual appetites of a human individual), or later at destroying my understanding... has come to nothing. From this... struggle between one weak man and God himself, I have emerged as the victor... because the Order of Things stands upon my side. (*Denkwürdigkeit eines Nervenkranken,* 61; Freud, "Psycho-analytic Notes," 19)

Soul murder, the destruction of understanding, and emasculation are, for Schreber, parallel assaults; because he wants to become a woman despite the dangers of so doing, he decomposes emasculation into two kinds, one authorized by the Order of Things (having as its grand purpose world redemption), the other contrary to that Order ("for the gratification of the sexual appetites of a human individual").[15] Schreber gets the Order of Things on his side by hyperlibidinizing his own body-soul—he is the apple of God's eye, however dubious the distinction—and risking the very reality of that body-soul, that is, its survival but also its prestige, its credibility, its ability to comprehend reality, in battle with the Other to end all others, that is, the divinized image without whose support his subjectivity cannot survive but whose existence *as* Other is equally threatening to Schreber's project of self-regeneration.

This God resembles the "bird-souls" to whom Schreber gives "girls' names" "because of their voluptuous bent": God demands a *"constant state of enjoyment"*; he is "childish" and completely ineducable.[16] He resembles Schreber in his shameful desires: "'Deuce take it! What a thing to have to say—that God lets himself be f—d!'" (Schreber, 194; Freud, 27 n. 2; Schreber is likewise mocked by rays of God: "So *this* sets up to have been a Senatspräsident, this person who lets himself be f—d!" [Schreber, 177; Freud, 20]). The specularity of this series of figures, and the theme of coercion that links them (the bird-souls are forced to say things they do not mean, it is against Schreber's will that he says nasty things about God), indicate that the fault in the creature is mirrored in a faulty Creator. With Schreber, the endlessness of the suffering associated with this decomposition of ideality pays homage to the irreparable nature of the wound thus dealt to the subject's capacity for certitude, and seeks to relieve that wound by demonstrating in the flesh—by substantiating—the subject's capacity to endure.

At the core of Schreber's rescue fantasy, then, is the question of a man's honor; and for Schreber this is an ethical question, that is, a question of educability. Schreber's reformulation of the symbolics of the rescuing and (self-)rescued subject is so testily carnal because Schreber is aware of a contradiction: sexual difference is part of the "Order of Things" (femaleness is shameful, etc. [Schreber, 55; Freud, 24–25]); but it is also negotiable, profane. Even God does not care about it when his *jouissance* is at stake, a fact that jolts Schreber to the core because he has had to pay a very high price (in the way of shame) for his bad habits, his ineducability, his femaleness. In an attempt to restore sexual difference (and reasonableness) to the Order of Things while recognizing that at the same time sex is changeable, Schreber pays for what he learns and likes about the mortality and contingency of powers by mortifying his flesh, ransoming his own and his deity's fecklessness through a perdurable suffering.

Schreber's carnal theodicy thus simultaneously excoriates and redivinizes creationism's phantasmic positing of man's identity with the field from which he originates. Schreber's response to the discovery that sex can be changed is to materialize an art of self-transformation addressed, as Lacan would put it, to the ethical question of what it means when "man" fashions the signifer ex nihilo. In other words, Schreber's story addresses the ethical problems raised not only by man's production of the artifact, but by man's (and God's) production, *through* ethics, as artifact, out of nothing: that is, man and his God emerge as such ex nihilo, out of that which they are not, as do their works—a fact that they are always trying to conceal, by passing the signifier off as that which it is not.

The later Middle Ages has been seen by some scholars as a particularly bad time for the notion of woman's capacity to exercise reason.[17] It has also been seen as a bad time for women rulers. Pauline Stafford argues that queenly power suffered from the diminishing importance of household politics; Paul Strohm writes that queens were "progressively excluded from affairs of state" and "compensated in sumptuous but highly inflated symbolic coin."[18] Increasingly, the queen, like Alceste in the Prologue to *The Legend of Good Women,* is patron and intercessor, and little else; Diane Bornstein explains that the *Speculum dominarum,* the first "mirror for the princess," develops the political role of the queen almost entirely in terms of charity—"her reputation for mercy should make her visits a welcome solace to the poor, the oppressed, and the unfortunate"—and teaches the queen "virtuous love" "of God, relatives, neighbors, fellow Christians, husband, and children."[19]

But "affairs of state" and "symbolic coin" are difficult to separate; power is not purely a matter of public administration, nor is the love a queen might inspire in her subjects necessarily easy to manage politically. Bornstein argues that courtesy books written by men emphasize women's "sexual and familial roles" out of "an anxiety about women overreaching their domain."[20] The late-medieval "mirror for the princess," with its inculcation of the "passive" virtues of "humility, obedience, modesty, piety, and chastity," is apotropaic; it tries to ethicize the queen's dangerous status as sublime object. And one aspect of her sublimity is the indeterminacy of her gender.

The queen is a paradoxical figure because she links sovereignty to the feminine. She is, as Ian Maclean puts it, a "point of contradiction," a "dislocation" in the "structure of thought."[21] Because of this, her power is fascinating. And as late-medieval representations of female patronage make evident, the problem of her pleasure likewise becomes exigent.[22] The ethicizing of queenship re-presents a compelling indeterminacy as dangerous but educable; the fantasy of the queen's benevolence specularly reassures the narcissism of those she can compel.[23] It is true that the figures of queenly petition and intercession lend sovereign authority to sexual difference and heterosexualize sovereignty; but despite such indications of a straightforward gendering of charity, the apotropaic figures of petition and intercession are perilously unstable, as their careful handling in royal ritual suggests.[24] To understand this fact, and its implications for Alceste in the *Legend,* we need to see the queen as part of a broad medieval ethicizing of the proximate other—the neighbor, consort, spouse, friend, brother; and we need in particular to explore the role of the lady in the ethics of courtly love.

As we have seen in previous chapters, *fin' amors* crafts an aristocratic subject whose pathos is the ground of its *ascesis,* who wills its own passional suffering. *Fin' amors* develops a sexuality—an identitarian stylization of sex, or, in this case, of not-yet-sex—for which temporality, and therefore the mortal suffering bound up with signification, is constitutive of the specific prestige of its pleasures.[25] The *finamen* possesses a special body capable of deferral and lack; it can endure, because it so chooses, and its endurance marks its special aliveness, its power of alteration over its own flesh. Thus the *finamen* can speak endlessly of its suffering flesh, of the "gentil herte" whose passion or "pite" defines a subject boundlessly aware of and inhabited by an intimate other. It is on the basis of this relation to the intimate other that *fin' amors* founds its ascetic timing and its ethics. Moreover, chivalric discourse usually presents the relation between the subject and its intimate other as one of service or rescue. It thereby ethicizes the honorable subject's finitude, its "ignoble origins," its mimetic dependence on the other, the limits on its ability to help or to be helped.[26] The subject's wish for rescue—a wish addressed to and by ethics—points to, but also amends, the finitude of the subject and the Other, "the Other whose primacy of position Freud affirms in the form of something *entfremdet,* something strange to me, although it is at the heart of me, something that on the level of the unconscious only a representation can represent" (71). The dependence of the subject's "experience of satisfaction" on the Other, the other as "*Nebenmensch,*" is, for Lacan, the insight fundamental to any understanding of charitable practices of (self-)rescue.[27]

Let us recall Lacan's argument about charity. When we recoil from the obligation to love our neighbor, we do so because of the "evil" that dwells within the neighbor, the "*jouissance*" we do not dare go near, but of which we have an inkling because some form of unspeakable evil dwells also within us (*Ethics of Psychoanalysis,* 186). Instead of love, all too readily we offer our neighbor the helping hand, whereby we re-create our neighbor according to the reassuring image of our own narcissism. Altruism thus secures the ideal image; through it

> I can avoid taking up the problem of the evil I desire, and that my neighbor desires also. That is how I spend my life, ... in my neighbor's time, where all the neighbors are maintained equally at the marginal level of reality of my own experience.
> ...what I want is the good of others in the image of my own.... the whole thing deteriorates so rapidly that it becomes: provided that it depend on my efforts. (187)[28]

This is why we are so easily turned back from the path of our *jouissance* (a question posed urgently in courtly literature, for example, by the *Legend*'s repeated amatory debacles): we retreat from the danger posed by *jouissance* either to self or to other, because self and other are always mutually implicated. We retreat "from assaulting the image of the other, because it was the image on which we were formed as an ego. Here we find the convincing power of altruism ... [and] the leveling power of a certain law of equality—that which is formulated in the notion of the general will."[29] The transitivism of charity seeks in the specular structure of benevolence to manage the finitude implied by the founding of the subject on the image of the other; it seeks the reassurance of equivalence, as though either the mortifying or exhilarating aspects of the subject's difference from the ideal image could be dealt with by adequating an image defined as common, capable of universal possession. This is why figures of the common good, and discourses of rescue, are so often related to the figure of the intimate stranger: hence the "apotheosis of the neighbor" in Christianity as well as in *fin' amors* (in the form of the *bon vezi*); hence, again, the repeatedly enjoined rescue, in treatises on chivalry, of widows, orphans, and the Eucharist—that figure of God as *Nebenmensch*, who divinizes the object's capacity to endure suffering, and takes on all the evil that lies in the hearts of all the neighbors.[30]

In courtly literature, the figure of near distance, in time or space, repeatedly marks the strange intimacy of the Other, the element of the unknown in the subject's desire. In *The Legend of Good Women*, for example, Cleopatra is "another wyf" (594); between Piramus and Tysbe "there nas but a ston-wal" (713); Dido's "pity" turns Aeneas the "straunger" into her "newe gest" and then her "dere herte" (1075, 1158, 1294); Procne finds her mutilated sister "in a litel stounde" (2376). As Lacan puts it, covetousness is addressed to the good that is our neighbor's, to an object valuable because it has "the closest possible relationship" to the field of the subject's desire, "to that in which the human being can rest"—"insofar," that is, "as it is the good in which he may find rest" (*Ethics of Psychoanalysis*, 83). The phantasm of repose in "the good" (in goods and in that which is defined as the good) is thus closely linked to restlessness, insofar as the good that seems to provide it is always in the possession of the neighbor.

Thus the *brevitas* of Chaucer's legends of good women—the haste with which they are narrated—marks them as taking place in the time of the neighbor. And in the legends, as in so much other courtly literature, the rescued or rescuing lady is nearby, that is, uncannily able to be found, but also impossible to stay with. Both proximity and distance are crucial to the lady's positioning, because she is "extimate": she marks not only the intimacy of the "I's" formation through the other, but also a limit, the "I's" distance from itself, from the stranger within. She is both inaccessible and next door; in the case of Alceste, she is in the possession of, but (in a figure that doubles her neighborliness) yet not the wife of, the God of Love.[31] And when the God of Love first addresses the narrator of the Prologue to the *Legend*, it is to challenge his nearness: "What dostow her / So nygh myn oune floure, so boldely? / It were better worthy, trewely, / A worm to neghen ner my flour than thow" (315–18).

The plasticity of the figure of the *Nebenmensch* is crucial to its role in the ethical structure of courtly love. Neighborliness is not identity; next door is not unknown territory. Insofar as the spatiality of the *Nebenmensch* is "over there," in a place that can be found but never secured, the beauty of the lady likewise marks the extimacy of the structuring of the subject according to the image of the other (Lacan, *Ethics of Psychoanalysis*, 216–17, 298). Her most rigorous and inhuman forms reveal that she is *not* to be equated with the good; she does not offer a phantasmic image of desire's closure, but rather of its relentlessness. Her arbitrary, capricious demands express the exactions of the ideal image, the impossibility of identifying with it fully, and therefore the endless labor involved in the ethical pursuit of (self-)rescue.

It is, moreover, continuous with the logic of extimacy that the image of beauty should, in some courtly poems, decompose altogether to reveal the "vacuole" of unimaginable desire, in the form of the knight's sodomitical encounter, via the *ascesis/jouissance* of shame, with the lady's "hole."[32] The "lady" can readily point to a desire that goes beyond certain limits, where sodomy serves as a figure for the abjection/jubilation of the extimacy of the body. Or the lady might be turned into an image of the "good," her virtue chivalrously rescued, her gender secured. If the obverse of shame is the glory of beautiful form, the result of such a rescue in the Prologue to the *Legend* is Alceste, whose status as heterosexual, female, constant, and salvific is established through the metamorphosis of a daisy, the "blisful sighte" of which "softneth" the "sorwe" of the narrator (who says of himself, "Ther loved no wight hotter in his lyve" [50, 59]) into a woman wearing a "whit corowne" (216). It could be argued that, whereas in Ovid the human body is transformed through the workings of desires that perpetually escape the confines of the ideal image, Chaucer does it to Alceste in reverse. But the Prologue's attempt to fix the mobility of desire is not entirely successful, and both the attempt and the failure are central to the Prologue's legendary beauty. The ethical poetics of *The Legend of Good Women* both assert and put into question the humanization, feminization, and heterosexualization of the indeterminate inhuman partner.

A number of critics have noted the importance of queenly intercession to the Prologue of *The Legend of Good Women*.[33] Critics have also drawn attention to the *Legend*'s apotropaic handling of the power of good women.[34] Repeatedly in the *Legend*, "pite" is placed in the heart of woman, and given to man: Alceste's pity saves the narrator (503); Dido's pity gives Aeneas a kingdom (1080); Hypermnestra's pity paralyzes her hands that "ben nat shapen for a knyf" (2684, 2692). "Pite" signifies the feeling of being bound to the other, as its derivation from *pietas* suggests.[35] When Alceste rescues the narrator from the anger of the God of Love, the God praises her: "pite renneth soone in gentil herte; / That maistow seen; she kytheth what she ys" (503–4). In an eagerly specular assent worthy of *The Book of the Duchess*, the narrator replies, "No moore but that I see wel she is good" (506). "Pite," crossing the line between subject and other, is linked with the specular construction of goodness and identity, and with the promise of their visibility or demonstrability ("she kytheth what she ys"); to open oneself up or pour oneself out is to show what one is and that one is.[36]

In the *Speculum dominarum* the queen's charity makes her "*praeclarissima, illustrissima*, and *excellentissima*": clear, beautiful, honorable, manifest.[37] "Kithen," too, means not only to reveal, but also to prove oneself, and to give alms.[38] "Pite" rushes in and reveals itself outwardly at the moment of perfected memory and identification: Alceste's pity not only shows that she is "good," that she "is what she is"; the narrator can now remember who she is. Pity binds subject to other; one is obliged to recognize it. Like "compassioun," "bounte," "merci," the signifier "pite" promises, and promises to signify, what Butler calls "the manageability of unspeakable loss."[39]

That the phantasmic promise of the good offered by these signifiers is unsustainable, that their promise of "semantic abundance" is unrealizable, is of course figured in the legends' repetitively failed unions, their ceaseless slippage from truth to treachery; despite the cradling framework of the "good" women's constancy, of the object's phantasmic capacity to endure, the wind of faction and betrayal blows throughout, as cruelly in the historical events that haunt the Prologue as in the sails that blow away the faith of pious Aeneas (1365).[40] The Prologue is glorious; but its semantics speak of, and do not clearly condemn, broken faith. The birds "deffye" the "foweler" (138; "defien" can mean to disavow a pledge, to renounce one's allegiance to a lord); the God of Love accuses the narrator of having "reneyed" his "lay" (336; "reneien" means to forsake one's beliefs, retract a pledge, withdraw one's devotion).[41] In the Prologue, cruelty afflicts the very earth, hurt by winter's "swerd of cold," "naked made and mat" (127, 126)—changed into the poor and shameful obverse of the magnificent outpouring of compassionate identity that is Alceste. The birds suffer from the "foweler," "that, for his coveytise / Had hem betrayed with his sophistrye" (136–37). But the evil in the heart of the "foweler" turns up in the hearts of certain of its prey: those "that hadde doon unkyndenesse— / As dooth the tydif, for newfangelnesse" (153–54).

It is consistent with the brilliant symbolicity of the Prologue, with the faith it lavishes on beautiful signifiers, that the promise, despite its springtime transience, asks for, and to some extent gets, our credence. The pain caused by the "foweler," displaced by the pain caused by the treachery of certain "foweles," is relieved through the birds' capacity to promise and thus to renew themselves: they "sworen on the blosmes to be trewe / So that hire makes wolde upon hem rewe" (157–58). Their reward: "Pitee, thurgh his stronge gentil myght, / Forgaf, and made Mercy passen Ryght" (161–62). And this masculinizing of pity is followed by a protestation as to its ethical status: "But I ne clepe nat innocence folye, / Ne fals pitee, for vertu is the mene, / As Etik seith; in swich maner I mene" (164–66).

But despite this pious affirmation of the "mene"—which promises to settle everything through its rhyming of "I mean" with the "mean" of virtue—the text implies that all the birds, not just particular ones that have "doon unkyndenesse," have been hateful: "And thus thise foweles, voide of al malice, / Acordeden to love, and laften vice / Of hate" (167–69). The referent of "thise foweles" is unclear—for example, does it include the pitying birds (presumably female, though pity is "stronge")? In the midst of this (re)generative pageant, the text's search for a figure of universality produces the implication of a universal capacity for betrayal and shame. Promise and pity make these birds into good neighbors; the signifier, in this case song, promises a perfection of redeemed and lawful pleasure ("Welcome, somer, oure governour and lord!" [170]); but part of the power of this much-admired passage is undeniably that, in it, we glimpse something unspeakable.

Almost without our noticing, prey turns into predator, and predators then turn into a chorus singing "alle of oon acord" (169). The poetics of the Prologue are both metamorphic (shape-shifting, but with the aim of recovering innocence) and specular (but the kind of mirroring that has something slightly different—the other—on the other side). This is why the narrator introduces his impossible vegetable love, the daisy, while introducing himself: "And as for me" (29); "Now have I thanne eek this condicioun / That, of al the floures in the mede, / Thanne love I most thise floures white and rede, / Swiche as men callen daysyes in our toun" (40–43). His "condicioun," his "mode of being," is to love "most" that which he repeatedly desires to see ("ther daweth me no day / That I nam up and walkyng in the mede / To seen this flour ayein the sonne sprede / Whan it upryseth erly by the morwe" [46–49]). He arises as she arises from the "derknesse" which she hates (63); the ritual re-creation and salvific protectiveness of his "reverence" in her "presence" involves a devotional seeing (51–52; "reverence" is respect, honor, but also specifically religious veneration).[42]

This seeing is transitivist, specularly vivifying: the "blisful sighte" of the daisy "softneth al [his]...sorwe" even as his "reverence" raises this "she," this "daisy," to "the dignity of the Thing." Its/her consolatory, restorative power mirrors the ritual attentiveness he provides it/her. Moreover, the ritual repetitiveness of his devotion is mirrored in her constancy *as* vision: it is "evere ilyke faire and fressh of hewe" (55); then the narrator says, "And I love it, and ever ylike new, / And evere shal" (56–57). "Ever ylike new" is indeed the ambition of the Prologue's beauty, through which the narrator constitutes both the mirage of the object's vitality and the reflected endurance of the devotional subject. The importance of visibility is emphasized even more when the narrator must run quickly not only in the morning but also in the evening "To seen this flour, how it wol go to reste, / For fere of nyght, so hateth she derknesse" (62–63). The figure of the daisy becomes a means to divinize the very conditions of visibility through which the screen of beauty may blind us, and point us to, the field of desire that lies beyond it: "Hire chere is pleynly sprad in the brightnesse / Of the sonne, for ther yt wol unclose" (64–65).

Like Schreber in relation to his God, the daisy is heliotropic—fully visible, "pleynly sprad" (the fantasy is of its perfect accessibility) in response to the eye of day, the sun. The daisy's own solar identity is made even more explicit when the narrator describes himself at a subsequent moment (a moment that reiterates previous devotions) as sinking down "softely" (178; the word used to describe the daisy's restorative power), "And, lenynge on myn elbowe and my side" (in other words, planted) / "The longe day I shoop me for t'abide / For nothing elles, and I shal nat lye, / But for to loke upon the dayesie, / That wel by reson men it calle may / The 'dayesye,' or elles the 'ye of day,' / The emperice and flour of floures alle. / I pray to God that faire mote she falle, / And alle that loven floures, for hir sake!" (178–87). The sublime object that is the daisy emerges as the day's eye under the eye of day at the moment when the narrator dedicates his day to eyeing her. And the specular nature of intercession and rescue is brought out again here when the narrator prays for the daisy's well-being ("faire mote she falle") and for "alle that loven floures," that is, for himself.

This narrator whose sorrow is softened by following the daisy's every movement, by gazing at it and at its own ocular receptivity, locates salvific power in visibility itself; visibility screens from view the hateful "derknesse" that frightens the daisy, despite her powers of resurrection. Visibility also calls attention to that darkness. The Prologue's desire for and deferral of the limit, of transformation—its pacifications of destructivity, its heteronormative pageantry, but also its passion for scoping daisies, not to mention its logophilia—are enacted in that moment of repose when the narrator "shoop" himself "for t'abide" "the longe day," in the sweetly inspired "joly month of May" (176), in which he thought he might, "day by day, / Duellen alwey" (175–76). *Dwellen* can mean "to remain," "live, dwell," but also "to procrastinate, delay, linger." It can mean to take time to tell something, a constant problem for the narrator ("I may not al at-ones speke in ryme" [102], though his richly artificed repetitions suggest that he is trying his hardest); but also "to hold back or restrain (lust)," to postpone, to desist, refrain or stay away from, to stop speaking of something—in short, "al at-ones," to linger *and* to leave, to dilate *and* to abbreviate.⁴³ When one dwells, one is either at home or away, or a bit of both: neighborly.

Dwellen epitomizes that saturated aspect of the poetic timing of the Prologue, its attempt to slow description down to the stillness of the captivating image. *Dwellen* epitomizes also the fantastic pleasure of a fullness of expectation conferred by deferral. The narrator gets up before daylight because he is "constreyned" with "gledy desir" (105), he "thursteth" (103), he runs home swiftly at night "erly for to ryse" (201). Being near, nigh, on the brink, is a matter of time as well as space, the time of the *Nebenmensch*.⁴⁴ Insofar as *dwellen* evokes both lingering and hastening away, dilating and abbreviating, the leisurely lyricism of the Prologue and the comparatively unadorned haste of the legends seem to split the verb apart; but this divide is adumbrated in the Prologue itself, in the almost comic (were it not so beautiful) dashing about the narrator has to do in order to follow the movements of his flower, "hastening" being what passes for the *finamen*'s ordeal in the earlier, comforting stages of the Prologue, and haste and rest being, apparently, his only two gears.⁴⁵

Thus the specularly heliotropic, "hot" narrator hastens home "To goon to reste, and erly for to ryse, / To seen this flour to sprede, as I devyse. / And in a litel herber that I have, / That benched was on turves fressh ygrave, / I bad men sholde me my couche make" (201–5). The daisy in effect puts the narrator to sleep, in an alluring image of the repose man seeks in the objects of his desire; but this image points uncannily to the potential destructivity of desire with respect to the "nothing I" of the subject, a destructivity from which the narrative then runs away. The narrator goes to bed in his "herber," with its newly dug earthern benches, but lest things get too deadly there, in the space of a few lines he wakes into a dream in daylight in the meadow, looking ("To seen this flour" [211]) instead of hiding his eyes (208).

The dream is a vision that raises the stakes of vision even further, by enhancing the daisy's solar properties; it/she is now both Alceste and a brilliant crown, a thing and a woman. There are apotropaic aspects to this transformation; an impossible object, an uncannily vivid plant, decomposes into images at once more human and more intricately insentient. Yet Alceste herself is a "relyke" (321). She signifies survival and its evanescence; she is a trace, a vestige, an aftereffect.⁴⁶ Being neighborly now means being a ghostly simulacrum, accessible even beyond the limit of life that the narrator now comes close to facing. Her solar properties are enhanced also through her association with the God of Love, whose "face shown so bryghte / ... unnethes myghte I him beholde," who steals the "gledy" narrator's fire (the God has two fiery darts, "gleedes rede," in his hands; his "lokynge" makes the narrator's heart cold) (232–33, 235, 240). *Cold* in such a context can mean "to lose warmth (as in death)" (the *MED* cites several uses of the verb *colden* in descriptions of dying), as well as "to be chilled, shocked, or overcome"; when used "of love, charity, joy," it means "to lose fervor, slacken."[47] *Colden* is thus one of the terms in the Prologue that form a rich semantic cluster around both charity (pite, compassioun, merciable, mek, tretable, benigne, bounte, comfort, releven) and aggressivity (peine, reneien, agreven, defien, disteinen, colden).

It is noteworthy that God's solar power freezes us in our tracks. What works on one level as a sanctification of sexual difference—whereby the mortality, the changefulness, that the signifier signifies, is made brilliant and merciable in the figure of Alceste, brilliant and terrifying in the case of the God of Love—reveals a transitivist structure, or, in other words, reveals the destructivity in the heart of the charitable neighbor. For Alceste's very excellence, even if what she excels in is pity, makes her as potentially lethal as the God of Love; *praeclarissima*, the *Balade* confers upon her a similar power to drain the heat and light, the life and visibility, from her rivals. Other good women are sentenced to be neither seen nor heard, even at the moment of their invocation (a sentence strangely fulfilled by the comparative lifelessness of the women in the legends): "Thy faire body, lat yt nat appere, / Lavyne"; "Maketh of your trouthe neythir boost ne soun"; "My lady cometh, that al this may dysteyne" (256–57, 267, 269). *Disteinen* can mean either to color or stain something *or* its reverse—to deprive something of color, brightness, beauty; figuratively, to dim or put in the shade.[48] Even more aggressively, it can mean to sully someone's reputation or to desecrate something worthy of honor; it is thus related to *defien* and *reneien*. The semantic range of this word tracks the specular relation between the God of Love and Alceste; for all their supposed differences of gender, of temper, they share a power of alteration, a power of brightening *and* of obscuring. *Disteinen* reveals the aggressivity of Alceste's image, of her status as image, largely hidden from view but emerging in the *Balade*—as if the terrifying (shameful, abjecting) implications for the admiring subject of

Alceste's superlative condition could only emerge openly in a structure even more formal, repetitive, and deliberately devotional than is the rest of the Prologue.

The doubleness of the ideal image—its promise of rescue, its rejection of everything that needs rescue—leaves its traces in a few of the Prologue's other words of praise (as well as in the abjecting of the good women of the legends). The meanings of *digne* (the word used by the God of Love to describe his ghostly "relyke" [321]) shade from "worthy of great honor or reverence" to "proud," "disdainful."[49] Alceste's "bounte," which, according to the God of Love, "doubleth" her "renoun" (522), is one of the terms linking Alceste's charity to the power of her identity, in the form of its capacity to manifest itself; bounte is "the quality of kindness, benevolence, mercy," "liberality in giving."[50] But other meanings of *bounte* hint at Alceste's participation in the aggressivity of which the God of Love is such a brilliant image: *bounte* can also mean "knightly prowess, strength, valor, chivalry." And even so benign a word as *benigne* (243) points to the brinksmanship of the Prologue: it can mean simply "gentle, kind, generous, merciful"; but, of an inferior, "meek, submissive"; of an animal, "friendly, gentle, tame," a range of meanings also registered in "meke": "gentle, quiet, unaggressive," of a woman; "modest," "merciful," "submissive, obedient, docile, amenable," of an animal; "tame," "lowly, poor, unimportant, abject," "weak, helpless."[51] *Benigne* tracks the transitivist crossings of the subject who helps and the subject who is helpless.

Helplessness thus haunts the Prologue, significantly in the form of poverty, described in the story of the birds who escape the fowler as one of the ills surmounted by the earth in springtime through the ability of "th' atempre sonne" to "releven" it: "Forgeten hadde the erthe his pore estat / Of wynter" (128, 125–26). The redress of poverty is one of the meanings of *releven* (hence the term "relief fund"): *releven* can mean "to alleviate wretchedness": to requite love, gratify; to provide for, help, give alms; to feed an animal or bird, to feed the soul, to bring deliverance, rescue; to spare from death, to free a land from hardship. *Comfort*, attributed to the "presence" of Alceste by the worried narrator (who at the same time prays for her [277–79]), can, like *releven*, refer to pleasure, gratification, invigoration; relief of poverty, illness, suffering, as when food comforts the bodies of beasts by warming them, or cool water comforts animals fleeing the hunt.

If solar privilege is the obverse, adversary, and comforter of poverty, it is not surprising that the narrator's dream also intensifies the ethical stakes of vision by mortifying the "nothing I" that the narrator earlier imagines himself to be ("ye ben verraily / The maistresse of my wit, and nothing I" [87–88]). The narrator is (in the eyes of the God of Love at least) less worthy than a worm "to neghen ner my flour" (318), more negligible than the kind of creature who burrows its way through earthy recesses. In *The Parliament of Fowls* "wormes corupcioun" is one of the insults flung at the lower-class birds who do not have "gentil hertes" and cannot "guess" what love is (614, 601–2). The prestige of this creature who is not even a worm is very low; but insofar as shame and beauty both point to the unspeakable desire that lies beyond them, the neighborly interest Alceste takes in this not-even worm—the way, from a distance, they mirror each other—is instructive. "Nothing" is indeed likely to be the condition of the "I" who gets too near the *Nebenmensch*, too near the nonknowing framed by the image of beauty.

In its way, the Prologue is as repetitious as the legends: daisies turn into crowns that look like daisies, "nothing I" turns into not-even worm, the narrator runs back and forth, he prays for his daisy, she prays for him. But the Prologue has seemed beautiful to many critics, whereas the legends have often seemed merely drab. The problem of beauty and drabness is not incidental to the *Legend*'s ethical concern with the evil that lies in the heart of the neighbor, but is, rather, its formal manifestation. The sheer concentration of the Prologue's sublime poetics, the very brilliance of its mirrors, points to the ethical meaning of artifice as such— the way beauty signifies symbolicity itself as that which must always emerge around the indeterminacy of desire; the way, as Lacan puts it, beauty reveals the "site of man's relationship to his own death" "in a blinding flash," because it is "insofar as the subject articulates a signifying chain that he comes up against the fact that he may disappear from the chain of what he is" (*Ethics of Psychoanalysis*, 295); the way there emerges, from and through the specularity of the Prologue, the transitivism that blocks but cannot be without mobility, in other words, the way metonymy takes over (the daisy becomes Alceste), the "change as such" that is desire (293).[52]

It is precisely the vitalization of the object's transience, the claim made on our desire by something that we know to be a fabrication, that powers the beauty of the Prologue, and makes Alceste not just a remembered image of the power of rescue, but also an image that "disteyneth." Because she is supremely illustrious and fatal to any figure that seeks to resemble her, she is displaced; though she revives the figure of sexual difference after the wonderful weirdness of the indeterminate it/she daisy, her position is equivocal—she goes to hell for her husband but appears to us as the consort of another man. And in keeping with the brinksmanship of the Prologue, her beauty courts disaster; some of the most awkward poetry of the Prologue is to be found in the lines that describe her crown, almost ready to topple from the weight of accumulated resemblance:

> For al the world, ryght as a dayesye
> Ycorouned ys with white leves lyte,
> So were the flowrouns of hire coroune white.
> For of o perle fyn, oriental,
> Hire white coroune was ymaked al;
> For which the white coroune above the grene
> Made hire lyke a daysie for to sene,
> Considered eke hir fret of gold above. (218–25)

And the visual center of this crowning accumulation of resemblance ("ryght as," "So were," "lyke" "for to sene") is the "o perle fyn," which almost stops our gaze by taking the "vacuole" one step further and re-visioning it as that for which emptiness is so often itself a screen: the pearl of jouissance, the site of the *bon vezi*'s pleasure. This is to put something in the place of "nothing," which might indeed have the same destabilizing effect on sexual difference as putting nothing in the place of something.[53] Something of the uncanniness of the daisy's opaque floral eye is transferred here, rarefied, but equally captivating.

The comparative drabness of the legends is not of a different aesthetic order from the beauty of the Prologue. Rather, the legends enact the failure of metamorphic promise, the loss of expectancy and *jouissance*, the weariness of the object condemned phantasmatically to charitable endurance. It is this "power to support a form of suffering," this re-creation of the *Nebenmensch* as a "double" "made inaccessible to destruction," that makes the legends suffer by comparison (Lacan, *Ethics of Psychoanalysis*, 261). The legends fail to be beautiful because they figure the exhaustion of the enduring form of the image. The depressed value of the signifier in the legends is the result of a certain decathexis of the signifier as such, that is, of its changefulness; the legends try to retain the signifier while stripping it of its power to escape.

It could be argued that Sade makes, as it were, much more vivid work of the image of suffering than do the legends; what bars this in Chaucer's poem is its unwillingness to relinquish the figure of rescue, so that the "good" stops us short of confronting the unbearable suffering of the image when we demand that it live on despite our attempts to destroy it. *The Legend of Good Women* fantasizes that good women, despite their suffering, have really been rescued, worthy of their textual resurrection because of their capacity for sacrifice. The narrator is their redeemer; though chivalric rescue fails within the legends, the legends are produced by a chivalrous rescuer of the reputations of women—at no small cost to himself, as the narrator repeatedly reminds us, because writing the legends is hard work. No wonder he wants to get through them as quickly as possible: they are for him precisely a sacrificial payment, the loss of *jouissance* in the neighbor's time.

The legends gender as feminine the suffering but never-obliterated "good" object, the loss of *jouissance* at stake in charitable donation. The women of the legends often begin their stories with substantial resources of affection, wealth, secret knowledge; by the end of their stories, they have usually been robbed, emptied, eviscerated. They are "benigne": rescuers so imperiled by the extent of their power to give themselves away that they cannot rescue themselves or be rescued by others. It is noteworthy that, despite what they do for others, good women seem helpless largely because they cannot help themselves; it is also noteworthy that, despite their goodness, their acts of pity can seem ethically equivocal.[54] But these facts only underscore the endlessness of the demand that impels charity. Help will always be flawed and disappointing; no power of wealth, rule, love, can redress the outrage of lost *jouissance*. And in the legends, the mortal creature's failure to secure rescue from the image of the other on whom it is founded is—it is an old story—given to the woman in her figure *as* helper.

In the legends, the impossibility of absolute rescue is re-presented as the frustration of heterosexual love. The difference that separates "men" from "women" and makes heterosexual union so charged, delicate, and desperate a matter stands in for finitude, turning limit into exploit, impossibility into irony, and producing thereby the truth of the genders that cannot seem to enter into relation with one another no matter how hard they try. Thus we might address the mystery of the poem's repetitively failed transactions, exchanges, and unions by proposing that these very failures, these breaches of contract, these endings of love in betrayal, of life in death, repetitively reinscribe the certainty of gender by insisting on the depth, variety, and intractability of the walls, oceans, fathers, gods, passions, and errors that keep men and women apart—and make their attempts to unite, however futile, so heroic and so tragic.

In other words, the legends try to make it look as though it is the walls, and not the emptiness between them, that pose the problem for good loving. The genders on which heterosexuality depends, and the ideologies of conception that deploy these categories, have as their central goal the explanation of why *jouissance* is never perfect and why the subject has its limits. This is why "prohibitions" seem to mandate that we join with those who bear our *proximate* image (i.e., again, the prohibition screens the impossibility of full coincidence); and this is why sexual difference so often becomes a question for ethics.

But, of course, to the extent that the gender divisions thus ontologized on behalf of conceptive certitude in fact cannot merge absolutely (though only because absolute merger is impossible), the displacement and displaceability of desire emerge as an irony within the apotropaic figure of irony. If "women" are to be constituted as such in relation to goodness—that is, in relation to a certain capacity for evisceration—"women" emerge precisely for that reason as displaced. In other words, they emerge as such, as a category, most strongly when they are displaced from their male counterparts, in the "*Balade*," where they are represented in a transitivist, invidious relation among themselves, along the axis of superlative visibility and invisibility, as the signifier itself—the mark that cannot be effaced and that nonetheless is never what it seems to be ("My lady cometh"; "Thy faire body, lat yt nat appere").

The comparative structure of the "*Balade*" acknowledges that appearing and disappearing, the power of illustration and its privation, are both at stake in acts of making. At the heart of the figure of union ("alle yfere" [263]) is envy, the evil that lies in the heart of my neighbor; and concomitant with this disclosure of extimacy is the disclosure of the fact that "woman" is a signifier—an artifact whose finitude has everything to do with its ethical implications for gendered subjects. It is an artifact that reveals something also exposed by the *Legend*'s distinction between the adventuring men of the legends and the chastised and rescuing narrator: honor's biggest lie is its representation as freedom, risk, adventure, the finitude that reappears elsewhere in the equally reassuring guise of rituals of submission to the law.

6

"Oure Owen Wo to Drynke"

DYING INSIDE IN *TROILUS AND CRISEYDE*

> *Therto we wrecched wommen nothing konne,*
> *Whan us is wo, but wepe and sitte and thinke;*
> *Our wrecche is this, oure owen wo to drynke.*
> —Criseyde

> We will see what an absolute choice means, a
> choice that is motivated by no good.
> —Jacques Lacan[1]

> What is done involuntarily is done with sorrow.
> —Saint Thomas Aquinas

Enjoyment exceeds the subject's awareness of desire and pleasure. While enjoyment shares some of the meanings of "intent" (*entente,* in Chaucer), that is, "will," "desire," the focus of *entente* is on specific mental acts of focusing, attending, purposing. Where *entente* concentrates the mind, narrows its focus, centers it on specific narrative possibilities, enjoyment participates ineluctably in the exteriorities of groups, of history and the signifying processes that work their way *through* subjects. But enjoyment does not just disseminate; it also concentrates. Desire depends on intensifications as well as multiplications of sentience. Moreover, intending is closely linked to wishing. Dissemination and fixation are not so much opposed as they are different aspects of the circulation of enjoyment—through exchange, for example. This is attested by the enormously rich semantic range of *will* in medieval psychology: the will is a point of intersection between desire and intention, between the dissolution of resolution into sensuality and the gathering of the appetites around a deliberate decision to make something happen.[2] Neither the tendency of enjoyment to take root, nor its tendency to proliferate, were lost on the Middle Ages.

One example of this version of the dialectic between repetition and difference is in Aquinas's *Commentary on the Nicomachean Ethics,* which, as we saw in chapter 5, reflects on the problem bad habits pose for ethical judgment. Clear or unqualified ethical action (e.g., the choice between continence and incontinence) only takes place when the person being judged has sufficient power of reason to exercise "universal judgment." This means being able to free one's mental activity from immersion in particulars, so that comparisons can be made. The abstract equivalents that enable different things to be compared are detectable only by universal judgment. This power is impaired in men with bad habits because of their "psychological sickness."[3] It is also a power impaired in women because of the weakness of their bodies and their consequent susceptibility to influence, which raises the question of whether women can be judged by the same standards as men—an idea Christine de Pizan takes up in *The Book of the City of Ladies.*[4] Whether as a consequence of habit or of physiological disposition, ingrained modes of enjoyment pose a challenge to ethical thought because something ingrained is difficult to change and to make choices about. To choose is to break free; only someone capable of breaking free of particulars is the kind of ethical subject whose decisions or intentions can be judged as such.

But classical and medieval ethical education meant to cultivate habit for the good, by means of the techniques of living that gave instruction on everything from scratching one's head first thing in the morning to the ideal of moderation. Late-medieval devotional technique likewise acknowledged that the devotee was malleable enough to be trained but obdurate enough to need it; as with mnemotechnique, striking images were needed, and a lifelong discipline of *imitatio*. We are sometimes tempted to think that the question of responsibility was less perplexing in the Middle Ages than it is now. The mitigation of sin or crime on the basis of opportunity or temptation was, on the whole, not popular in the Middle Ages. Even the idea that a starving pauper could be forgiven a theft on the basis of "necessity" became a major bone of contention in the thirteenth century.⁵ But penitentials and confessional manuals thrived on qualification. In one early English penitential, "every learned priest of Christ" is seriously urged that

> not all are to be weighed in one and the same balance ... but there shall be discrimination ... between rich and poor; freeman, slave; little child, boy, youth, young man, old man; stupid, intelligent, layman, cleric, monk; bishop, presbyter, deacon, subdeacon, reader, canoness, or nuns; the weak, the sick, the well. He shall make a distinction for the character of the sins of the men; a continent person or one who is incontinent willfully or by accident; [whether the sin is committed] in public or in secret; with what degree of compunction he [the culprit] makes amends by necessity or by intention; the places and times [of offenses].⁶

Not only did medieval psychologies see the subject's choices as highly conditioned by circumstance, they also clearly thought one reason for this was the subject's terrible vulnerability to invasion and influence—by demons, angels, the stars, the effusions of plants, and the gazes of certain birds, to say nothing of the words of the other. The choices made by subjects thus possessed could *not* be judged in the same way as those of the self-possessed. But only the self-possessed were full ethical subjects, and only their sacrifices counted fully.

The picture that emerges is somewhat confusing. The orthodoxy of the doctrine of free will was established decisively by Saint Augustine in the fifth century, but the doctrine of original sin complicated the judgment of judgments, because it gave authority to the intuition of a primal fault, of fracture and loss of self-possession as *constitutive* of the postlapsarian subject. Adding paradox to contradiction was the idea that only grace (a generosity exceeding all human economies) could restore full self-possession. How secure could our wholeness, or our participation in the wholeness of the mystical body, ever be if it is always in the form of a gift we cannot take for granted? These problems have been talked over for centuries, and many elaborate theological solutions have been proposed. What interests me is the question of how to read the fault line between medieval society's fascination with influence, on the one hand,

and right judgment, for example, freedom from (undue) influence, on the other. Medieval society loved endless complications of responsibility; it also loved the sensation, entailed in choice, of freeing oneself from complications, responsibilities, habits, dispositions, histories. Choice was, to this degree, a line of flight, a deterritorialization of sentience, a "becoming-universal." But choice thereby enjoined on the subject an ever more rigorous calculation of demands and obligations.

Atonement theology depends on a similar structure of incitement: the more we pay, the more we owe, the more we *can* pay. We can spend more and more, because more and more is asked of us. The (Christian) fantasy of an infinitely generous hypereconomy, able to break free of calculation altogether, always seems to collect its reward in the other scene of a higher place.[7] But even if debt and (re)payment are only displaced rather than disappeared, the displacement accomplishes something. Medieval Christianity raised solvency—freedom from debt, understood as payment of debt—to the dignity of the Thing. Solvency sublimed means that when the debt of sin is paid, the debtor is freed not only from her specific debts, but from the very logic of debt itself (projected onto the Old Law of the Jews and/or the devil who wants his contracts honored)—which unfortunately does not protect her altogether from falling back into debt. The devil's law is the law as drive—mortifying, inexorable, mechanical. Freedom from the law of death and debt displaces judgment to a "higher" law, but one that still requires calculation if only to measure its departures from calculation. Subliming judgment—making it a matter of life and death, or, even more important, of access to or denial of enjoyment—intensifies the claims of the conditions from which judgment breaks free. The consequent spiraling of value is the form of enjoyment that ultimately reproduces solvency in the sublime form of redemptive power, where the kind of owing-nothing that depends on paying everything off turns into the kind of surplus that can afford to sacrifice everything on behalf of an entire community of exchange. All that is required is an "agency that rewards," in every possible way.

These remarks may begin to indicate why Criseyde's status as ethical subject can be treated sublimely even if Criseyde herself is desublimed, and why consent and exchange are therefore the chief narrative and critical cruxes in *Troilus and Criseyde*. *Troilus and Criseyde* sees the exchange of sentient objects from the standpoint of the Thing by asking what kinds of judgments can be made by and about objects of exchange whose sentience is constrained by conditions. In other words, it sees from the standpoint of the Thing the ethics of the economy of sentient exchange. This vision produces questions such as the following: Does Criseyde consent, and does she do so freely? Is she coerced or responsible, and why does she "open her heart" and show Troilus "her *entente*" during the scene in which this question is urged most powerfully (Book III)? Does Criseyde's exchange produce surplus redemptive power because of her sacrifice, or does her status as (sentient) object of exchange compromise the clarity of her sacrifice? Does she sacrifice or is she sacrificed?[8] The ambiguities attendant on choice in *Troilus and Criseyde* enable the sublimity of the poem's approach to the question of the "good"—to the question of what is good for us, and whether this good and the goods that seem to embody it are necessarily the factors that motivate exchange, (e)valuation, and judgment. Criseyde's status as ethical subject can be treated sublimely because *Troilus and Criseyde*'s enjoyment is caught up not in the *objet a* but in the *objet a* as (sentient) object of exchange. This necessitates, or at least produces in *Troilus and Criseyde*, a constant oscillation between sublimation and desublimation. And if *Troilus and Criseyde* "sees"—is able to deterritorialize—the *jouissance* of judgment in an epic tradition about the consequences that result from nonpayment of debt, what does *Troilus and Criseyde* see about the relations between rape and war, on the one hand, and judgment on the other?

In *The Body in Pain,* Elaine Scarry argues that consent distinguishes torture from war because people suffering torture can almost never be imagined as consenting to their ordeal, whereas soldiers can be imagined as consenting to being injured as well as injuring.[9] Victims of torture are extreme cases of sentient objects: their sentience is exacerbated to the point of unbearability by treating them as objects devoid of the power of judgment. Discourses of "atrocity" commonly address the war-related suffering of civilian populations who likewise cannot be imagined to have consented to participation in the scene of injury, and therefore also stand as extreme examples of sentient "objection."[10] Pain, Scarry argues, can exacerbate sentience to the point of unbearability at which the "self," its "world," its objects, and hence its capacity to make choices, begin to collapse into a radical experience of embodiment, a "becoming-body." Choice, by contrast, depends on "self-extension." By this logic, sacrifice is the kind of choice that triumphs over the radical embodiment experienced by the sentient object.

The subject that can sustain sacrifice is a hypersubject. But something wicked this way comes. The hypersubject of sacrifice has a twin: the subject of *jouissance,* who also seeks the unbearable exacerbation of sentience and, "becoming-body," risks the "little death" of self, its world, and its objects. Thus the hypersubject of sacrifice must be willing to endure agony but at the same time not "want" to endure agony. The semantic range of "will," which goes all the way from suffering something to be done to intending that something be done, enables these fine discriminations and allows them to shade into each other. *Troilus and Criseyde* sees that the exacerbation of sentience works for enjoyment in a bewildering number of directions. It sees that the scenes of "love" and "war" act out the instability of the distinctions between suffering, allowing, consenting, desiring, purposing. (Is sight passive or active? When Troilus sees Criseyde, is he invaded by eye-beams or does he send his out into the world?)[11] The scenes of love and war make explicit the connection between states of sentience and the perplexities of the will. Both presuppose, even if they avoid or defer, the extreme exacerbation of sentience. And this is why *raptus* and atrocity haunt an epic tradition about the nonpayment of debts.

It is the business of chivalric culture to develop techniques for anticipating, inducing, and cultivating extreme states of sentience. This accounts for the intimacy of atrocity and rescue in chivalric discourse. Chivalric treatises seek to distinguish between atrocity and legitimate violence, giving knights special responsibilities, not merely to avoid injuring, but to protect from injury, those who cannot protect themselves. Those incapable of self-defense include those incapable of consent, or deprived of powerful voices to speak for them at law—in particular, orphans and widows, whose uncertain positions in exchange make them anomalies and thus limit-cases of sentient objecthood.[12] Orphans and widows, that is, belong to no one, but are for that very reason up for grabs. Chivalric treatises display the difficulty of distinguishing between atrocity and rescue when loyalties are conveyable (which is to say, always) and sentience is at a premium. Lamentation over the widespread devastation of civilian populations in France during the Hundred Years' War is interior to chivalric discourse, which zealously promulgates, in de Certeau's phrase, the "law of a certain technique." Chivalric writing—Honoré Bonet's *The Tree of Battles* is a good example—draws intensively on legal codes and rhetoric, reinforcing the links medieval societies made between the privilege of bearing arms and privilege at law, including the privilege of administering justice.[13] The international law also developed in such treatises is a logical, not a surprisingly benign, outcome of medieval warrior society and its stylizations of power: war by every means. Chivalric ordinance, like the law of courtly love, designs the *jouissance* of the warrior; there is no inherent conflict between ordinance and destructivity. The proliferation of law and its related technologies does not signal a departure from the passional violence of the Middle Ages, but a development of it. Ordinance groupifies the chivalric body, working out the terms of a group sentience, of a circulation of sentience such that pain, consent, intent, and responsibility can be passed on. And it is the circulation that matters above everything else; the group can tolerate failure and excess because when an unfulfilled duty is transferred to the account of another group member, the value of fulfilling it is intensified. Sacrifice thrives on the group's power of relay.

Because consent can be understood as turning befallenness into sacrifice, it plays a central role in the rituals that initiate knights into their lives of sovereign mortality. Ordination transforms the identity of the aspirant, into someone whose "new life" now belongs to the Other—the lord, and the law of the knightly order.[14] The assumption of the new life through the chivalric gift of death involves a blood pact, which binds the life of the knight to the lives of all the other knights, thus sanctifying his anticipated injuries as his own sacrificial gift to the group body. Sovereignly mortal, the chivalric body grows by means of ritual violence—the slap, the wound—that dramatizes the intimacy between aggressivity and pacts of dominance and submission. Another of the contentions of this chapter is therefore that Troilus's submission to the Trojan state represents not a conflict between enjoyment and duty but the enjoyment of duty itself.

The rites of blood and blade make a knight by dramatizing and exacerbating sentience, which in turn authenticates consent (consenting to injury is *beyond* consent). These rites make a difference between the hypersentient group and the dead/unfeeling/uncanny object-body that has not been thus remade. The sanctification of the martial encounter with death abjects techniques of survival and risk avoidance, techniques associated with the sentient object. To survive by protecting sentience at all costs is, because it is a "becoming-body," to live a facsimile of hypersentient life, to be undead rather than reborn or twice-born. But this is the kind of life the knight is enjoined to protect, that of the sentient object. There is a bond of some kind between the undead and the born-again, which reveals the importance to martial experience of points of crossover between *jouissance* and the law of the group. Not the object itself, but the extraordinarily complicated character of the object in martial culture—already lost to life insofar as it is defined as an object of rescue, already sacrificed and therefore bearing the mark of doom—is always sublimed when the warrior mourns. Chivalric treatises repeatedly, sometimes movingly, honor the strength of the wish to live. But this privilege is always adjudicated vis-à-vis the overriding "obligation" of knights to "pour out their blood for their brothers" and their lords.[15] Spectacular enactments of the death drive, however, are not simply consolation prizes for the loss of life or limb. As the equivalent, on the psychic level, of pained sentience, loss is one of the chief goals of chivalric enjoyment, and consent to loss one of its chief mechanisms.

To create the hypersentient subject, chivalric techniques of living cultivate preparedness, the reverse of befallenness, in the form of an intentional relationship to violence. The fact that this may result in inflicting as well as suffering injury is a difficulty that emerges from this fundamental orientation. What becomes absolutely necessary for the chivalric subject is to demonstrate that he is always prepared for violence, that violence is always a reflex of his intent and never something that simply befalls him. The contrast between lawful and unlawful violence obscures the fact that, at least in chivalric culture, violence is always already intended, and to that extent always already participates in the law. The transformation of passivity into activity, of suffering into sentience sublimed, is exciting as well as consoling, because it activates the law that guides the movements of enjoyment. In fact, it "fulfills" the meaning of the law—supplying its lack, animating it—by locating that meaning in the prospective power of the law, its intentionality, its importance to group as well as individual preparedness (knights must be trained this way and not that way, etc.). The sublimation and desublimation of *compliance* impels the narrative of *Troilus and Criseyde*. It is well known that Chaucer brought out Criseyde's consent *as a problem*, whereas in Boccaccio she is more straightforwardly eager and in charge of the narrative that brings about the fulfillment of "her" desires, "double" in what is presented as an *intentional* difference between depth and surface. Chaucer, on the other hand, doubles his ambiguation of Criseyde's consent by making Troilus's compliance with the Trojan state's reasons an equally puzzling crux. Again, it is the judgment of judgments that is first in enjoyment in *Troilus and Criseyde*. What has not always been so clear, however, is the extent to which the crux of Criseyde's consent to love parallels the equally puzzling crux of Troilus's consent to the Trojan state's reasons.

Chaucer's narrator assumes that we will be shocked by Criseyde's "sodeyn" love for Troilus, despite the suddenness of Troilus's love for Criseyde in Book I—indeed, despite the fact that Criseyde's love does not seem sudden at all. But the narrator is thereby able to present the drawn-out delectation of the *question* of Criseyde's desire as chivalrous defense of the lady against the "envious" who "jangle" (II, 666). Everything needs a beginning, he remarks; a bit later on, Criseyde will also mark the historicity of love: "That erst was nothing, into nought it torneth" (II, 798). Book II re-begins Criseyde's story (as the story of her coming-to-desire) with the narrator's famous meditation on change. From this moment on, Criseyde embodies (or encharacters) the historicity and sociality of desire, the shiftiness of entente, the susceptibility of the soul to influence. She bears the charge of the poem's enjoyment of the impossibility of pinpointing the moment when consent is given.

When Troilus falls in love at first sight, it is a total scene; his vulnerability to engraving is staged dramatically (by comparison with Criseyde's death by a thousand cuts) as wound (Cupid's dart) and then again as penetration/emanation of eye-beams. When Troilus loses his freedom, his lack of lack, and falls prey to desire, it might seem that he also loses his status as sovereign subject. The question is whether he in fact has a greater chance of becoming a hypersubject if he can bear love's unbearable exacerbation of his sentience. (For many readers, this question is never settled, which points to the exquisite equipoise needed by the hypersubject if he is to show that he can bear an unbearable desire he did not ask for—that is, he is not a masochist—but at the same time that he is prepared for wounds of any kind, owing to his a priori intent with respect to violence.) But the import of the contrast between Troilus's and Criseyde's fallings-into-desire is partly to show that, in one way, there is no difference between them. The impossibility of pinpointing the moment when desire awakens is in no way incommensurate with its traumatic decisiveness.

Sometimes trauma produces structures of enjoyment that distribute shock away from the center of injury (one of the roles of the group is to absorb these shock waves, e.g., the "goosish" women who visit Criseyde in Book IV). Even more important, though, trauma is an experience that has no beginning, middle, or end. It ruptures time rather than taking place within it. The experience of trauma is most ambiguous—when did it happen, why, how?—when it is most destructive. Narratives establishing or disestablishing consent supply a time for trauma, the time needed by the law to judge the formation of intentions. Giving consent the power to *decide* truth, even though consent in relation to trauma is indecidable, delivers the excitement of passional reassemblage (with its appearance of ambiguity) *and* the animation of the law (with its demand for judgment) at the very same time. The law enjoys adjudicating violation by treating desire as if it were decidable. One result is the legitimation of doubt, whether in the form of the "reasonable doubt" that we might feel about Troilus's and Pandarus's machinations, or in the form of the sacrifice of belief that sublimes Troilus at the end of Book V ("Who shal now trowe on any othes mo?" [V, 1263]). But *Troilus and Criseyde* shows, through Troilus's submission in Book IV, that the state rests precisely on the *arbitrariness* of its reasons and the demands it makes on our consent. *Troilus and Criseyde* makes a powerful contribution to the literature of rape not by clarifying consent but by *showing* its difficulty.

The importance of intent to militancy means the importance of interiority and its prosthetic resources. The preoccupation of *Troilus and Criseyde* with intimate desires, private spaces, secret conversations, and innermost thoughts has inspired a critical tradition more concerned with the vicissitudes of love than war.[16] The narrator tempts this reading: "But how this town come to destruccion / Ne falleth nought to purpos me to telle" (I, 141–42). Indeed, the interior terrain of courtly love is set out with enchanting richness in *Troilus and Criseyde,* and psychoanalytic criticism has not escaped the lure.[17] But this "litel...tragedye" shows us the importance to the chivalric group subject of the interiority of the warrior. *Troilus and Criseyde* manifests the later Middle Ages' foregrounding of the sacrificial aspects of signification and chivalric culture's interest in the exacerbation of sentience by showing interiority to a hitherto unprecedented degree. But this interiority is the group subject turned inside out. Tragedy reanimates the dying group by producing a purified remnant; Chaucer's "litel... tragedye" plays out the production of the purified remnant within the prosthetic interior space already mapped out by courtly love and philosophically sublimed by Boethius. At stake is a sentience whose survival is not banal but exciting, a sentience that survives as such (in the apotheosis tradition, it matters that the surviving spirit *sees* and *hears* more than it could before), but in the mode of triumph.

In contrast to this apotheosis of sentience, Cassandra's warnings will always have fallen on deaf ears. She speaks but no person hears her entente. In the legend of Troy, nothing assures woman's ability to animate the group body, because she is the epitome of the sentient object—uncanny, undead.[18] It may seem paradoxical that when she wants to survive, she can easily get in the way of the groupifying thrill of tragedy, ending in a banal way, with a new boyfriend. But tragedy is the epitome of *sublime* loss, of the dignifying of loss into something that produces redemptive power, and it is this sublimity that is in question where woman is concerned. What does it mean to have foresight and not be understood? It is to be oracular, to be on the level of *das Ding* where the law means nothing but form and the drives just keep on pulsating. (The Trojans cannot listen to Cassandra because doing so would reveal that their attempt to keep their "gains" is really a death drive.) Oracular intelligibility, on the other hand, means that meanings are being supplied; speech can make truth claims that can be judged, and the conditions of possibility for entente emerge.

In Freud's essay "The Theme of the Three Caskets," the mythical motif that represents woman at three different stages of life (young, old, and in-between) is read as an apotropaic reversal of the subject's befallenness.[19] These figures are uncanny because they epitomize sentient objecthood, which is often indicated by privation of sentience (Cordelia cannot heave her heart into her mouth; she anticipates the silence of the grave). The death drive keeps time for the relentless forward motion of the sentient object through the stages of life, and powers the apparent fickleness of Fortune's wheel. The illusory variety of the trifold woman's guises signifies her function in ideological fantasy as the medium through which *das Ding* mutters the truth of the primacy of the signifier, the mark as such, as opposed to meaning, reasons, and so on. Criseyde is vulnerable to the voice of "al the town" in *Troilus and Criseyde* because she bears the burden of the oracle, the faithlessness of which is first acted out by the mortal father, Calchas (I, 86). (The oracle could care less who wins and who loses, because from its point of view, "winner" is a signifier.) Like Cassandra, Criseyde poses an oracular challenge to interpreting signifiers in moments of "decision"; they always threaten to become opaque.

In Book IV, for example, the status of her speech when she explores the possibilities for future reunion with Troilus is bizarrely overdetermined. Her words are already opaque in the sense that whatever their function is, it is obviously *not* to explore possibilities for future reunion with Troilus. Planning and intentions are completely overshadowed by the inexorability of the end; the terminal pole of human life is devouring the middle. It is as though she already knew *without knowing* that everything they might do to divert Troy's march to destruction will ultimately lead to the same end. The empty speech of reassurance (also a feature of the garrulity of Pandarus and the narrator) reassures by offering itself as sacrificial gift of time to the Other. What reassuring speech "says" is that the speaker will sacrifice the time of her life to spinning out patterns of destinerring signifiers as though doing so could keep Atropos's scissors closed. But reassurance cannot convey this gift without showing that somewhere, the Thing knows better. So there is a strangely anticlimactic, almost comic, feeling in Book IV; everything is finished already, trauma time is over without our knowing exactly when it happened, there is nothing left except the realization as tragedy of what Book IV presents as farce: *Romeo and Juliet* manqué. This anticlimax is what Troilus hears; perhaps it is because he is already so close to the end that he can sense the closeness of Criseyde's speech to unintelligible oracularity, without (by the same logic) really understanding why. The capacity of the courtly "lady" to shift between subject and object of loss can be accounted for by her role as stand-in *for* the destinerring signifier, for what it means to be-as-signifier, including what it means to be a signifier in the discourse of the Ōther: to be oneself and yet other, human yet inhuman, sentient yet insentient: the always exchangeable, always objectifiable subject.[20]

If the humanity of the oracular lady is in question, so is her gender, which makes her fascinating; beauty converges on monstrosity, as with Alceste in *The Legend of Good Women* and Fortune in *The Book of the Duchess*. The lady is always threatening to "fall," that is, to lapse out of meaning into the real obscenity of the meaningless signifying chains that structure enjoyment. Guinevere, in Malory, is *repeatedly* shamed and vindicated, tried and rescued; the significance of her function emerges as a consequence of this repetition, which ties her to the rhythms of the death drive, now (in Malory) in the form of an oscillation between safety and danger, pleasure and *jouissance*.[21] To bring the fallen creature back to life and good fame is to reanimate the sentient object. But, as in *Frankenstein*, there is no telling how uncanny the results will be, and Chaucer reminds us in *The Book of the Duchess* that raising the dead/fallen is not always the fire of our desire. Saving fallen women can be good for the group (as Lacan argues, the sublime object is always chosen by the group), but anybody in Troy knows that it is a tricky project, for it involves presenting one's own particular stolen undead object (Helen) as worthy of groupified sublimation—an *aventure* that Troilus, unlike Paris, does not finally undertake.[22] It is Criseyde's failure to become the group object that sets her adrift, in Book V, into silence.

Criseyde's legend is a bit of a paradox, an antilegend: the legend of the woman who cannot be sublimed, of the object the group (including her critical tradition) chooses not to sublime. One reason for this is that Helen, structurally speaking, blocks the way. Criseyde might be a reprise of Helen, but she is not a pure repetition. As sublime object, Helen can cause catastrophe, launch a thousand ships; Criseyde can "only" cause heartbreak. She repeats Helen with the difference of an erotic particularity (Troilus's desire for her) treated as anticlimax. But another way of putting this is that, as reprise or spin-off of Helen, her very function is to threaten the special uniqueness of the sublime object (particular, but *for the group,* and therefore not limited to the term of one love affair or two lifetimes).

Crisdeyde's "beginnings" in two different women of the *Iliad* (Chryseis and Briseis), both of whom are objects of problematic exchanges, indicates this paradoxical, originally anticlimactic character. The attempt to substitute Chryseis for Briseis does not work because, for Achilles, Briseis is *particular;* he is not captivated by the desire of the Ōther, he does not want whatever value might accrue from circulating her and having her come back as Chryseis. But as signifier in the discourse of the Ōther (i.e., seen from the standpoint of the symbolic order), the sentient object circulates on behalf of *jouissance,* by means of displacements—substitutions—that depend on a powerful element of repetition. The story, moreover, does its own "falling" after Chaucer (Henryson, Shakespeare); its downward curve includes increasing obscenity, overfamiliarity, desublimation, excessive proximity, the repetitiveness of the drive: "truth tired with iteration."[23]

But exchangeability is the common fate of men and women, and the sentient economies of medieval aristocracies make this evident enough. Daughters and sons are both used to further alliances through marriage; it makes a difference that sons usually stay in the family domain and daughters do not, but the difference it makes does not change the fact that a deal's a deal. One can be given away without having to go away. When one becomes a signifier, taking up one's position in language as an "I," one also *becomes* exchangeable. Once one is an "I," one can be spoken of by others; one's life is never entirely free of determination by one's position in the symbolic order, as "son" or "subject" or "Trojan." The ambiguity Lévi-Strauss famously notes in relation to "woman" as object of exchange—that, unlike signs, things, and other exchangeable objects, she is also a "person" and "generator of signs"—is also true of men, and openly so in *Troilus and Criseyde*.[24]

In Book II, Criseyde registers some surprise that Pandarus actually *wants* her to love a *finamen*, noting (in effect) that when the symbolic order is in its patriarchal attire, it does not want women to love out of place no matter who the lover is: "Allas! I wolde han trusted, douteles, / That if that I, thorugh my dysaventure, / Hadde loved outher hym or Achilles, / Ector, or any mannes creature, / Ye nolde han had no mercy ne mesure / On me" (II, 414–19). It is another Chaucerian moment when we see, Schreber-like, that the big Other does not even care about its own rules when its *jouissance* is at stake. *Au contraire:* breaking the rules *and* being constrained by them are significant modes of enjoyment for rule makers, if only because transgression requires something to transgress. And pointing out to powerful male aristocrats that they like to play fast and loose with the rules they equally enjoy is perhaps not going to shock them as much as we lesser beings (including Criseyde here) might think. But there is something about the way Criseyde makes her point that could really raise problems for the boys' enjoyment. It is that when she is pointing out that the big Other does not want her to choose anyone to love, she lets loose a series of substitutions that make the alternatives all look alike: Troilus or Achilles, Hector or absolutely anybody, Greek or Trojan, town hero or anonymous, who cares? No man is important enough to disturb the doings of the big Other (and this is perhaps really true, insofar as enjoyment is always linked to signifiers through and beyond the subject).

The belated Troilus, the younger son, is not quite Hector—a point belabored sufficiently by *Troilus and Criseyde* to have been taken up by Shakespeare as one of the master tropes of his revision. Although Troilus's name obviously points to an identification with Troy, it does so partly to mark a slippage: Troilus, the generic Trojan, bears the name of the Other, comes "after," like any signifier participating in exchange. This appears to be the reason why his heartbreak cannot entirely serve as sublime subject of catastrophe: in an ironic but inevitable movement, the generic hero precisely epitomizes what it means to be just another signifier, and therefore cannot stand in for group enjoyment. So he can only have "just another" death. The point is made harshly; he is killed by the same man who kills his brother Hector, but Achilles does not matter to Troilus, and Troilus's death, though mourned, is not the one that brings down the town. It does not even bring down his rival Diomede, whom he tries so hard to establish as his mortal foe. What a fate, to be killed in an ordinary way by one's older brother's enemy. But in *Troilus and Criseyde*, Troilus gets to speak from the heavens. Not only does he see and hear from a long way off, but he also acquires the power to communicate with the living, namely, us. He sounds a little like a hypersubject. Criseyde instead slips off into silence. Is *Troilus and Criseyde* sustaining or showing how the fantasy of sexual difference is used to differentiate access to technological power, including the power to write poetry?

Kathryn Gravdal describes "life" as it appears in the records of the Abbey of Cerisy in Normandy during the time of the Hundred Years' War, and the difficulties women faced in seeking reparation for violence inflicted on them:

> We find a picture of poverty, broken family structures, quotidian sexual violence, incest, demoralization, and social instability. The court is notably lax in sentencing, practically flaunting canon law. The names of the jurors in any given sitting frequently include those of men convicted of criminal behavior in the preceding sessions.[25]

The *Registre Criminel de la Justice de Saint-Martin-des-Champs à Paris* "clearly suggest[s] that women, who commit far fewer crimes, receive the death penalty three times more frequently than men." Their punishments were burial alive (in order to shield their modesty from hanging) for "lesser offenses," as when in 1342 Ameline La Soufletiere is buried alive for the theft of a man's purple cloak, and burning at the stake for "grave" offenses. When Criseyde is introduced in Chaucer's poem, and the town, angered by her father's betrayal, wants to burn her—"al his kyn"—"fel and bones," this cruel detail is not obviously the result of mob excess alone (I, 91).[26] Shulamith Shahar writes that women died "by the cruellest methods of execution known to the cruel society of the Middle Ages"; Gravdal remarks of medieval French law: "Slow to protect and quick to punish, this society gives every sign that it values female life less than male."[27] In one of the rape cases tried by the court of the Abbey of Cerisy, the accused man was convicted and fined for rape, and the woman in question fined three times as much for allowing him to have carnal knowledge of her.[28]

Widows were the most frequent victims of rape because they were "unprotected" by father or husband; relatives, guardians, and friends were often sources of violence as well as of protection.[29] Of the witnesses present on Chaucer's behalf at Cecily Champain's well-known release of Chaucer from "*omnomodas assiones tam de raptu meo tam* [sic] *de aliqua alia re vel causa*—'actions of whatever kind either concerning my rape or any other matter'"—Donald Howard remarks that they were "some very big guns indeed, which means he thought the matter grave." If Cecily was the stepdaughter of Alice Perrers, who had been the mistress of Edward III, "it means that Chaucer raped or seduced the stepdaughter of an old friend who had done him many favors.... Or it means that his old friend's stepdaughter brought against him a vindictive accusation."[30] It is not easy to know what to make of the fact that Chaucer gives the Man of Law the job of declaring his distaste for tales of "unkynde abhomynacions" ("Introduction" to *The Man of Law's Tale*, 88).

Georges Duby has argued of medieval France that incest was not so much a stigmatized aberration or even an overlooked occasional vice, but a central practice and sign of seigneurial power.[31] John of Ireland's *Meroure of Wyssdome,* an advice book for princes, includes an ecstatic description of the Annunciation, in which ladies are by the by warned to eschew "worldly plesance" in the form not only of the company of strange men, but also that of kinsmen and friends, because "gret perell js ... to be allane with [th]ame jn sacret placis and tyme."[32] As a scene, the Annunciation links the dangers of intimacy with the apotheosis of consent, which crosses the desire of the subject with the desire of the Other. Consent bestows the kind of inner life necessary to allegiance; one offers up one's interior to transformation by the Other's desire, risking the very borderline between strangeness and intimacy that consent is often thought capable of determining. The Marian vessel points to, by enclosing, this vanishing point; it/she mystifies, but depends on, the enjoyment of submission to the law's extraordinary demands. Her "delectation" depends on the trial of her consent. She makes herself into the secret place of God's—and her own—*jouissance* by becoming his "humyll chaumerere, and seruand.... In all things j me conforme to his haly will and plesaunce.... humely j consent [th]arto." This act of consent gives her "gret powere and strenthe," whence she was able to conceive "hire blist sone without doloure; sche had gret and merwalus dilectacioune and plesaunce in [th]at, baithe naturall and spirituale." But in this, Mary is no more than the epitome of the subject-*as*-vessel, the sensorium that takes shape around emptiness, and thus puts form up to the ruse of identifying *das Ding* with mere emptiness, instead of with mute, indifferent, inaccessible enjoyment.

This ruse plays a role in shaping the narrative of *Troilus and Criseyde*. In *Troilus and Criseyde* as well as in the *Meroure*, consent shapes the vessels, the verbal intimacies and private places, that dissimulate our captivation by arbitrary power. In *Troilus and Criseyde* each consent to the betrayal of an intimacy takes us more deeply inside—into thoughts, chambers, hiding places. But each anticlimax rewrites the apparent richness of interiority as empty of value. The "is-that-all" of interiority can be blamed on the very nature of the object: the vanity of the *temporalia*, the world's littleness. Finally, turning outward instead of inward, flown to the eighth sphere, we refer our desire to the divinity who consents to die for us. The alibi of emptiness, like Fortune's arbitrariness, allows readers of *Troilus and Criseyde*, and participants in chivalric culture, to make the vanity of human wishes and objects responsible for knightly melancholia, destructivity, and so forth. One has sacrificed, one has perhaps lost one's head, and for what? Vainglory? Chivalry is always impelled to de-sublime the objects on whose behalf it sacrifices. But what if anticlimax and indifference were produced by an encounter not with emptiness but with the abjection of the Real? With the insentient materiality of enjoyment that can be designed but not absorbed by the signifier? So that we would find, after each betrayal of intimacy, our *jouissance*? Surely the problem of the evil that lies within our hearts is a bit more terrifying than the vanity of human wishes?

Histories of war often mourn the loss of a clear and honorable front.[33] As a corollary, they often represent civilian casualty as "by-product" of a war that is "really" being conducted between soldiers.[34] But complaints about atrocity and injustice during the Hundred Years' War really tempt one to believe that the Hundred Years' War was an extraspecial catastrophe for the "people," a decisive step toward the *jouissance* of massacre as the only way to make war.[35] In *The Tree of Battles,* Honoré Bonet grieves that "in these days all wars are directed against the poor labouring people."[36] The war made on the civilian population was cruelest in France, whose "unhappy fate" it was "to provide the battleground for much of the war," as Chaucer knew, having participated in the 1359 campaign.[37] But for England as well as for France, "[w]ar... had by now come to pervade all the ranks of those societies in or between which it was being fought."[38] England was attacked frequently and brutally during the later fourteenth century, and there was great fear of a full-scale invasion.[39] Although Richard II's pacific policies were greeted in some quarters of the realm with real enthusiasm, the vulnerability of England to invasion during his reign was highly anxiogenic, especially given the appearance of decline in England's military fortunes after the spectacular successes of Edward III's solemnly *sportif,* adventurist reign (despite the fact that England's misadventures probably had as much to do with Edward III's assemblage of hypermasculine sons as with the grandson who embraced the arbitrariness of the law and demanded "absolute choice").

Scarry argues that injuring is the central activity of war. The opening of the body—the emergence of what is "in us more than ourselves"—promises to make substantial the cultural fictions that wars contest.[40] A cultural fiction is a "sublimation," that is, a group consensus about what is sublime (has the dignity of the Thing) and what is not. Wounding is an extreme exacerbation of sentience, the inescapability of which seems to certify decisions and obligations that might be open to doubt. The implication of Scarry's formulation is that the wound serves for us both as passageway and as link between the Thing and the symbolic order; as passageway, it structures retrospection and anticipation; as link, it seems to substantiate (and thus also to make sense of) the relation between the Real and the signifier. *The Knight's Tale* displays the importance of the wound to chivalric culture when the course of the narrative changes because of the trauma of Arcite's shattered breast and his sacrificial consent to this loss/excess. Trauma is both result and psychic counterpart of the wound. As Laplanche and Pontalis note, the term comes from the Greek word for wound, which in turn derives from the word for "to pierce": "[trauma] generally means any injury where the skin is broken as a consequence of external violence, and the effects of such an injury upon the organism as a whole."[41] Trauma, whether physical or psychic, entails "the idea of a violent shock, the idea of a wound and the idea of consequences affecting the whole organisation."[42]

Traumatic shock may result from unbearable loss, separation, violation, ecstasy; what causes the trauma is not so much the specific nature of the event but the unbearable excitation it produces. Hence, as noted previously, trauma's power to confuse and obscure: the excitation produced by an overwhelming onset of desire is not readily distinguishable from excitation produced by physical injury. Moreover, the anxiogenic object often cannot be signified: it is repressed, impossible to determine, both. The impossibility of finding signifiers adequate to the "working through" of shock, breach, enormity means that the traumatic experience "remains in the psyche as a foreign body." The excitation and anxiety caused by a traumatic event are thus capable not simply of disturbing but of remaking subjectivity. Paradoxically, the radical nature of these effects is what confers on trauma its ability to confer, in turn, the quality of inescapability and the apparent power to disambiguate.

Anxiety designates excitation when it concerns the future; it works in the register of entente; it is capable of remaking a life, organizing it around expectation, preparedness. Excitation likewise propels the repetition compulsions that seek to transform helplessness into enjoyment. These are among the most important means by which the wound can receive its sacrificial reasons, its *"jouis-sense"* (the enjoyment of "making sense" out of the arbitrary). Consent, we have suggested, depends for its psychic and cultural power on trauma and the indeterminacy of intention or will associated with it: "I am not the person who endures this catastrophe, instead I am the person who inflicts the wound; I agree to it, I take it on, indeed I ask for it." Traumatic indeterminacy also extends to the object. The object may be anxiogenic if it is perceived as capable of rescuing the subject from anxiety because it raises hopes it may not ultimately satisfy. For this reason the psychic line between the rescuing and the persecuting object is extraordinarily fine; and it becomes even easier to confuse them because both kinds of object will be "overvalued," for good or for ill.

Troilus and Criseyde shares with many other instances of courtly discourse a knowledge of the tight bond between desire and trauma. The poem juxtaposes signifiers of consent and coercion, love and war, without clarifying the relations between them. In *Troilus and Criseyde* the figure of the wound is not only prominent but prominently polyvocal. Moreover, *Troilus and Criseyde* sometimes intensifies these phenomena all the way back around to indifference. For many readers, the treatment of the onset of Troilus's desire in Book I is overkill, but overkill that threatens to tire with iteration—perhaps because the anxiogenic nature of his object of desire is correlated too closely with its arbitrariness (why this person? Why now?). In *Troilus and Criseyde* I, IV, and V, the poem's fascination with the idiocy of rule (its senselessness in the strict sense, i.e., its lack of "reasons") and the desire of the "peple" exposes the reliance of the machinery of state on the enjoyment of consensual sacrifice. *Troilus and Criseyde* shows how deeply chivalric literature responds to, indeed, makes art out of, trauma.

The Hundred Years' War, like the Trojan War, came to pervade "femenye." During the English siege of Limoges in 1370, the Black Prince, "borne in on his litter, watched while the soldiers, on his orders, ran about killing the citizens—men, women, and children."[43] Such tableaux suggest that if the Hundred Years' War made fear newly popular among the weaponless, the unleashing of calamity on the helpless may have been, not its by-product, but its desire: the "war machine" on the loose.[44] Prior to the advent of feminist approaches to *Troilus and Criseyde*, criticism—like Pandarus—often isolated Criseyde's anxieties from their historical contexts and desires that made them, castigated or patronized Criseyde for her "choices," and thus repeated the effect of anticlimax traced by *Troilus and Criseyde*'s militant structuring of enjoyment.[45] Either Criseyde's emotions are "second-rate," or she is the epitome of feminine anxiety in need of rescue. According to C. S. Lewis, Chaucer

> so emphasized the ruling passion of his heroine, that we cannot mistake it. It is Fear—fear of loneliness, of old age, of death, of love, and of hostility; of everything, indeed, that can be feared. And from this Fear springs the only positive passion which can

be permanent in such a nature; the pitiable longing, more childlike than womanly, for protection, for some strong and stable thing that will hide her away and take the burden from her shoulders.[46]

But Criseyde's fear has a function that makes Lewis's fantasy of rescue helpful as indication if not precisely as analysis. Her fear stands for the anxieties of the very "peple" so apparently willing to do her in. To a significant degree, she figures group desire in the form of anxiety and (excessive/inadequate) emergency preparedness. The diffuse, uncanny sentience of the group subject is mirrored in the uncertain political status of the traitor's daughter, and in both cases takes the anxiogenic shape of the subject who does not know what (the right thing is) to do.

When Pandarus arrives at Criseyde's house to tell her of Troilus's love, she says "is than th'assege aweye? / I am of Grekes so fered that I deye" (II, 123–24). The scene invokes literary powers of preparedness; she is listening to Statius, a text that ought to have a sobering effect. However, Criseyde's fear is rendered anticlimactic by the nature of the business that follows. The good news delivered in the moment of annunciation remakes her fears of violation: the only men she need worry about now are her uncle and one of the princes of Troy. The sublimity of group catastrophe to which this scene of reading at least alludes is scaled down with comic rapidity, but to what? Something *almost* overfamiliar: easy intimacy pushed to excess, linked to something unaccountable at the heart of home. The narrative rhythms of *Troilus and Criseyde* depend on oscillations between safety and danger, familiarity and over/underfamiliarity. Objects of anxiety multiply, gain and lose significance, seem less and more real. Hyperbole (subliming that gets itself noticed) trivializes Pandarus's threats that he and Troilus will die if Criseyde does not consent; but the final effect of his courtly overkill is to shift and diffuse the sense of menace into a more "free-floating" uneasy atmosphere.

This comedy makes us feel that those in charge pursue enjoyment, not "reasons." It is not simply that they desire, but that their enjoyment takes the form of entente; they are ravenous for plots, plans, intrigue, willing, wishing, and their desire for entente as such means that their schemes always have an air of the arbitrary. Everyone who reads this poem knows that the Polyphete ruse that Pandarus uses to bring Criseyde and Troilus together at Deiphebus's house is zealously overcomplicated.

The interiority of the love plot enables this focus on the obscenity of the law, the *jouissance* of rule, which means also its pervasiveness, its everywhere-and-nowhere quality. The prosthetic role of interiority, scene of sentience, its exacerbation, and the desires and fears that make and are made by war, is signaled also by the extraordinary prominence *Troilus and Criseyde* gives here and elsewhere to the messenger function. The role of prosthesis in extending intimacy, thus in extending the possibilities for trauma's ambiguating work, is fully on display, made evident by the amount of time Book II devotes to Criseyde's "working over" of Pandarus's overture.

The time it takes Criseyde to fall in love pushes consent in the direction of narrative, as though the instantaneousness of choice and the impossibility of determining when it occurs could be turned into the kind of story that enables but also defers judgment—the story of entente in which Troilus and Pandarus delight but do not want to see "fulfilled." Criseyde must be lured into encounter with her *un/heimlich* prince. The relatively lengthy and uncertain onset of her desire draws out the moment of consent, repeating the remaking of traumatic befallenness into a more trivial genre. The threat of fusion posed *by* joining a group body and adoring one's ruler (the anonymous, fused character of the "peple" in *Troilus and Criseyde* seems linked to its desires for draconian solution) is interiorized as a *jouissance* of terror on behalf of community, the sort of thing that might captivate one into staying inside one's doomed town, where one would be so afraid of the enemies at the gates that one could die, precisely because it is the only place where just such a *jouissance* might be found. But for *Troilus and Criseyde* to make the point that consensual submission (which includes residence, insofar as residence implies choice of community) is a structure of enjoyment, the poem must invoke the law, and the pleasures the law takes and gives through acts of obedience.

The early books focus on seduction and thus make fear erogenic, bringing home (in premature triumph) war's raptures—a mode of preparedness that makes direct use of trauma's excitations. The furor of the war machine is remade as interior *jouissance*. Troilus goes off to fight and comes back covered with broken arrows, riding a wounded horse: "Who yaf me drynke?" says Criseyde, rendering as love potion the idea of an exquisitely painful transformation just the other side of pleasure

(II, 651). But the ethical thrust of these early books is not to show a tragic "forgetting" of the point of these arrows, except insofar as it is the business of really interesting tragedy to remind us that although remembering may be necessary for rescue, it cannot guarantee our safety and is inevitably ambiguous. The scene rather reminds us that war, in and perhaps because of all its furor, is always already masked, always already capable of attaching passional excitation to the most arbitrary of signifiers (e.g., Helen); war happens because of an intensification of interiority (sentience), not because wits have fallen asleep. On this score, as the structure of Chaucer's scene suggests, the theatrical character of war recalls the mask of love.

Troilus and Criseyde, then, brings out the erotic potential of the gift of death. It is not too hard to understand why we would enjoy triumph; we enjoy the sovereignly mortal insofar as its wounds mark a death already confronted, the afterimage of which gives us not only the *jouissense* of "mastered" excitation, but also—and note that it amounts to the same thing—enhanced power to commune with the dead (because we are now, though the more alive, on their wavelength). But this power to commune with the dead/Thing along the path of the wound can channel something stranger, that is, the desire for an "other" sentience, the desire to traffic with the differently animated. Something or someone that has passed the barrier between life and death is what is wanted: something inhuman, perhaps a signifier. Even as the poem is entertaining us indoors, it shows us the arbitrariness of hometown law, the lack in Trojan sovereignty, the absurdity of submission thereto. Because this arbitrariness is the basis for the obscene enjoyment of allegiance, and also reveals the state's and the law's dependence on excitation (the meaningless furor of the war machine), exposure of sovereign lack intersects with the traumatic dis/replacements of the terrors of love and war, and makes the Trojan interior into a site of multiple investments in outrage.

This is why Calchas is, at the same time, such an oddly prosaic and remote character. Deprived of the sublimity that might otherwise surround the oracular, he embodies the fact that the law is calculating and indifferent; it makes its demands *irrespective* of persons. The long delay between his defection to the Greeks and his request for Criseyde is one signal that Calchas normally does not speak or ask for particular attachments. And yet he is particular about himself as well as his daughter.

The father enjoys; Calchas is the father who will not give his daughter away, and thus is associated with the endogamous-incestuous-interiorizing register of the poem.[47] As a consequence he is more anticlimactic than Sibylline, especially in the discourse of the poem's betrayed children, Troilus and Criseyde. But *Troilus and Criseyde* knows all about the intimacy between calculation and furor, anticlimax and tragedy. Indeed, a similar anticlimax attends Criseyde after her return to Calchas's authority; once she leaves Troy, the value of her consent is degraded even before she "falses" Troilus because, as noted earlier, we can already hear that it is all over as soon as the news is out. *Troilus and Criseyde* shows that it is possible to structure desire in such a way that to leave one's group *is* to leave *jouissance* for "mere" survival. On this score, Criseyde's desublimation is inevitable. Chaucer's lingering, in *Troilus and Criseyde* II, over Criseyde's destinerring thoughts works over as comedy the trauma of "love's fatal glance" in Book I, but it does so by tracing in time the transferences between the prosaic and the sublime that determine the traumatic poetics of *Troilus and Criseyde*. Moreover, because the poem takes such pains with the complexity of her consent, we come to understand the uselessness of adjudicating Troilus's actions on such a basis.

To treat fear as a characterological matter where Criseyde is concerned is to avoid the question of why chivalry (including that of Chaucer's narrator) fails to protect her. Does chivalry only protect women whose families have unimpeachable reputations? Women whose place in the symbolic order is already secure? Why would they need so much protection then? If they are already admirable, where is the sacrificial surplus to be gained from treating abject women in the same way a knight would treat a pillar of the community? Malory understands all this; his Lancelot *repeatedly* champions a woman who likely does not "deserve" rescue (any more than he "deserves" to champion her successfully), the risk being whether Malory can pull off the sublimity *of* this senselessness. *Troilus and Criseyde* may be asking a different question: does the triumphant warrior *want* to rescue the girl? Yes but no, precisely *because* Criseyde's image as widow, dressed in samite brown, is also an afterimage. Where Criseyde is concerned, befallenness has always already happened, which is what makes her susceptible to rescue in the first place; she has even already been rescued by Hector before there is any question of her needing Troilus's powers of rescue. Not only, then, traumatic object of Troilus's desire and premier representative of "woman's" power to befall man, but also epitome of the (feminized) subject as constituted by trauma, Criseyde will even, as signifier of the destinerrings of the traumatic signifier (at once result and cause of trauma), be "shent" in her afterlife, by books.

Thinking now of the image as a form of the signifier, we can recognize the extent of *Troilus and Criseyde*'s preoccupation with the power of the image to magnify, and thus to provide the protection of prosthesis. The image makes things larger than life, if only by reexpressing them, and thus can seem to promise rescue; we *take refuge* in images. Moreover, images magnify themselves, before or along with anything else. But they do so by relaying magnification from one image to the next, and thus cannot stay fixed. In the zone between life and death, the zone of trauma, form appears as such, we appeal to its power of magnification; so does the mutability of form, and thus its power to resignify the event of befallenness. The power of the signifier depends, paradoxically, on its iterability. And "more than one," the "next," like Troilus (who follows Hector/Paris) and Criseyde (who follows Helen), cannot help but register anticlimax, or at least can be used to do so.

Posttraumatic laughter, as trivialization or anticlimax or wit or the compromising mimesis of Pandarus's hand under the sheets, runs throughout the poem, changing places with its sublimings and tragedifyings. The repeated marking and dissemination of threat structure the plot of *Troilus and Criseyde*: the fictions of Polyphete and "Horaste," the near-death experiences of Book IV, even Troilus's cartoonish pursuit of Diomede. The slide between distinctiveness and belatedness characteristic of traumatic signification also explains why combat itself is treated equivocally throughout *Troilus and Criseyde,* even before its *ascesis* at the end of the poem: the question of whether Troilus is right to fight on behalf of the sublime erotic image instead of the sublime body of the group; the fact that Pandarus, a dubious angel on the score of militancy as well as messengering, is nonetheless perfectly willing to go out and fight from time to time, as though his participation were a casual matter from the standpoint of the group body. The unevenness of *Troilus and Criseyde*'s texture, like that of *The Book of the Duchess,* registers an alternation between indifference and desire—an alternation not only acted out by

Criseyde but disseminated across the poem through the militarized group body of Troy, hence, as we shall see, finding its way into the representation of the sublime military body of Troy's Troilus. But inside those private Trojan spaces in which love is pursued, the potential for violence against Criseyde is brought before us to be turned into *jouissance,* partly so that we will not notice, and partly so that we will, the queerness of the analogue of military *jouissance.*

The alternations between fear or premonition and *jouissance* are always signaled by a foregrounding of form—an exacerbation of the image, or a multiplying intertextuality. When we first see Criseyde in Book I, form is outermost: we see her as image, sublime visibility itself, seen for the first time, emerging virginally from her own and her family's (dubious) past, her brightness emphasized by contrast with the darkness of widow's weeds or the family's loss of reputation. She has the power of the signifier, the "work," to rupture the world (that has Troilus in it). But she is seen for the first time *twice;* and she emerges from her own past, she has already been sad. And at this time, when her appearance as image is at its height, Criseyde is threatened with burning, "fel and bones," for her father's treachery.

The sliding of the signifier in relation to trauma persists in Book II. As we noted earlier, Criseyde announces her fear of the Greeks while listening to Statius. Pandarus's first physical violencing of his intimacy with Criseyde is to thrust a letter into her bosom ("And in hire bosom the lettre down he thraste" [II, 1155]). When he tries to terrify her on the score of her mortality—"And therfore er that age the devoure, / Go love" (II, 395–96)—he does so by invoking the image of the mirror, and by quoting the king's fool. Book II opens when Pandarus, feeling "his part of loves shotes keene" (II, 58), is awakened to his "grete emprise" by the song of the swallow, Procne. She "so neigh hym made hire cheterynge, / How Tereus gan forth hire suster take, / That with the noyse of hire he gan awake" (II, 68–70).[48] The allusion is rendered in such chillingly neutral tones that it is difficult to believe either that Chaucer expected his audience to draw the inference or that he did not; the allusion simply joins a chain of stories of violence and rape whose import is rendered ambiguous.

But the links among intertextuality, danger, and awakening have been made, with decisive consequences for the reader's understanding of the constitutive relation between allusion and trauma. In a further tableau that alludes to the tableau of Pandarus's awakening, Criseyde listens to the song of Procne's raped and mutilated sister, Philomela, in the form of the "nyghtyngale"—here described by Chaucer as male, and as singing "*Peraunter* [emphasis added] ... a lay / Of love" (II, 921–22). Philomela sings just before Criseyde falls asleep and dreams (II, 925–31) of the eagle who painlessly rips out her heart and leaves his behind—an image of overwhelming invasive power and apparent reciprocity ("herte left for herte" [II, 931]).

One of the most important stagings in *Troilus and Criseyde* of what Lynn Higgins and Brenda Silver refer to as the "elision of the scene of violence" characteristic of literature about rape is the consummation scene in Book III.[49] The possibility of rape is raised by Troilus himself—"Now yeldeth yow, for other bote is non!"—and then seems to vanish when Criseyde utters the words that might seem to confirm her consent, not only to her "capture" at this moment, but to the entire course of the affair: "Ne hadde I er now, my swete herte deere, / Ben yolde, ywis, I were now nought heere!" (III, 1208, 1210–11). The moment is introduced by prior signs of trouble, when the narrator asks: "What myghte or may the sely larke seye, / Whan that the sperhauk hath it in his foot?" (III, 1191–92). The narrator adds that "Criseyde, which that felte hire thus itake, / ... Right as an aspes leef she gan to quake" (III, 1198, 1200).

We now know, having read Book II, that such an accumulation of avian and pastoral metaphors is a warning. Images that mark the presence of the image as such as well as its iterability and plasticity (the "olde romaunce" [980], the *pastourelle,* the *Natureingang*) also and thereby announce the ability of the image to mask trauma (pastoral as hiding but also signing vulnerability to predation).[50] This warning might awaken us to a lasting state of preparedness were it not for the poem's repeated dissemination of predation through the enjoyment of pastoral. Yet only when pastoral has become genre, or at least convention—hence iterable, movable—do we "know" that pastoral hides or does not fully anticipate danger.[51] Only by means of stories that destineer beyond the "original" trauma can we be warned of dangers that might repeat themselves. The destinerring of the traumatic signifier does not just pose problems for the understanding of trauma; it actually enables it, because only by tracing their swerves and deviations can we understand what signifiers of trauma *do*—that is, they swerve and deviate—and thereby how they construct subjectivity. We positively must learn to read what is, strictly speaking, indecidable—as Freud sought to do with his interminably patient listening—if we are to understand what it means to be creatures whom events can befall.

The exquisite pastoral images used to describe the lovers' pleasure in Book III (1226–32) are followed by a simile that compares Criseyde's language to that of the nightingale:

> And as the newe abaysed nyghtyngale,
> That stynteth first whan she bygynneth to synge,
> Whan that she hereth any herde tale,
> Or in the hegges any wyght stirynge,
> And after siker doth hire vois out rynge,
> Right so Criseyde, whan hire drede stente,
> Opned hire herte and tolde hym hire entente. (III, 1233–39)

It is possible to hear, behind Criseyde's inaudible (to us) voicing of her "entente," the mutilated mouth of Philomela. The undead voice of the survivor calls collect; Philomela, Procne, and Criseyde all survive to tell and, in one way or another, to warn, but their iterated voices (textile, legend, birdsong, avian poetry) are variously received. The possibility of Criseyde's rape is spoken in *Troilus and Criseyde* through intertextual haunting. Is this a groupification of trauma through intertextuality, an attempt to disseminate (dispel *and* relay) shock and responsibility? The difficulty of deciding on the meaning of this voice at any given moment is partly owing to such dissemination: trauma is redistributed, but also magnified, given a history. But this does *not* mean that the signifier simply occludes wound, or body, or woman, nor that sublimation simply follows trauma. The signifier, however wayward, will always be accompanied by the drive it designs. Without a doubt, we create forms to design and "contain" our destructivity; but our destructivity is always already formal. Events and bodies—Tereus's acts of violence, and the feminine body they violate—are always already signifiers in addition to all the other things they are, and must be so in order to do all the things they do.

The haunting voice, the oracular signifier warn us—but as to what? Is anything helped by recognizing that the oracular signifier foregrounds the oracularity of all signifiers—their insistence that something always lies ahead, and that the "we" we are now will not be the same then? And what of the fact that the oracular signifier is also the mnemonic signifier—that we remember in order (not) to repeat in the future? If we cannot know exactly for what eventuality the oracular/mnemonic signifier wants to prepare us, it is not because no violation has "really" occurred, nor is it because the signifier is incapable of pointing to instances of violation. It is because the inscriptions of trauma within the unconscious are forever subject to reassemblage, indeed, to the reassembling activity of intertextuality. The voice of the survivor makes warning signs; this is one definition of art, a definition foregrounded by tragedy. And what these warning signs tell me is both that violence can be repeated on me or by me, and that I cannot limit either my responsibility or my response to the fiction of a fixed representation or an absolutely finished event. If voice can never stabilize—if the voice of the survivor, inevitably altered by its trauma, can never stably describe an unstable event—responsibility does not disappear; rather, its multiplicity emerges and insists, we learn that responsibility is a relational matter for subject and socius.

Book III of *Troilus and Criseyde* might be likened to the garden in Book IV of *Daphnis and Chloe,* which John Winkler so beautifully called "a microcosm of the pastoral world—protected, fertile, flowering, with a structure of recollected violence in the center." According to Winkler, the pastoral romance discloses that "sexual violence is not merely an unhappy accident that might be avoided, but is a destiny written into the very premises of socially constructed reality."[52] Tragedy, in its own way, also makes "accident" into something meaningful, whether the reality in question is "socially constructed," as it is for Dollimore, or something superreal. But how much does it really help to identify "destiny" with "socially constructed reality," any more than with superreality? To what extent does the historicizing or culturalizing move *in and of itself* disturb the valorizing of intention, simply by redefining the nature of the reality that has "us" in its sights? Don't we also need to emphasize that very reality's failures of purpose, its destinerrings?

The revelation that reality is socially constructed does not *inevitably* perform subversive work. *Troilus and Criseyde* does not make it at all hard to imagine reality, or at least some crucial bits of it, as socially constructed. Hector chivalrously opposes Criseyde's exchange, failing to persuade the very community whose customs he invokes. He thereby enacts chivalry's bid for the power to define the meaning of exchanges. This in turn discloses chivalry's dependence on exchange, a point made also by the "everyday" exchange of male prisoners, the arbitrariness of which practice, had Criseyde's "extraordinary" exchange not drawn our attention to it, might have gone unremarked. Troilus himself, as Scanlon points out, complains about the power of power to be both arbitrary and nonnegotiable.[53] Does "destiny" name simply this: one cannot exchange without being also exchangeable? But this does nothing to eliminate the destinerring of exchange; on the contrary, it guarantees the impossibility of pure equivalence, even of male prisoners. But the further point is that the symbolic order does not care that its exchanges are not perfect, because the symbolic order is not going anywhere in particular; form does not imply telos. Bad signs will always be reassembling, and the destinies they write take nothing personally.

To associate destiny with social reality can sometimes, then, simply rationalize, via what currently counts as knowledge, our desire to substantiate the inhuman and purposeless formality of the law. *Troilus and Criseyde* goes beyond representing social reality as constructed, by suggesting the role of rationalization in enjoyment—that is, dissimulating the obscene enjoyment of submitting to a law that has no purpose and is not necessarily destinal or even, paradoxically, regular. Despite or because of his complaints, Troilus's consent to this destinerring law is as absolute as Criseyde's; and this obscene consent is the basis of the poem's structuring of enjoyment. The poem is telling us, and not very quietly, that all symbolic pacts are negotiable, because they have no particular substance; they concern nothing in particular. As is true, again, of Schreber's universe, there's no "order" in *Troilus and Criseyde* that is not willing to give up on the law in order to pursue its *jouissance*. No pact in particular is necessary; what is inevitable is only that desire loves to make pacts, so much so that we are usually prompted to decorate them with sense. But chivalry's passion for insentience always makes itself powerfully felt with respect to the pact: absurd vows, fighting to the death, the paradoxical delectation of shame, all exacerbated by the indeterminate status of the object (and hence the subject). But whether a particular pact will be the recipient of such fervor is hard to predict; it "depends," but on what? After all, we are here because Troy once tried to get out of paying its debts to the gods.

The pact makes legible the idiocy and simplicity of desire. Desire, as Lacan puts it, wants to be "deprived of something real" (*Ethics of Psycho-*

analysis, 150). And, at some level, Troilus's desire *wants* to let Criseyde go; Troy's desire *wants* to let the "traitor" out of its sight and thus let the death drive run loose in the world. This is the most straightforward way to understand why Troilus does nothing to keep Criseyde, and why Troy is so famously stupid about its own downfall. In *Troilus and Criseyde*, enjoyment depends on the loss of the object. Submission/resistance to the state is thus not a sublimation of amorousness, but rather an enhancement of it. Both courtly love and military preparedness are "service," and that is why the Trojan state can confuse Troilus about what he ought to do about Criseyde. Ostensibly puzzling choices between obligations to the "common" good and to one's particular objects are just so much diversionary fun, for both depend on the inescapably erotic dimension of submission. But submission to the common good is more readily dissimulated as consensual sacrifice than is courtly service, because of the magnifying effects of the relay of the particular object through the group body. This rewiring of the group sensorium through consent—enacted in *Troilus and Criseyde* by expanded transmissions (gossip, messengering, the voice of the "peple," parliament)—transforms mourning and protest into a "consensus" against befallenness.[54] But if coerced relations are structures of enjoyment, and no chosen relation can be scoured clean of submission, victims of violence nonetheless cannot be said to "deserve" their fate, even if the state demands it. If anything, it is to say that one does not even necessarily "deserve" what one enjoys.

When, in Book III of *Troilus and Criseyde*, the narrator tells us that Criseyde speaks her "entente," but does not tell us what that "entente" is, Chaucer draws attention to the inaudibility at the core of this most voluble poem. In *Troilus and Criseyde* III, consent begs for analysis; violation is adjudicated by means of the signifier (vows, testimony) and structured by it. Because of the signifier's interdependence with *jouissance* (hence destructivity), we cannot adjudicate violence from a position "outside" signification; violence is always already gestural. In this field (of the agency of the signifier) lie also *Troilus and Criseyde*'s defensive garrulities. The rationalizations that crest in Book IV, the logophilia of Pandarus and the narrator, pass around, but also potentially magnify, the shock of the (endlessly repeated) encounter between *jouissance* and the law of the signifier. The consummation scene of Book III shows that distinctions between violence and the signifier—whereby violence is "real," the signifier not—cannot do justice to heterosexual masculinity's demands on "feminine" *jouissance*. At least, this is true insofar as heterosexual masculinity fantasizes that consenting and being forced are two different things, and that its own desires could therefore possibly be free. What freedom, after all, brings *Troilus* into that bedchamber? It is symptomatic of something terrible indeed that, if we acknowledged the limited nature of Troilus's freedom, someone might feel we were trying to get him off the hook. The only actions that will ever require our judgment are the actions of finite beings, where freedoms are never absolute.

The legends of Troy are not sure whether Helen was abducted or whether she eloped of her own free will, and also are not sure whether Achilles is a hero or a pawn. These uncertainties, as noted earlier, impel the offshoot legend of Troilus and Criseyde. Criseyde, as feminized embodiment of the perplexities of being an exchangeable subject, acts out the nonabsolute status of freedom and the structuring role of constraint in the designing of desire. As noted earlier, in this Criseyde follows the example of Helen, who, while confirming the sad fact that objects men exchange can change hands, also reveals that those who exchange themselves become exchangeable. Menelaus, Paris, who cares? Hector, Troilus—what's the difference? As erotic objects, men can substitute indifferently for each other just as coolly as when they are prisoners. In *Troilus and Criseyde,* moreover, the exchangeability of male prisoners coolly anticipates subsequent desublimating exchanges: Criseyde's exchange of Troilus for Diomede; the substitution of Achilles for Diomede as Troilus's mortal foe. The question of Criseyde's and Helen's consent mystifies *and* marks the difficulty of choosing between Menelaus and Paris, Troilus and Diomede, and, for that matter, Palamon and Arcite—a difficulty that arises from warrior culture's own work of defining the equivalences between warriors that make them exchangeable (despite the need also to calculate their differences). The sacrificial construction of *pro patria mori* sublimes the sweet expendability of being-as-signifier.

Troilus and Criseyde's moral dimension emerges partly through its participation in a series of repetitions about the need to avoid repetition. This is one way of describing the forewarning work of traumatic repetition and the element of futility built into it (which does not at all mean that it gets nowhere). The plot of the poem averts one tragic outcome by refusing to repeat the "ravyshhyng" of women. But this refusal to repeat is itself part of that series of repetitions-about-the-need-to-avoid-repetition which *is* the secondhand story of *Troilus and Criseyde*—a story that in any case merely realizes by a certain doubling-with-a-difference the Helen legend's absorption by the question of the object's previousness, its having-already-been-possessed, which is itself an alibi for the exchangeability of the "possessors." Troilus and Criseyde struggle not to repeat a tragic story, and tragically fail to find an alternative; tragedy can thus be made out of Troilus's refusal to ravish, in the form of a chivalrous *ascesis* of predation. But, in Chaucer's version of the legend, it is not so much that the alternatives are destructive as it is that destructivity itself is what is wanted, in the very form of passivity.[55]

This *does* get us somewhere. By clarifying in so many ways the nature of the delectation of inaction, Chaucer's poem asks us to understand that the aristocratic gift of death testifies neither to a historical inanition of aristocratic power nor to its increasing sophistication, but more simply to the extraordinary resourcefulness of its modes of enjoyment. The poem warns, as it were proleptically, against histories of chivalry that make feud and sex precede law and courtly love—in other words, the sublimating narratives of European political history and ethnography. The poem's exploration of the aristocratic gift of death, in the form of the sublimation myth, the apparent "substitution" of enlightenment for action (Troilus, eighth sphere; narrator, to "yonge fresshe folkes" on the true meaning of sacrifice), is related to the voyeurism (apparent voyeurism? does he watch, or does he deflect the voyeuristic gaze by reading?) of Pandarus's behavior in Book III. The ambiguity of his turn to old romance points to a link between the theory of sublimation and that of perversion: unable to gain satisfaction from "real" erotic objects, Pandarus pursues vicarious enjoyment through fictions, whether of his own making, or (same thing) twice-told: "And with that word he drow hym to the feere, / And took a light, and fond his contenaunce, / As for to looke upon an old romaunce" (III, 978–80).

This reminder of the *jouissance* of vision, which clarifies what is at stake in Troilus's later enlightenment, is related to another particularly notorious moment of undecidability: on the morning after, the moment that *might* be read, but could never *definitively* be read, as Pandarus's incestuous dalliance with Criseyde:

> With that she gan hire face for to wrye
> With the shete, and wax for shame al reed;
> And Pandarus gan under for to prie,
> And seyde, "Nece, if that I shal be ded,
> Have here a swerd and smyteth of myn hed!"
> With that his arm al sodeynly he thriste
> Under hire nekke, and at the laste hire kyste.
>
> I passe al that which chargeth nought to seye.
> What! God foryaf his deth, and she al so. (III, 1569–77)

From the pastoralization of violence, to the avuncularity of incest? Chaucer's poem indeed treads the finest of lines between threat and safety, reminding us that whereas narratives of sublimation posit art as the safe haven that frustrated or otherwise menaced desire might seek, *Troilus and Criseyde*—and the Chaucerian narrator in general—knows that there is nothing safe or reliably diversionary about the play of the signifier. After all, our lamentations over the ineffectuality of the signifier should not be allowed to obscure how often we take refuge in the safety of art's putative irrelevance to pain. The signifier renders inaudible "that which chargeth nought to seye," just as in Book III it renders inaudible the "entente" of Criseyde's open heart. Again, this is because the emergence of the signifier cannot help but reassemble all the other signifiers that remember and portend. The link made in Book III between Pandarus and the *galeotto* of canto v *Inferno* is relevant here—does he merely look on or does he make desire happen where it would not? Is he responsible for sexual violence, has he tried to cover up its traces? "kep the clos" (III, 332).[56] Unheroic avuncularity—"erand" rather than "grete emprise" (II, 72–73)—is not a promising alternative to charismatic masculine violence. But if the signifier threatens to divert us from the event of violation, it also leaves a trail that we can follow, at least as far back as the story of Philomena.

Chaucer's poem makes this clearer than any other version of the legend. Even Shakespeare only gets so far as keeping us fixed for a time in the rock bottom of disappointment, the exhaustion of repetition's uses ("truth tired with iteration").[57] Chaucer's narrators, Pandarus included, see in ways that reveal the intimacy of menace and enjoyment. *The Legend of Good Women* shows the Chaucerian narrator "nearing" his inhuman love in the time "before" his punishment, when he is still getting away with having written *Troilus and Criseyde;* the latter poem thus signifies a *jouissance* menacing enough to lead to the trauma of judgment. (The narrator's penance for offending the sublime object is to rewrite the *jouissance* of discipline as the discipline of *jouissance.*) The unthreatening cuteness or desexualized gallantry ("Men seyn—I not") of the Chaucerian narrator does not fool the God of Love. He knows that the narrator is after something that belongs to him, and we should believe him.

The narrator's working over of befallenness as posttraumatic survival gets arrested in this Prologue. But the arrest makes explicit that the signifiers of the comic body are signifiers of anxiety. Given that traumatic repetition tries to work through, and hence also to sustain, overwhelming excitation, there is a complicity between *Troilus and Criseyde*'s comically garrulous attempts to speak the *jouissance* of sacrifice, and the figures of *ascesis* that crowd its only apparently more streamlined ending. If relaying excitation is a mode of defense, its point is to make excitation bearable; and one way of making it bearable is to say good-bye to it, as does Book V, in a hundred different ways. The *ascesis* of *Troilus and Criseyde*'s ending is not merely a way of containing the excitation let loose elsewhere in the poem. Neither the concept of "containment" nor that of "occlusion" can do full justice to the role of *ascesis* in preserving excitation. But can we be more precise? How does the premise of the interdependence of the law with *jouissance* explain the quality of *Troilus and Criseyde*'s ending?

To address this question, we need to focus again on the nature of sacrificial enjoyment. Communities group together and fall apart in the course of their attempts to get as close to *jouissance* as possible. The ability of communities to relay desire means that they endlessly transgress their own limits. The signifier of "community"—fatherland, nation, country, people, public good—is the signifier in the name of which the excessive or heterogeneous becomes lawful or homogeneous. The reverse is also true: simply by withdrawing its presence, if only for a moment, the signifier of community can flood a place of worship with desire. Because of this, the signifier of community has immense power to put desire through its paces.

In his essay "Thoughts on War and Death," Freud explained civilian depression during World War I by suggesting that wartime exposed the criminality, the *jouissance,* of the state. In peacetime, the subject could interpret the trouble with her desire—guilt, or enervation—as the result of a sacrifice of *jouissance* on behalf of a state that forbade private violence and overly intrepid sex. In wartime, however, the state, and/or its proxies, reveals itself as allowed to do these very things, in the name of "necessity." As we noted in our discussion of *The Knight's Tale,* sacrifice requires the fantasy of the big Other; but the big Other is there not only to give *to* (by which means, putatively, we restrain our passions), but also to protect us *from* the realization that *jouissance* is not so easy to come by as all that. When the fantasy of the big Other fails us, we are liable to depression because we need another account of the trouble with our desire. (This is the state of melancholy that afflicts Troilus after his death.) Lack in the big Other reveals the arbitrariness of the law on behalf of which we sacrifice. This revelation of arbitrariness is destabilizing because submission to the arbitrary law, to its unreasonability, gets us as close to unconscious enjoyment as anything can.

The coincidence of idealism with atrocity in chivalric culture is thus no mystery; it is what gives rise to the enjoyment of the state as well as of war. The group subject is "entitled" to a *jouissance* denied particular subjects, and this entitlement takes place through the medium of the law. And since codification implies the group—it is always addressed to "the community"—codification is a great way to mobilize. It mobilizes by clarifying how and when a signifier can be groupified and empowered to act as switchpoint between heterogeneous and homogeneous, communal and individual, forms of desire. *Troilus and Criseyde* gets its aesthetic and ethical power—including its power as tragedy—from its multiplication and foregrounding of such signifiers, chief of which are the names "Troilus" and "Criseyde." Troilus's and Criseyde's awareness of themselves as signifiers in a destinerring chain is part of the poem's chain of formal reflections on the meaning of submission: to fate, law, group meanings, the Trojan parliament, and (same thing) the destinerrings of desire. "Tragedye" is another such signifier; in Chaucer's poem, it marks the complicity, not the alienation, of private desire and public good. If sacrifice is recuperated by the narrator's turn to the constant love of Jesus, fruit of Marian consent, there is at least no doubt of the fact that Troilus has been royally screwed by Troy.

As Freud notes, rescuing the work of the fathers gives them new life.[58] But the life they are given is the uncanny life of the signifier that survives the life of the body. *Troilus and Criseyde* is full of intentional encounter with the nearly dead or the recently alive (the old but close-to-home examples narrated by Cassandra; the old (with the emphasis on *old*) men whose hands lay heavily on the futures of the young (Priam, Calchas); the dead husband who is never mentioned once. But, in keeping with the uncanny, oracular life of the signifier, nothing meaningful comes through on these channels. What are we to make of all this insignificance? Is it possible that, rather than bringing out the exchangeability of the masculine subject, the poem wants us to see Troilus as even more finely lost than Hector? Is this a rarefaction and interiorization of epic and tragedy (not easily distinguished in the Middle Ages), such that the group consequences so important to tragedy are simply, but intensely, named by Troilus's name and its destinerring in books? (V, 585).[59] Is this to say, to "Troy Novant," that the signifier's exchangeability might perhaps after all be recuperable as the iterability of legend, or as *translatio*, rather than as the mark of the ordinary, the proper subject of comedy? Perhaps, in losing even the public meaning of his sacrifice, Troilus's *ascesis* is all the greater; and this in turn may power the legend of his desire. But it is not clear that the uncertain futures crowding this ending do not just deterritorialize, by a precise appeal to the sacrifice of trust, the field of risk sanctified throughout chivalric discourse. Book V reveals that what Žižek calls "the second yes," the "yes" not only to honorable sacrifice but then also to the sacrifice of honor (i.e., giving up the chance to be appreciated for one's sacrifice), does not necessarily push the logic of sacrifice to destabilizing extremes.[60] Arguably, the only thing achieved by the second yes—we might call it the "second consent"—is the further rarefaction of sacrifice, through interiorization and/or "extratextual" relay. If the second yes is witnessed—and it cannot not be witnessed, if we know about it—the honor of sacrifice cannot finally be sacrificed. The masculine chivalric subject's loss of loss is, at least potentially, part of the logic of contest; its function may simply be to attest the lengths to which it is prepared to go to defend its faith, all the way to the sacrifice of faith in the faithless object.

At the end of Book V, when Troilus seems so alone with his fate, his revenance has him virtually transmitting by satellite. The narrator is still there to listen, and we ourselves read the traces in the book made of his life. To this extent, Troilus's story is still structured by the economy of sacrifice: it is devoted to recovering, with a difference that is also a bonus, whatever he relinquishes. The bonus is enhanced sentience and prosthetic power. Having crossed the line, Troilus can not only see and hear in a new way; he can commune with the living, because we can hear him. Chaucer's art, not just Troilus's, is implicated. Art, war, and love seem to share the enjoyment of a chosen chance to lose: "Go, litel bok" (V, 1786). To choose to lose is to reverse befallenness or melancholy into activity so active as to be godlike creativity or redemption. The *aventure* of making—perhaps the *aventure* of vernacularity, and/or that of tragedy writing, either of which could close the little book down or make it a media success—shares this much with sacrifice.

The sacrificial production of "the gift of the signifier" is at stake in many narratives about artistic creation and sublimation, narratives that repeatedly end mourning with the acquisition of symbolicity.[61] The structuring of historical writing on the arts through sublimation and subliming of melancholy is one of the most important and most naturalized frameworks for criticism on *Troilus and Criseyde*. As noted in previous chapters, the notion of Chaucer's "bent for play"—his lack of "high seriousness," his oscillation between "the sublime and the ridiculous"—has centrally shaped his literary-historical role as the "father of English poetry."[62] The "father of enjoyment," whose crude obscenities bespeak the barbarism of his age, but also the paternal ideal, whose perfect temper polishes whatever is rude, Chaucer is the split figure of origin through whom English cultural history has presented the plot of the sublimation of the nation. The split emerges, in fact, with the Renaissance, when the "*iuvens pater*" begins to show signs of corruption. Sixteenth-century English writers are the first to remark the rudeness and antiquity of Chaucer's work.[63]

The humanist could identify an ideal paternity in the reflectiveness and literacy of the classical philosopher—the *skola* as suspension of the world—and project onto the medieval past an excessive bent for action, thus screening the coerciveness of his own rhetoric. Stephanie Jed argues that "It is important to understand the humanistic codification of classical narratives of political violence not as a screen isolating humanists from authentic political activity, but as a particular political strategy in its own right, a strategy of suppression."[64] The idealization of a distant classical paternity resubjected the "man of letters" to the violence of the state while assigning cruelty to the medieval man of war and rudeness to medieval arts and letters. *Troilus and Criseyde* anticipates this future in its end: the new work of English tragedy finds itself anticlimactic compared to classical *auctores* and vulnerable to future misreading; the narrator himself is no more a "divinistre" than is the Knight. But the enjoyment of subjection at stake in humanist melancholy nonetheless owes a great deal to the medieval chivalric subject it disavows. In the Middle Ages, "melancholy" already suffuses discourses of desire, power, and knowledge: *tristitia, amor hereos, acedia,* but also the work of reflection and memory, are all conditions of exacerbated interiority serious (and often exalted) enough to signify, and to merit interpretation.[65] Chivalric subjectivity, that is, already exposes the interdependence of greatness and submission, melancholic reflection and violent action.

Certainly, *Troilus and Criseyde* seems to anticipate something of the association of sublimation with the transcendence of crisis that we find in some contemporary accounts of mourning (e.g., Kristeva's *Black Sun*).[66] To artifice the signifier, to get to be the giver of life in the symbolic order, is perhaps some reward for being one (though the downside of being a signifier has been greatly exaggerated by those who still want the self-present subject to stay in one piece). Chivalric rescue fantasy, as in Hector's eloquent attempts to make exchange a respecter of persons, tries for sublimation in Book V. Criseyde, on the other hand, living on the fumes of Hector's gift of life/death, fears risk. She survives, but *as* a failure at sublimity; her sacrifice of sacrifice does not tragedify her. She divines that, so far from achieving virtuosity with the signifier, her textual afterlife will be one of vilification—"thise bokes wol me shende" (V, 1060). But how are we to understand the poem's mutually exclusive distribution of life and good literary reputation? If submitting to "the first death" enables transmission between the living and the dead, is Chaucer going for it?

Possibly. One effect of *Troilus and Criseyde* is to problematize its characters' access to sublimity as a way of exacerbating tragedy's relation to *das Ding*. Might we not get closer to *das Ding* with tragic characters who do not entirely deliver on catastrophe? Is Criseyde not perhaps the sublime object manqué who gets us as close to *das Ding* as possible by abandoning the group altogether for the faithless oracular law itself, that is, Calchas, and the come-lately Diomede?[67] *Troilus and Criseyde* effects a certain desublimation—a delivering of enjoyment by writing the obscenity of the sacrificial pact, and hence of the group in whose name the subject sacrifices. If the signifier can never be securely distinguished from the patterning of the drives, making this evident is how a poem that "serves" love and enjoys its submission breaks out of the sacrificial economy. In doing so, *Troilus and Criseyde* denies any possibility of using "consent" to disambiguate the meaning of violence.

EPILOGUE

SOME THOUGHTS ON THE HUMANITIES

ENJOYING THE MIDDLE AGES

A number of the academics I have talked to about the movie *Babe* lay claim to it, but usually in a roundabout way; they feel that the movie revives something old that was also revived during their own period of study. Some think it is a pastoral, others a georgic. For me, *Babe* echoes the tropes of antiutilitarian medievalism in the nineteenth century.[1] *Babe* celebrates love between master and servant (these days, animals have to stand in for the peasants), and rural life as the scene in which such love might be rediscovered. It expresses distaste for technology, presenting the gift of a fax machine to Babe's farmer as epitome of the technophilia of arrogant youth. But *Babe* recuperates the fax; the fax saves the day by getting Babe into the sheepdog contest at the last minute. The movie also recuperates discipline as an aspect of the relation between master and man, or pig; Babe must work, learn, and prove himself, even if his talent issues in the first instance from his kind heart. As would antiutilitarian medievalist discourse of the nineteenth century, the film associates empty speech with commercialism and disbelief in the remarkable, and meaningful speech with Babe's taciturn but loving farmer—a man behind the times who nonetheless succeeds because he recognizes the distinctive gifts of his animals, even when they want to do the work of the "other" (when Babe wants to do the work of a sheepdog, or the duck the work of a rooster).[2]

An envious feline "thief of enjoyment" at one point explains to Babe that cats, because they are beautiful, need not be useful, and therefore are not eaten. Pigs, on the other hand, are destined to be food, and this was the fate of Babe's family. This information severely depresses Babe's desire to compete on his farmer's behalf in the upcoming sheepdog trials. There follows a scene in which Babe has to be convinced that his farmer loves him, that his relation to this other is not merely instrumental. Babe is not persuaded by food. Babe is persuaded that he is loved by the other only when the other produces art for him, that is, sings and dances for him. There is elaborated in the shockingly jubilant scene that follows the whole array of meanings Lacan brings out through his notions of the mirror stage and the design of the subject's desire by the signifier: a wild morning song lures Babe into life, love, and work, a song of promise that allows Babe to refind the lost *oikos* in his master: *If I had the words to make a day for you / I would sing you a morning golden and true / I would make this day last for all time for you.*

Babe suggests that sublimation does not redirect to the arts a drive that originates elsewhere, but rather arises in relation to the same designs on *jouissance* that structure subjectivity itself—the captivating images of the imaginary, or the protean divertissements of signifying chains. Sublimation arises through the same processes that construct the subject's desire of, for, and through the other, in short, through the subject's sociality. There is never a time when we are not artificed by arts, never a time when desire is fully separable from the desire to entertain and to be entertained: to engage the desire of the other and/or the Other. The subject is an auditor from the beginning; she is also a maker, and product of artifice and artifacts saturated with enjoyment through the economies of infant survival, economies that, like any other, must always overshoot their mark. *Babe*, moreover, suggests how closely artifactuality is connected with justice, in the form of the distribution of resources—functions, powers, wealth. Fortunately, medievalists on the whole do not need to be told that sublimation is intricately related to production, in part because of medievalism's history of attentiveness to the problem of alienation of labor, in the form of the distinction between artisanal and industrial production. More generally, it is the inescapable artfulness of subjectivation and sociality that the disciplines of the humanities are moved to study, and sophisticate, and make ever more artful.

Our enjoyment of the signifier is at the heart of our practice in literary and cultural studies; these disciplines, and their institutional matrices, are themselves modes of enjoyment. But we have permitted our attention to the issue of enjoyment to flag somewhat, partly because of the decisive critiques of formalism and aestheticism launched in recent decades from a variety of historicist and theoretical quarters. If, however, the dangers of divorcing the study of beauty from the study of sociality are now abundantly clear, the value of reclaiming the issue of enjoyment *for* culturalist projects seems to me also irresistible. When the humanities seeks to define the social and historical efficacies of its work, we too often elide the issue of our enjoyment by repeating oppositions between productivity and pleasure that privilege the former term at the expense of the latter—oppositions many of us would be unlikely to tolerate in our work.

It is not altogether surprising that we have, on the level of our institutional discourses, been prone to adopt rhetorics of need, utility, and productivity. These rhetorics are interior to the very historicisms—materialist and otherwise—that have shaped literary studies in the last two centuries. There are also reasons for such a susceptibility exterior to our disciplines: some of the celebrations of productivity we engage in on the level of theory and method converge with the powerful demand the humanities have faced in recent years that we demonstrate our public utility. In the last decade or so, we have become all too familiar with notions such as the following: the University of California really does not "need" (as though "necessity" had not been a term under strenuous philosophical review for centuries) graduate programs in women's studies at all of its campuses, nor for that matter in German. Such discussions inevitably reveal themselves as legacies of the tactics of cultural dispossession that operated so powerfully in Anglo-American politics of the 1980s. Had we altogether accepted the terms of "accountability" thus conceived, like Lear we would have ended up stripped down indeed.

Not all humanists, of course, admire the brilliant analyses of the notions of utility and necessity written by Marx, Bataille, Baudrillard, and Lacan.[3] Not all will be drawn to Donald's argument about the dependence of technological development on the human ability to dramatize counterfactual situations (he argues that dramas and fictions were vital in the acquisition of fire- and tool-making skills), or to Jacobs's arguments about the primacy of play, ornament, and élan in the development of technology.⁴ Jacobs cites Cyril Stanley Smith's argument that the "roots of invention are to be found... in motives like... 'esthetic curiosity.'"⁵ Smith contends that the demand for utilitarian or "realistic" (i.e., predictable, reassuring) outcomes can easily destroy inventions in their infancy, unless aesthetic curiosity protects these fragile "ventures" (our relation to "progress" is highly ambivalent). How, indeed, do we account for the astonishing fact that "man has the possibility of making his desires tradeable or salable in the form of products.... How is it possible?"⁶

But the recent turn to technology in the humanities often seems the result of a simple desire to associate our work with the glamour of robotics, the Internet, genetics research, virtual life, and the like (*anything* having to do with cyberspace, really); we do not *enact* the radical possibilities of these technologies for our institutional arrangements, teaching, or understandings of history.⁷ Even those of us enthusiastic about these topics, therefore, can miss the work being done in these very fields on enjoyment (e.g., Laurence A. Rickels, *The Case of California,* Daivd E. Nye, *American Technological Sublime*), to say nothing of our willingness to admire historians of science such as Michel Serres or Bruno Latour but ignore altogether the adventuresomeness of their historiographical methods.⁸ On the whole, the humanities qua institution continues to act as if it valorized work and its related figures of sacrifice and debt, accepting the canon of utility as though it functioned as a "real" index of value in any domain, and invoking necessity precisely so that the unnecessary, the luxurious, and the wasteful might be calculated and pared away.

But insofar as these strategies are designed to oppose and sometimes abject enjoyment, they are more likely than not to prove inimical, practically and theoretically, to the future of cultural and literary studies. The situation is complicated for medievalism per se because it has a history in reactionary as well as progressive antiutilitarian thought and practice. It is also complicated for progressive cultural studies because of the extent to which feminist, race, postcolonial, and queer theory have critiqued aestheticism, and have been associated with killjoy politics, whereby coalition formation must inevitably be a sacrifice of pleasure to political duty, and any desire for difference or change must be scrutinized for exoticism and expansionism. The extent to which race, class, gender, and sexuality theories have sought to remake and extend enjoyment, including enjoyment of literature and its interpretation, seems to have been largely muffled by the academy's own reprise of the discourse of "political correctness," a situation exacerbated by assumptions that psychoanalysis (home of enjoyment), or theory in general (home of totalization, never of critique thereof), are somehow more Western than the historical and cultural alteritism (Ireland *cannot* be discussed in the same terms as Scotland; "race" was not an issue as such during the Middle Ages); and research methodologies (recording, archiving, editing, appreciating) we learned chiefly from the nationalist/imperialist philologies of nineteenth-century Europe. (Of course, only if one approaches enjoyment in a certain way can one fully appreciate the fact that rigor on the political/cultural left has as much to do with the *jouissance* of the law as does rigor on the right. And why shouldn't we have our fun?) Further, the association of the topic of the humanities with the interests of not-very-interesting whites has not been helped by John Guillory's use of feminist theory and identity politics as foils for his attempt at an apparently bloodless (but in fact satisfyingly severe) understanding of the academy and its canons as *institutional*—as if institutions were not themselves structures of enjoyment, whose bids for power are as likely to be as passional and self-destructive, motivated by "no good," as are those of larger human polities; as if the privileging of certain texts had no points of connection with the circulation of signifiers constituting institutional practices of enjoyment.[9] It is one thing to say that *Paradise Lost* caused its place in the canon and quite another to say that there is nothing in *Paradise Lost* that speaks in particular to institutionalizers of knowledge/enjoyment. The poem is, after all, one lecture after another; it can barely wait to answer its own rhetorical questions, it is so excited by certainty: "The Serpent it was."

Despite associations of progressive academics with various thefts of enjoyment, few belletrists *or* basilisk-eyed latter-day Marxians have ever spoken more passionately *and* critically about the arts, and hence about the history and politics of *form*, than Toni Morrison in her literary criticism, or Eve Sedgwick in hers, to say nothing of Hortense Spillers, bell hooks, Sara Suleri, Luce Irigaray, Julia Kristeva, David Halperin, Lee Edelman, Edward Said—all barrier-breakers whose profound attachments to attachment and the power of words/images to bring it about are beyond question. If we study enjoyment *and* its social, political, and economical effectivities, we cannot helpfully cede its significance at the level of the academy's own local and national, sexual and ethnic, politics—especially, once again, if our disciplines have been formed as much by the nineteenth century's valorizing of passion as by its passion for technique.

For the most part, what we try to deliver to our audiences is the excitement of knowledgeable discourse (or "pleasurable analysis"), including knowledgeable discourse on excitement.[10] We are formidably helped in this by the extensive role played by knowledge creation in human play (the basic manual for the Dungeons and Dragons game called *Baldour's Gate* is 156 pages long) and by pleasure in human learning (we are wired to like to learn, however badly this can turn out in practice). It is crucial that we not idealize the connection between knowledge and enjoyment, or turn to another facile reconciliation of *dulce et utile*. Of course, it can be pleasurable for us to know useful things because they benefit and improve our lives. But are we sure we know what useful things and activities are, or that they exist independently of our creative activity? They seem to change all the time. There is something about the human activities of invention and production that is irreducibly gratuitous, excessive, fascinating. Luxurious things, and the luxuriousness of creativity, lead rather than follow "practical applications," nor are the latter the final cause of the former.

It is crucial, therefore, that we not give way to the discourse of crisis over our failures or marginality. Although specifics can vary—language departments, increasingly under threat of closure, might have few majors but many students; enrollment numbers can fluctuate from year to year, discipline by discipline, or in consequence of the recessions historically unfavorable to the humanities—we have not, on the whole, been losing positions because we lack students. We do not lack students. It is not even the case that the students who flock to us are either indolent or foolish; a classics major turns out to be one of the best preparations for law school, or at least the most promising indicator of future success.[11] But we all know that if humanities faculties have not been losing workload, at least compared to science faculties, we have been losing funding. (Some of the losses inflicted by the recession of the early 1990s have been recouped, but overall the humanities has lost ground, and federal funding agencies have atrophied almost completely.) This is not because of our irrelevance to managerial interests—if anything, the reverse is proving to be true—but because the value of (critical thinking about) enjoyment and symbolicity has come under attack in the course of attempts to deprive the "labor pool" of its discursive power, or, to be more precise, in the course of attempts to goupify and manage its discursivities and pleasures, including its pleasure in discursivity. I am sorry to sound paranoid, but when Shakespeare makes it big in popular culture but new funding for teaching and research on Shakespeare is scanty, something funny is going on. The draining of funding from humanities departments and its "return" in the form of masters in liberal arts programs inspired and funded by corporate interests is one of the clearest examples of this phenomenon.

Meanwhile, our mathematical knowledges, hence our expertise in relation to the signifier in that register, produce ever more brilliant prostheses of subjectivity, but disavow the passions at stake in, and set in train by, this project. Despite the similarity between the ambivalences that attend theoretical discourse in physics as well as in humanities, many scientists perplexingly ascribe relativism to humanistic approaches to the history and discourse of science. Despite the importance of recent scientific research demonstrating that the signifier can alter brain chemistry *and* vice versa (e.g., that psychotherapy can be very helpful, even without benefit of medication, in many instances of depression), many psychology departments continue ironically to "scientize" themselves by repudiating clinical work as just so much mumbo jumbo. Sociology departments often play out internally these supposed oppositions between the verbal and mathematical signifier.

But the thick presence of enjoyment that has always been characteristic of science is just as disavowed as ever. The August 2000 issue of *Scientific American* features as its second full-spread ad (for a company that sells patent validity insurance) a photograph of a faceless young lady in a form-fitting black dress encircled with loop after loop of ignited fuse. (Scientists like to take risks, it seems, but should still protect their "intellectual property transactions," which are symbolized—why not?!—by young ladies with slicked-down red hair.) The flourishing on the Internet of pornography and highly skilled vandalism indicates that the symbolicity of cyberspace designs, and is designed by, *jouissance* as prosthesis for the unconscious itself, as does the national discourse about "addiction" to cyberspace and our double-binding rhetorics of fear that our children will become obsessed and fear that they will be left behind in the race to "keep up" with the newest technology.[12] Focusing our analytical work on either the regulatory power or the liberatory potential of cybersignification will only obscure the intrications of mechanicity and passion, and the ethical ambiguities, at stake in how and why we produce "works" and put them into the world. Our enjoyment is first and foremost with and of the signifier, as is obvious when one spends more than one second talking to a theoretical physicist about the idea of "elegance."

For us to foreground symbolicity and enjoyment, and to insist on their sociality, is to get to the heart of the human matter, unfortunately (for our funding) by making problems for the many necessitarian and utilitarian rhetorics that sustain the *jouissance* of capitalism. But the evidence suggests that we have gained very little by capitulating to the discourses of knowledge institutions with which we are, or are soon to be, *competing*, except, of course, the enjoyment of destructivity and/or of dispassion for our work, both of which have not been unexampled within the academy in the last two decades. Classics—who needs 'em? (except for aspiring attorneys). So that we can win the enrollment numbers game (enrollment numbers have proved to be good sticks to beat ourselves with, but what exactly are the demonstrated financial rewards of swelling classroom size?), let's cut those unpopular classics requirements out of our major, and while we are at it, let's get rid of the Middle Ages too. German (pace the European Union)—why bother? Everyone speaks English, because it is globalizing. Never mind the fact that nothing about the history of language change supports the notion that a "world language" is going to provide the alibi we seem to be seeking on this score, or that the fastest-growing languages now are Arabic and Chinese.

Very simply, then, we would do well to teach and write more explicitly about enjoyment. We should also be more enjoyable. I want to be clear, though, that by "more enjoyable" I do not mean "more pleasurable" or "easy." If this book has accomplished anything, I hope it has clarified that pleasure is only one of the forms—the most homeostatic one—that enjoyment takes. It is not that we should scorn pleasure, but its pursuit as a goal in and of itself, particularly in the context of pedagogy, must inevitably yield the *regulation* of enjoyment as its primary result. One of the central functions of pleasure is protection from trauma, which means the minimizing of unfamiliarity. Pleasure therefore always poses a potential threat to experiences of curiosity and wonder, to risk, to work that has not yet become habitual (pleasure can be quite comfortable with the latter). The survival of the humanities in the academy depends on our power to provoke curiosity and wonder. Let's take more risks with our enjoyment, with the fact that what makes our work distinctive is precisely its *foregrounding* of enjoyment.

The humanities in general, and medieval studies in particular, *must* put more of a premium on teaching, by every means possible. (I do not mean to pit research against teaching; most of the good teachers I know are also good scholars.) It is also crucial that we not wield canons of utility or necessity like blunt objects when we rethink our institutional arrangements and the subjects we teach and research. If we want the humanities to have a future, we have to see through the false promise that if we are *highly* efficient and productive and eager to retrain and regroup, we will ipso facto be rewarded with smaller classes, better pay, and actual clerical assistance. These goals might be worthy, but reaching them guarantees nothing because it is the United States today's structure of knowledge/enjoyment that we are up against, not rational calculations of interest (except insofar as the latter provide the former). Let's teach more about modes of knowledge/enjoyment, in the Middle Ages or any other time. What was the "elegance" of scholasticism for those who loved it, and why did they love it so much? We should take up even more generally the question of the *jouissance* of the academy, rather than assuming that it is our ethical task to discipline *jouissance* out of the academy. For one thing, we *cannot* discipline *jouissance* out of the academy, because discipline is always permeated with enjoyment. So why give ground on our enjoyment?

In medieval studies, as noted in chapter 1, our current treatment of the "problem" of popular medievalism is perhaps the biggest symptom of our hesitation. We ask ourselves how we can make use of historically licentious mass-culture medievalisms to lure students into courses that will correct their impressions but not extinguish their enthusiasms. Is popular medievalism really of no interest to medieval studies except as lure? Isn't it the lure that made many of us medievalists, even those of us who became medievalists because of our religious faith, or apostasy? What is the status of a lure that populates a discipline? Medievalism today is a limit case in contemporary discourses of instructional utility partly because of its own role in the history of utilitarian thought. It is also because of this history that medievalism still has the power to promise both protection and risk. Through the form of the benign paternalism of masters (or wizards), as well as through the figure of armored combat and the meaningful "front," medievalism "screens," in both senses, *jouissance*.[13] It points the way to the ecstatic location where we, as "moderns," come to an end, and defends against the deadliness of that ecstatic possibility. The relentless association, from the Renaissance onwards, of the Middle Ages with the "hypereconomy" of the gift (with whatever exceeds calculation or rationality), for good or for ill, has made the Middle Ages a marker of fantasy and excess, including excessive privation. It continues to have a vast cultural address in the contemporary United States precisely as a figure of the unnecessary and the extraordinary, the curious and the wondrous.[14] As, then, a preeminent symptom, in Las Vegas, in Marx, and in Joseph Warton's *Essay on the Genius and Writings of Pope* (1756/1782), of the passional quality of economic thought and practice, the Middle Ages of modernity still can inspire a thinking of the interdependence of need and desire, conservation and (in Bataille's sense) "expenditure."

The Middle Ages is not just one index among others of the power of fantasy to make history. When we consider how the imaginaries of contemporary popular medievalism might be negotiated by academic medievalism—especially in that the latter is usually powered by the histories we love, by what entertains us as children—we should remember the crucial role nineteenth-century medievalism played in laying the groundwork for the welfare state, including public funding of education. We still "think" the "role of government" in the terms of medievalist critiques of capitalism and utilitarianism (including those of Marx and William Morris) and responses thereto. Medieval discourses of charity were resituated in nineteenth-century rhetorics of responsibility for the other, which in turn informed Romanticist and Victorian historiography, as well as more recent alteritisms. Insofar as medieval culture spoke relentlessly of love and its just deserts, it still haunts our discussions of responsibility to the other, and instances how powerfully the memorial inscriptions of history can move us to read them.

Responsibility, attachment, the polis, enjoyment—these questions have been central to academic discourse at least since Socrates:

> The gift *(doron)* of Mnemosyne, Socrates insists, is like the wax in which all that we wish to guard in our memory is engraved in relief so that it may leave a mark, like that of rings, bands, or seals. We preserve our memory and our knowledge of them; we can then speak of them, and do them justice, as long as their image *(eidolon)* remains legible.[15]

Socrates wishes for a mark that will be legible, for an interior writing of memory that will be a true representation. This true representation dwells within us; it is a matter of property:

> [E]ven the best of writings are but a reminiscence of what we know, and... only in principles of justice and goodness and nobility taught and communicated orally for the sake of instruction and graven in the soul, which is the true way of writing, is there clearness and perfection and seriousness, and... such principles are a man's own and his legitimate offspring.[16]

The truth of this memorializing representation that is not mere "reminiscence" enables a proper repetition—"we can then speak of them"—so that the life will continue, "offspring," a living speech of the dead who live on through proper representation and repetition.

And thus "justice" (*dike*) will be done; justice or "right," which depends on a true representation, on the repeatability of the *eidolon* so that it can be properly adjudicated. One of the early senses of *dike* is "custom"; there is traceable in its history the transformation of custom into ideality, a transformation also being pursued in the *Phaidros*, where the spoken—what is graven in the heart, the principles by which one must live—is not less true than the laws that are fixed in stone, that anyone can read, but more so, because they live and breathe. So those who are truly within the customary principles of their culture, because those customary principles are truly within them, are those who can defeat the differences that threaten proper repetition, and thus can guard and protect the *eidolon*. This question of who is in and who is out, of who has the habitus engraved in the heart and who, as outsider, learns it only from tablets, is pursued as a question about communicative technologies—what Middleton refers to, in the context of medieval studies, as the "circumstance[s] of production, dissemination and reception."[17] In short, it is a question for "philology."

Derrida will go on to ask:

> Is the most distressing, or even the most deadly infidelity that of a *possible mourning* which would interiorize within us the image, idol, or ideal of the other who is dead and lives only in us? Or is it that of the impossible mourning, which, leaving the

other his alterity, respecting thus his infinite remove, either refuses to take or is incapable of taking the other within oneself, as in the tomb or the vault of some narcissism? (*Memoires*, 6)

The interiorization of the *eidolon* described by Socrates, and also by Freud in "Mourning and Melancholia," might involve a deadly infidelity because no perfect repetition of the *eidolon* is possible. "Within us" is such a different place from "in itself"; "only" the image of what is lost survives; and it "only" survives within us. The ethical crisis that attends mourning is the same that attends creation in general, including the production of art, of the aestheticized as well as mnemonic signifer. Socrates longs for the living as well as the engraving. At least, he reinscribes the material circumstances of textual production within the body—a culture and cultivation of the heart—in order to certify, to substantiate, the infinite repeatability of the immaterial *eidolon*.

But it is best to say, not that we have nothing in the *eidolon*, but that the categorical distinction between it and the living presence to which it refers is not clear. Should the trajectory of mourning be read as the replacement of living presence by signifier? I think rather it should be read as the attempt to signify the finitude of creatures who bear the signifier. The surplus or leftover signifier could not exist without that once-living presence having lived, nor could that former living presence have lived the way it did without this signifier, this "nothing," this paradoxical marker of the intrication of repeatability and unrepeatability that is signification itself and hence is memory. Mourning makes this passion of the signifier painfully apparent. The dead do not live on in us through our images of them, and yet they do, because the form of their living on is the form of their very unrepeatability. They live on, that is, only insofar as they are interiorized, in a mode that indicates their being as something unrepeatable that will be subjected to endlessly inventive technologies of repetition. There is no way for the alterations made in us by our fidelity to the loved other not to be grievous. But part of our guilt is that loving and honoring the other is inseparable from the dedication of our enjoyment to "form": to the activity of resignification and the status of the other as signifier, to the other's mode of "being as signifier" (Lacan, *Ethics of Psychoanalysis*, 214).

It is when we are most anxious to preserve the past that we know we have not done justice and cannot properly "speak of them." To speak of them seems to set aside their set-apartness. Yet we cannot not speak of them, and also they cannot not remain other to us, in part because of the mnemonic imperative of signification itself. We cannot not change them, because they do live on in us, and yet they cannot be changed, certainly their deadness cannot be changed, the life they lead now is not the life they once led. And yet they could not have led either life without the very vicissitudes of the signifer that produce this paradoxicality in the first place. The deadly or inhuman limit that is the Other, the unconscious, inhabits the living subject. We live in relation to the inanimacy of the signifier, and this is what we memorialize.

In renewing the old customs whereby "our" culture "recovered" the past, "the new philology," as announced in the January 1990 special issue of *Speculum*, sought specifically to recover the very means whereby medieval culture preserved itself, remembered itself, guarded and protected its past—and did not. This latter-day philology repeated in the register of the signifier what romanticism registered as love; instead of trying to remember a lost age of fidelity, we try to remember its means of remembering. We mount a defense: a phobic valorizing of philological practice as capable of "standing in for" the failed relation to the object, whether it be an object of love, of reference, or of historicist reconstruction. The enhancement of philological technique through the already-duplicated form of a recuperation of *medieval* philology marks the spot of the death drive of our discipline—a term that seems justified by the somewhat mixed results of the philological *renovatio* in terms of medieval studies' reputation for liveliness. We vivify ourselves by tasting, by trying on, the catastrophe of the ending that would be our *jouissance*. We seek to live through our simultaneous embrace and denial of the deadliness and nonjustice at the heart of the mnemonics of sublimation. The question I find most urgent at the moment is whether we even know how to enjoy our symptom, let alone work through it. The emphasis one sometimes finds on the "playful" aspects of textuality in discussions of manuscript culture, for example, seems a failure in this respect, that is, a repression precisely of the cruelly passional aspects of play, as inexorably present in the signifying play of calculus as in that of children.

The institutional significance of the emergence, in the last decade or so, of the new philology, this elaboration of mnemotechnique for the true representation of mnemotechnique, seems, then, to be in part the thrill of technique itself, that is, the hyperdisciplining of access to the deadly mechanicity of *jouissance:* the thrill of our "subject's" extinction, and of our continuing ability, as ghostly survivors, to talk about it. We situate ourselves as about-to-be postapocalypse, our medievalism therefore as much a part of our time as the medievalism of Mad Max or *Screamers.* Our lamentations about the marginality of medieval studies are concomitants of our valorization of technically enhanced communication with the dead—the founders of our discipline as well as the forephilologists of the Middle Ages. The *Speculum* issue on the new philology remains a fascinating document of our "true discourse" on how we skirt the edge of extinction. Nichols remarks that "the consensus seems to be that medieval philology has been marginalized by contemporary cognitive methodologies" and asks philology to "minimize the isolation between medieval studies and other contemporary movements in cognitive methodologies"; Patterson says that "medieval studies is a marginalized institution."[18] We need to decipher in medieval studies' *self-*marginalization both the destructivity within us and the enjoyment produced by our management of it, by the rarefaction of our phantasmic modes of triumph over deadliness: medievalism's gift of death.

Insofar as history is always and inevitably retrospectively constituted, insofar as the work of signification is inseparable from memory and desire, insofar as the passional and the technical coincide in the register of our *jouissance,* we could not, even if we wanted to, stop creating, or more properly re-creating, new prostheses of memory. I hope we will continue reflecting on the relations between philology and other forms of medievalism, including popular medievalism, and that we will explore rather than assume differences between contemporary medievalisms on the score of technique and knowledge. Otherwise, we will find ourselves in the mode of Socratic cultivation, saying that those who do not possess philological skills do not possess worthy ways of remembering the past, because they are forced to rely on the now-discredited, dead, humanistic "text" instead of on the living exuberance of medieval "textuality." Should we not seek to understand more carefully here the many forms of cruelty—the passional exactions of memory, the murderous resituations of life and death—that intimately, or "extimately," haunt our fidelity to, our loving of, what is gone, especially when what is gone is that period marked for us, by itself and by later centuries, as the very time of love?

NOTES

INTRODUCTION

1. Jacques Lacan, *The Seminar of Jacques Lacan: Book VII: The Ethics of Psychoanalysis, 1959–1960*, ed. Jacques-Alain Miller, trans. Dennis Porter (New York: Norton, 1992), 3.

2. "Mode of enjoyment" is Slavoj Žižek's phrase. See *The Sublime Object of Ideology* (New York: Verso, 1989), 114–16. "Enjoyment" is often used to translate *jouissance*. Žižek's term "mode of enjoyment," however, seems to designate any organized relationship to *jouissance*, including pleasures and methods of avoidance ("Eastern Europe's Republics of Gilead," *New Left Review* 183 [1990]: 50–62, at 52).

3. Julia Kristeva, "Psychoanalysis and the *Polis*," trans. Margaret Waller, in *The Critical Tradition: Classic Texts and Contemporary Trends*, 2d ed., ed. David Richter (Boston: Bedford, 1998), 1075–86, at 1076.

4. Ibid.: "Only one theoretical breakthrough [psychoanalysis] seems consistently to *mobilize* resistances, rejections, and deafness."

5. On techniques of living—vocational, ethical, religious, affective, political—see Sigmund Freud, *Civilization and Its Discontents*, trans. James Strachey (New York: Norton, 1961), 26–34; see also Michel Foucault, *The History of Sexuality*, vol. 3, *The Care of the Self*, trans. Robert Hurley (London: Allen Lane/Penguin, 1986), on the development of the "art of existence" "under the theme of the care of oneself" (44), wherein "one is called upon to take oneself as an object of knowledge and a field of action," so as to transform, correct, and purify oneself, and find salvation (42).

6. Lacan, *Ethics of Psychoanalysis*: "why is it necessary that thinkers in the field of ethics always return to the ethical problem of the relation of pleasure to the final good . . . ?" "How does one explain that internal demand which constrains the ethical philosopher to try to reduce the antimonies [sic] associated with this theme"? (36) See also 292–93 on the "demand for happiness" in the context of Aristotelian ethics.

7. Dante Alighieri, *De Monarchia*; in *Those Who Fought: An Anthology of Medieval Sources*, ed. Peter Speed (New York: Italica, 1996), 41; hereafter cited in the text as *Those Who Fought*.

8. Jacques Derrida discusses the economy of sacrifice in *The Gift of Death*, trans. David Wills (Chicago: University of Chicago Press, 1995), 94–102.

9. Slavoj Žižek, "From the Courtly Game to *The Crying Game*," *re:Post* 1 (1993): 7.

10. The big Ōther is Lacan's term for the symbolic structures into which we are born. I use the following style: "Ōther" refers to the symbolic order and/or the unconscious structured by it; "Other" is the fantasy O⁻ther that is full, consistent, and all-knowing; "other" refers to particular others—objects, people, figurations thereof—which can bear the significance of either the "Other" or the "Ōther." The Ōther ("barred") refers to the symbolic order as *itself* lacking, senseless, unconscious, and the Other ("unbarred") to a fantasy of the symbolic order as ordered by Reason or at least by reasons.

11. *Jouissance* is pleasure so intense and overwhelming that it verges on, or becomes, unpleasurable. "Ecstasy" and "rapture" are analogous, but *jouissance* refers to corporeal experience, and its most specific meaning is orgasm. The term is discussed more fully later in this section. The formal patterning of body/drive/subject in relation to pleasure is a highly important theme in developmental psychology. See Daniel N. Stern, *The Interpersonal World of the Infant: A View from Psychoanalysis and Developmental Psychology* (New York: Basic Books, 1985), on the organization of "domains [of relatedness]... as distinct forms of experiencing social life and self" (31–33).

12. Gilles Deleuze and Félix Guattari write that "There is, in fact, a joy that is immanent to desire as though desire were filled by itself and its contemplations" (*A Thousand Plateaus: Capitalism and Schizophrenia*, trans. Brian Massumi [Minneapolis: University of Minnesota Press, 1987], 155). See also Julia Kristeva, *Tales of Love*, trans. Leon S. Roudiez (New York: Columbia University Press, 1987), who argues that the song of the troubadour "carries no referential, objective signification, it is the meaning of joy" (282).

13. Lacan discusses Romans 7:7 in *Ethics of Psychoanalysis* at 83–84: "The dialectical relationship between desire and the Law causes our desire to flare up only in relation to the Law, through which it becomes the desire for death."

14. Lacan argues that classical ethics offers well-regulated pleasure in return for the sacrifice of *jouissance* (ibid., 27).

15. Deleuze and Guattari, *A Thousand Plateaus*, 155.

16. Jacques Lacan, *The Four Fundamental Concepts of Psycho-analysis*, trans. Alan Sheridan (New York: Norton, 1977/1981), 115. As Freud puts it, "In the individual's mental life someone else is invariably involved, as a model, as an object, as a helper, as an opponent; and so from the very first individual psychology... is at the same time social psychology as well" (Sigmund Freud, *Group Psychology and the Analysis of the Ego*, trans. and ed. James Strachey [New York: Norton, 1959], 1).

17. Žižek, "Eastern Europe's Republics of Gilead," 56.

18. Eugen Weber, *Apocalypses: Prophecies, Cults, and Millennial Beliefs through the Ages* (Cambridge: Harvard University Press, 1999), 52–53, 77.

19. On cognition as group process, see Edwin Hutchins, *Cognition in the Wild* (Cambridge: MIT Press, 1995), for example, xii, "cognition [is] socially distributed"; on ethics as group process, see Irvin D. Yalom, *The Theory and Practice of Group Psychotherapy*, 4th ed. (New York: Basic Books, 1970/1995): "norms are created relatively early in the life of a group" (112).

20. Michel de Certeau, *The Writing of History*, trans. Tom Conley (New York: Columbia University Press, 1988), 61.

21. Foucault's *Care of the Self* is an important example; also David Halperin, *Saint Foucault: Towards a Gay Hagiography* (New York: Oxford University Press, 1995); *Pink Freud*, ed. Diana Fuss, *Gay and Lesbian Quarterly* 2 (1995); *Ethical Politics*, ed. Vassilis Lambropoulos, special issue of *South Atlantic Quarterly* 95 (1996); Judith Butler, *Bodies That Matter: On the Discursive Limits of "Sex"* (New York and London: Routledge, 1993). *Constructing Medieval Sexuality*, ed. Karma Lochrie, Peggy McCracken, and James A. Schultz (Minneapolis: University of Minnesota Press, 1997), is a good collection of medievalist work on these topics; see also *Premodern Sexualities*, ed. Louise Fradenburg and Carla Freccero (New York: Routledge, 1996), and see Judson Boyce Allen, *The Ethical Poetic of the Later Middle Ages: A Decorum of Convenient Distinction* (Toronto: University of Toronto Press, 1982).

22. Stephen Orgel, *The Illusion of Power: Political Theater in the English Renaissance* (Berkeley: University of California Press, 1975); Jonathan Goldberg, *James I and the Politics of Literature: Jonson, Shakespeare, Donne, and Their Contemporaries* (Baltimore: Johns Hopkins University Press, 1983); Richard C. McCoy, *The Rites of Knighthood: The Literature and Politics of Elizabethan Chivalry* (Berkeley: University of California Press, 1989).

23. Paul Strohm, *Social Chaucer* (Cambridge: Harvard University Press, 1989) and *Hochon's Arrow: The Social Imagination of Fourteenth-Century Texts* (Princeton, N.J.: Princeton University Press, 1992); David Wallace, *Chaucerian Polity* (Stanford, Calif.: Stanford University Press, 1997); Lee W. Patterson, *Chaucer and the Subject of History* (Madison: University of Wisconsin Press, 1991); Carolyn Dinshaw, *Chaucer's Sexual Poetics* (Madison: University of Wisconsin Press, 1989); Gayle Margherita, *The Romance of Origins: Language and Sexual Difference in Middle English Literature* (Philadelphia: University of Pennsylvania Press, 1994).

24. Judith Butler, *The Psychic Life of Power* (Stanford, Calif.: Stanford University Press, 1997); Robert Miklitsch, ed., *Psycho-Marxism: Marxism and Psychoanalysis Late in the Twentieth Century*, special issue of *South Atlantic Quarterly* 97 (1998).

25. The "history of the signifier" is my term for Lacan's idea of a history of how the function of marking has been realized in relation to enjoyment; see *Ethics of Psychoanalysis*, 139–45, and Lacan, *The Four Fundamental Concepts of Psycho-analysis*, 208.

26. Merlin Donald, *Origins of the Modern Mind: Three Stages in the Evolution of Culture and Cognition* (Cambridge: Harvard University Press, 1991).

27. Jean-Charles Hûchet, *Littérature médiévale et psychanalyse: pour une clinique littéraire* (Paris: Presses universitaires de France, 1990); Lee W. Patterson, *Negotiating the Past* (Madison: University of Wisconsin Press, 1987); Jonathan Goldberg, *Queering the Renaissance* (Durham, N.C.: Duke University Press, 1994), 5–6 (see also his brilliant essay "The History That Will Be," in Fradenburg and Freccero, *Premodern Sexualities*, 3–21); María Rosa Menocal, *Shards of Love: Exile and the Origins of the Lyric* (Durham, N.C.: Duke University Press, 1994); Carolyn Dinshaw, who breaks the mold in *Getting Medieval: Sexualities and Communities, Pre- and Postmodern* (Durham, N.C.: Duke University Press, 1999); Kathleen Biddick, *The Shock of Medievalism* (Durham, N.C.: Duke University Press, 1999).

28. Elaine Scarry develops these meanings in *The Body in Pain: The Making and Unmaking of the World* (New York: Oxford University Press, 1985); see esp. 285–306.

29. Scarry, *The Body in Pain*, argues that sentience extends itself through prostheses—buildings, telescopes, clothing, computers—whereas pain disables this activity. See also Freud on prosthesis in *Civilization and Its Discontents*, 41–43. Freud theorized the relation between vitality and libidinality in terms of *anaclisis*, the notion that libido is "propped" upon the drives that work for survival (Jean Laplanche and Jean-Bertrand Pontalis, *The Language of Psychoanalysis*, trans. Donald Nicholson-Smith [London: Karnac and the Institute of Psycho-Analysis, 1973/1988], s.v. "Anaclisis"). See also Stern's discussion of "vitality affects" in *The Interpersonal World of the Infant*, 53ff.

30. Deleuze and Guattari, *A Thousand Plateaus*, 273.

31. "The developed tool is the nascent form of the non-I. The tool brings exteriority into a world where the subject has a part in the elements it distinguishes" (Georges Bataille, *Theory of Religion*, trans. Robert Hurley [New York: Zone, 1992], 27–28).

32. Lacan, *Ethics of Psychoanalysis*, 293.

33. Derrida, *Gift of Death*, 65; Lacan, *Ethics of Psychoanalysis*, 119ff., on "the question of what man does when he makes a signifier" (119); "everybody knows what may emerge from a vase or what can be put in one. And it is obvious that... optimism is in no way justified by the way things function in the human world, nor by what is born of its works. Thus it is around the question of the benefit or the cost of a work that the crisis of consciousness has crystallized" (122).

34. *Dépense* ("expenditure") is Bataille's term for the *jouissance* of destruction, of giving away and giving way. The prestige-producing destruction of goods on ritual occasions—potlatch, the sacrifice described in Frederick II's Preamble—are examples of *dépense*, *jouissance* unleashed thereby, but in Bataille's view do so in order to maximize returns. See Georges Bataille, "The Notion of Expenditure," in *Visions of Excess: Selected Writings, 1927–1939*, ed. and trans. Allan Stoekl (Minneapolis: University of Minnesota Press, 1985), 116–129. For the Preamble to the Constitutions of Melfi, see *Those Who Fought*, 43.

35. Scarry, *The Body in Pain*, 13–14.

36. On the godsend, see Jacques Derrida, "My Chances/Mes Chances: A Rendezvous with Some Epicurean Stereophonies," in *Taking Chances: Derrida, Psychoanalysis, and Literature*, ed. Joseph Smith and William Kerrigan (Baltimore: Johns Hopkins University Press, 1984), 4–31, for example, 5; hereafter cited in the text as "My Chances/Mes Chances."

37. Law code of Alfonso the Wise, King of Castile and Leon, ca. 1254, in Speed, *Those Who Fought*, 40.

38. Scarry, *The Body in Pain*, 31.

39. Friedrich Nietzsche, *The Birth of Tragedy*, trans. Francis Golffing (New York: Anchor, 1956), 29.

40. See Bataille, *Theory of Religion*, on "the common project of developing the means of production" (93).

41. Sigmund Freud, *Beyond the Pleasure Principle*, trans. James Strachey (New York: Norton, 1975).

42. Suicide is the second most common cause of death among adolescents in the United States today; anyone of any age is more likely to die by means of suicide than homicide; and the intimacy of suicide with the signifier is beyond question, because 80 percent of reported suicides talk about killing themselves before they do so. See Jerrold S. Maxmen and Nicholas G. Ward, *Essential Psychopathology and Its Treatment* (New York: Norton, 1995), 23–24.

43. See Žižek, *Sublime Object of Ideology*, 76–79, on that which is "in you more than yourself."

44. See Laurence A. Rickels, *The Case of California* (Baltimore: Johns Hopkins University Press, 1991), 193–94, on "Freud's conviction that indifference toward objects antedates any libidinal orientation. Here... lies the first dim representation of an urge to die."

45. Jacques Lacan, *The Seminar of Jacques Lacan: Book II: The Ego in Freud's Theory and in the Technique of Psychoanalysis, 1954–55*, ed. Jacques-Alain Miller, trans. Sylvana Tomaselli (New York: Norton, 1991), 7. Lacan emphasizes that "[d]iscontinuity... is the essential form in which the unconscious first appears to us as a phenomenon... something is manifested as a vacillation" (*Four Fundamental Concepts of Psycho-analysis*, 25).

46. Geoffrey Chaucer, *The Parliament of Fowls*, l. 602. All citations to Chaucer's poetry are from *The Riverside Chaucer*, 3d ed., ed. Larry D. Benson (Boston: Houghton Mifflin, 1987).

47. Charles Homer Haskins, *The Renaissance of the Twelfth Century* (Cambridge: Harvard University Press, 1927).

48. Kristeva, *Tales of Love*, 280. Sarah Kay explores "the problem of origins" in "The Contradictions of Courtly Love and the Origins of Courtly Poetry," *Journal of Medieval and Early Modern Studies* 26 (spring 1996): 209–53, esp. 209–12. See also Roger Boase, *The Origin and Meaning of Courtly Love* (Manchester: Manchester University Press, 1976).

49. On narratives about the romance, see Sarah Kay, *The Chansons de Geste in the Age of Romance: Political Fictions* (Oxford: Clarendon Press, 1995), 2.

50. See John M. Graham, "National Identity and the Politics of Publishing the Troubadours," in *Medievalism and the Modern Temper*, ed. R. Howard Bloch and Stephen G. Nichols (Baltimore: Johns Hopkins University Press, 1996), 57–94.

51. Kristeva mourns the passing of courtly love and our "post-romantic nostalgia" in *Tales of Love*, 296.

52. Menocal, *Shards of Love*, emphasizes medieval vernacularity and "the strongly historical specificity of medieval literatures and... cultures" (38).

53. Žižek, "From the Courtly Game to *The Crying Game*," 5. See also his discussion of "Repetition in History" in *Sublime Object of Ideology*, 58–62.

54. Deleuze and Guattari, *A Thousand Plateaus*, 155.

55. Lacan, *Ethics of Psychoanalysis*, 146–50.

56. Žižek's most entertaining discussion of the Lacanian concept of the Real is *Looking Awry: An Introduction to Jacques Lacan through Popular Culture* (Cambridge: October/ MIT Press, 1991). "Social reality is... nothing but a fragile, symbolic cobweb that can at any moment be torn aside by an intrusion of the real" (17). The Real is unconscious to either group or individual subjectivity, escaping the categories (subject versus object, ani-

mate versus inanimate) that structure the symbolic order. Lacan remarks that "the real is beyond the *automaton*, the return, the coming-back, the insistence of the signs, by which we see ourselves governed by the pleasure principle. The real is that which always lies behind the automaton" (*Four Fundamental Concepts of Psycho-analysis*, 53–54).

57. Lacan discusses the function of the *stain*, one example of which is the power of the eyes of a predatory insect to *impress* its prey. This instance marks "the pre-existence to the seen of a given-to-be-seen," just as the intense colors of the butterfly constitute "a gratuitous *showing*, in which is marked for us the primal nature of the essence of the gaze" (*Four Fundamental Concepts of Psycho-analysis*, 74–76). "Showing" refers to a "showing off" independent of the intentions of a self-present subject, and is thus a useful term for the elaborate disguising that goes on in love and war (disguising in its primal senses, both attracting and occluding vision): "Modifying the formula I have of desire as unconscious—*man's desire is the desire of the Other*—I would say that it is a question of a sort of desire *on the part of* the Other, at the end of which is the *showing*" (ibid., 115). "Showing" displays on the level of the signifier; it does not explain or mean, but rather attracts the gaze and unfolds a visual structure in relation to it. The functions of this structure run the gamut from deception to threat to gratuitous brilliance, arbitrarily fascinating. Language "shows" verbally, not necessarily intending certain meanings, but rather displaying a structure and process of marking as such.

58. See Barbara Johnson, "Writing," in *Critical Terms for Literary Study*, 2d ed., ed. Frank Lentricchia and Thomas McLaughlin (Chicago: University of Chicago Press, 1990/1995), 42.

59. The *finamen* of the *trobairitz* (the women troubadours) is not always masculine; Meg Bogin includes poems written by women to women in *The Women Troubadours: An Introduction to the Women Poets of Twelfth-Century Provence and a Collection of Their Poems* (New York: Norton, 1980); see also John Boswell, *Christianity, Social Tolerance, and Homosexuality: Gay People in Western Europe from the Beginning of the Christian Era to the Fourteenth Century* (Chicago: University of Chicago Press, 1980), esp. 370–74. See chapter 5 for discussion of Alceste in this regard.

60. The object, as Bataille explains it in *Theory of Religion*, "is strictly alien to the subject.... It is the subject's property, the subject's thing, but is nonetheless impervious to the subject" (29).

61. "Subliming" is the process by which it is possible "to give an object, which in this case is called the Lady, the value of representing the Thing" (Lacan, *Ethics of Psychoanalysis*, 126; see also 112, 118–19, 158). As object, the Lady "stands for" the continuity of the human order with that of the signifier.

62. This recognition need not take place on the level of the subject, but on the level of the signifiers themselves, which "know" how to do what they do (as cells "know" what to let inside their borders and what to keep out). This emphasis on the significance of "code" or "information" is central to Lacan's decentering of the subject and the privilege of "knowledge" as it has been linked there.

63. Lacan, *Four Fundamental Concepts of Psycho-analysis*, 20, referring to the work of Claude Lévi-Strauss. According to Lévi-Strauss, Nature's signifiers are organized into "themes of opposition." Lacan's work is generally interested in many signifying techniques: ratios,

equations, topologies, and the "homeomorphic" and "heteromorphic" orders of identification discussed in his famous essay "The Mirror Stage as Formative of the I" (in *Écrits: A Selection*, trans. Alan Sheridan [New York: Norton, 1977], 1–7).

64. For example, the difference between the voiced or unvoiced alveopalatal stop, <d> and <t> respectively, enables English speakers to distinguish between *dot* and *tot*.

65. Slavoj Žižek, *Enjoy Your Symptom!: Jacques Lacan in Hollywood and Out* (London: Routledge, 1992), "Why Are There Always Two Fathers?" (149ff.).

66. The term *imago*, in psychoanalysis, refers to an internalized image sufficiently powerful to restructure the subject, most likely by means of identification.

67. Chaucer, *Boece*, book 2, prosa 1, 50–53.

68. Peter of Blois, Letter to the Royal Chaplains of Henry II, in Speed, *Those Who Fought*, 52.

69. Ibid., 52–53.

70. The account is in ibid., 56–57, citing Gabriel Tetzel, *The Travels of Leon von Rozmital*.

71. Ibid., 105. Frederick H. Russell, *The Just War in the Middle Ages* (Cambridge: Cambridge University Press, 1975), is the classic study.

72. See Žižek, *Sublime Object of Ideology*, 81–82. The obscenity of submission to the law is retroactively constituted; that is, it is obscene from the point of view of a subject capable of distinguishing between the senseless and the sensible.

73. Foucault, *The Care of the Self*, 42–43, 46–47.

74. Ibid., 51.

75. Žižek, *Sublime Object of Ideology*, 115.

76. See ibid., 164, and Lacan, *Ethics of Psychoanalysis*, 149–52, for a discussion of courtly love's transformation of "the impossible" into "the prohibited" through sacrifice. What is impossible because it lies beyond our reach is re-presented as what "must" be given up because of the mandate of the Other. We find it easier to believe in the demands of the Other than to accept finitude.

77. See Derrida, *Gift of Death*, 14–15. The Freudian term *melancholic* refers to a denial of loss thoroughgoing enough to restructure the subject; in this context, not only a lost object (compare "imago"), but death itself, is "incorporated" into the subject, so that it can be watched over and given new interior life.

78. On the role of death in establishing particularity, see ibid., 41. I use terms such as *particularity* or *specificity* to refer to constructs. Particularity is the quality of an object that has been named, or designed to be, or functions as, particular to an other: set apart, distinctive. Because such an object appears to be irreplaceable, it can be mourned. On the role of particularity in mourning and attachment, see John Bowlby, *Attachment*, vol. 1 of *Attachment and Loss* (New York and London: Tavistock Institute, 1982).

79. *Groupification, groupify* are terms used by Rickels to designate the work of transforming desire into the (phantasmatically) controlled relay system of group identification. See, for example, *Case of California*, 48, where Rickels elaborates on the role of introjection and projection in forming group structures of enjoyment. Introjection and projection are Freud's terms for our two earliest techniques of living: taking things into ourselves (the basis for identification) and spitting things out of ourselves (the basis for projective disiden-

tifications e.g., "this danger comes from within you, not from within me"). See Sigmund Freud, *The Ego and the Id,* trans. Joan Riviere (New York: Norton, 1961).

80. See Arthur Stephen McGrade, "Enjoyment at Oxford after Ockham: Philosophy, Psychology, and the Love of God," in *From Ockham to Wyclif,* ed. Anne Hudson and Michael Wilks (Oxford: Basil Blackwell for the Ecclesiastical History Society, 1987), 63–88.

81. Karma Lochrie, *Margery Kempe and the Translations of the Flesh* (Philadelphia: University of Pennsylvania Press, 1991), 6; 33, citing Richard Misyn's fifteenth-century translation of Richard Rolle's *Incendium Amoris.*

82. Scarry, *The Body in Pain,* 213. Scarry argues that the rhetoric of the Gospels emphasized healing, but in my view she underestimates the rewounding of the devotional subject through *imitatio Christi.*

83. Valerie Flint, *The Rise of Magic in Early Medieval Europe* (Princeton, N.J.: Princeton University Press, 1991), 173–77.

84. Ibid., 178, citing Rabanus Maurus, *De Laudibus Sanctae Crucis, Patrologia Latina* 108, 84–85.

85. Ibid., 183.

86. Lacan (*Ethics of Psychoanalysis,* 202) remarks that Sade shows an image of "eternal punishment" in which the victim's body is not broken into "part-objects," but rather "appears in the fantasm as the indestructible...Other." "Whatever happens to the subject is incapable of spoiling the image in question, incapable even of wearing it out."

87. Freud, *Group Psychology and the Analysis of the Ego,* 32–35: with "artificial groups," "a certain external force is employed to prevent them from disintegrating and to check alterations in their structure" (32).

88. Norbert Elias, *The Civilizing Process,* vol. 1, *The History of Manners,* and vol. 2, *Power and Civility,* trans. Edmund Jephcott (New York: Pantheon, 1982); also *The Court Society,* trans. Edmund Jephcott (New York: Pantheon, 1983). See also Stephen Jaeger, *The Origins of Courtliness: Civilizing Trends and the Formation of Courtly Ideals, 939–1210* (Philadelphia: University of Pennsylvania Press, 1985). On brotherhood, see Sharon Farmer, *Communities of Saint Martin: Legend and Ritual in Medieval Tours* (Ithaca, N.Y.: Cornell University Press, 1991).

89. Ramón Lull, *The Book of the Order of Chivalry,* in Speed, *Those Who Fought,* 93; Lull's work was translated into English by William Caxton as *The Book of the Ordre of Chyualrye* (Westminster: Caxton, 1486?). Painter dates the "beginning of religious chivalry" to the period after the eleventh century (Sidney Painter, *French Chivalry: Chivalric Ideas and Practices in Mediaeval France* [Baltimore: Johns Hopkins University Press, 1940], 66–67).

90. Sister Marie de Lourdes Le May, "The Allegory of the Christ-Knight in English Literature" (dissertation, Catholic University of America, Washington, D.C., 1932), and Rosemary Woolf, "The Theme of Christ the Lover-Knight in Medieval English Literature," *Review of English Studies* 12 (1962): 1–16.

91. Aryeh Grabois, "*Militia* and *Malitia:* The Bernardine Vision of Chivalry," in *The Second Crusade and the Cistercians,* ed. Michael Gervers (New York: St. Martin's Press, 1992), on Bernard's *De laude novae militiae.*

92. Georges Bataille discusses "heterogeneity" and "homogeneity" as characteristics of sovereignty in "The Psychological Structure of Fascism," in *Visions of Excess,* 137–60.

The sovereign must be representative, similar to the neighbors he rules, but must also be special—a sign of *jouissance* beyond the proper and everyday.

93. Text and translation of Geoffroi de Charny's treatise may be found in Richard W. Kaeuper and Elspeth Kennedy, eds., *The Book of Chivalry of Geoffroi de Charny: Text, Context and Translation* (Philadelphia: University of Pennsylvania Press, 1996). See also Sir Gilbert de la Haye's *The Buke of Knychthede*, which includes an allegorization of the "habilliamentis" of knighthood (J. H. Stevenson, ed., *Gilbert of the Haye's Prose Manuscript [A.D. 1456]*, vol. 2, *The Buke of Knychthede and the Buke of the Governaunce of Princis* [Edinburgh: Blackwood, 1914]); for discussion, see Louise Olga Fradenburg, *City, Marriage, Tournament: Arts of Rule in Late Medieval Scotland* (Madison: University of Wisconsin Press, 1991), 202–4. Compare also the description of the arming of Sir Gawain and the symbol of the pentangle in *Sir Gawain and the Green Knight*.

94. H. Ansgar Kelly, *Ideas and Forms of Tragedy from Aristotle to the Middle Ages* (Cambridge, England: Cambridge University Press, 1994), 180–82; citing Philippe de Mézières, *Oracio tragedia seu declamatoria Passionis domini nostri Jhesu Christi*, Paris, Bibliothèque Mazarine MS 1651, fols. 129–209bis, at "Prologue," fol. 137v; 4.6 (fol. 197), 2.9 (fol. 155v).

95. Foucault, *The Care of the Self*, 42. Prudence, in Chaucer's *Tale of Melibee*, counsels her irate husband/lord to "enelyne and bowe youre herte to take the pacience of our Lord Jhesu Crist," who "hath suffred for us." She remarks: "it is good as now that ye suffre."

96. Lacan, *Ethics of Psychoanalysis*, 186–87, 262. For readings of Christ's body in the later Middle Ages, see Sarah Stanbury, "Regimes of the Visual in Premodern England: Gaze, Body, and Chaucer's *Clerk's Tale*," *New Literary History* 28 (1997): 261–89; and Sara Beckwith, *Christ's Body: Identity, Culture and Society in Late Medieval Writings* (New York: Routledge, 1993).

97. On the distinction between the deserving and undeserving poor, see Louise O. Fradenburg, "Needful Things," in *Medieval Crime and Social Control*, ed. Barbara A. Hanawalt and David Wallace (Minneapolis: University of Minnesota Press, 1999), 49–69, at 56–57.

98. Lacan, *Ethics of Psychoanalysis*, 186–87. Lacan notes that although the "general will ... is no doubt the common denominator of the respect for certain rights ... it can also take the form of excluding from its boundaries, and therefore from its protection, everything that is not integrated into its various registers" (195). Cf. Rickels's notion of groupification in *The Case of California*.

99. Saint Thomas Aquinas, *De regimine principum*, chap. 1, in *St. Thomas Aquinas on Politics and Ethics: A New Translation, Backgrounds, Interpretation*, trans. and ed. Paul E. Sigmund (New York: Norton, 1988), 14–15.

100. Ibid.

1. Becoming Medieval

1. Gerald of Wales, *The Journey through Wales/The Description of Wales*, trans. Lewis Thorpe (Harmondsworth, England: Penguin, 1978), 117–18.

2. Ibid., 116–17.

3. Meilyr recovers his health in "the Church of St. David's, thanks to the virtues of the saintly men of that place" (ibid., 117).

4. Julia Kristeva, *Powers of Horror: An Essay on Abjection*, trans. Leon S. Roudiez (New York: Columbia University Press, 1982), characterizes phobic language as a libidinalizing of symbolic activity in place of the object that has been lost or frightened away; but the lost object returns and "threatens us from the outside" (41, 44–45).

5. On acting "as if," see Slavoj Žižek, *The Sublime Object of Ideology* (New York: Verso, 1989), 33–35.

6. Michel de Certeau, *The Writing of History*, trans. Tom Conley (New York: Columbia University Press, 1988), 61.

7. The geographer Jane Jacobs, in *Cities and the Wealth of Nations: Principles of Economic Life* (New York: Random House, 1984), emphasizes the role of drift and play in the history of technological invention (221).

8. Julia Kristeva, "Psychoanalysis and the *Polis*," trans. Margaret Waller, in *The Critical Tradition: Classic Texts and Contemporary Trends*, 2d ed., ed. David Richter (Boston: Bedford, 1998), 1075–86, at 1079.

9. Derrida problematizes the idea "that to be responsible, free, or capable of deciding cannot be . . . conditioned or conditional . . . historicity . . . must not touch the essence of an experience that consists precisely in tearing oneself away from one's own historical conditions" (*The Gift of Death*, trans. David Wills [Chicago: University of Chicago Press, 1995], 5).

10. On the nineteenth-century historian's "mission" to mediate "the uniqueness . . . of historical phenomena," see Lionel Gossman, "History as Decipherment: Romantic Historiography and the Discovery of the Other," *Studies in Historical Change* 18 (1986): 23–57, at 23, 26; on "historical authenticity," see Stephen Bann, "The Sense of the Past: Image, Text, and Object in the Formation of Historical Consciousness in Nineteenth-Century Britain," in *The New Historicism*, ed. H. Aram Veeser (New York: Routledge, 1989), 102–15, at 108.

11. Alexandre Leupin, "The Middle Ages, the Other," *diacritics* 13 (1983): 30.

12. Norman T. Macdougall writes that "True historical scholarship . . . did not really begin until . . . 1729" ("The Sources: A Reappraisal of the Legend," in *Scottish Society in the Fifteenth Century*, ed. Jennifer M. Brown [Wormald] [New York: St. Martin's Press, 1977], 10–32, at 10–11). See also Steven Justice, *Writing and Rebellion: England in 1381* (Berkeley: University of California Press, 1994), especially "Insurgent Literacy" (13–66), on documentary cultures.

13. Michel Foucault, *The History of Sexuality*, vol. 1, *An Introduction*, trans. Robert Hurley (New York: Vintage, 1978), referring to the village fool who "had obtained a few caresses from [a] little girl," remarks on "the fact that this everyday occurrence in the life of village sexuality, these inconsequential bucolic pleasures, could become . . . the object not only of a collective intolerance but of a judicial action, a medical intervention, a careful clinical examination, and an entire theoretical elaboration" (31–32). For critical readings of the strategic nature of Foucault's point, see Karma Lochrie, "Desiring Foucault," *Journal of Medieval and Early Modern Studies* 27 (1997): 1–16; and Carolyn Dinshaw, "Michel Foucault's Middle Ages," in *Getting Medieval: Sexualities and Communities, Pre- and Postmodern* (Dur-

ham, N.C.: Duke University Press, 1999), 191–206. See also *Premodern Sexualities*, ed. Louise Fradenburg and Carla Freccero (New York: Routledge, 1996).

14. De Certeau, *The Writing of History*, 31.

15. These concepts are developed most fully in Raymond Williams, *Marxism and Literature* (Oxford: Oxford University Press, 1977).

16. John Guillory, *Cultural Capital: The Problem of Literary Canon Formation* (Chicago: University of Chicago Press, 1993), 53.

17. Kristeva, "Psychoanalysis and the *Polis*," 1076.

18. Barbara W. Tuchman's epigraph in *A Distant Mirror: The Calamitous Fourteenth Century* (New York: Knopf, 1978) is: "*For mankind is ever the same and nothing is lost out of nature, though everything is altered*" (John Dryden, "On the Characters in the Canterbury Tales").

19. Umberto Eco, *Travels in Hyper Reality: Essays*, trans. William Weaver (New York: Harcourt Brace Jovanovich, 1986), 63.

20. Lee Patterson, *Negotiating the Past: The Historical Understanding of Medieval Literature* (Madison: University of Wisconsin Press, 1987), 157–58.

21. Deleuze and Guattari's "lines of flight" are also called "deterritorializations." Deterritorializing does not mean linear, unidirectional movement from one distinct form to another. Rather, it is the creation of a rhizomatic "alliance." Deleuze and Guattari contrast "rhizomatic" models with "arborescent" ones (the growth patterns of tubers rather than trees); the former model changes as open-ended, capable of ending but then starting up again in the same place, or moving to some alluring point of intersection elsewhere in the rhizome. "Alliance" links together two different forms—such as the wasp and the orchid—in an open-ended, mutual collaboration that continually transforms both wasp and orchid. Alliance "deterritorializes" both wasp and orchid; while wasp and orchid are working together, they are on lines of flight that knock them loose from "being orchid" and "being wasp" and thereby permit a surprising and productive convergence. "Becoming" is a related concept. See Gilles Deleuze and Félix Guattari, *A Thousand Plateaus: Capitalism and Schizophrenia*, trans. Brian Massumi (Minneapolis: University of Minnesota Press, 1987), 10 and n. 79 below.

22. Jacques le Goff, *History and Memory*, trans. Steven Rendall and Elizabeth Claman (New York: Columbia University Press, 1992), 68.

23. See A. J. Minnis and A. B. Scott, with David Wallace, eds., *Medieval Literary Theory and Criticism, c. 1100–c. 1375: The Commentary Tradition*, rev. ed. (New York and London: Oxford University Press and Clarendon Press, 1991); also A. J. Minnis, *Medieval Theory of Authorship: Scholastic Literary Attitudes in the Later Middle Ages* (London: Scolar, 1984).

24. William Caxton, *The Prologues and Epilogues of William Caxton*, ed. W. J. B. Crotch, Early English Text Society, e.s. 176 (Millwood, N.Y., and London: Oxford University Press, 1928), 64–65. Caxton's edition is a modernization of John of Trevisa's translation into English of Higden's *Polichronicon*; see *Polychronicon Ranulphi Higden monachi Cestrensis, together with the English translations of John of Trevisa* ..., ed. Churchill Babington (New York: Kraus Reprints, 1964–75).

25. See Frances Yates, *The Art of Memory* (Chicago: University of Chicago Press, 1966), on the role of the *imagines agentes* in the arts of memory (66).

26. In Lacanian theory, imaginary modes of enjoyment focus on the "other" when the other appears to be (potentially) an image of the self; the thrust of fantasy in the imaginary is toward completion, unity, perfection of form, relationship as fusion. The foundations for Lacanian conceptions of identification and the imaginary are to be found in "The Mirror Stage as Formative of the I": "we have only to understand the mirror stage as an *identification*, in the full sense that analysis gives to the term: namely, the transformation that takes place in the subject when he assumes an image" (in *Écrits: A Selection*, trans. Alan Sheridan [New York: Norton, 1977], 2). The *imago* is capable of making, of producing "formative effects" that enter and modify the symbolic order. The symbolic differs from the imaginary, however, because difference and incompletion are fundamental to its processes and hence to the ways it structures enjoyment.

27. The term *groupify* is from Laurence A. Rickels, *The Case of California* (Baltimore: Johns Hopkins University Press, 1991), 48.

28. Ernst H. Kantorowicz, *The King's Two Bodies: A Study in Mediaeval Political Theology* (Princeton, N.J.: Princeton University Press, 1957), 232–71.

29. "Wound" is of course also a signifier, but "good" in this passage is *seeking* an expanded meaning that goes beyond the well-being of the body.

30. *The Tree of Battles of Honoré Bonet*, ed. G. W. Coopland (Cambridge: Harvard University Press, 1949).

31. Gaines Post, "Two Notes on Nationalism in the Middle Ages," *Traditio* 9 (1953): 281.

32. Caxton, *The Prologues and Epilogues of William Caxton*, ed. Crotch, 77.

33. Derrida discusses the longing for a meaningful front in *Gift of Death*, for example, 70. This longing is often expressed as a "loss" of medieval or chivalric styles of combat. On this topic in discussions of World War I, see Paul Fussell, *The Great War in Modern Memory* (New York: Oxford University Press, 1975). See also Louise Olga Fradenburg, "A Royal Legend," in *City, Marriage, Tournament: Arts of Rule in Late Medieval Scotland* (Madison: University of Wisconsin Press, 1991), on the terms used to describe the difference between late-medieval and early-modern warfare.

34. Constance Penley, personal communication.

35. Foucault, *The History of Sexuality*, vol. 1, *An Introduction*, 124, 147–49.

36. "*Yes, I have been my father and I have been my son*," in Gilles Deleuze and Félix Guattari, *Anti-Oedipus: Capitalism and Schizophrenia*, trans. Robert Hurley, Mark Seem, and Helen R. Lane (Minneapolis: University of Minnesota Press, 1983), 15; "fantasy is never individual; it is *group fantasy*" (30).

37. Jonathan Goldberg, "The History That Will Be," in Fradenburg and Freccero, *Premodern Sexualities*, 3–21.

38. On the sexual politics of Renaissance "antiquity," see Earl Jackson Jr., *Strategies of Deviance: Studies in Gay Male Representation* (Bloomington: Indiana University Press, 1994).

39. "[O]ur thesis is that history has to be read retroactively: it is only the emergence of masochism... towards the end of the [nineteenth]... century, that enables us to grasp the libidinal economy of courtly love" (Slavoj Žižek, "From the Courtly Game to *The Crying Game*," re: *Post* 1 [1993]: 43).

40. "Unnatural participation" is Deleuze and Guattari's term for connections/disconnections made between bodies/things in the course of their metamorphoses (Deleuze and Guattari, *A Thousand Plateaus*, 240).

41. Foucault describes *The History of Sexuality* as an "archaeology of psychoanalysis" (vol. 1, *An Introduction*, 30). See Eugene Vance, "Medievalism: Testing Ground for Historicism(s)? Roundtable discussion with Peter Haidu, Alexandre Leupin, and Eugene Vance," *Paroles Gelées: UCLA French Studies* 9 (1991): 24–25.

42. Leupin, "The Middle Ages, the Other," 28–29. See also Jean-Charles Hûchet, *Littérature médiévale et psychanalyse: pour une clinique littéraire* (Paris: Presses universitaires de France, 1990).

43. Guillory, *Cultural Capital*, 53.

44. See Louise O. Fradenburg, "Criticism, Anti-Semitism and *The Prioress's Tale*," *Exemplaria* 1 (1989): 69–115.

45. Hûchet, *Littérature médiévale et psychanalyse*, 7, 9.

46. Guibert of Nogent, notorious misanthrope, xenophobe, and mariolater, gives special attention to his and his mother's beauty in the hilariously titled "*De vita sua*, or *Monodiae* (Songs for One Voice)"; see Joost Baneke, "Transference Figures in Medieval Literature: The Madonna of Guibert of Nogent," in *Fathers and Mothers in Literature*, ed. Henk Hillenaar and Walter Schonau (Amsterdam: Rodopi, 1994), 92–94, and Steven Kruger, "Medieval Christian (Dis)identifications," *New Literary History* 28 (1997): 185–203. On late-medieval psychology, see Arthur Stephen McGrade, "Enjoyment at Oxford after Ockham: Philosophy, Psychology, and the Love of God," in *From Ockham to Wyclif*, ed. Anne Hudson and Michael Wilks (Oxford: Basil Blackwell for the Ecclesiastical History Society, 1987).

47. Fredric Jameson analyzes medieval romance and exegesis in *The Political Unconscious: Narrative as a Socially Symbolic Act* (Ithaca, N.Y.: Cornell University Press, 1981), 29–33, 105, 130–31. On Lacan's medievalism, see Hûchet, *Littérature médiévale et psychanalyse*, 19–21. Judith Butler's most influential discussion of identity remains *Gender Trouble: Feminism and the Subversion of Identity* (New York: Routledge, 1990); for Carolyn Dinshaw's discussion, see *Chaucer's Sexual Poetics* (Madison: University of Wisconsin Press, 1989), esp. 28–64, "Reading Like a Man: The Critics, the Narrator, Troilus, and Pandarus."

48. David Wallace, *Chaucerian Polity: Absolutist Lineages and Associational Forms in England and Italy* (Stanford, Calif.: Stanford University Press, 1997), 9–11. Anne Middleton speaks, apparently approvingly, of medieval literary studies' resistance to "imported critical paradigms and the transferred master narratives of other disciplines" in Stephen Greenblatt and Giles Gunn, eds., *Redrawing the Boundaries: The Transformation of English and American Literary Studies* (New York: Modern Language Association of America, 1992), 15. Steven Justice alludes, also somewhat murkily, to the "Foucauldian gloom of some recent historicisms" (*Writing and Rebellion*, 5). Wallace links theory to "discipleship" in *Chaucerian Polity*, 265. On academic high theory in the Middle Ages, see Lois Roney, *Chaucer's Knight's Tale and Theories of Scholastic Philosophy* (Tampa: University of South Florida Press, 1990); Ross G. Arthur, *Medieval Sign Theory and Sir Gawain and the Green Knight* (Toronto: University of Toronto Press, 1987); Eugene Vance, *Mervelous Signals: Poetics and Sign Theory in the Middle Ages* (Lincoln: University of Nebraska Press, 1986).

49. *Medievalism and the Modernist Temper*, ed. R. Howard Bloch and Stephen G. Nichols (Baltimore: Johns Hopkins University Press, 1996); Norman F. Cantor, *Inventing the Middle Ages: The Lives, Works, and Ideas of the Great Medievalists of the Twentieth Century* (New York: William Morrow, 1991). See also Kathleen Biddick's discussion of the "fathers," and of *Medievalism and the Modern Temper*, in *The Shock of Medievalism* (Durham, N.C.: Duke University Press, 1999), 2–4.

50. María Rosa Menocal calls for "two epistemological adaptations: first, that we reconceive our own relationship to earlier texts and culture as part of our fundamental personal and present histories... second... that our 'study' of medieval literature restore... the radical presentness of the medieval past just beneath our consciousness"; we recover some aspects of the lyricism and polyglossia of medieval vernacular culture by "embracing our own history and time and songs" (*Shards of Love: Exile and the Origins of the Lyric* [Durham, N.C.: Duke University Press, 1994], 17–18). Commenting on the philology of Dante and Vico, she adds that "narrative can be constructed lyrically, that philosophy can be contingent, that history can be anachronic, and that the love song and the hermetic poem can be acts of deep political engagement" (141). This summarizes Menocal's hopes for medieval studies.

51. Charles Méla, "Poetria Nova et Homo Novus," in *Modernité au Moyen Âge: Le Défi du passé*, ed. Brigitte Cazelles and Charles Méla (Geneva: Droz, 1990), 207–32, at 213, 218.

52. Leupin, "The Middle Ages, the Other," 24, 27. See Roger Dragonetti, *Le Gai Savoir dans la rhétorique courtoise: Flamenca et Joufroi de Poitiers* (Paris: Seuil, 1982).

53. Alexandre Leupin, *Barbarolexis: Medieval Writing and Sexuality*, trans. Kate M. Cooper (Cambridge: Harvard University Press, 1989), 5–6 and 238 n. 10; Leupin, "The Middle Ages, the Other," 29. For more on medieval textuality, see Carol Braun Pasternack, *The Textuality of Old English Poetry* (Cambridge, England: Cambridge University Press, 1995), and A. N. Doane and Carol Braun Pasternack, eds., *Vox Intexta: Orality and Textuality in the Middle Ages* (Madison: University of Wisconsin Press, 1991).

54. Jacques Derrida, "My Chances/*Mes Chances:* A Rendezvous with Some Epicurean Stereophonies," in *Taking Chances: Derrida, Psychoanalysis, and Literature*, ed. Joseph Smith and William Kerrigan (Baltimore: Johns Hopkins University Press, 1984), 16: "In the destination... there is... a principle of indetermination, chance, luck, or of destinerring."

55. On courtly love's restyling of the signifier, see Jacques Lacan, *The Seminar of Jacques Lacan: Book VII: The Ethics of Psychoanalysis, 1959–1960*, ed. Jacques-Alain Miller, trans. Dennis Porter (New York: Norton, 1992), 123–25, 148–51.

56. Alexandre Leupin, "The Powerlessness of Writing: Guillaume de Machaut, the Gorgon, and *Ordenance*," *Yale French Studies* 70 (1986): 143; Leupin, *Barbarolexis*, 13.

57. For an account of Lacanian historicity that emphasizes the imaginary register, see Teresa Brennan, *History after Lacan* (New York: Routledge, 1993); on trauma, see Christine Boheemen-Saaf, *Joyce, Derrida, Lacan and the Trauma of History* (Cambridge, England: Cambridge University Press, 1999).

58. Slavoj Žižek, *The Sublime Object of Ideology* (New York: Verso, 1989), 32–33.

59. Karl Marx and Friedrich Engels, *The German Ideology*, in *Karl Marx: Selected Writings*, ed. David McClellan (Oxford: Oxford University Press, 1977), discuss the historicality of need at 165–66. See Michel Mollat, *The Poor in the Middle Ages: An Essay in Social History*,

trans. Arthur Goldhammer (New Haven: Yale University Press, 1986), on definitions of need in discourses of medieval poverty.

60. Jacobs, *Cities and the Wealth of Nations*, 222–23.

61. Julia Kristeva, *Nations without Nationalism*, trans. Leon S. Roudiez (New York: Columbia University Press, 1993), 3–4.

62. Ibid., 4.

63. Sigmund Freud, "Letter to Binswanger," in *Letters of Sigmund Freud*, ed. E. L. Freud (New York: Basic Books, 1960); cited by Lorraine D. Siggins, "Mourning: A Critical Survey of the Literature," *International Journal of Psychoanalysis* 47 (1966): 14–25, at 17.

64. On Deleuze and Guattari's definition of "becoming," see n. 79 below.

65. Julia Kristeva, "Motherhood according to Giovanni Bellini," in *Desire in Language: A Semiotic Approach to Literature and Art*, ed. Leon S. Roudiez, trans. Thomas Gora, Alice Jardine, and Leon S. Roudiez (New York: Columbia University Press, 1980), 236–70.

66. I am solely responsible for this paraphrase of Frank Gardiner's views.

67. An important example of current work in religious studies is Catherine Bell, *Ritual Theory, Ritual Practice* (New York: Oxford University Press, 1992).

68. Kristeva, "Psychoanalysis and the *Polis*," 1081. Kristeva problematically links "reality" with "the exigencies of the moment and developments dictated by the needs of the majority," and I am not sure that the desires interpreted are only utopian ones; but her overall point remains important, that is, that for a discourse to succeed widely, it has to "read" the desires it addresses, and thus a kind of knowledge is involved—knowledge that works on the level of group subjectivity.

69. On the injunction to leave father and mother, Kristeva cites Genesis 2:24, Matthew 19:5, Mark 10:7, Ephesians 5:31; see Kristeva, *Nations without Nationalism*, 4, 22.

70. Kristeva, *Nations without Nationalism*, 24, 21.

71. See n. 10.

72. Sarah Stanbury, "Regimes of the Visual," "Regimes of the Visual in Premodern England: Gaze, Body, and Chaucer's *Clerk's Tale*," *New Literary History* 28 (1997): 261–89. 268, 279; Kathleen Biddick, "Genders, Bodies, Borders: Technologies of the Visible," *Speculum* 68 (1993): 405, 409; Karma Lochrie, *Margery Kempe and the Translations of the Flesh* (Philadelphia: University of Pennsylvania Press, 1991), 6, 33, citing Misyn's translation of Rolle's *Incendium Amoris*.

73. An instance of pathologizing is William Ober, "Margery Kempe: Hysteria and Mysticism Reconciled," *Literature and Medicine* 4 (1985): 24–40.

74. Caroline Walker Bynum, *Holy Feast and Holy Fast: The Religious Significance of Food to Medieval Women* (Berkeley: University of California Press, 1987); for example: "women manipulated far more than their own bodies through fasting.... It was a part of suffering; and suffering was considered an effective activity, which redeemed both individual and cosmos" (207). Religious women "strove not to eradicate body but to merge their own humiliating and painful flesh with that flesh whose agony, espoused by choice, was salvation" (246). From my perspective, what these women manipulated was not "far more than their bodies," but rather enjoyment, which is always simultaneously material *and* part of the order of the signifier.

75. Biddick, "Genders, Bodies, Borders," 389–418, at 415.

76. On heterogeneity, homogeneity, and sovereignty, see Georges Bataille, "The Psychological Structure of Fascism," in *Visions of Excess: Selected Writings, 1927–1939*, ed. and trans. Allan Stoekl (Minneapolis: University of Minnesota Press, 1985), 137–60; and Louise Olga Fradenburg, *City, Marriage, Tournament: Arts of Rule in Late Medieval Scotland* (Madison: University of Wisconsin Press, 1991) 68, 286 n. 2.

77. The decisive article on this Foucauldian view of subversion and containment was Stephen Greenblatt's "Invisible Bullets: Renaissance Authority and Its Subversion," *Glyph* 8 (1981): 40–61. "Genuine" and "radical" "subversiveness" is "generated in the midst of apparently orthodox texts and simultaneously contained by those texts and thus by the power it would appear to threaten" (41, 48).

78. There are many exceptions, including Saul Friedlander's classic *History and Psychoanalysis: An Inquiry into the Possibilities and Limits of Psychohistory*, trans. Susan Suleiman (New York: Holmes and Meier, 1978); see also Dominick LaCapra, *Representing the Holocaust: History, Theory, Trauma* (Ithaca, N.Y.: Cornell University Press, 1994) and *History and Memory after Auschwitz* (Ithaca, N.Y.: Cornell University Press, 1998). For a recent general discussion, see Jacques Szaluta, *Psychohistory: Theory and Practice* (New York: P. Lang, 1999); for bibliography, though not up to date, *A Bibliography of Psychohistory*, ed. Lloyd de Mause (New York: Garland, 1975).

79. "A becoming is not a correspondence between relations. But neither is it a resemblance, an imitation, or, at the limit, an identification.... To become is not to progress or regress along a series. Above all, becoming does not occur in the imagination, even when the imagination reaches the highest cosmic or dynamic level.... Becomings-animal are neither dreams nor phantasies. They are perfectly real.... What is real is the becoming itself... not the supposedly fixed terms through which that which becomes passes" (Deleuze and Guattari, *A Thousand Plateaus*, 238).

80. Freud argues, however, that religion "restricts the play of choice and adaptation" necessary to the quest for happiness, because it imposes equally on everyone its own path to the acquisition of happiness and protection from suffering; another of religion's tools is "mass delusion" (*Civilization and Its Discontents*, trans. James Strachey [New York: Norton, 1961], 36). Laurence A. Rickels, commenting on Freud's *Group Psychology and the Analysis of the Ego*, argues that religion "groupifies," that is, melancholically constructs a group identity that cannot lose the way individuals can; and Christianity's doubling of the power of identification is where its "modernity" resides: "The Christian church introduces modern group psychology... [It] not only brings about group identification among the faithful... but also enforces identification with Christ; every Christian must love the other Christians just as Christ loves them" (*The Case of California* [Baltimore: Johns Hopkins University Press, 1991], 55).

81. Deleuze and Guattari, *A Thousand Plateaus*, 273.

82. Those familiar with polemics among French psychoanalysts will know that Deleuze and Guattari critique Freud and Lacan (most notably in *Anti-Oedipus*) on the score of their attempts to domesticate or systematize becoming. But the Freudian concept of the polymorphous perverse and the Lacanian notion that "Desire *is* change" seem to me to be try-

ing to capture the same mobility as does "becoming," and I have yet to be convinced that an analysis of subjectivation—of subject-construction—is inevitably also an *act* of subjectivation possible to eschew. Is analyzing inevitably also replicating or reenacting what is being analyzed? Those in favor of analysis would probably answer in the negative.

83. D. Vance Smith, "Irregular Histories: Forgetting Ourselves," *New Literary History* (spring 1997): 171.

84. Justice, *Writing and Rebellion*, 7.

85. Barbara Johnson, "Opening Remarks—Difference," in *The Critical Difference* (Baltimore: Johns Hopkins University Press, 1980), ix–x.

86. Deleuze and Guattari, *A Thousand Plateaus*, 257.

2. "My Worldes Blisse"

1. These poems, along with *The Knight's Tale* and *The Manciple's Tale*, also share a significant number of sources: Virgil, Ovid, Boethius, and Boccaccio, in addition to Machaut, Deschamps, Guillaume de Lorris, and Jean de Meun, were most decisive for Chaucer's conception of what tragic verse might be.

2. Henry Ansgar Kelly, *Chaucerian Tragedy* (Woodbridge, Suffolk: D. S. Brewer, 1997), critiques Willard Farnham's contention that because Chaucer's treatment of love is courtly, it "excludes itself from any ethical consideration except the loyalty of lover to beloved," and hence is wanting as tragedy (144; citing Farnham, *The Medieval Heritage of Elizabethan Tragedy* [Berkeley, 1939], 159).

3. For a study of elegy and *The Book of the Duchess*, see Louise O. Fradenburg, "'Voice Memorial': Loss and Reparation in Chaucer's Poetry," *Exemplaria* 2 (1990): 169–202.

4. Laurence A. Rickels invents the term and related forms throughout *The Case of California* (Baltimore: Johns Hopkins University Press, 1991), for example, at 48.

5. *Jouissance*, as it is developed in Lacanian psychoanalysis, refers to the libidinal condition that precedes the constitution of the subject, and which, once designed by the image/signifier, is forever transformed, but can be reapproached through experiences like orgasm. *Jouissance* is not identical with pleasure, because it can reach unpleasurable levels. See note 11 to the Introduction.

6. David Wallace remarks suggestively in *Chaucerian Polity: Absolutist Lineages and Associational Forms in England and Italy* (Stanford, Calif.: Stanford University Press, 1997) that "Chaucer...seems...concerned to interrogate the vertical space that sets *vires illustres* [great men] apart from, or over, the rest of humanity" (311).

7. On the courtly lady as *bon vezi*, good neighbor, see Jacques Lacan, *The Seminar of Jacques Lacan: Book VII: The Ethics of Psychoanalysis, 1959–1960*, ed. Jacques-Alain Miller, trans. Dennis Porter (New York: Norton, 1992), 151. See also Sarah Kay, "The Contradictions of Courtly Love and the Origins of Courtly Poetry: The Evidence of the *Lauzengiers*," *Journal of Medieval and Early Modern Studies* 26 (1966): 209–53.

8. Larry D. Benson, ed., *The Riverside Chaucer* (Boston: Houghton Mifflin, 1987). Subsequent references to Chaucer's poetry are from this edition and will be cited in the text by line number.

9. Georges Bataille discusses "heterogeneity" and "homogeneity" as two characteristics of sovereignty in his essay "The Psychological Structure of Fascism," in *Visions of Excess: Selected Writings, 1927–1939*, ed. and trans. Allan Stoekl (Minneapolis: University of Minnesota Press, 1985), 137–60.

10. Jacques Derrida, "My Chances/*Mes Chances:* A Rendezvous with Some Epicurean Stereophonies," in *Taking Chances: Derrida, Psychoanalysis, and Literature*, ed. Joseph H. Smith and William Kerrigan (Baltimore: Johns Hopkins University Press, 1984), 1–32, at 5. Hereafter, references are cited in the text. A good discussion of falling in Chaucer's *The Book of the Duchess* is John M. Fyler, "Irony and the Age of Gold in the *Book of the Duchess*," *Speculum* 52 (1977): 314–28.

11. Valerie Flint, *The Rise of Magic in Early Medieval Europe* (Princeton, N.J.: Princeton University Press, 1900), 171, 162.

12. Rickels, *Case of California*, 139, citing Sabina Spielrein, *Die Destruktion als Ursache des Werdens* (Tübingen Edition Diskord-Tübingen, 1986), 9; hereafter, references to Rickels are cited in the text.

13. Rickels comments on "Freud's conviction that indifference toward objects antedates any libidinal orientation. Here...lies the first dim representation of an urge to die, later a wish to die, to die someone else" (ibid., 194). "Preparedness...protects against... the state of indifference," that is, against a preference for insentience, but by that very token tries also to keep sentience from becoming unbearable (192). "Right away, at birth, aggression emerges in the effort to master (via identification and projection) the traumatic state of helplessness which birth introduces" (193).

14. Henry Ansgar Kelly, *Ideas and Forms of Tragedy from Aristotle to the Middle Ages* (Cambridge, England: Cambridge University Press, 1994), 14, citing J. V. Cunningham, *Woe or Wonder* (Denver: Swallow, 1951), reprinted in *The Collected Essays of J. V. Cunningham* (Chicago: Swallow Press 1976), 30. The phrase *fugienda vita* is from the treatise on tragedy by Evanthius that is included in Donatus's commentary on Terence [*Aeli Donati Commentum Terenti*, ed. Paulus Wessner, 2 vols. (Leipzig, 1902–5, repr. Stuttgart, 1963–66). Kelly glosses this phrase as referring to "the sort of life depicted in the [tragic] play," that is, "it is the characters in the tragedy who wish to flee from their life." I like the more general reading.

15. Kelly, *Ideas and Forms of Tragedy*, 136, citing Albertino/Alberto Mussato, Epistle I, lines 105–18; in *Opera Poetica*.

16. Jacques Derrida, *The Gift of Death*, trans. David Wills (Chicago: University of Chicago Press, 1995). For an explanation of my style with regard to "Other," "other" in what follows, see n. 10 to the Introduction.

17. Maurice Blanchot, *The Space of Literature*, trans. Ann Smock (Lincoln: University of Nebraska Press, 1982); hereafter, references are cited in the text. Blanchot writes of man's attempts to master death: "it does not suffice for him that he is mortal; he understands that he has to become mortal, that he must be mortal twice over: sovereignly, extremely mortal" (96).

18. Lacanian psychoanalysis posits that the subject comes into life when its *jouissance* is engraved by the laws that structure the play of the signifier. Although the subject's desire is, forever after, inextricable from this experience of submission to a senseless and arbitrary law, she will seek to make sense of the law, to give it reasons, purposes, a "face." Desire is

thus intimate with, not controlled by, the law as a separate faculty of restraint. This is crucial to understanding Lacan's conception of *das Ding:* as that portion of *jouissance* made inaccessible to the subject when she identifies with the signifier, *das Ding* is "extimate," both interior and exterior to the subject, inhabiting her but unknowable. Lacan remarks that *"das Ding* presents itself at the level of unconscious experience as that which already makes the law.... It is a capricious and arbitrary law, the law of the oracle, the law of signs in which the subject receives no guarantee from anywhere" (*Ethics of Psychoanalysis,* 73).

19. See Rickels, *Case of California,* on the Marquis de Sade's "law of sexual pleasure, which decrees that every body be at everybody's disposal, [and] guarantees that the pleasure to be had will be enjoyed only by the Other" (56); and Lacan, *Ethics of Psychoanalysis,* on the role of the Sadean object as "an indestructible support. Analysis shows clearly that the subject separates out a double of himself who is made inaccessible to destruction," who has "the power to support a form of suffering, which is in itself nothing else but the signifier of a limit. Suffering is conceived of as a stasis which affirms that that which is cannot return to the void from which it emerged" (261).

20. Michel Foucault, *The History of Sexuality,* vol. 3, *The Care of the Self,* trans. Robert Hurley (New York: Vintage, 1988), 42–43, 46–47.

21. Sigmund Freud, *Civilization and Its Discontents,* ed. James Strachey (New York: Norton, 1961), 62–66; discussed by Rickels, *Case of California,* 55. See also Louise O. Fradenburg, "Be not far from me": Psychoanalysis, Medieval Studies and the Subject of Religion," *Exemplaria* 7 (1995): 41–54, at 50–52. I use terms such as *particularity* or *specificity* to refer to constructs. Particularity is the quality of an object that has been designed to be, or in certain contexts functions as, particular to an other: set apart, distinctive. Because such an object appears to be irreplaceable, it is "mournable," capable of being mourned. On the role of particularity in mourning and attachment, see John Bowlby, *Attachment,* vol. 1 of *Attachment and Loss* (New York and London: Tavistock Institute, 1982). The "sublime object" theorized by Lacan and Žižek as an object "raised to the dignity of the Thing" can be understood as deriving its power from a certain universalization of something merely particular: a lady "stands in" for *jouissance.* But *jouissance* also gains, so to speak, by being thus particularized. Only *this* lady can deliver me to my *jouissance;* but because I can mourn her endlessly, I am bound to the travail of my desire. See Lacan, *Ethics of Psychoanalysis,* 149–52; and Slavoj Žižek, "From the Courtly Game to *The Crying Game, re:Post* 1 (1993): 5–9. The importance of particulars in the formation of images is fundamental to much Aristotelian medieval psychology and epistemology; Aquinas says that "Man cannot understand without images *(phantasmata);* the image is a similitude of a corporeal thing, but understanding is of universals which are to be abstracted from particulars." The image mediates between particularity and corporeality on the one hand, and universality and spirituality on the other. See Saint Thomas Aquinas, *In Aristotelis libros De sensu et sensato, De memoria et reminiscentia commentarium,* ed. R. M. Spiazzi (Turin/Rome: Marietti, 1973; ca. 1950), 85ff.; cited by Frances A. Yates, *The Art of Memory* (Chicago: University of Chicago Press, 1966), 70.

22. Rosemary Woolf, "The Theme of Christ the Lover-Knight in Medieval English Literature," *Review of English Studies* 12 (1962): 1–16.

23. Lacan, *Ethics of Psychoanalysis,* 186–87. Lacan's notion of the formation of the subject according to the image of the other in "The Mirror Stage" is central to his analysis

of charity in *The Ethics of Psychoanalysis;* see Jacques Lacan, *Écrits: A Selection,* trans. Alan Sheridan (New York: Norton, 1977), 2.

24. On the senselessness of the law, its intimacy with desire, and the obscenity of submission to it, see Slavoj Žižek, *The Sublime Object of Ideology* (London: Verso, 1989), 81–82, 113–15.

25. Charlton T. Lewis [Lewis and Short], *A Latin Dictionary* (Oxford: Clarendon Press, 1879, 1984), s.v. "pietas."

26. *Pite* appears frequently in Chaucer's poetry, 122 times, in a wide range of contexts (legal, petitionary, amorous, devotional); see Larry D. Benson, ed., *A Glossarial Concordance to the Riverside Chaucer,* 2 vols. (New York: Garland, 1993), s.v. "pite."

27. Saint Augustine, *Confessions,* trans. R. S. Pine-Coffin (Harmondsworth, England: Penguin, 1975), book 3, chap. 2, 56–57. See also Kelly's discussion of the comments on tragedy and the problem with pity in Aelred of Rievaulx's *Speculum Caritatis* (2.17.50), ed. A. Hoste and C. H. Talbot, *Aelredi Rievalensis opera omnia* (*Ideas of Tragedy,* 85–86). Rickels discusses the undoing of "the personalized" by language, and the role of "unconscious generalization or mythification which replaces [the personalized] . . . , makes it replaceable. . . . In love one has survived oneself and now turns back toward life—toward the witness, neighbor, or friend one likes to be like" (*Case of California,* 142).

28. Sarah Beckwith, *Christ's Body: Identity, Culture, and Society in Late Medieval Writings* (London: Routledge, 1993), notes the importance of compassion in late-medieval passional devotion.

29. Kelly, *Ideas and Forms of Tragedy,* 180–82, citing Philippe de Mézières, *Oracio tragedia seu declamatoria Passionis domini nostri Jhesu Christi,* Paris, Bibliothèque Mazarine MS 1651, fols. 129–209bis, at "Prologue," fol. 137v; 4.6 (fol. 196v–197), 2.9 (fol. 155v). The conquest of Alexandria by Peter I (Lusignan) of Cyprus took place on October 10, 1365; it is one of the battles mentioned in the portrait of the Knight in Chaucer's "General Prologue." *The Riverside Chaucer* notes that Alexandria was "abandoned a week later, after great plundering and a massacre of its inhabitants" (801 n. 51).

30. Gaston Bachelard, *The Poetics of Space,* trans. Maria Jolas (Boston: Beacon Press, 1969): "it is through their 'immensity' that . . . two kinds of space—the space of intimacy and world space—blend"; there is "correspondence between the immensity of world space and the depth of 'inner space'" (203, 205). Hereafter, references are cited in the text.

31. Part I of Foucault's *The Care of the Self,* "Dreaming of One's Pleasures," is devoted to Artemidorus's treatise (4–36).

32. Kelly, *Ideas and Forms of Tragedy,* 114, citing Saint Thomas Aquinas, *In octo libros Physicorum Aristotelis expositio,* Marietti edition, ed. P. M. Maggiòlo (Turin: Marietti, 1954), 6.11.6. Horace associates tragedy "with bloated mouth" when acknowledging that "even comedy raises her voice at times, and Chremes when angered quarrels with bloated mouth" ("Interdum tamen et uocem Comoedia tollit, / Iratusque Chremes tumido delitigat ore") (Horace, *Ars Poetica* [Cambridge, Mass.: Loeb Classical Library, 1900], 93–94; for Placidus, see *Glossae,* ed. J. W. Pirie and W. M. Lindsay, *Glossaria latina,* vol. 4 (Paris, 1930, repr. 1965), 34; both cited by Kelly, *Ideas and Forms of Tragedy,* 6–7.

33. Medieval discourses on dreaming and magic were fascinated by the openness of the psychic interior to demonic or angelic intervention; the reliability of dreams depended

on which sort of agency had inspired the dreamer. See Richard Kieckhefer, *Magic in the Middle Ages* (Cambridge, England: Cambridge University Press, 1989, c 1990), 176–87; Steven Kruger, *Dreaming in the Middle Ages* (Cambridge, England: Cambridge University Press, 1992), 16.

34. On the mnemonic image, see Yates, *The Art of Memory*, esp. 16–18. On medieval memory, see also Mary Carruthers, *The Book of Memory* (Cambridge, England: Cambridge University Press, 1990).

35. Sigmund Freud, "Mourning and Melancholia," in *The Standard Edition of the Complete Psychological Works of Sigmund Freud*, trans. James Strachey (London: Hogarth Press and the Institute for Psycho-Analysis, 1953–73), vol. 14, 152–70, esp. 161.

36. Blanchot, *The Space of Literature*, 32–33: "fascination is passion for the image"; "what one sees seizes sight and renders it interminable"; it is "the relation that the gaze entertains...with sightless, shapeless depth."

37. On the "development of the art of living under the theme of the care of oneself," see Foucault, *The Care of the Self*, 45.

38. See Yates, *The Art of Memory*, 64–66, for discussion of the mnemonic role of wonder in Albertus Magnus and Aquinas; also Raymond Dilorenzo, "Wonder and Words: Paganism, Christianity, and Consolation in Chaucer's *Book of the Duchess*," *University of Toronto Quarterly* 32 (1982): 20–39, at 23 and 36 n. 8. Geoffrey de Vinsauf agrees that the art of memory is a psychological art: the "little cell that remembers...craves what is delightful"; it is important for the writer to "fashion signs for yourself, whatever kind your own inclination suggests," because "enjoyment alone makes the power of memory strong" (*Poetria Nova of Geoffrey of Vinsauf*, trans. Margaret F. Nims [Toronto: Pontifical Institute of Mediaeval Studies, 1967], 87, 89).

39. Albertus Magnus, *De bono*, in *Opera omnia*, ed. H. Kuhle, C. Feckes, B. Geyer, and W. Kubel (Monasterii Westfalorum in aedibus Aschendorff, vol. 28, 1951), Solution, point 20, p. 249; Yates, *The Art of Memory*, 67. Yates stresses the "introduction of a devotional atmosphere" as one aspect of the medieval reception of the art of memory (76); memory techniques became particularly important in late-medieval passional devotion.

40. Flint, *The Rise of Magic in Early Medieval Europe*, 30, citing Origen, *Contra Celsum*, trans. H. Chadwick (Cambridge: Cambridge University Press, 1953), 35.

41. Kruger, *Dreaming in the Middle Ages*, 48, citing Saint Augustine, *De Genesi at litteram libri duodecim*, ed. Iosephus Zycha, Corpus Scriptorum Ecclesiasticorum Latinorum, vol. 28, section 3, Part I (Prague and Vienna: F. Temsky, and Leipzig: G. Freytag, 1894), Book XII.13.18, 196. See also Flint, *The Rise of Magic in Early Medieval Europe*, 161–62.

42. Saint Augustine, *The Divination of Demons* 3, 5, trans. R. W. Brown, in R. J. Deferrari, ed., *St. Augustine: Treatises on Marriage and Other Subjects* (Washington, D.C.: Fathers of the Church, 1955), 426, 430; cited by Flint, *The Rise of Magic*, 148. See also Kruger, *Dreaming in the Middle Ages*, 49.

43. Gregory the Great, *Moralia in Iob*, ed. Marc Adriaen, Corpus Christianorum, series latina, 143, 143A, 143B (Turnholt: Typographi Brepols Editores Pontificii, 1979–85), VIII. 24–43; *Morals on the Book of Job*, 3 vols., A Library of Fathers of the Holy Catholic Church, trans. Members of the English Church (Oxford: John Henry Parker, and London: F. and J. Rivington, 1844–50), 449–50; cited by Kruger, *Dreaming in the Middle Ages*, 49.

44. Calcidius, *Timaeus a Calcidio translatus commentarioque instructus*, ed. J. H. Waszink, Corpus Platonicum Medii Aevi: Plato Latinus (London: Warburg Institute, and Leiden: E. J. Brill, 1962), chap. 251; "imagines locorum simulacraque hominum tam uiuentium quam mortuorum"; cited by Kruger, *Dreaming in the Middle Ages*, 25.

45. Calcidius, *Timaeus*, chap. 256; Kruger, *Dreaming in the Middle Ages*, 30; "When we read this one commandment, *You shall love your neighbor as yourself*, we experience three kinds of vision: one through the eyes, by which we see the letters; a second through the spirit, by which we think of our neighbor even when he is absent; and a third through an intuition of the mind, by which we see and understand love itself," *De Genesi* (Book XII.6.15, 185), cited by Kruger, *Dreaming in the Middle Ages*, 37; and Robert Holkot, *In librum sapientiae regis Salomonis praelectiones CCXIII* (Basel: Jacobus Ryterus, 1586), esp. *lectio* 103, 350–51; cited by Kruger, *Dreaming in the Middle Ages*, 95.

46. Mary Wack, *Lovesickness in the Middle Ages: The "Viaticum" and Its Commentaries* (Philadelphia: University of Pennsylvania Press, 1989), argues that the medicalization of love in the High Middle Ages contributed to the dignifying of aristocratic sensibility.

47. Pascalis Romanus, *Liber thesauri occculti*, ed. Simone Collin-Roset, "Le *Liber thesauri occulti* de Pascalis Romanus (un traité d'interprétation des songes du XIIe siècle)," *Archives d'Histoire Doctrinale et Littéraire du Moyen Âge* 30 (1963): 111–98, book 1, chap. 11; cited by Kruger, *Dreaming in the Middle Ages*, 74.

48. Fradenburg, "'Voice Memorial,'" 179. For a recent example of this tendency, see Glenn Burger, "Reading Otherwise in the *Book of the Duchess*," *Exemplaria* 5 (1993): 325–41.

49. See *The Riverside Chaucer*, notes to lines 2375–98 to *The Monk's Tale*, and David Wallace's discussion in *Chaucerian Polity: Absolutist Lineages and Associational Forms in England and Italy* (Stanford, Calif.: Stanford University Press, 1997), 315–17.

50. In his notes on Dora's case, Freud asks: "What are transferences? They are new editions *(Neuauflagen)* or facsimiles *(Nachbildungen)* of the impulses and phantasies which are aroused and made conscious during the progress of the analysis ... they replace some earlier person by the person of the physician" (*Standard Edition*, vol. 7, 116). Laplanche and Pontalis also note that "In his first general exposition of transference Freud stresses that it is connected with 'prototypes' or imagos" (Freud, "The Dynamics of Transference," *Standard Edition*, vol. 12, 100.c, cited by Jean Laplanche and Jean-Bertrand Pontalis, *The Language of Psycho-Analysis*, trans. Donald Nicholson-Smith [London: Karnac and the Institute of Psycho-Analysis, 1973/1988], 458, s.v. "transference").

51. Lisa Kiser discusses Chaucer's "highly creative sleeping" in "Sleep, Dreams, and Poetry in Chaucer's *Book of the Duchess*," *Papers on Language and Literature* 19 (1983): 3–12, at 6.

52. On the territorial properties of sound, see Gilles Deleuze and Félix Guattari, "Of the Refrain," in *A Thousand Plateaus: Capitalism and Schizophrenia*, trans. Brian Massumi (Minneapolis: University of Minnesota Press, 1987), 310–50.

53. See Henry Ansgar Kelly, *Chaucerian Tragedy* (Woodbridge, Suffolk: D. S. Brewer, 1997), 6.

54. See *The Riverside Chaucer*, nn. 389–96, pp. 969–70.

55. Ibid. In Machaut's *Jugement du Roy de Behaigne*, on which *The Book of the Duchess* is closely modeled, a "lady's little dog runs barking to Guillaume," the narrator, because

the dog has "accidentally overheard sad accounts of love"; and Machaut has a lion who is compared to a little dog, and "join[s] his ears when patted." See Rickels, *Case of California*, 40–41, for his discussion of Ernst Kris's "psychoanalytic theory of caricature which presupposes the interchangeability of comic and manic effects" (Rickels references Ernst Kris, *Psychoanalytic Explorations in Art* [New York: Schocken Books, 1964], 213 n. 12, 221–24: ghosts animate caricature; the grimace "places itself... in charge of the imitation of a corpse"; "this pleasurable liberation of aggression... results from the underlying comparison, the likeness in deformity, for which the resemblance between humans and animals has been a model. Doubled over with laughter, the caricaturist's audience takes a turn in becoming animal... the laughter itself becomes the sole content or... the sealing of the pact").

56. The critical crux of the narrator's apparent stupidity at the end of the poem (the Man in Black has said that his lady is dead, but the narrator just does not seem to get it until the last minute) is perfectly intelligible if one considers that the poem's virtuosity might lie in making something sensible out of the insensible. The need for repetition points to the vulnerability of communication, but repetition is meant to be no dead end; rather, it is meant to "magnify" through expression, replication.

57. Jacques Derrida, *Politics of Friendship*, trans. George Collins (New York and London: Verso, 1997), 7, 12–13.

58. *Dépense* ("expenditure") is Bataille's term for the *jouissance* of destruction—for example, the prestige-producing destruction of goods on ritual occasions. See Georges Bataille, "The Notion of Expenditure," in *Visions of Excess: Selected Writings, 1927–1939*, ed. and trans. Allan Stoekl (Minneapolis: University of Minnesota Press, 1985), 116–29.

59. Derrida, *Politics of Friendship*, 8–9.

60. The term "power of alteration" is Elaine Scarry's, in *The Body in Pain: The Making and Unmaking of the World* (New York: Oxford University Press, 1985), 189. I am indebted to Scarry's understanding of sentience.

61. A. J. Minnis, *Chaucer and Pagan Antiquity* (Totowa, N.J.: D. S. Brewer/Rowman and Littlefield, 1982), 34, cites Vincent of Beauvais's *Speculum Morale:* "First, [idolatry]... proceeded from inordinate affection.... This reason is intimated in the Book of Wisdom 14:15: 'For a father being afflicted with bitter grief, made to himself the image of his son who was quickly taken away, and him who had then died as a man, he began to worship as a god'; the second reason... was the great delight in representation which is a facet in human nature."

62. Sampson is in *The Monk's Tale;* the story of Dido is retold in *The Legend of Good Women* and *The House of Fame*, at considerably greater length and with, as Jahan Ramazani notes, considerable attention paid to the pathos of suffering interiority ("Chaucer's Monk: The Poetics of Abbreviation, Aggression, and Tragedy," *Chaucer Review* 27 [1993]: 260–76, at 265). In *The Book of the Duchess*, Dido is summarily dismissed: "which a fool she was!" (734).

63. The "number" of friendship—the number of "true" friends one may have—is, as Derrida notes, unsettled in its philosophical tradition; but this very fact sets the friend apart from the spouse or the lady, at least in the later Middle Ages (*Politics of Friendship*, 2–3). Of all models of friendship, "heroic friendship" most closely resembles the valorized

relation to the spouse: an insistent coupling (only two), a life-and-death pact. Nonetheless, William Burgwinkle argues that medieval romance often presents heroic friendship as a kind of endogamous, untroubled bond, in contrast to the troubles brought on by the comparative exogamy of heterosexual marriage (and alliance) ("Knighting the Classical Hero: Homo/Hetero Affectivity in Eneas," *Exemplaria* 5 [1993]: 2–43). I am interested in showing how sameness and alterity work as figural resources in the development of courtly interiority and its purchase on "immensity"; I hope thereby to indicate the plasticity of those figures. My purpose is definitely *not* to assert the reality of sexual difference, or of the putatively greater sameness of "same-sex" coupledom.

64. Freud, "Mourning and Melancholia," 159–60.

65. "We wonder more at unfamiliar things and the soul is more strongly and vehemently held by them; whence it is that we remember better things seen in childhood" (Saint Thomas Aquinas, *Summa Theologiae*, II, II, Quaestio XLIX, *De singulis Prudentiae partibus: articulus I, Utrum memoria sit pars Prudentiae;* cited in Yates, *The Art of Memory*, 74).

66. Foucault, *The Care of the Self:* "the work of oneself on oneself and communication with others were linked together" (51).

67. Larry Scanlon, "Sweet Persuasion: The Subject of Fortune in *Troilus and Criseyde,*" in *Chaucer's Troilus and Criseyde:* "Subgit to Alle Poesye": *Essays in Criticism,* ed. R. A. Shoaf (Binghamton, N.Y.: Medieval and Renaissance Texts Society, 1992), 211–23.

68. On "prosthetic maternity," see Derrida, *Politics of Friendship,* 11.

69. On queenship, charity, and beauty, see Louise Olga Fradenburg, "Sovereign Love," in *City, Marriage, Tournament: Arts of Rule in Late Medieval Scotland* (Madison: University of Wisconsin Press, 1991), 67–83.

70. For discussion, see ibid., 251. This pageant also looked to the future; it was presided over by Jeanne de Laval, for whom the emprise was secretly arranged and who married René in 1455.

71. Lacan describes courtly love itself as "anamorphosis," and develops the idea in a discussion of Holbein's painting *The Ambassadors,* which portrays the expected group of powerful men but, when viewed from one unusual angle, shows a death's-head. Anamorphosis permits the visualization of the simultaneously Real and "empty" Thing. See *Ethics of Psychoanalysis,* 135, 139–154.

3. The Ninety-six Tears of Chaucer's Monk

1. Larry D. Benson, ed., *The Riverside Chaucer* (Boston: Houghton Mifflin, 1987). All references to Chaucer's poetry are taken from this edition and are hereafter cited by line number in the text.

2. Sabina Spielrein, *Die Destruktion als Ursache des Werdens* (Tübingen: Edition Diskord, 1986), 9, associates the feeling of anticlimax with transference and its "specific form of anxiety: one senses the enemy inside oneself, it is one's own passion which imposes upon one as constraint of necessity what one does not want: one senses the end, the transience from which one in vain would wish to flee into some unknown distance. Is that

all? one would like to ask. Is that the highpoint, the climax, and nothing more beyond that?" Cited by Laurence A. Rickels, *The Case of California* (Baltimore and London: Johns Hopkins University Press, 1991), 139. *The Case of California* is hereafter cited in the text.

3. Chaucerian comedy is discussed in chapter 2 of this volume. See Rickels, *Case of California*, 40–41, for his discussion of Ernst Kris's "psychoanalytic theory of caricature which presupposes the interchangeability of comic and manic effects" (Rickels references Ernst Kris, *Psychoanalytic Explorations in Art* [New York: Schocken Books, 1964], 213 n. 12, 221–224: ghosts animate caricature; "the grimace places itself... in charge of the imitation of a corpse"; "this pleasurable liberation of aggression... results from the underlying comparison, the likeness in deformity, for which the resemblance between humans and animals has been a model. Doubled over with laughter, the caricaturist's audience takes a turn in becoming animal... the laughter itself becomes the sole content or... the sealing of the pact."

4. Jacques Derrida, "My Chances/*Mes Chances:* A Rendezvous with Some Epicurean Stereophonies," in *Taking Chances: Derrida, Psychoanalysis and Literature*, ed. Joseph H. Smith and William Kerrigan (Baltimore: Johns Hopkins University Press, 1984), 5; hereafter cited in the text.

5. The "gift of death" is Derrida's phrase for the transformation of death's "necessity" into a gift of life that (re)structures the subject as one who keeps watch over his life in preparation for death. See Jacques Derrida, *The Gift of Death*, trans. David Wills (Chicago: University of Chicago Press, 1995).

6. A. J. Minnis, *Chaucer and Pagan Antiquity* (Totowa, N.J.: D. S. Brewer/Rowman and Littlefield, 1982), 34.

7. *Ovid: Metamorphoses*, trans. Frank Justus Miller (Cambridge: Harvard University Press and London: Heinemann, 1984), 2d ed., vol. 2, 161–62, lines 577–86;

> omnibus illa quidem superis pia tura ferebat,
> ante tumen cunctos Iunonis templa colebat
> proque viro, qui nullus erat, veniebat ad aras
> utque foret sospes coniunx suus utque redinet,
> optabat, nullamque sibi praeferret; at illi
> hoc de tot votes poterat contingere solum.
> At dea non ultra profuncto morte rogari
> sustinet utque manus funestas arceat aris,
> "Iri, meae" dixit "fidissima nuntia vocis,
> vise soporiferam Somni velociter aulam.

8. For a reading of similar issues in the poetry of James Foullis, see Louise Olga Fradenburg, *City, Marriage, Tournament: Arts of Rule in Late Medieval Scotland* (Madison: University of Wisconsin Press, 1991), 57–61. David Wallace's *Chaucerian Polity: Absolutist Lineages and Associational Forms in England and Italy* (Stanford, Calif.: Stanford University Press, 1997) discusses Chaucer's travels at a number of points, but see especially 362–63 on Chaucer's internationalism. *Chaucerian Polity* is hereafter cited in the text.

9. Rickels, *Case of California*, uses the term *groupify* to refer to an action capable of producing or maintaining the group as imaginary group body. The term does not refer to

all modes of association or alliance formation. See, for example: "'California' is the endopsychic reflection" of the shift of Freudian theory "from the myth complexes of the first system into the group identifications of the second system," that is, the shift "into another theoretical format—that of the group *inside* the death cult which has doubled (on contact with) the surrounding outside which is thus also internally (eternally) groupified" (48).

10. Maurice Blanchot, *The Space of Literature*, trans. Ann Smock (Lincoln: University of Nebraska Press, 1982), 96; hereafter cited in the text.

11. For Lacan, "the death drive is to be situated in the historical domain; it is articulated at a level that can only be defined as a function of the signifying chain," that is, in terms of the iterability and therefore variability of the signifier. It is not a biologistically conceived instinct and does not, as a conception, support an opposition between "drive" and law; quite the reverse (Jacques Lacan, *The Seminar of Jacques Lacan: Book VII: The Ethics of Psychoanalysis*, ed. Jacques-Alain Miller, trans. Dennis Porter (New York: Norton, 1992), 211–13; hereafter cited in the text).

12. See Henry Ansgar Kelly, *Chaucerian Tragedy* (Woodbridge, Suffolk: D. S. Brewer, 1997), 30, and *De casibus virorum illustrium*, facsimile of the ca. 1520 Paris edition, ed. Lewis Brewer Hall (Gainesville: University of Florida Press, 1962), 1 (pp. 25–26). Boccaccio's *De casibus* was probably Chaucer's chief model for *The Monk's Tale*, but "it was Chaucer who hit on the idea of calling these narratives tragedies, shortly after Boccaccio released the *De casibus* to the public" (Kelly, *Chaucerian Tragedy*, 9).

13. See Derrida, *Gift of Death*, 41–45, on the role of death in the creation of the responsible subject.

14. Lacan, *Ethics of Psychoanalysis*, 32, on the linguistic structure of the unconscious. For the most part, I use the term *law* in the Lacanian sense of the law as "symbolic order"—the signifying systems that enable language, kinship arrangements, economies, and so forth. The symbolic order is referred to as the "barred O" because, although it is systematic, it is open-ended and always changing, however subtly. By contrast, the "unbarred O" refers to the *fantasy* of the law as full, constant, and omnipotent.

15. For discussion of Chaucer's *Parliament of Fowls* in this context, see Fradenburg, *City, Marriage, Tournament*, 123–29. See also Sarah Kay, "The Contradictions of Courtly Love and the Origins of Courtly Poetry: The Evidence of the *Lauzengiers*," *Journal of Medieval and Early Modern Studies* 26 (1966): 209–53. The power of the envious word, in courtly culture, could be not only magical but fatal. Courtiers often officially or unofficially claimed training as magicians and astrologers, and it was assumed that "[t]hose seeking royal favor might use sorcery in doing so"; "magical assassination and love magic were common allegations in the French court during the early fourteenth century, and they were not uncommon in the English court throughout the later Middle Ages" (Richard Kieckhefer, *Magic in the Middle Ages* [Cambridge, England: Cambridge University Press, 1992], 96).

16. Slavoj Žižek, *The Sublime Object of Ideology* (New York and London: Verso, 1989), 81–82, on the "obscene enjoyment at work in [the]...act of formal sacrifice," that is, in submission to the form, the formality of, the law, not to any of its putative contents. Žižek distinguishes between *jouissance* as the signifier of an impossible "full" *jouissance* imaginable as preceding the subject's encounter with the law, and the "surplus enjoyment" or "*plus-de-jouir*," what is left of *jouissance* after it has been designed by the signifier. An "ideo-

logical fantasy" is not illusory, but rather a "work," whether of verbal or material signifiers, that participates in turn in the design of modes of enjoyment, and indeed of "worlds" for subjects to live in.

17. Henry Ansgar Kelly, in *Ideas and Forms of Tragedy from Aristotle to the Middle Ages* (Cambridge, England: Cambridge University Press, 1993), describes Salisbury's extended treatment of the world-as-stage as follows: "periods of time are acts in which the characters play out their parts until the roles in the play assigned to them by joking Fortune are finished. But the way in which Fortune casts the roles ... makes John think that the life of men is more like a tragedy than a comedy, because almost everyone's end is sad" (79; referring to John of Salisbury, *Policraticus* 3.7–3.8, in *Patrologia latinae ...*, ed. J. P. Migne [Paris], 199, and ed. C. C. J. Webb [Oxford, 1909]; and Ernst R. Curtius, *European Literature and the Latin Middle Ages*, trans. Willard R. Trask [London: Routledge and Kegan Paul, 1953], 138–40). Kelly discusses some other medieval instances of this motif at 57.

18. Lacan refers the "ex nihilo" to the emergence of the signifier, which must be "at one stroke": language does not evolve out of cries and whispers. First there is the word. See *Ethics of Psychoanalysis*, 121–22.

19. Kelly, *Chaucerian Tragedy*, 52, 71, 77.

20. Michel Foucault, *The History of Sexuality*, vol. 3, *The Care of the Self*, trans. Robert Hurley (London: Allen Lane/Penguin, 1986), 46.

21. Saint Augustine, *Confessions*, trans. R. S. Pine-Coffin (Harmondsworth, England: Penguin, 1961), III, 2, 55–56.

22. On the disavowal of rhetoric in *The Consolation of Philosophy*, see Larry Scanlon, "'Sweet Persuasion': The Subject of Fortune in *Troilus and Criseyde*," in *Chaucer's Troilus and Criseyde:* "Subgit to Alle Poesye": *Essays in Criticism*, ed. R. A. Shoaf (Binghamton, N.Y.: Medieval and Renaissance Texts and Studies, 1992), 211–23.

23. See Friedrich Nietzsche, *The Genealogy of Morals*, trans. Francis Golffing (New York: Anchor/Doubleday, 1956), on the "progressive sublimation and apotheosis of cruelty which ... characterizes [and constitutes] the whole history of higher culture" (198); "In order to ... dispose of the possibility of any secret, unwitnessed suffering, early man had to invent gods ... who could ... see in the dark, and who would not readily let pass unseen any interesting spectacle of suffering" (200).

24. Ibid., 196.

25. Augustine, *Confessions*, 55–56.

26. Willard Farnham, *The Medieval Heritage of Elizabethan Tragedy* (Oxford: Basil Blackwell, 1963), 2.

27. In *The Ethics of Psychoanalysis*, Lacan asks, "Who is there who in the name of pleasure doesn't start to weaken when the first half-serious step is taken toward *jouissance*?" (185); "the only thing one [feels] guilty of is giving ground relative to one's desire" (321).

28. Kelly, *Chaucerian Tragedy*, 140–41, and *Ideas and Forms of Tragedy*, 110.

29. Farnham, *Medieval Heritage*, 14.

30. Ibid., 29.

31. Augustine, *Confessions*, 56.

32. Jonathan Dollimore, *Radical Tragedy: Religion, Ideology and Power in the Drama of Shakespeare and his Contemporaries* (Chicago: University of Chicago Press, 1986), 190–91.

33. Scanlon, "'Sweet Persuasion,'" 216–17.

34. Thomas Walsingham, *Chronicon Angliae*, ed. Edward Maunde Thompson, Rolls Series 64 (London, 1874), 206, 301, 312; cited by Kelly, *Ideas and Forms of Tragedy*, 170.

35. Henry IV, *Epistolae*, ed. Carl Erdmann, *Die Briefe Heinrichs IV*, Deutsches Mittelalter I (Leipzig, 1937), letter 37, 50; cited by Kelly, *Ideas and Forms of Tragedy*, 61, 89.

36. See *Riverside Chaucer*, nn. 2375–98, *Monk's Tale*, 932. Kelly, *Chaucerian Tragedy*, discusses the "modern instances" at e.g., 73–74.

37. On *imagines agentes*, see Frances A. Yates, *The Art of Memory* (Chicago: Chicago University Press, 1966), 10, 16–17.

38. Jahan Ramazani points out the aggressivity of the Monk's appearance in "Chaucer's Monk: The Poetics of Abbreviation, Aggression, and Tragedy," *Chaucer Review* 27 (1993): 260–76, at 269.

39. Ibid., 266, 271.

40. On anamorphosis, see Lacan, *Ethics of Psychoanalysis*, 135–42: "any kind of construction that is made in such a way that by means of an optical transposition a certain form that wasn't visible at first sight transforms itself into a readable image" (135).

41. Wallace argues that the Host wants to see the Monk as a man of destiny; Harry Bailey is "initally seduced by his own fantasy of 'a myghty man,' ... who (so the fantasy runs) will ease the painful memory of past failures, public and domestic" (*Chaucerian Polity*, 300).

42. See Rickels, *Case of California*, 209, citing William Spring, "Observations on World Destruction Fantasies," *Psychoanalytic Quarterly* 8 (1939): 48–56, at 52: "To face a murder wish against an actual person is far more difficult than to face a wish to injure a whole community or the whole world. To destroy the world is therefore an act of self-injury." Ramazani, "Chaucer's Monk," argues that while Chaucer "explores the openness of human temporality," the Monk wants to reduce "temporal event and contingency to the timeless structure of a totality," "by transforming the horizon that individualizes us—death—into a thing ... that happens to everyone and therefore to no one in particular" (265).

43. Ramazani, "Chaucer's Monk," 262.

44. Ibid., 261.

45. Philotheus Boehner, O.F.M., trans., *Philosophical Writings: A Selection: William of Ockham* (Indianapolis and Cambridge: Hackett, 1990), xxx–xxxvii, xlviii–xlix.

46. Ockham reformulated the Aristotelian proposition that "a proposition is true when that which is said to be is" by saying "that a proposition is true when subject and predicate stand for (have *suppositio* for) the same thing." See ibid., xxxvi.

47. Ibid., xxxii–xxxiii.

48. Alfred W. Crosby, *The Measure of Reality: Quantification and Western Society* (Cambridge: Cambridge University Press, 1997), 14. Even Saint Bonaventure, in saying that "God is light in the most literal sense," meant that "it functioned *uniformly* throughout time and space" (228; on Saint Bonaventure, citing David C. Lindberg, "The Genesis of Kepler's Theory of Light: Light Metaphysics from Plotinus to Kepler," *Osiris*, n.s. 2 [1986]: 17).

49. Ibid., 202; see also Janet Thormann's fine article "The Circulation of Desire in the 'Shipman's Tale,'" *Literature and Psychology* 39 (1993): 1–15.

50. Hilary M. Carey, *Courting Disaster: Astrology at the English Court and University in the Later Middle Ages* (New York: St. Martin's Press, 1992), 91; referring to John North, *Chaucer's Universe* (Oxford: Oxford University Press, 1988), 7–8, 19, 286, 325, 452.

51. Crosby, *The Measure of Reality*, 234.

52. Kieckhefer, *Magic in the Middle Ages*, 100.

53. Ibid., 101; see also 107–9, 112.

54. Carey, *Courting Disaster*, 100.

55. Crosby, *The Measure of Reality*, 12.

56. Derrida, "My Chances/*Mes Chances*," 28; citing Sigmund Freud, *The Psychopathology of Everyday Life*, in *The Standard Edition of the Complete Psychological Works of Sigmund Freud*, trans. James Strachey (London: Hogarth Press and the Institute for Psycho-Analysis, 1953–73), vol. 11, 136–37, on Leonardo da Vinci, *A Memory of His Childhood*.

57. Lacan, *Ethics of Psychoanalysis*, 177, 214. "Being as signifier" refers to the idea of a way and kind of being that takes up the signifier, enters into its order, and can never go back on its acceptation. The human subject is an embodied signifier.

58. Peggy Knapp, *Chaucer and the Social Contest* (New York: Routledge, 1990), 48.

59. Lee W. Patterson, *Chaucer and the Subject of History* (Madison: University of Wisconsin Press, 1991), 242.

60. F. Anne Payne, *Chaucer and Menippean Satire* (Madison: University of Wisconsin Press, 1981), 155.

61. Dolores Warwick Frese, *An Ars Legendi for Chaucer's Canterbury Tales: Reconstructive Reading* (Gainesville: University of Florida Press, 1991), 102.

62. Donald R. Howard, *Chaucer: His Life, His Works, His World* (New York: E. P. Dutton, 1987), 438.

63. Wallace, *Chaucerian Polity*, 299.

64. H. Marshall Leicester Jr., *The Disenchanted Self: Representing the Subject in the Canterbury Tales* (Berkeley: University of California Press, 1990), 387–88.

65. Michaela Paasche Grudin, *Chaucer and the Politics of Discourse* (Columbia: University of South Carolina Press, 1996), 141–45.

66. Ibid., 146.

67. Wallace, *Chaucerian Polity*, 319. See also Donald Fry, "The Ending of the *Monk's Tale*," *Journal of English and Germanic Philology* 71 (1972): 355–68.

68. See Kelly, *Chaucerian Tragedy*, 75–78.

69. See Louise O. Fradenburg, "Voice Memorial: Loss and Reparation in Chaucer's Poetry," *Exemplaria* 2 (1990): 169–202, at 179. For a more recent example of this tendency in criticism on *The Book of the Duchess*, see Glenn Burger, "Reading Otherwise in the *Book of the Duchess*," *Exemplaria* 5 (1993): 325–41.

70. Ramazani, "Chaucer's Monk," 264–65, 260, 274.

71. Ibid., 265; and 264: "The Monk mercilessly abbreviates every tale he sets his hands on." On Chaucer's treatment of Dido, see Marilynn Desmond, *Reading Dido: Gender, Textuality, and the Medieval Aeneid* (Minneapolis: University of Minnesota Press, 1994), 128–62.

72. Wallace, *Chaucerian Polity*, 300.

73. Ibid., 310–12.

74. Cf. Patterson on Chaucer's concern with historical "recursion," in *Chaucer and the Subject of History*, 23–24, 47ff.

75. Žižek, *Sublime Object of Ideology*, 5.

76. Lacan, *Ethics of Psychoanalysis*, 3, 212, 213, 7, 8. Žižek concludes *The Sublime Object of Ideology* by locating "that radical change which, according to Lacan, defines the final stage of the psychoanalytic process: 'subjective destitution.' What is at stake in this 'destitution' is precisely the fact that *the subject no longer presupposes himself as subject*" (230). Kristeva locates in Freud a new "foreignness, an uncanny one, [which] creeps into the tranquility of reason itself, and, without being restricted to madness, beauty, or faith any more than to ethnicity or race, irrigates our very speaking-being, estranged by other logics, including the heterogeneity of biology" (*Strangers to Ourselves*, trans. Leon S. Roudiez [New York: Columbia University Press, 1991], 170).

77. Žižek, *Sublime Object of Ideology*, 5.

78. Kristeva, *Strangers to Ourselves*, 170.

4. Sacrificial Desire in Chaucer's Knight's Tale

1. On medieval theories of charity, see Michel Mollat, *The Poor in the Middle Ages: An Essay in Social History*, trans. Arthur Goldhammer (New Haven: Yale University Press, 1986).

2. The phrase "scapegoat for his debtor" is Friedrich Nietzsche's, *The Genealogy of Morals*, vol. 13 in *The Complete Works of Friedrich Nietzsche*, ed. Dr. Oscar Levy (New York: Gordon Press, 1974), 111; cited by Jacques Derrida, *The Gift of Death*, trans. David Wills (Chicago: University of Chicago Press, 1994), 113–14, where Derrida takes up the question of the "irreducible experience of belief," the "history of *credence* or credit" (115). On God's absurd and infinite love, see Julia Kristeva, *Tales of Love*, trans. Leon S. Roudiez (New York: Columbia University Press, 1987), esp. 139–50. Slavoj Žižek discusses the subject's submission to the law at many points; see *The Sublime Object of Ideology* (New York and London: Verso, 1989), esp. 37, 81–82, 113, and 115.

3. Saint Augustine's commentary on the Sermon on the Mount takes great pains with the problem of who the enemy is that one is commanded to love without promise of redress for injury; see *St. Augustine: Our Lord's Sermon on the Mount, according to Matthew*, trans. William Findlay, revised by D. S. Schaff; in Philip Schaff, ed., *A Select Library of the Nicene and Post-Nicene Fathers* (Grand Rapids, Mich.: Eerdmans, 1974), where heretics are not blessed through persecution, in other words they make no meaningful sacrifice (Book I, chap. v., sec. 13, p. 7); and see also I.xx.63, p. 27: "Nor are we... precluded from inflicting such punishment [requital] as avails for correction, and as compassion itself dictates."

4. Jacques Lacan, *The Seminar of Jacques Lacan: Book VII: The Ethics of Psychoanalysis, 1959–1960*, ed. Jacques-Alain Miller, trans. Dennis Porter (New York: Norton, 1992), 5, 39.

5. Lacan's notion of the formation of the subject according to the image of the other, explored in "The Mirror Stage" (in *Écrits: A Selection*, trans. Alan Sheridan [New

York: Norton, 1977], 1–7), is central to his analysis of charity in *The Ethics of Psychoanalysis*, 195–96.

6. Žižek, *Sublime Object of Ideology*, 113–15.

7. See ibid., 164, and Lacan, *Ethics of Psychoanalysis*, 149–52, for a discussion of prohibition in courtly love, specifically of the transformation of "the impossible" into "the prohibited" through sacrifice. That which is impossible because it lies beyond the limit of finitude is re-presented as what "must" be given up because it is the mandate of the Other; according to Lacan, we find it easier to tell ourselves stories of what the powerful Other has desired from us or made us do than to act in a field whose limits, including the limits of its interest in us, we acknowledge.

8. On the sublime body of the Stalinist, see Žižek, *Sublime Object of Ideology*, 145. The editors of *Knyghthode and Bataile: A XVth Century Verse Paraphrase of Flavius Vegetius Renatus' Treatise "De Re Militari"* (ed. R. Dyboski and Z. M. Arend, EETS o.s. 201 [London: Oxford University Press, 1935; rpt. New York: Kraus, 1971]) note that the author deviates from Vegetius in his "most enthusiastic references to the imagined ranks and orders of angels, introduced sometimes by way of comparison and analogy between knightly hosts in heaven and on earth" (xxxii). For a discussion of this text, see Patricia Ingham, "Military Intimacies: The Pleasures and Pains of Conquest," in *Sovereign Fantasies: Arthurian Romance and the Making of Britain* (Philadelphia: University of Pennsylvania Press, 2001).

9. Ockham, Holkot, and other fourteenth-century psychologists questioned whether enjoyment (*fruitio*, the act of inhering in love with something for its own sake) could be distinguished from the pleasure the self takes in enjoyment; see Arthur Stephen McGrade, "Enjoyment at Oxford after Ockham: Philosophy, Psychology, and the Love of God," in *From Ockham to Wyclif*, ed. Anne Hudson and Michael Wilks (Oxford: Ecclesiastical History Society, Basil Blackwell, 1987), 63–88.

10. Elaine Scarry, "Counting in an Emergency," paper delivered at the University of California, Santa Barbara, 1995.

11. For discussion of the critical tradition on *The Knight's Tale*, see Anne Laskaya, *Chaucer's Approach to Gender in the* Canterbury Tales (Cambridge, England: D. S. Brewer, 1995), esp. 58; an analysis of the tradition in the context of historical writing on chivalry can be found in Lee W. Patterson, *Chaucer and the Subject of History* (Madison: University of Wisconsin Press, 1991), 171–75.

12. Catherine La Farge, "Women and Chaucer's Providence: *The Clerk's Tale* and *The Knight's Tale*," in *From Medieval to Medievalism*, ed. John Simons (Houndmills and London: Macmillan, 1992), 69–81, at 75.

13. See Ernst H. Kantorowicz, "*Pro Patria Mori*," in *The King's Two Bodies: A Study in Mediaeval Political Theology* (Princeton, N.J.: Princeton University Press, 1957). For fuller discussion of historical writing on chivalry, see Louise Olga Fradenburg, *City, Marriage, Tournament: Arts of Rule in Late Medieval Scotland* (Madison: University of Wisconsin Press, 1991), 192–98.

14. On the contrast between terrestrial and celestial economies, see Derrida, *Gift of Death*, 98–99.

15. Frederick H. Russell, *The Just War in the Middle Ages* (Cambridge: Cambridge University Press, 1975), 17, 247, 260, 278.

16. On beauty, see Lacan, *Ethics of Psychoanalysis*, 295–98. Dyboski and Arend, in *Knyghthode and Bataile*, note that among the translator's digressions from his original are lengthy discussions of "remedies against... seditious movements" among soldiers, "a proof [of] how fully our author (himself a member of the strictly organised ecclesiastical body) appreciates [that]... aspect of military life, viz. the principle of unconditional subordination and rigorous discipline" (xxxii). On Christ the Lover-Knight, see Rosemary Woolf, "The Theme of Christ the Lover-Knight in Medieval English Literature," *Review of English Studies* 12 (1962): 1–16. Woolf notes that the "popularity of the theme undoubtedly arose from its exceptional fitness to express the dominant idea of medieval piety, that Christ endured the torments of the Passion in order to win man's love" (1; see also p. 2 on the relevance of the theme of chivalric rescue of the helpless).

17. On the "mourning for the front," see Derrida, *Gift of Death*, 17–18.

18. Bronislaw Geremek, *The Margins of Society in Late Medieval Paris*, trans. Jean Birrell (Cambridge: Cambridge University Press, 1987), 31–36.

19. As Derrida notes in one chilling passage in *The Gift of Death*, the "monotonous [ethical] complacency" of modern societies can occlude all too readily the extent to which they are organized *for* the sacrifice of millions of children, men, animals, women (86). Sacrifice plays a major role in political change through its power to sacralize what has not been sacred before, conferring plenitude, authority, the promise of union on new (or old) "political signifiers" whose hypereconomic, "surplus" value will be founded on the very terrestrial palpability of the injuries suffered in their "name." Judith Butler's chapter "Arguing with the Real" in *Bodies That Matter: On the Discursive Limits of "Sex"* (New York: Routledge, 1993) discusses the concept of the "political signifier" in Žižek's work. See also Elaine Scarry, *The Body in Pain: The Making and Unmaking of the World* (New York: Oxford University Press, 1985), for a discussion of how injury lends substantiation to the cultural fictions at stake in war (95–96).

20. "Deterritorialization" is Deleuze and Guattari's term; see Gilles Deleuze and Félix Guattari, *A Thousand Plateaus: Capitalism and Schizophrenia*, trans. Brian Massumi (Minneapolis: University of Minnesota Press, 1987), 326, on pilgrimage. Lacan discusses foreclosure in relation to the bomb—"at the end of physics"—in *Ethics of Psychoanalysis*, 131.

21. On the sacrifice of the *oikos*, see Derrida, *Gift of Death*, 94–95. The semantic field of the "sacred" is instructive on this score; the *Oxford English Dictionary* notes the "wider sense" of "sacrifice" as "the surrender to God or a deity, for the purpose of propitiation or homage, *of some object of possession*" (*OED*, s.v. "sacrifice"; emphasis added; see also *Middle English Dictionary (MED)*, s.v. "sacrifice"). Lewis and Short note the following Latin proverbs: "Hereditas sine sacris, i.e. *a great profit without trouble*," i.e., "*a rose without thorns, meat without bone, etc.* (because the keeping up of the sacra privata [the private religious rites of a gens, family] was attended with great expense)" (Charlton T. Lewis, [Lewis and Short], *A Latin Dictionary* [Oxford: Clarendon Press, 1879, 1987], s.v. "sacer"). "*Sacramentum*" in juridical usage referred to "the sum which the two parties to a suit at first deposited, but afterwards became bound for, with the *tresviri capitales;* so called because the sum deposited by the losing party was used for religious purposes, esp. for the *sacra publica;*... or, perh[aps] more correctly, because the money was deposited in a sacred place" (Lewis and Short, s.v. "sacramentum").

22. Russell, *The Just War in the Middle Ages*, 258–60. Lewis and Short note that one of the classical meanings of *sacramentum* in military discourse was the "preliminary engagement entered into by newly-enlisted troops," and thus the term was also used to designate "an oath, a solemn obligation or engagement"; hence, in ecclesiastical and late Latin, "something to be kept sacred" (Lewis and Short, *A Latin Dictionary*, s.v. "sacramentum," II).

23. Lacan describes *das Ding*, the Thing, as "that which in the real suffers from [the] ... fundamental, initial relation [to the signifier]" (*Ethics of Psychoanalysis*, 134). The Thing is "intimate exteriority" or "extimacy" (139). See also p. 52, where the Thing is "the element that is initially isolated by the subject in his experience of the *Nebenmensch* as being by its very nature alien, *Fremde*." On that which is in the subject more than the subject, see Žižek, *Sublime Object of Ideology*, 180.

24. Lacan, *Ethics of Psychoanalysis*, 150; see also Slavoj Žižek, "From the Courtly Game to *The Crying Game*," *re:Post* 1 (1993): 5–9, at 5.

25. John of Salisbury heaps a good deal of abuse on tyrants but admits that they are "ministers of God, who by His ... judgment has willed them to be in the place of highest authority in one sphere or the other, that is to say over wicked souls or over bodies, to the end that by their means the wicked may be punished, and the good chastened and exercised" (*John of Salisbury: Policraticus: The Statesman's Book*, ed. Murray F. Markland [New York: F. Ungar, 1979], 141). See also Russell, *The Just War in the Middle Ages*, 224–34.

26. Sigmund Freud, *On Creativity and the Unconscious: Papers on the Psychology of Art, Literature, Love, Religion*, ed. Benjamin Nelson (New York: Harper and Row, 1958), 63–75. Analyzing, among other texts, *The Merchant of Venice* and *King Lear*, Freud comments on the theme of choice as follows: "Choice stands in the place of necessity, of destiny. In this way man overcomes death.... No greater triumph of wish-fulfillment is conceivable. A choice is made where in reality there is obedience to a compulsion; and what is chosen is not a figure of terror, but the fairest and most desirable of women" (299).

27. *OED*, s.v. "win." God is said to win the world; Langland's wasters are ordered to work and "wynne [th]at [th]ei wasteden" (*OED*, citing Langland's *Piers Plowman*, A. v. 25).

28. *OED*, s.v. "host." The word appears several times in the opening movement of *The Knight's Tale* and rarely elsewhere in Chaucer; the exception is *Troilus and Criseyde*, where *host* is used usually to refer to the Greek army, there retaining its more hostile inflection. See Larry D. Benson, ed., *A Glossarial Concordance to the Riverside Chaucer*, 2 vols. (New York: Garland, 1993), s.v. "host." Middle English "host," as in "a victim for sacrifice," or the Eucharist, derives from Latin *hostia*, "victim, sacrifice" *(OED)*; for Latin *hosticus*, Lewis and Short give "of or belonging to a stranger, strange, foreign"; *hostimentum* is "a recompense, requital"; *hostire* is "to make even, return like for like, recompense, requite; also to strike." *Hostis* is a "stranger, foreigner," an enemy, "an enemy in arms or of one's country" as opposed to a private enemy; related to the Sanskrit root *ghas*, "to eat, consume, destroy."

29. D. W. Robertson Jr., *A Preface to Chaucer: Studies in Medieval Perspectives* (Princeton, N.J.: Princeton University Press, 1962), 467.

30. Medical rhetoric was one of the preeminent (and ethicized) languages for the "care of the self" during the Middle Ages, for the minimizing of fear and other passions, and the maximizing of proper enjoyment; see Glending Olson, *Literature as Recreation in the Later*

Middle Ages (Ithaca, N.Y.: Cornell University Press, 1982): "hygiene is ethical activity, for it both reveals and reinforces a properly functioning hierarchy within the individual" (54).

31. *MED*, s.v. "divinistre," "divinen."

32. Laura Kendrick notes the theme of the triumph of age over youth in *The Knight's Tale* in *Chaucerian Play: Comedy and Control in the* Canterbury Tales (Berkeley: University of California Press, 1988), 116, 118, 122.

33. See *OED*, s.v. "assent."

34. Marcel Mauss, *The Gift: Forms and Functions of Exchange in Archaic Societies*, trans. Ian Cunnison (Glencoe, Ill.: Free Press, 1954).

35. In Latin the relevant term for "heigh...entente" would be *"alta mente,"* used in royal charters; see Fradenburg, *City, Marriage, Tournament*, 58.

36. *OED*, s.v. "due."

37. *OED*, s.v. "grutch." See Steven Justice, *Writing and Rebellion: England in 1381* (Berkeley: University of California Press, 1994), on the association of rumor and noise with the rebels of 1381, and on scholarly characterizations of the rebels' unintelligibility (130).

38. *OED*, s.v. "foul."

39. *OED*, s.v. "heaviness," "heavy"; also s.v. "hele," "[s]ound bodily condition; freedom from sickness; health," "safety," "prosperity," as also "[s]piritual health, well-being, or healing; salvation." See Scarry, *The Body in Pain*, 36, 46, on the association of embodiedness and inarticulate voice with the disempowered, and the corresponding association of super-real powers of articulation with those who claim authority.

40. See Fradenburg, *City, Marriage, Tournament*, 200–201.

41. *OED*, s.v. "amen": "used adverbially 'certainly, verily, surely,' as an expression of affirmation, consent, or ratification of what has been said by another"; "[r]etained in the Bible from the original, as a title of Christ," that is, the "faithful one", citing Wycliffe *Rev.* iii.14, "Thes thinges seith Amen the feithful witnesse."

42. La Farge, "Women and Chaucer's Providence," 75.

43. Robertson, *A Preface to Chaucer*, 375–77. Robertson argues that this conception of marriage is "developed first" in *The Knight's Tale*, and its "manifold implications" are developed "in the subsequent tales." He also links "chaste" marriage to the "New Song" (127, and see n. 142, where the "New Song" is, of course, charity, and the "Old Song" cupidity).

44. Derrida cites Jan Patocka, *Essais hérétiques sur la philosphie de l'histoire*, trans. Erika Abrams (Lagrasse: Verdier, 1981; limited Czech edition, Prague: Petlice, 1975); see *Gift of Death*, 3 for a discussion of the relation between sexual desire and the history of responsibility. Judith Butler's *Gender Trouble: Feminism and the Subversion of Identity* (New York: Routledge, 1990) offers a very rich and psychoanalytically informed analysis of subjective processes of mournful incorporation of repudiated forms of enjoyment. See esp. "Freud and the Melancholia of Gender," 57–66.

5. Loving Thy Neighbor

1. D. W. Robertson Jr., *A Preface to Chaucer: Studies in Medieval Perspectives* (Princeton, N.J.: Princeton University Press, 1962), 25; citing his translation of Saint Augustine, *On Christian Doctrine* (New York: Liberal Arts Press, 1958), 3, 10, 16.

2. Michel Foucault, *The History of Sexuality*, vol. 3, *The Care of the Self*, trans. Robert Hurley (London: Allen Lane/Penguin, 1986), 41–42. On medieval hygiene as "ethical activity," see Glending Olson, *Literature as Recreation in the Later Middle Ages* (Ithaca, N.Y.: Cornell University Press, 1982), 54.

3. Lacan uses "creationism" to refer to ethical traditions that rationalize the emergence of humanity and of the signifier; see Jacques Lacan, *The Seminar of Jacques Lacan: Book VII: The Ethics of Psychoanalysis, 1959–1960*, ed. Jacques-Alain Miller, trans. Dennis Porter (New York: Norton, 1992), esp. 3, 120–25. Other important contemporary readings of creationist discourse include Elaine Scarry, *The Body in Pain: The Making and Unmaking of the World* (New York: Oxford University Press, 1985); Judith Butler, *Bodies That Matter: On the Discursive Limits of "Sex"* (New York: Routledge, 1993), esp. 27–55; Jean-Joseph Goux, *Symbolic Economies* (Ithaca, N.Y.: Cornell University Press, 1990), esp. 213–43; and Kenneth Burke, *The Rhetoric of Religion: Studies in Logology* (Berkeley: University of California Press, 1970).

4. Chaucer, F-Prologue, *The Legend of Good Women*, line 166; hereafter cited in the text.

5. Saint Thomas Aquinas, *Commentary on the Nicomachean Ethics*, trans. C. I. Litzinger, O.P. (Chicago: Henry Regnery, 1964), vii.l.v:c 1374–75, pp. 641–42.

6. Ibid., 1376, p. 642.

7. See Butler, *Bodies That Matter*, 50–51, on resemblance.

8. Saint Thomas Aquinas, *Summa Theologica*, trans. Fathers of the English Dominican Province, 5 vols. (Westminster, Md.: Christian Classics, 1981), vol. 1; part 1, question 92, article 1, 466; hereafter cited in the text.

9. On the common good, see Paul Strohm, *Social Chaucer* (Cambridge: Harvard University Press, 1989), 145–47; on the pleasures of the ruler in mirrors for princes see Olson, *Literature as Recreation*, 53–83. The best current treatment of medieval theories of charity is Michel Mollat's *The Poor in the Middle Ages: An Essay in Social History*, trans. Arthur Goldhammer (New Haven: Yale University Press, 1986).

10. Sigmund Freud, "Psycho-analytic Notes on an Autobiographical Account of a Case of Paranoia (Dementia Paranoides)," in *The Standard Edition of the Complete Psychological Works of Sigmund Freud*, trans. James Strachey (London: Hogarth Press and the Institute for Psycho-Analysis, 1953–73), vol. 21; hereafter cited in the text. Freud cites Schreber's *Denkwürdigkeiten eines Nervenkranken: nebst Nachträgen* (Leipzig: Oswald Mutze, 1903), 409; the translations from Schreber are Strachey's and are hereafter cited in the text.

11. Freud, "Psycho-analytic Notes," 65, 72. See Butler, *Bodies That Matter*, 64–65 on how prohibitions structure the form of the body as "an allegory of prohibited love, the *incorporation* of loss"; 98–99 on disidentification with libidinal positions that seem "too saturated with injury or aggression."

12. Elaine Scarry uses the term "power of alteration" in *The Body in Pain*, 189.

13. "Introduction" to Schreber, *Denkwürdigkeiten eines Nervenkranken*, 4; Freud, "Psycho-analytic Notes," 32 n.1; Freud notes that Schreber's identification with Jesus Christ appears only at a very late stage (Schreber, 338, 431; Freud, 28). On Schreber's association of femaleness with disgrace, see Freud's citation of Dr. Weber's report (Freud, 16–17, and Schreber, 127, Freud, 20).

14. Schreber is supported throughout his ordeal by the belief that until his transformation into a woman is complete, his personality will "remain indestructible" (Freud, "Psycho-analytic Notes," 7, 48).

15. Schreber explains in a footnote to the words *"contrary to the Order of Things"* that he hopes to show that "emasculation for quite another purpose," a "purpose *in consonance with the Order of Things,*" "is within the bounds of possibility" (Freud, "Psycho-analytic Notes," 20).

16. Schreber, 208–14, Freud, 35–36; Schreber, 283, Freud, 34; Schreber, 188, Freud, 52 n. 3; Schreber, 333, Freud, 27.

17. Prudence Allen, *The Concept of Woman: The Aristotelian Revolution, 750 BC–AD 1250* (Montreal: Eden Press, 1985), 415, 470–71.

18. Pauline Stafford, *Queens, Concubines, and Dowagers: The King's Wife in the Early Middle Ages* (Athens: University of Georgia Press, 1983), 196; Paul Strohm, *Hochon's Arrow: The Social Imagination of Fourteenth-Century Texts* (Princeton, N.J.: Princeton University Press, 1992), 95.

19. Diane Bornstein, *The Lady in the Tower: Medieval Courtesy Literature for Women* (Hamden, Conn.: Archon Books, 1983), 81–82. The *Speculum dominarum* (Bibliothèque Nationale, manuscrits latins 6784) was written for Jeanne de Navarre by her confessor, Durand de Champagne, early in the fourteenth century; it was translated into French with the title *Miroir des dames* (Bibliothèque Nationale, f. fr. 610). Stafford's work makes clear that patronage was also a very important aspect of early queenship (*Queens, Concubines, and Dowagers,* 99, 101, 108–9).

20. Bornstein, *The Lady in the Tower,* 120; she notes that Christine de Pisan's *Livre de trois vertus* is the only mirror for the princess to give serious consideration to the queen's economic and political activities.

21. Ian Maclean, *The Renaissance Notion of Woman: A Study in the Fortunes of Scholasticism and Medieval Science in European Intellectual Life* (Cambridge: Cambridge University Press, 1980), 60, 66.

22. See Judson Boyce Allen, *The Ethical Poetic of the Later Middle Ages: A Decorum of Convenient Distinction* (Toronto: University of Toronto Press, 1982), 28; and Olson, *Literature as Recreation,* 210.

23. On the indeterminacy of queenship, see Louise Olga Fradenburg, *City, Marriage, Tournament: Arts of Rule in Late Medieval Scotland* (Madison: University of Wisconsin Press, 1991), 75–90. On the role of virtue in rendering "invisible" the "traumatic, intolerable dimension" of "the Lady," see Slavoj Žižek, "From the Courtly Game to *The Crying Game,*" *re:Post* 1 (1993): 5–9; and Lacan, *Ethics of Psychoanalysis,* 194.

24. See John Carmi Parsons, "Ritual and Symbol in the English Medieval Queenship to 1500," in Louise O. Fradenburg, ed., *Women and Sovereignty, Cosmos* 7 (Edinburgh: Edinburgh University Press, 1992), 60–77, for a discussion of how medieval queenship rituals both acknowledge and limit queenly power.

25. See Lacan, *Ethics of Psychoanalysis,* 152, on the "ethical function of eroticism" as displayed in courtly love's "sexual valorization of the preliminary stages of the act of love." Mary Wack theorizes the medicalization of *amor hereos* as an effort to substantiate the reality of the condition of passionate love among the nobility (*Lovesickness in the Middle Ages:*

The Viaticum and Its Commentaries [Philadelphia: University of Pennsylvania Press, 1990]); and see John Livingston Lowes, "The Loveres Maladye of Hereos," *Modern Philology* 11 [1913–14]: 1–56/491–546).

26. Lacan's notion of the formation of the subject according to the image of the other in "The Mirror Stage" (in *Écrits: A Selection*, trans. Alan Sheridan [New York: Norton, 1977], 2) is central to his analysis of charity in *The Ethics of Psychoanalysis*.

27. See Lacan, *Ethics of Psychoanalysis*, 139, on "the intimate exteriority or 'extimacy,' that is the Thing."

28. Butler discusses "the ambivalence at the heart of political forms of altruism" in *Bodies That Matter*, 99.

29. The "general will" promotes the "respect for certain rights," but Lacan's concern is that "it can also take the form of excluding from its boundaries, and therefore from its protection, everything that is not integrated into its various registers" (*Ethics of Psychoanalysis*, 195).

30. See ibid., 152, on the "apotheosis of the neighbor" in Christianity and on the *bon vezi*, Guillaume de Poitiers's term for his beloved; 261–62 on sadism's construction of a double of the self made phantasmatically inaccessible to destruction, and the crucifixion as the "apotheosis of sadism," the "divinization" of that "limit in which a being remains in a state of suffering."

31. The notion that when the "lady" is a married spouse something astonishing has occurred in the annals of courtly love is an overreaction; though the distinction between the wife and the neighbor's wife—and the neighbor's wife is herself a neighbor—is important insofar as it figures the proximity or distance involved in coveting what lies in the field of the other, the crucial element is the "extimacy" of the lady, and the wife can figure that too, by a number of different ruses, for example, Blanche's deadness in *The Book of the Duchess*.

32. Like its obverse, beauty, shame marks the limit of the ideal image and points, comically or punitively, to what lies beyond it (ibid., 298). Lacan remarks of a poem by Arnaut Daniel in which the lover is asked to "put his mouth to [the lady's] trumpet" that "the idealized woman ... finds herself suddenly and brutally positing, in a place knowingly constructed out of the most refined of signifiers, the emptiness of a thing in all its crudity, ... the one that is to be found at her very heart in its cruel emptiness" (162, 163). See also Fradenburg, *City, Marriage, Tournament*, 260–62, for a related reading of Dunbar's poem "Ane Blake Moir."

33. Strohm, *Hochon's Arrow*, 113–17, discusses Alceste's role as intercessor and her relation to Queen Anne. David Wallace, in *Chaucerian Polity: Absolutist Lineages and Associational Forms in England and Italy* (Stanford, Calif.: Stanford University Press, 1997), reads Alceste as part of Chaucer's broad concern with wifely eloquence and its power to subdue masculine violence. See also Robert Burlin, *Chaucerian Fictions* (Princeton, N.J.: Princeton University Press, 1977), 40–41, and Allen, *The Ethical Poetic of the Later Middle Ages*, 268.

34. Carolyn Dinshaw's reading of *The Legend of Good Women* emphasizes Chaucer's "excising of the women's acts of honor and virtue, or recrimination and revenge" (*Chaucer's Sexual Poetics* [Madison: University of Wisconsin Press, 1989], 86). Elaine Hansen stresses the *Legend*'s preoccupation with the instability of gender roles in *Chaucer and the Fictions of*

Gender (Berkeley: University of California Press, 1992), 1–10; see also Jill Mann's important discussion of gender and pity in the *Legend*, in *Geoffrey Chaucer* (Atlantic Highlands, N.J.: Humanities Press, 1991), 39–48, and Sheila Delany, *The Naked Text: Chaucer's* Legend of Good Women (Berkeley: University of California Press, 1994), 153–64.

35. *Pietas* is "dutiful conduct toward the gods, one's parents, relatives, benefactors, country, etc., *sense of duty*," "love"; in later Latin, "*Gentleness, kindness, tenderness, pity, compassion*" (Charlton T. Lewis [Lewis and Short], *A Latin Dictionary* [Oxford: Clarendon Press, 1879, 1987], s.v. "pietas"). Though often linked to "charite," "pite" appears more often in Chaucer's poetry (122 times) and in a wider range of contexts (legal, petitionary, amorous, devotional) than does "charite" (26 occurrences). See Larry D. Benson, ed., *A Glossarial Concordance to the Riverside Chaucer*, 2 vols. (New York: Garland, 1993), s.v. "pite."

36. Mann notes that "Alceste's 'pitee' is the very mark of her identity" (*Geoffrey Chaucer*, 41).

37. Lewis and Short, *A Latin Dictionary*, s.v. "praeclarus," "illustris," "excellens"; Bornstein, *The Lady in the Tower*, 81.

38. *Middle English Dictionary (MED)*, s.v. "kithen."

39. Butler, *Bodies That Matter*, 209.

40. See ibid. on Slavoj Žižek's notion of "political signifiers," their posturing as a "site of radical semantic abundance," and the inevitable "disappointment or disidentification" that follows in their wake (*The Sublime Object of Ideology* [New York and London: Verso, 1959], 208–9).

41. *MED*, s.v. "defien," "reneien."

42. *MED*, s.v. "reverence."

43. *MED*, s.v. "dwellen."

44. *MED*, s.v. "neigh"; as an adjective "neigh" can mean "near by kinship, friendship, or allegiance," "reconciled," as well as spatially proximate; as an adverb, "almost," "closely"; as a preposition, "close to, near to," as in the senses of "close to the political rank of," "in the confidence of," "on the brink of."

45. The Prologue is full of what Freud called "primal words" ("words with two meanings, one of which says the exact opposite of the other") ("'The Antithetical Sense of Primal Words': A Review of a Pamphlet by Karl Abel, *Über den Gegensinn der Urworte*, 1884," in Sigmund Freud, *On Creativity and the Unconscious: Papers on the Psychology of Art, Literature, Love, Religion*, ed. Benjamin Nelson [New York: Harper, 1958], 55–62).

46. *MED*, s.v. "relik."

47. *MED*, s.v. "colden."

48. *MED*, s.v. "disteinen."

49. *MED*, s.v. "digne."

50. *MED*, s.v. "bounte."

51. *MED*, s.v. "benigne," "mek."

52. Lisa Kiser gives a finely detailed reading of the figurative transformations in the Prologue, in *Telling Classical Tales: Chaucer and the* Legend of Good Women (Ithaca, N.Y.: Cornell University Press, 1983); see esp. 28–49 and 58.

53. The pearl is the vacuole "filled in" with rare, sublime matter, as if to say that *jouissance* can always destabilize the $\pm$ phallus on which binary sexual difference depends.

"The idealized woman" posits "a thing that reveals itself in its nudity to be the thing, her thing" (Lacan, *Ethics of Psychoanalysis*, 163). The clitoris "queers" sexual difference by upsetting the assumption that the female genital is "not."

54. See Delany, *The Naked Text*, 231–32 on the legends' "Pauline-Augustinian orthodoxy."

6. "OURE OWEN WO TO DRYNKE"

1. Jacques Lacan, *The Seminar of Jacques Lacan: Book VII: The Ethics of Psychoanalysis, 1959–1960*, ed. Jacques-Alain Miller, trans. Dennis Porter (New York: Norton, 1992), 240.

2. John Bowers argues of the later Middle Ages that "[n]ot since Augustine's attack upon the Pelagians in the fourth century had theologians argued so heatedly over the faculty which determines the extent of man's power to act [and] ... to accomplish what is right" (41). He notes especially Robert Holcot and Adam of Woodham, whose "conclusion was to invest in the will the powers of cognition and reasoning in addition to its usual acts of wishing, intending, choosing, and moving of man's other potencies" (54). See John M. Bowers, *The Crisis of Will in Piers Plowman* (Washington, D.C.: Catholic University of America Press, 1986).

3. Saint Thomas Aquinas, *Commentary on the Nicomachean Ethics*, trans. C. I. Litzinger, O.P. (Chicago: Henry Regnery, 1964), vii.l.v:c 1374–75, pp. 641–42.

4. Christine de Pizan, *The Book of the City of Ladies* (New York: Persea, 1982). The idea that the morally weak may be judged by gentler standards is a topos in medieval moral philosophy.

5. See Michel Mollat, *The Poor in the Middle Ages: An Essay in Social History*, trans. Arthur Goldhammer (New Haven: Yale University Press, 1986): "By the beginning of the thirteenth century it was generally accepted that the starving thief was innocent of any crime" (111).

6. John T. McNeill and Helena M. Gamer, trans., *Medieval Handbooks of Penance: A Translation of the Principal Libri Poenitentiales and Selections from Related Documents* (New York: Columbia University Press, 1938), from *The Penitential Tentatively Ascribed by Albers to Bede* [early eighth century], 221, 223. The notion that just penance depended on fine discriminations of condition was a feature of the penitential manuals throughout the Middle Ages.

7. Derrida discusses the "hypereconomy" of Christian exchange at a number of points in *The Gift of Death*, trans. David Wills (Chicago: University of Chicago Press, 1995), for example, "This [celestial] capital that cannot be devalued will yield an infinite profit" (98); the "economy of sacrifice ... always presupposes a calculation that claims to go beyond calculation" (107).

8. The consent of the sacrificed entity is a vexed issue long before Christianity. Marcel Detienne, "Culinary Practices and the Spirit of Sacrifice," in *The Cuisine of Sacrifice among the Greeks*, ed. Marcel Detienne and Jean-Pierre Vernant, trans. Paula Wissing (Chicago: University of Chicago Press, 1989), 1–20, writes that, among the ancient Greeks, "the sacrifice is carried out in an atmosphere of uneasy caution, as can be seen in words and ges-

tures laden with ambiguity"; for example: "The animal selected as victim is led without apparent constraint in a procession to the altar at the same pace as the future diners and the ritual takes care to obtain the animal's consent by a sign of the head. The usual procedure puts the animal in contact with pure water and the fruits of the earth, but suddenly and by surprise. When the cold water splashes on the animal, it shudders...which among the Greeks is a sign of agreement" (9).

9. Elaine Scarry, *The Body in Pain: The Making and Unmaking of the World* (New York: Oxford University Press, 1987), 21, 149–57.

10. By "objection" I mean "the making of a sentient creature into an object."

11. On the easy interchange between passivity and activity in medieval [amorous] optics, see Sarah Stanbury, "The Lover's Gaze in Troilus and Criseyde," in *Chaucer's Troilus and Criseyde: "Subgit to alle Poesye": Essays in Criticism*, ed. R. A. Shoaf with Catherine S. Cox (Binghamton, N.Y.: Medieval and Renaissance Texts and Studies, 1992), 224–38. Whether Troilus is the victim or the wielder of "Love's Fatal Glance" is finally undecidable: "The gaze seems to fracture the boundaries of the private self" (227). This "intersubjectivity" is "the experience central to the ethics of the western love tradition" (231).

12. See C. T. Allmand, ed., *Society at War: The Experience of England and France during the Hundred Years War* (Edinburgh: Oliver and Boyd, 1973), 26–27 for an example of an oath taken by an aspirant to a military order founded by the Duc de Bourbon "to maintain the honour of womanhood,...and to do this with our bodies, if need be."

13. G. W. Coopland, ed. and trans., *The Tree of Battles of Honoré Bonet* (Cambridge: Harvard University Press, 1949).

14. See "The Blessing of the New Knight" in *Chaucer: Sources and Backgrounds*, ed. Robert P. Miller (New York: Oxford University Press, 1977), 171–73: "Just as he is raised from an inferior station to the new honor of chivalry, so, putting off the old man with his deeds, he will put on the new man,...to obey the articles of his oath lawfully in all things, and to fulfill his office justly" (172).

15. John of Salisbury, *Policraticus*, in Murray F. Markland, ed., *John of Salisbury: Policraticus: The Statesman's Book* (New York: Ungar, 1979), 82: "But what is the office of the duly ordained soldiery? To...pour out their blood for their brothers (as the formula of their oath instructs them), and, if need be, to lay down their lives."

16. The work of the last two decades has, however, focused more carefully on social contexts: David Aers's influential discussion of Criseyde in *Chaucer, Langland, and the Creative Imagination* (London: Routledge and Kegan Paul, 1980); Lee W. Patterson's reading of the poem as a meditation on historical process (*Chaucer and the Subject of History* [Madison: University of Wisconsin Press, 1991], 84–164); Paul Strohm's treatment of the poem's audience, and its "critique of temporality," in *Social Chaucer* (Cambridge: Harvard University Press, 1989); Jill Mann's feminist criticism in *Geoffrey Chaucer* (Atlantic Highlands, N.J.: Humanities Press, 1991); Gayle Margherita's rereading of historicity in *Troilus and Criseyde* in *The Romance of Origins: Language and Sexual Difference in Middle English Literature* (Philadelphia: University of Pennsylvania Press, 1994), 100–128. Christian moral readings have sometimes treated Troilus's forgetting of the war as spiritual failure; see D. W. Robertson Jr., *A Preface to Chaucer: Studies in Medieval Perspectives* (Princeton, N.J.: Princeton University Press, 1962), 478, on Troilus's "neglect of duty."

17. Douglas B. Wilson's "The Commerce of Desire: Freudian Narcissism in Chaucer's *Troilus and Criseyde* and Shakespeare's *Troilus and Cressida*," *English Language Notes* 21 (1983): 11–22, primarily analyzes character; Helen Corsa's "Is This a Mannes Herte?" *Literature and Psychology* 16 (1966): 81–88, reads *Troilus and Criseyde* in light of the Oedipus complex. Michael Masi's "Troilus: A Medieval Psychoanalysis" contends that in the Middle Ages, "the understanding of human psychology is a philosophical study" (*Annuale Medievale* 11 [1970]: 81–82).

18. David Wallace stresses how often Chaucer's poetry gives audience to eloquent women; see *Chaucerian Polity: Absolutist Lineages and Associational Forms in England and Italy* (Stanford, Calif.: Stanford University Press, 1997), 212–46.

19. Sigmund Freud, "The Theme of the Three Caskets," in *On Creativity and the Unconscious: Papers on the Psychology of Art, Literature, Love, Religion,* ed. Benjamin Nelson (New York: Harper and Row, 1958), 69.

20. Slavoj Žižek, *Enjoy Your Symptom!: Jacques Lacan in Hollywood and Out* (New York: Routledge, 1992), 171ff.

21. Sigmund Freud, "Three Contributions to the Psychology of Love," in *On Creativity and the Unconscious*, 162–205, discusses desires to rescue fallen women.

22. Lacan stresses the role of the group in defining the sublime object in *Ethics of Psychoanalysis*, 145, 149.

23. William Shakespeare, *Troilus and Cressida*, 3.2.163 (in *The Norton Shakespeare*, ed. Walter Cohen, Jean Howard, and Kathy Maus [New York: Norton, 1997]). Gretchen Mieszkowski, "The Reputation of Criseyde 1155–1500," *Transactions of the Connecticut Academy of Arts and Sciences* 43 (1971) (New Haven: Archon Books), demonstrates that Criseyde's reputation for faithlessness was well established by the time Chaucer wrote *Troilus and Criseyde*. On repetition and identity in Shakespeare's *Troilus and Cressida*, see also Mihoko Suzuki, *Metamorphoses of Helen: Authority, Difference, and Epic* (Ithaca, N.Y.: Cornell University Press, 1989); and Linda Charnes, *Notorious Identity: Materializing the Subject in Shakespeare* (Cambridge: Harvard University Press, 1993).

24. Claude Lévi-Strauss, *The Elementary Structures of Kinship*, trans. James Harle Bell, John Richard von Sturmer, and Rodney Needham (Boston: Beacon Press, 1969), 496. Gayle Rubin, "The Traffic in Women: Notes on the 'Political Economy' of Sex," in *Toward an Anthropology of Women*, ed. R. R. Reiter (New York: Monthly Review Press, 1975), is now a classic; see also Carolyn Dinshaw, *Chaucer's Sexual Poetics* (Madison: University of Wisconsin Press, 1989), 96–99.

25. Kathryn Gravdal, "The Poetics of Rape Law in Medieval France," in *Rape and Representation*, ed. Lynn A. Higgins and Brenda R. Silver (New York: Columbia University Press, 1991), 211. See also Gravdal's *Ravishing Maidens: Writing Rape in Medieval French Literature and Law* (Philadelphia: University of Pennsylvania Press, 1991), 124–25, 126.

26. Ibid., 215–16; Shulamith Shahar, *The Fourth Estate: A History of Women in the Middle Ages*, trans. Chaua Galai (London: Methuen, 1983), 21.

27. Gravdal, "The Poetics of Rape Law in Medieval France," 216. For a broad review of the treatment of rape in medieval law, see Shahar, *The Fourth Estate*, 16–17.

28. Gravdal, "The Poetics of Rape Law in Medieval France," 213.

29. Ibid., 217.

30. Donald R. Howard, *Chaucer: His Life, His Works, His World* (New York: E. P. Dutton, 1987), 317, 318. See also Christopher Cannon, "*Raptus* in the Chaumpaigne Release and a Newly Discovered Document concerning the Life of Geoffrey Chaucer," *Speculum* 68 (1993): 74–94, and "Chaucer and Rape: Uncertainty's Certainties," *Studies in the Age of Chaucer* 22 (2000): 67–92.

31. See Georges Duby's chapter "Incest, Bigamy and Divorce among Kings and Nobles," in *Medieval Marriage: Two Models from Twelfth-Century France*, trans. Elborg Foster (Baltimore: Johns Hopkins University Press, 1978).

32. *The Meroure of Wyssdome...by Johannes de Irlandia*, ed. Charles Macpherson, vol. 1 (Edinburgh: William Blackwood and Sons, for the Scottish Text Society, 1926), 137; hereafter cited in the text. See Louise Olga Fradenburg, *City, Marriage, Tournament: Arts of Rule in Late Medieval Scotland* (Madison: University of Wisconsin Press, 1991), 76, 88–90, for fuller discussion of this text's treatment of Marian consent.

33. On mourning the loss of the front as "historic figure for [the] *polemos* that brings enemies together as though they were conjoined in the extreme proximity of the face-to-face," see Derrida, *Gift of Death*, 17.

34. Scarry, *The Body in Pain*, 65ff.

35. C. T. Allmand writes that "one of the biggest changes in warfare which occurred at this period was the way in which, as the scale of war continued to expand, this expansion was made to embrace larger proportions of the populations of both England and France than ever before" (*Society at War*, 9). See also Maurice Keen, *Chivalry* (New Haven: Yale University Press, 1984), 228: the "passage of armies...made the ravages of war into a factor of social and economic importance at least comparable with the effect of plague."

36. Coopland, *Tree of Battles of Honoré Bonet*, chapter cii, 189.

37. Howard, *Chaucer*, 69–73.

38. Allmand, *Society at War*, 13.

39. Ibid., 9, 11.

40. Scarry, *The Body in Pain*, 63ff.

41. Jean Laplanche and Jean-Bertrand Pontalis, *The Language of Psycho-analysis*, trans. Donald Nicholson-Smith (London: Karnac and the Institute of Psycho-Analysis, 1973/1988), s.v. "trauma."

42. Ibid., s.v. "trauma." See also entries "anxiety neurosis" and "helplessness."

43. Howard, *Chaucer*, 128. See also Keen, *Chivalry*, 230, and Patterson, *Chaucer and the Subject of History*, 177. It should be remembered that women were not simply victims of war. Landed women often had the responsibility of defending holdings when, as was often the case, husbands were making law or war elsewhere; by the fifteenth century, a "rising" woman such as Margery Paston would learn how to conduct siege warfare.

44. See Gilles Deleuze and Félix Guattari, *A Thousand Plateaus: Capitalism and Schizophrenia*, trans. Brian Massumi (Minneapolis: University of Minnesota Press, 1987), "Treatise on Nomadology," 351–423. Their revision of the idea that the state comes to dominate private feud argues that the war machine is *always* present, always appropriable, but never containable by the state's quite different styles of power.

45. A good discussion of some aspects of *Troilus and Crisyede*'s earlier critical tradition is "Reading Like a Man," in Dinshaw, *Chaucer's Sexual Poetics*, 28–64.

46. C. S. Lewis, *The Allegory of Love: A Study in Medieval Tradition* (New York: Oxford University Press, 1958), 185; cited in Alice R. Kaminsky, *Chaucer's Troilus and Criseyde and the Critics* (Columbus: Ohio University Press, 1980), 145–46; for bibliography on the question of Criseyde's fear, see Kaminsky, 200 nn. 58, 59.

47. On the father's reluctance to give up the daughter, see Lynda Boose, "The Father's House and the Daughter in It: The Structures of Western Culture's Father-Daughter Relationship," in *Daughters and Fathers*, ed. Lynda E. Boose and Betty S. Flowers (Baltimore: Johns Hopkins University Press, 1989), 19–74.

48. The story is told in Ovid's *Metamorphoses* 6 of how Tereus, married to Procne, raped her sister Philomela, subsequently imprisoning her and cutting out her tongue so that she could not accuse him of his crime. Philomela weaves a tapestry telling her story and sends it to her sister; they revenge themselves upon Tereus and are turned into a swallow (Procne) and a nightingale (Philomela). The story is also told in Chaucer's *Legend of Good Women;* he leaves out the sisters' revenge against Tereus. See Patricia Joplin's influential reading of the myth in "The Voice of the Shuttle is Ours," in *Rape and Representation*, ed. Lynn A. Higgins and Brenda R. Silver (New York: Columbia University Press, 1991), 35–64.

49. "Introduction: Rereading Rape," in Higgins and Silver, *Rape and Representation*, 5.

50. On the *pastorelas*, see Joan Ferrante, "Male Fantasy and Female Reality in Courtly Literature," *Women's Studies* 11 (1984): 70–72.

51. David Aers's groundbreaking discussion of Book III recognized the possible implications of the narrator's question; Aers argues that in *Troilus and Criseyde*, "the effects of male domination and egotistic predatoriness, legitimized in social practice and ideology, are reflected even in the most personal acts where there is genuine love." But Aers writes too lyrically about this scene, positing a "genuine love" that can be distinguished from "social practice and ideology," even if the latter is to be found reflected in the former (Aers, *Chaucer, Langland, and the Creative Imagination*, 127–28).

52. John J. Winkler, "The Education of Chloe: Erotic Protocols and Prior Violence," in Higgins and Silver, *Rape and Representation*, 15–34, at 25.

53. See Larry Scanlon, "Sweet Persuasion: The Subject of Fortune in Troilus and Criseyde," in Shoaf and Cox, *Chaucer's Troilus and Criseyde*, 211–223, at 222.

54. On the transformation of "coerced relations" into "elective" and "reciprocal" ones, see Pierre Bourdieu, *Outline of a Theory of Practice*, trans. Richard Nice (Cambridge: Cambridge University Press, 1977), 171.

55. Patterson remarks that "Thebanness is a fatal doubling of the self that issues in a replicating history that preempts a linear or developmental progress" (*Chaucer and the Subject of History*, 77).

56. Karla Taylor, "A Text and Its Afterlife," in *Chaucer Reads the Divine Comedy* (Stanford, Calif.: Stanford University Press, 1989), 50–77.

57. Shakespeare, *Troilus and Cressida*, III, ii, 66.

58. Sigmund Freud, "A Special Type of Object Choice," in *On Creativity and the Unconscious*, 170.

59. Henry Ansgar Kelly, *Chaucerian Tragedy* (Woodbridge, Suffolk: D. S. Brewer, 1997), 6.

60. I disagree with Žižek on this point; see *Enjoy Your Symptom!*, 165–79.

61. Writing of the role of "paternal intervention" in the elegy, Peter Sacks, following Lacan's "elaboration of Freud's Oedipus scenario," emphasizes the "submission of the child to society's 'symbolic order' of signs," in *The English Elegy: Studies in the Genre from Spenser to Yeats* (Baltimore: Johns Hopkins University Press, 1985), 8.

62. Joseph Warton famously complained about Chaucer's "very sudden transitions from the sublime to the ridiculous" in his "Essay on the Genius and Writings of Pope," cited in Derek Brewer, *Chaucer: The Critical Heritage*, vol. 1, *1385–1837* (London: Routledge, 1978), 212; Matthew Arnold, equally famously, complained of Chaucer's lack of "high seriousness," "General Introduction" to *The English Poets*, ed. T. H. Ward (1880); rpt. *Essays in Criticism*, 2d series (1888), xxx–xxxvi; cited in Brewer, *Chaucer: The Critical Heritage*, vol. 2, *1837–1933* (London: Routledge, 1978), 220. Byron described Chaucer as "obscene and contemptible" (T. Moore, *The Life, Letters, and Journals of Lord Byron*, 1830/1860, ch. 5, p. 49; cited in Brewer, *Chaucer*, vol. 1, 249).

63. Wallace argues in *Chaucerian Polity* that differences in time and sophistication between Chaucer and "Renaissance" poets such as Petrarch have been greatly exaggerated; the effect has been to redistribute the cultural and political diversity of fourteenth-century Europe along a timeline favoring the idea of the "emergence" of early modern absolutism and its administrative technologies (9–11). Sir Philip Sidney remarks of Chaucer that he had "great wants, fitte to be forgiuen, in so reuerent antiquity" (*An Apologie for Poetrie*, ed. G. T. Shepherd, 1965; cited in Brewer, *Chaucer*, vol. 1, 120). See also Seth Lerer, *Chaucer and His Readers: Imagining the Author in Late Medieval England* (Princeton, N.J.: Princeton University Press, 1993), on fifteenth- and early sixteenth-century receptions of Chaucer's work.

64. Stephanie Jed, "The Scene of Tyranny: Violence and the Humanistic Tradition," in *The Violence of Representation: Literature and the History of Violence*, ed. Nancy Armstrong and Leonard Tennenhouse (London: Routledge, 1989), 40. This work is reprised in Stephanie H. Jed, *Chaste Thinking: The Rape of Lucretia and the Birth of Humanism* (Bloomington: Indiana University Press, 1989).

65. Susan Snyder, "The Left Hand of God: Despair in Medieval and Renaissance Tradition," *Studies in the Renaissance* 12 (1965): 18–59, notes that for Saint Paul, for patristic writers, for medieval mystics and theologians, *tristitia* is both a deadly sin and—insofar as the Christian must sorrow for his sins before he can be forgiven—a necessary part of Christian life. *Tristitia*, as *fruitful* sorrow for sin, forms part of a narrative of *ascesis* and reward—of renunciation and compensation; in the form of despair, *tristitia* goes nowhere, "works death." On *amor hereos*, see Mary Wack, *Lovesickness in the Middle Ages: The Viaticum and Its Commentaries* (Philadelphia: University of Pennsylvania Press, 1989). See also Frances Yates, *The Art of Memory* (Chicago: University of Chicago Press, 1966); Mary Carruthers, *The Book of Memory* (Cambridge: Cambridge University Press, 1990); and Siegfried Wenzel, *The Sin of Sloth: Acedia in Medieval Thought and Literature* (Chapel Hill: University of North Carolina Press, 1967).

66. Julia Kristeva, *Black Sun: Depression and Melancholy*, trans. Leon Roudiez (New York: Columbia University Press, 1989), 6.

67. I associate Diomede with the "bad side" of *das Ding* because his come-lately status, along with the promiscuity of his speech and his desire's awareness of its dependence on precedent, gives him some of the properties of the destinerring signifier.

Epilogue

1. On medievalism and social thought in the nineteenth century, see Alice Chandler, *A Dream of Order: The Medieval Ideal in Nineteenth-Century Literature* (London: Routledge and Kegan Paul, 1971), 3–4, 7.

2. Clifford Siskin made this point about Babe and the "work of the other" in "The Work of Writing," a paper delivered at the "Conference on the Directions of Scholarship: Virginia Graduates Confront the Profession," University of Virginia, October 1996, also the venue where I presented the first version of this epilogue.

3. Karl Marx and Friedrich Engels, *The German Ideology*, in *Karl Marx: Selected Writings*, ed. David McClellan (Oxford: Oxford University Press, 1977), 165–66; Georges Bataille, "The Notion of Expenditure," in *Visions of Excess: Selected Writings, 1927–1939*, ed. and trans. Allan Stoekl (Minneapolis: University of Minnesota Press, 1985), 116 ("there is nothing that permits one to define what is useful to man"); Jean Baudrillard, *The Political Economy of the Sign*, in *Jean Baudrillard: Selected Writings*, ed. Mark Poster (Stanford, Calif.: Stanford University Press, 1988), 75, 79, on need and the centrality of the structure of the sign to commodity production. Lacan discusses utilitarianism in Jacques Lacan, *The Seminar of Jacques Lacan: Book VII: The Ethics of Psychoanalysis, 1959–1960*, ed. Jacques-Alain Miller, trans. Dennis Porter (New York: Norton, 1992), 187, 216, 228–29.

4. Merlin Donald, *Origins of the Modern Mind: Three Stages in the Evolution of Culture and Cognition* (Cambridge: Harvard University Press, 1991); Jane Jacobs, *Cities and the Wealth of Nations* (Harmondsworth, England: Penguin, 1986), 221.

5. Jacobs, *Cities*, 222.

6. Lacan, *Ethics of Psychoanalysis*, 293.

7. Kathleen Biddick, *The Shock of Medievalism* (Durham, N.C.: Duke University Press, 1998), 165–201. Beyond the field of medieval studies, see Joseph Tabbi, *The Postmodern Sublime: Technology and American Writing from Mailer to Cyberpunk* (Ithaca, N.Y.: Cornell University Press, 1995); Joseph Tabbi and Michael Wutz, eds., *Reading Matters: Narratives in the New Media Ecology* (Ithaca, N.Y.: Cornell University Press, 1997), and N. Katherine Hayles, *How We Became Posthuman: Virtual Bodies in Cybernetics, Literature, and Informatics* (Chicago: University of Chicago Press, 1999).

8. Michel Serres, for example, *The Birth of Physics*, trans. Jack Hawkes, ed. David Webb (Manchester: Clinamen, 2000), and Bruno Latour, *We Have Never Been Modern*, trans. Catherine Porter (Cambridge: Harvard University Press, 1993).

9. My chief difficulties with John Guillory's *Cultural Capital: The Problem of Literary Canon Formation* (Chicago: University of Chicago Press, 1993) are these: first, its implicit assumption that power is an effect of rational interests (insitutions want to perpetuate and extend themselves, they are fundamentally indifferent as to how they do so, they are not

motivated by enjoyment to any significant degree); that institutions do not on the whole share spheres of influence or activity (presumably, this helps institutions to be powerful, because they do not have to deal with much interference from outside, nor do they desire the outside except insofar as they can make it work for their interests); that institutions take shape and keep themselves going by means of signifying activities is not salient, nor do the signifying activities that sustain the institution in general have any important points of connection with signifying activities (literary texts) that circulate *through* the institution. I disagree with each of these positions, not because they are Marxian, but because they ignore the implications of Marx's critique of utility and rigidify Marx's attempt to understand the specific articulations and differentiations of human productive activity, while adopting identity politics as foil instead of confronting the more immediately relevant challenge of Ernesto Laclau's and Chantal Mouffe's highly influential work *Hegemony and Socialist Strategy: Toward a Radical Democratic Politics*, trans. Winston Moore and Paul Cammack (London: Verso, 1985).

10. Michel Foucault, *The History of Sexuality*, vol. 1, *An Introduction*, trans. Robert Hurley (New York: Vintage, 1978), 71.

11. For a discussion of recent research on the effects of training in the humanities, see Anthony Dangerfield and James Engell, "The Market-Model University: Humanities in the Age of Money," *Harvard Magazine* (May/June 1998): 48–111.

12. Freud theorizes technology as prosthesis with respect to memory: "With every tool man is perfecting his own organs, whether motor or sensory, or is removing the limits to their functioning.... In the photographic camera he has created an instrument which retains the fleeting visual impressions, just as a gramophone disc retains the equally fleeting auditory ones; both are at bottom materializations of the power he possesses of recollection, his memory" (*Civilization and Its Discontents*, trans. James Strachey [New York: Norton, 1961], 41–42).

13. On the "mourning for the front," see Jacques Derrida, *The Gift of Death*, trans. David Wills (Chicago: University of Chicago Press, 1994), 17–18. Lacan develops the notion of beauty as something that "stops us, but ... also points in the direction of" "the unspeakable field of radical desire that is the field of absolute destruction," the field of *das Ding* (*Ethics of Psychoanalysis*, 216–17).

14. On the fantasy of the "hypereconomy" of the gift versus the "terrestrial economy" of "simple" exchange, see Derrida, *Gift of Death*, 105–7.

15. Jacques Derrida, *Memoires for Paul de Man*, trans. Cecile Lindsay, Jonathan Culler, and Eduardo Cadava (New York: Columbia University Press, 1986), 3; hereafter cited in the text.

16. Plato, *Phaidros*, 274ff.

17. Ann Middleton, "Medieval Studies," in *Redrawing the Boundaries: The Transformation of English and American Studies*, ed. Stephen Greenblatt and Giles Gunn (New York: Modern Language Association of America, 1992), 35.

18. Stephen G. Nichols, "Philology in a Manuscript Culture," *Speculum* 65 (1990): 1; Lee W. Patterson, "On the Margin: Postmodernism, Ironic History, and Medieval Studies," in *The New Philology*, ed. Stephen G. Nichols, *Speculum* (special issue, 1991), 87–108, at 87.

Index

abbrevatio: in *MKT,* 148
abject, the: and the sublime, in Swift's Celia poems, 19
abjection, 75, 186, 215; of body, 186; and Gaze, 75; of the real, 215
absence: and death, 119; in dreams, 91; of our good, 17; recuperated, in *KT,* 172; spectral, and the Thing, 21
abstraction: and law of signifier, 86
absurdity of law, 173, 221
academy, 69, 243–44, 246–47
accountability, 172, 241
acedia, 237
Achilles, 211–13, 230
"acting-out," 74–75
action, 147, 178, 200, 231
active life, 133
activity, 244; mourning as sociable, 100; and passivity, 206, 292n11; productive, 298n9; of signifier, 21, 25; symbolic, 262n4
adventure/*aventure,* 198, 211, 236
Aelred of Rievaulx, 86
Aeneas, 185, 187–88
Aers, David, 292n16, 295n51; use of psychoanalysis, 11
aestheticism, 241–42
aestheticization, 171
aesthetics: ethics of, 19
afterlife: and knowledge of death, 91; world of, 88
agency, 28, 52, 74, 75, 129, 202; of subject, limits to, 29; that rewards, 39, 52, 75, 202; of women, 74

aggressivity, 156, 160, 193, 205; and altruism, 85; in Monk's portrait, 134; return of, 93; and sacrifice, 161
Alceste, 171, 182–83, 186–88, 191–92, 210; as intercessor, 289n33; and *showing,* 21
Alcibiades, 109
Alcyone, 93, 149; and death wish, 118–19; obsessive waiting of, 117; prayer to Juno of, 115
Alexandria: loss of, 36
alienation: Marx's theory of, 13; in mirror stage, 27; and the subject, 28
aliveness, 15, 82, 89, 107, 115–16, 123, 133, 184; awareness of, 12; in courtly love, 18–20; after falling, 137, 151; insignificance of, in tragedy, 122; and "living beyond" death, 33; of medieval objects of exchange, 23; pleasures of, 17; of survivor, 99; trauma of, 16; and our "works," 13
allegiance, 163, 215, 221; and circulation of signifier, 28; sacrifice of, 66
allegorization: and courtly sensibility, 105
allegory: of ordination into knighthood, 36; and premodernity, 107
alliance, 174, 212, 263n21; formation and exchange of, 22
Allmand, C. T., 292n2, 294n35
alms, 187, 193
alteration: and courtly interiority, 276n63; of the dead, 250; of Fortune, 102; of object, 22; of the past, 45, 48; power of, 180, 184, 192, 275n60
alteritism, 45, 48–49, 63, 243, 248

alterity, 63–65, 77, 250, 264n33; in Caxton, 59–60; and courtly interiority, 276n63; of dead, 250; of Fortune's "stroke," 125; Hûchet on, 64; of object, 22; of past, 45, 48; and tragedy, 81; and transitivism, 264n33
altruism, 85, 184–85; Butler on, 289n28; and neighbor, 38
ambiguity, 53, 54; of the mark, and ethics, 126
ambivalence, 52–53, 56, 57
"Amen," 174; and consent, 286n41
amor hereos, 91, 237
amour courtoise, 2
anaclisis, 256n29
anamorphosis, 152; courtly love as, 276n71; and the Monk, 134–36, 144
aneconomy, 14
angelic foresight, 90
angel(s): hosts, 160; and prosthesis, 81
animation, 16; and anxiety, 115; suspended, and fascination, 104
Annunciation, 214
anticipation, 170, 216
anticlimax: in *BD*, 93, 95, 110, 113; Spielrein on, 276n2; in tragedy, 222; and transmission, 111
Antigone, 127
antiquity, 264n38; and techniques of living, 89
anxiety(ies), 52–53, 58, 183, 217–19, 233; about animation, 115; of *finamen*, 18; and oneiric images, 91; and sacrificial identification, 39; and tragedy, 83, 117; and transference, 276n2
apocalypse, 15, 40; and spectacle, 134
apotheosis, 174, 185, 209; of guilt, and crucifixion, 34; of neighbor, 86, 289n30; of sadism, 37
appeal, 95, 116
appetite(s), 4, 17, 121, 200
Aquinas, St. Thomas, 177–79; on childhood, 106; *De regimine principum*, on the sign, 40; on images, 271n21; on tragedy, 88

arbitrariness, 53, 142, 234; of Fortune, 128–29; vs. justice, 16; of the law, 22, 26, 28, 151 (*see also* law)
archives, 54
Arcite, 22, 164, 166–68, 170–71, 174, 230
aristocracy, 129, 212; communities of, and marriage, 109; and figure of neighbor, 80; patrons from, 79; sorrow of, 99
Aristotle, 4, 101, 178; on tragedy, 144
Arnold, Matthew, 296n62
ars moriendi, 153
Artemidorus: on dreams, 87, 272n31
art(s), 69, 129, 227, 232, 236, 240, 250, 263n25; Arthurian, 105; of attentiveness, in *BD*, 112; in courtly culture, 10, 28–29; devotional, 34; history of, 20; of living, 107, 273n37; of memory, 88–90, 102, 132, 139, 273nn38–39; and sentience, 18; and vision, in tragedy, 84
artifact, 24, 54, 182, 197–98; and the cross, 34; deadness of, 83; and *jouissance*, 41; knowledge as, 10; loss of, and exchange, 23; opacity of, 13; production of, 120; and sacrificial violence, 35; and sentience, 18, 96
artifactuality: and justice, 240
artifice: ethical meaning of, 194; and groupification, 151; and *jouissance*, 18
artificing: of life, 80, 103; and signifier, 90
artisanship: in Chaucer's poetry, 34
ascesis, 32, 163, 175, 180, 183, 186, 223, 231, 233, 235; as art of memory, 90; vs. enjoyment, 17; and the group, 41; and prosthesis, 105; of rivalry, 101; and *tristitia*, 296n65
asceticism, 133, 137, 151
"as if," 45, 72, 262n5
assemblage(s), 32, 64
assent, 171, 173, 187
astrology, 141
astronomy, 141
atemporality: as time of sacrifice, 14
atrocity, 203, 204, 216, 234

attachment(s), 243; particular, to objects, 130, 221, 259n78; prosthetic, 105
attention: in Chaucer's poems, 115; and Fortune, 104; and image, 117; techniques of, in *BD*, 114; vigilance as, 92
attentiveness, 104, 109, 112
auctoritas, 57
Augustine, Saint, 14, 73, 86, 176, 201, 282n3; *Confessions*, critique of tragedy in, 125–28, 136, 149
authority, 45, 163, 173, 183; and the law, 26, 163
awareness, 12, 15, 33; and transference, 93; and wonder, 89

Babe, 239
Bachelard, Gaston: on the forest, 98; on immensity and intimacy, 87, 272n30; on oneiric experience, 89
Bacon, Roger, 51
Bailey, Harry: and the Monk, 132–33, 135, 145, 147
"Balade": in *LGW*, 192, 197
Bann, Stephen, 262n10
barbarism: of Chaucer's age, 236
Bataille, Georges, 66, 241, 256n31, 256n40, 258n60, 260n92; on alterity of object, 13; on *dépense*, 275n58; on sacrifice, 15; on utility, 297n3
Baudrillard, Jean: on utility, 241
beauty, 160, 164, 171, 186–87, 189, 194–95, 210, 241; and charity, 107, 276n69; love of, and the death wish, 89; and shame, 289n32
Beckwith, Sarah, 11, 261n96
becoming, 76–78, 204, 263n21, 269n82
befallenness, 97, 102, 124, 146, 206, 209, 220, 222, 229, 233, 236; and art of memory, 90; and history, 153; inscription of subject by, 106; and law, 121, 151; and signifier, 142; trauma of, 126
being, 27, 32, 36, 98, 108, 176, 179; corporeal, and subject(ivity), 20, 30; and signifier, 23–24, 61, 143, 174, 230, 281n57

belief, 72, 157, 163, 173, 208
benevolence, 185, 193; charitable, 178; chivalric, 175; as form of enjoyment, 101; of queen, 183
Benjamin, Walter, 11, 51
Bernard of Clairvaux, Saint, 35
betrayal, 110, 188, 197, 214
Biddick, Kathleen, 12, 74
Binswanger, Ludwig, 70
birth, 18, 36
Black, Man in. *See* Man in Black
Black Prince, 131, 218
Blanche, 92, 107, 289n31; deadliness of, 99; and Fortune, 123
Blanchot, Maurice: on being sovereignly mortal, 118; on passion for image, 273n36; and suicide, 136; on vigilance, 91
blood, 63, 167, 205, 292n15
Boccaccio, 132, 166, 206; *De casibus*, review of dead in, 119; and discipline, 133
body(ies), 24, 50, 67, 75, 81, 100, 123, 135, 139, 167, 177, 180, 200–201, 216, 233, 250, 265n40; angelic, 157; and "becoming," 77; chivalric, 205; of Christ, 37, 161, 261n96; comic, 233; in crusade, 161; dead, 57, 167; death and resurrection of, 115; engraved, 143; feminine, 226; of *finamen*, 183; and form, 27–28; group, 33, 37, 118, 120, 129–33, 135, 209, 224, 229; helpless, 87; of knight, 35; lost, of past, 64; military, 157, 165, 224; of neighbor, 153; of the other, 98; penalized, 34; prosthetic, 26, 63; and signifier, 57, 226, 234–35; sublime, 161, 174, 224, 283n8; of victim, 168, 260n86
Boethius: *Consolation of Philosophy*, 124, 209. *See also* Chaucer, *Boece*; Lady Philosophy
Bogin, Meg, 258n59
bon vezi, 40–41, 80, 86, 185, 195
Bonaventure, Saint, 280n48

bond: between calculation and aneconomy, 15; between desire and law, 4, 9–10, 143; male-male, 96
Bonet, Honoré, 205, 216
Boose, Lynda, 295n47
Bornstein, Diane, 182–83, 288nn19–20
bounte, 193
Bourdieu, Pierre, 10, 72, 295n54
Bowers, John, 291n2
Bowlby, John, 259n78, 271n21
Bradwardine, Henry, 178
Brennan, Teresa, 266n57
brevitas, 185. See also *abbrevatio*
Briseis, 211
Brooks, Cleanth, 52
brotherhood, 33, 260n88
Burger, Glenn, 274n48
Burgwinkle, William, 276n63
Burke, Kenneth, 10, 287n3
Butler, Judith, 11, 66, 287n11; on altruism, 289n28; on identity, 265n47; on loss, 187, 286n44; on political signifiers, 284n19
Bynum, Caroline Walker, 74, 267n74

Calchas, 210, 221–22, 235, 237
Calcidius: on loving our neighbor, 274nn44–45
calculation, 160, 222, 247; Christian, 156, 202; of interests, 247; and *jouissance*, 141, 159; and sacrifice, 4, 15, 291n7
calculus, 140, 251
Capellanus, Andreas: *Art of Courtly Love*, 10, 23–24, 41, 120
capital: of body of Christ, 161
capitalism: *jouissance* of, 246
care: for neighbor, 39; for objects, and indifference, 134; of self, 58, 125, 273n37, 285n30; of sovereign for subjects, 116
Carey, Hilary, 141
caricature: Chaucerian, 114; and stereotypy, 122
caritas, 73
Cassandra, 110–11, 209–10, 235

catastrophe, 211, 213, 237, 251; and grief, 112; and group, 135, 219; in medieval studies, 251; in *NPT*, 122–23; and tragedy, 122–23, 237
Cato, 61
Caxton, William, 59–62, 64
Cerisy, Abbey of, 213
certainty, 27–28, 180, 243
certitude, 182, 197
Ceyx (Seys), 93–94, 117–18
chain: signifying, 143, 194, 240
chance, 97, 114, 122–23, 142, 144, 236, 266n54; and tragedy, 82, 127
Chandler, Alice, 297n1
change, 179, 207; as desire, 6, 156, 194; historical, 19, 75; in language, history of, 246; and memory, 70; and "works," 61
character: and Monk, 148; in tragedy, 151
charity, 31, 40, 155, 161, 171, 176, 185, 192–93, 196; and beauty, 107; and befallenness, 103; gendering of, 183, 187, 276n69; and *jouissance*, 32; Lacan on, 184, 289n26; Mollat on, 287n9; and pity, 290n35; resemblance to Monk, 148; and sacrifice, 158; and *showing* of subject, 38
Charnes, Linda, 293n23
Chaucer, Geoffrey, 88, 116, 133, 147, 236–37, 274n51, 277n8, 278n12; appearances in poems, 115; art of, and loss, 236; and astrology, 141; biographies of, 49–50; and charity and pity in, 290n35; and Cecily Chaumpain, 214; and comedy, 222; cuteness of, 111, 114, 151; as father of English poetry, 236; obscenity of, 236; poetics of, 79; poetry of, 269nn1–2, 296n62; reception of, 80; and relation between sacrifice and signifier, 34, 41; revisions of Ovid, 94–95; self-images, 97–98; and *sentiment*, 112; in 1359 campaign, 216; and tragedy, 124, 127, 130. Works: *Boece*, 107, 122–26;

Chaucer, Geoffrey *(continued)*, *The Book of the Duchess*, 79, 81, 92, 109, 113–21, 123, 132, 147, 187, 211, 223, 289n31; *The Canterbury Tales*, 79, 135, 147–48, 150–51, 154; *The Franklin's Tale*, 141; *The General Prologue*, 145, 147; *The House of Fame*, 115, 123, 275n62; *The Knight's Tale*, 21–22, 79, 216, 234; *The Legend of Good Women*, 21, 79, 114, 144, 148, 187–88, 232, 275n62; *The Manciple's Tale*, 79, 147, 269n1; *The Man of Law's Tale*, 214; *The Monk's Tale*, 79, 92, 114, 130, 133–35, 137–39, 142–52, 275n62; *The Nun's Priest's Tale*, 122–23, 147; *The Pardoner's Prologue and Tale*, 40; *The Parliament of Fowls*, 18, 80, 120, 194, 278n15; *The Shipman's Tale*, 141; *The Squire's Tale*, 141; *The Tale of Melibee*, 261n95; *The Tale of Sir Thopas*, 105; *Treatise on the Astrolabe*, 141; *Troilus and Criseyde*, 21–22, 79, 92, 141, 147, 238
Chaucer, Lewis, 141
Chaucerian *brevitas*, 114; narrator, 111, 118, 135; tragedy, 138, 144
Chaucer studies, 10
Cheney, Lynne, 56
childhood, 62, 106
chivalry, 215, 222, 227, 231, 260n89, 283n11, 283n13, 292n14; Christ's, 35–36; critiques of, 174; and exchange, 227; groupified in later Middle Ages, 41; history of, 159–60, 231, 283n11, n13; treatises on, 185
choice, 49, 202–4; and necessity, in Augustine, 136; in "The Theme of the Three Caskets," 285n26
chora, 24
Christ, 36–37, 44, 284n16; being like, 85; crucified, 37–38; and crusader, 37; endurance of pain, 38; and gift of life/death, 32, 84, 165; as lover-knight, 35–36, 85, 160, 284n16; mystical body of, 37; as sublime, 34, 41, 161; wounds of, 33

Christian church, 33–34
Christianity, 3, 58, 72, 185, 268n80; apotheosis of neighbor in, 40, 86, 185; and group identification, 32
Christine de Pizan, 200, 288n20
Chryseis, 211
circulation, 40; of desire, 66; of enjoyment, 199; of signifier, 28, 243
Cistercianism, 41
class, 81, 112, 129, 178
classics, 244, 246
clinamen, 143
clitoris: and pearl, 290–91n53
closure, 95, 186
code, 55; and sentience, 151; and signifier, 20, 77, 258n62; and Thing, 23
codification, 24, 120, 234
coin, 158, 182–83
collector: and loss, 150–51; Monk as, 139
combat, 223, 247
comedy, 111, 222, 235
communication, 14, 29, 56, 110, 139, 146, 275n56; courtly, 116; with dead, 252; and group, 108; as sign, in Aquinas, 40; and transference, 93
community, 40, 108, 161, 165, 171–72, 220, 223, 227, 234; and *jouissance*, 223; sacrificial economy of, 173
complaint: and courtly love, 99
condensation, 25
confession, 115. *See also* Augustine, Saint
consent, 48, 202, 204, 238; and Annunciation, 214–15; Criseyde's, 222, 225; of group, 205, 229; to loss, 14; Marian, 234, 292n32; and narrative, 220; sacrificed entity, 291–92n8; and trauma, 208, 217; Troilus's, 228
consolation, 36, 73, 80, 100–101, 116, 153, 170; and attentiveness, 109; and group, 31, 104
consort, 183, 195; tragic, 109
Constance (daughter of Pedro of Spain), 92
"containment": as form of desire, 7; vs. subversion, 48, 76, 233

contemptus mundi, 16, 128
contest, 102, 104, 235
continence, 177, 200
corpse, 94, 108, 118
correction, 125, 160, 163
counsel, 59–60, 115
couple: dead end of, 94, 95, 104; heterosexual, vs. friendship, 100; vs. male-male, 94
court, 80, 116; Arthurian, 105; culture of, 106, 110; entertainment at, 141; and the law, 26, 110
courtliness: ideology of, 106
courtly love. *See* love, courtly
courtly vigil, 99; yearning, 93
courtoisie, 18
creation, 55, 69, 89, 161, 179, 236, 244, 250
creationism, 48, 287n3
creativity, 69, 236, 244
creator, 89, 157, 163, 178, 181
creature(s), 5, 17, 98, 163, 250; and sacrifice, 161
credence, 156, 163, 172–74, 188
Criseyde, 219–20, 222–25, 231, 295n46; anxieties of, 218; and Calchas, 221; consent of, 203, 206, 222, 225; her dream of eagle, 225; *entente* of, 229, 232; exchange of, 227–28; faithlessness of, 293n22; fear(s) of, 219, 237; 295n46; language of, 226; as nonsublime object, 202, 211, 222–23, 237; and oracle, 210; and sacrifice, 203, 237
crisis: in the academy, 244; over matter, 14
Crosby, Alfred, 140, 142
cross, 36, 73; and gift of death, 33; as signifier of sacrifice, 32
crucifixion: as apotheosis of sadism, 37, 289n30; tragedy of, 87
cruelty, 188, 236, 252; of Fortune, 125–26
crusader: tragedy of, 36–37, 87
culture(s): chivalric, 159, 160, 204, 206, 215, 217; Christian, 71, 156; court(ly), 100, 106, 110–11, 129; and enhanced sentience of, 35; intellectual, in fourteenth century, 140; and *jouissance* of submission, 29; military, groupification of, 87; and neighbor, 51; rarefies aliveness, 18; sacralizing of lay, 32; and tragedy, 110
curiosity, 16, 52, 246
cuteness: of the animal, 97; in Chaucer's poetry, 111, 114, 151
cybersignification, 245–46
cyberspace, 245

Daedalus (Dedalus) 101–2
daemon, 94, 118
daimons, 125
daisy, 186, 190–91, 195; as sublime object, 190
danger, 100, 211, 219, 224–25; of identification, 39
Dangerfield, Tony: and James Engell, 298n11
Daniel, Arnaut, 19, 289n32
d'Anjou, René, 109
Dante, 4, 119, 131, 232
dead, the, 48, 51, 56, 58; communication with, 58, 221, 252; knowledge of, 91; and rule, 116; and signifier, 57; transmission to, 237
deadness, 101
death, 33–34, 99, 111, 119, 136–37, 153, 170, 173, 194, 202, 204, 254n13; anticipation of, in *The Knight's Tale*, 169; Arcite's, 166; desire for, 254n13; and economy of sacrifice, 119; "first" and "second," 56–57, 167–68, 174, 237; and Fortune, 123; gift of, 16, 22, 30, 32–33, 36, 118, 123, 157, 164–65, 169, 171, 174 (*see also* gift); of God, 72; and group, 62, 92; of kings, and sacrifice, 118; law of, 202; as leveler, 40; of the other, 89, 95, 120; and pain, 16; and particularity, 259n78; and philosophy, 158, 168, 170; preparedness toward, 102; and repetition, 115; and responsibility, 278n13;

death *(continued)*, vs. resurrection, 115; as signifier, 63, 83, 121; and sovereign mortality, 134; and the subject, 31, 259n77; of Troilus, 213
death drive, 16–18, 25, 28, 47, 83, 118–19, 146, 153, 206, 209, 211, 229, 251; and being-as-signifier, 121; designed by signifier, 226; and desire for knowledge, 119; historical dimension of, 25, 68–69, 278n11; and indifference, 151; and law, 28, 119, 202; as passion for number, 142; and repetition, 212; and responsibility, 278n13; and tragedy, 82. *See also* drive
death wish(es), 88, 91, 97, 128, 137; in *Boece*, 125; as ghosts, 132; of Monk, 134; turned into sacrifice, 135. *See also* wish
debt, 57, 158, 173, 203–4, 228, 242; and Christian hypereconomy, 202; and cross, 34
de Certeau, Michel, 46, 50–52, 55, 61; on (academic) disciplines, 10, 205
de Charny, Geoffroi, 35–36
decision: concept of, 48; in *TC*, 210
Dedalus. *See* Daedulus
defense, 233, 251; of/against life, 79, 83, 88; prosthesis as, 81
deferral, 100, 116, 171–72, 183, 191; sacrificial, 171; and transference, 114
Deleuze, Gilles: on becoming, 76–77; on courtly love, 10; and Félix Guattari, 7, 63, 274n52; on joy of desire, 6, 254n11; on sadomasochism and group subject, 20; on unnatural participation, 265n40; on war machine, 294n44. *See also* deterritorialization(s)
demand, 30, 157, 186, 202; and charity, 196; sacrificial, 175
demon. *See* daemon
dependence, 156, 221, 227
dépense, 256n34, 275n58; of courtly manners, 100; dead object as, 105
depression, 233–34
de Roet, Philippa, 92

Derrida, Jacques, 161, 175, 276n68; on chance and tragedy, 81–82, 114, 122; on economy of sacrifice, 4, 9, 14, 254n8; on falling objects, 114; on gift of death, 82–83, 86, 157, 164–65, 168–71, 174, 205, 231, 277n5; on historicity, 262n9; on history of credence/credit, 282n2; on hypereconomy, 155; on iteration, 152; on mourning for the front, 264n33; on Nature, 142–43, 148, 153; and new historicists, 10; on responsibility, 48, 262n9, 278n13
desire(s), 16, 19, 24, 39, 44, 47–48, 50, 52, 55, 64, 66, 81, 83, 90, 116–17, 151, 161–62, 164, 167, 180, 191, 215, 217, 228, 234, 242; as change, 156, 194, 269n82; circulated, 37; and death wish, 119; and discipline, 7; ecstasy of, 6; to end desire, 92; to entertain, 240; and exchange, 9, 61; giving way on, 3, 297n27; and group(s), 40, 48, 219, 259n79; and history, 44–45; and identification, 86; and indifference, 108, 138; and the law, 4, 10, 28, 35, 143, 164; to live, 18; object(s) of, 5, 191; of the other/Other/Ōther, 7, 29–30, 258n57; particularity of objects of, 99; religious, 71; to rescue, 85; role in economic activity, 68–69, 77, 242; and sacrifice, 2, 4, 9, 156; of sadist, 168; and sentience, 199; structured by language, 10; and subject, 3; for submission, 162; for suffering of other, and pity, 86; and technologization, 121; and trauma, 142, 208, 218
destination, 90, 165–66, 169, 227–28
destiny, 90, 217, 228
destruction, 133, 135, 195
destructivity, 44, 104, 119, 129, 152, 160, 179, 190, 192, 231, 252; and chivalric ordinance, 205; of courtly culture, 106; and death drive, 17; of desire, 191; enjoyment of, 246; and group, 37, 100; of *jouissance*, 37; and sacrifice, 161; and signifier, 229

desublimation, 203, 206, 237, 212, 222, 237
deterritorialization(s), 73, 161, 202, 263n21; and pilgrimage, 284n20
Detienne, Marcel, 291n8
de Vinsauf, Geoffrey, 273n38
devotion: massification of, 87; passional, 37, 85, 273n39; process of, memory as, 105, 110; and subliming of chivalaric culture, 35
Dido, 148, 185, 187, 275n62
difference(s), 27, 45, 65, 77, 172, 242, 249; and Christian identification, 32; in court, 80; and ethics, 63; and exchange, 14, 30; and indifference, 98; and the Other, 75; sexual, 94, 177–78, 63, 180, 182–83, 192, 195, 213, 290n53; and signifier, 15; and symbolic order, 264n26
dignitas, 73
dignity, 88, 93, 178; of Thing, 18, 108, 141
Ding, das, 139, 215, 271n18; and beauty, 298n13; and the law, 28, 121, 162; and the signifier, 209, 285n23; and symbolic order, 20; and technology, 141. *See also* Thing
Dinshaw, Carolyn, 11, 61, 66, 262n13, 265n47, 289n34
Diomede, 213, 223, 230, 237, 297n67
discipline(s), 17, 90; academic, 10, 12, 45–46, 49, 53, 244; in *Babe*, 239; and enjoyment, 8, 53, 233, 241; military, 160; religious, 58, 200; sadomasochistic, and group, 10, 20
discourse, 69, 244–45, 248; analysis, 145; chivalric, 60, 235; courtly, 112
dissemination, 9, 48, 53, 64, 116, 226
distinctiveness, 109; pleasure of, 98
divination, 44, 90; as prosthesis, 115
divinity, 15, 156
divinized: love as, 105
Dollimore, Jonathan, 128–29, 227
dominance, 119, 205
domination, 75, 129, 152

Donald, Merlin, 11, 241
Donatus, 270n14
Dragonetti, Roger, 64, 67
dream(s), 62, 96, 191, 194, 225; medieval discourse on, 272n33
dream world, 111; demonic, 90; and group, 62; interiority of, 96
"drift," 46, 262n7
drive, 70–71; and anaclisis, 256n29. *See also* death drive
Dryden, John, 263n18
Duby, Georges, 214
Duns Scotus, 66
duty, 4, 7, 205

Eco, Umberto, 55
economy(ies), 17, 160, 173, 240, 298n14; aristocratic, 22; of feudal subsistence, 23; and gift, 15, 114; of infant survival, 240; libidinal, of courtly love, 19; from perspective of Thing, 23; and sacrifice, 4, 14, 100, 119, 171, 173–74, 235, 291n7; sentient, of Middle Ages, 211; of work, 15
ecstasy, 7, 217; of desire, 217
educability, 182
education: medieval, 200
Edward III, 92, 214, 216
Egeus, 170–71
ego, 17, 85, 185
eidolon, 250
elegy: and love lament, 80
Elias, Norbert, 10
embodiment, 67, 203; and sentience, 18; and signification, 12
Emelye, 22, 164, 166, 173–74
emotion(s), 177, 218
empathy, 103, 152
Empson, William, 53
emptiness, 93, 195
enchantment, 91, 97, 147
endurance, 99, 184, 195; of body of group, 38; limit of, and *jouissance*, 7
enemy, 161, 165; Augustine on, 282n3; love of, 160; and pity, 171

Engels, Friedrich. *See* Karl Marx
engraving: in *BD*, 107; and body, 87, 143; and falling, 81
enjoyment, 4–5, 16–17, 24, 45, 53, 56–57, 62, 64, 75–76, 150, 156, 158, 163–64, 170, 181, 199, 207, 212, 215, 218, 219, 228–29, 242–43, 246, 248, 253n2; aristocratic, 231–32; in *Babe*, 240; in Chaucer's work, 41; chivalric, 29, 206; and comedy, 219; courtly, 19; of crucified Christ, 37; of duty, 205; and exchange, 30; father of, 26, 236; and form, 104, 250; and *genre*, 121; group, 213, 259n79; and history (discipline of), 44–45, 74; and history of signifier, 58, 210–11, 241, 246, 255n25; humanist, 237; and the humanities, 242, 246; of identification, 60; and the law, 8; of loss, 206, 236; in medieval studies, 252; and memory, 273n38; moral sense as, 2–3; of pity, 39, 86; pleasure as form of, 31, 246; of rank, 23–24; and religion, 71; religious, 132; of repetition compulsion, 217; and sacrifice, 2, 12, 30, 45, 158, 168, 233, 237–38; and science, 245; and sentient object, 203; of submission to law, 28–29, 151, 162, 172, 221, 215; and suffering, 73; surplus, 156, 164; theft of, 132–33; and tragedy, 106, 125; and trauma, 90, 208; and the unconscious, 234
entente, 199, 207, 217, 219–20, 286n35; Cassandra's, 209; Criseyde's, 203, 226, 229, 232
envy, 62, 197
epic, 203, 235
equality, 35, 185; law of, 185; of members of group, 85
equivalence, 32, 35, 185
equivalent(s), 58, 200
ethics, 10, 11, 160–61, 253n6, 254n14; of courtly love, 183, 184; of historical study, 48, 56, 78; and the law, 121; political, 19; and sacrifice, 4, 136; and sexual difference, 197

Eucharist, 29, 34, 58, 185
evil, 37–38, 135, 158, 179, 188, 194; in heart of neighbor, 84–86, 103
excess, 75, 167, 214; and sacrifice, 15; and tragedy, 88
exchange, 10, 12, 30–31, 157–58, 159, 161, 298n14; aristocratic, 171; in *Art of Courtly Love*, 23–24; of Chryseis and Briseis, 211; consolatory, 100; of Criseyde, 227; and desire, 9; of enjoyment, 30, 199; and gift of death, 171; and group, 14; Hector's refusal of, 237; imaginary, 39; of men, 21–22, 228; objects of, 9, 23, 34, 203; and sacrifice, 22, 197; and sentience, 34, 203; and signifier, 61, 213
exchangeability, 212, 230, 235
exteriority, 24, 88, 96, 105, 113, 124, 136, 142, 163; and the group, 76; in mirror stage, 27; and prosthesis, 26; and tragedy, 81
"extimacy," 30, 135, 163, 186, 197, 285n23; of *das Ding*, 121; and lady, 289n31

faith, 72, 173, 188, 235; knights of, 156, 158, 164; and signifier, 174
fall, 119, 137; and *jouissance*, 121; into life, 88, 102, 114; in tragedy, 146
fallenness, 84, 138
falling, 103, 112; fear of, 151; in tragedy, 81
fantasy, 55, 62, 109, 116, 128, 280n42; of agency that rewards, 75; of chivalric culture, 29, 237; and chivalry, 160, 175–76; group, 31, 71, 76, 264n36; and history, 69–70; ideological, 65, 68, 121, 129, 279–80n16; and the imaginary, 264n26; and *jouissance*, 141; Middle Ages as, 248; and the O/Other, 157, 234; of queen's benevolence, 183; redeemer, 179; and religion, 71; of rescue, 101, 168, 180, 182, 237; of sexual difference, 213
Farmer, Sharon, 260n88
Farnham, Willard, 126–28, 269n2

fascination, 19, 27, 29, 75; and consolation, 116; and the image, 89, 273n36; and lost object, 104
fate, 32, 122, 234–35; in tragedy, 127
father(s), 67, 127, 170, 197, 234, 295n47; of English poetry, 236; of enjoyment, 26, 236; and signifier, 172; who sees in secret, 157, 169
fault, 177, 179, 181, 201; in tragedy, 127
fear(s), 93, 220, 245; and group, 151; and tragedy, 122
Ferrante, Joan, 295n50
fiction(s), 52, 54, 231; cultural, 15, 216, 284n19
fidelity, 251–52; as enjoyment, 101
finamen, 18, 120, 183–84, 191, 258n59; and exchange, 22; beyond the good(s), 23; interior of, 113; vs. lady, 100
fin' amors 183–85. *See also* love, courtly
finitude, 29, 83, 89, 104, 152–53, 156, 164, 184, 198; and prosthesis, 116; and sexual difference, 196–97; and signifier, 250; of subject, 86; and symbolic order, 156; and tragedy, 82
flesh, 158, 167, 182, 184; submission of, to signifier, 34
foresight, 90, 102, 142, 209
form, 28, 118, 186, 122, 223, 243; enjoyment and, 27, 104, 224, 250; group, 100, 143; history of, 243; *jouissance* of, 121, 150; of law, 164; and rule, 137; submission to, 27
Fortune, 80, 87, 102–3, 108, 124–25, 139, 209, 210, 215; in courtly culture, 129; and death wish, 126; *jouissance* of, 123; as O̅, 26; and refusal of life, 128; stroke of, 124, 126; and tragedy, 80–81, 84, 138, 143–44, 148, 151, 279n17
Foucault, Michel, 10, 50, 72, 84, 253n5, 262n13; on Artemidorus's dream treatise, 87, 272n31; on care/work of self, 29, 106, 273n37; on psychoanalysis, 64, 265n41

Fradenburg, Louise O. (L. O. Aranye), 92, 265n44; "'Be not far from me,'" 271n21; *City, Marriage, Tournament*, 264n33, 276n69, 277n8, 278n15, 283n13, 286n35, 288n23, 289n32, 294n32; "Criticism, Anti-Semitism, and *The Prioress's Tale*," 265n44; "Voice Memorial," 269n3, 274n48; *Women and Sovereignty*, 288n24
Franciscanism, 33, 41
freedom, 5, 48, 198; from the law, 202; and responsibility, 48
Frese, Dolores, 144
Freud, Sigmund, 2, 3, 70, 76, 96, 105, 120, 152, 226, 234, 254n16, 257n44, 290n45; on charity, 32; *Civilization and Its Discontents*, 31, 38, 76, 84; death drive, 17; groups, 29, 34, 260n87; history, 11; indifference, 257n44; insistence on particularity, 48; megalomania, 179; "Mourning and Melancholia," 250; *Nebenmensch*, 20; new historicism, 10; philology, 12; prosthesis, 256n29, 298n12; religion, 71, 268n80; Schreber, 177; social psychology, 254n16; techniques of living, 84, 253n6; "The Theme of the Three Caskets," 164, 209, 285n26; "Thoughts on War and Death," 233; transference, 76–77, 274n50; unconscious, 25
Friedlander, Sol, 11
friend(s), 100, 106, 112; courtly, 101; and help, 153; vs. lady, 275n63; and the survivor, 95
friendship, heroic, 276n63
fruitio, 31
fugienda vita, 82
future (the), 57, 62, 90; as gift, 136; and sacrifice, 175
Fyler, John, 270n10

Gamer, Helena M., 291n6
Gardiner, Frank, 71
Gaunt, John of, 92, 99, 131

gaze, 75, 163, 168, 172, 231; of the law, 164; of Other, 30; and *showing*, 258n57
gazing: and the undead, 89
Gehry, Frank, 54
gender, 11, 22, 73, 74, 178, 197; indeterminacy of, 183, 192, 210; of lady, 186, 210; and pity, 290n34
genealogy, 57, 65; of psychoanalysis, 3, 10
generality: of form, 27; insentient, 107
generalization, 272n27; and law of signifier, 86
generation, 178
generativity, 177–78
genre, 110, 142, 144; and enjoyment, 121; stereotypy of, 132; of tragedy, 106, 127
Geoffrey de Vinsauf, 66–67, 74
Geoffrey of Monmouth, 43–44, 49, 55
georgic, 239
Gerald of Wales (Giraldus Cambrensis), 43–44, 55
Geremek, Bronislaw, 284n18
ghostliness, 93
ghost(s): as death wishes, 132–33
gift, 136, 156, 160, 171–72; and construction of identity, 86; of death, 16, 30, 33, 38, 82–83, 92, 94, 104, 110, 114, 111–19, 123, 125, 136, 145, 157, 160, 165, 168, 169, 171, 174, 201, 205, 221, 231, 236–37, 248, 252, 277n5; of enjoyment, 156; hypereconomy of, 248; of knowledge, 115, 118; of life, 16, 30, 36, 82–83, 157, 237; opposed to commerce, 159, 171; and pity, 86; and sacrifice, 15, 210; of signifier, 236; specularity of, 157
glory, 60, 160
g/God, 34, 75, 156, 180, 183, 192; and apotheosis of neighbor, 86; death of, 72; and enjoyment, 75; interest in subject of, 4; of Love, 21, 186, 192, 233; love of, and pleasure, 31; love of creatures, 32, 84; as neighbor/*Nebenmensch*, 37, 185; of Sleep, 117–18
Goldberg, Jonathan, 10, 64, 255n27

Good/good(s), the, 15, 185, 196; common, 60–61, 161, 178, 179, 185, 229, 287n9; and *jouissance*, 7, 123; vs. the Lady, 186; and pleasure, 4, 253n6; public, 234; and sacrifice, 61, 136; and sublimity, 203
goodness: Blanche as, 108; of lady, 99
Gossman, Lionel, 262n10
Goux, Jean-Joseph, 287n3
grace, 155, 158, 201; and work, 15
Gravdal, Kathryn, 213–14
Greenblatt, Stephen, 268n77
grief, 73, 112
groupification, 139, 143, 149, 109, 259n79; of military culture, 87; and sacrifice, 135; of trauma, 226
groupifying power of image, 99
group(s), 20, 25, 30, 34, 39–40, 44, 48, 62, 76, 99, 99–101, 104–5, 107, 130, 234, 254n19, 277–78n9; Aquinas on, 40; artificial, 260n87; and becoming, 77; body of, 33, 37–38, 120, 133, 135, 223; and care for self, 58; in courtly love, 80; and death drive, 47, 119; defines sublime object, 293n22; enhanced by historiography, 59–60; and identification, 31–32; and knowledge, 47; and the law, 9–10, 46, 95, 108, 206; and love, 80; militarized, 224; modes of enjoyment of, 47, 199; never mourns, 33, 85; and pleasure, 150; power to relay, 35, 37; and sacrifice, 34, 136, 238; and signifier, 57; subject(ivity) of, 28–29; and survival, 222; talk, 117–18; thought, 12; and transmission, 98; and trauma, 47, 208; unity of, 9
Grudin, Michaela, 145
Guattari, Félix. *See* Gilles Deleuze
Guibert of Nogent, 65, 265n46
Guillaume de Poitiers, 289n30
Guillory, John, 51, 68, 243, 297–98n9
guilt, 72, 104–5, 111, 152; and the Passion, 34, 75; and the state, 234
Guinevere: in *Le Morte d'Arthur*, 211

habit(s), 177, 180, 182
Hansen, Elaine, 289nn34–35
"hap," 114, 123
happiness, 4, 253n6
heart, 97, 101, 160, 163, 166–67, 171, 177, 250; broken, of penitential subject, 156, 161, 167; gentility of, 18; of neighbor (Nebenmensch), 37, 158, 185, 192, 194, 197; pity in, 187
Hector, 212–13, 222–23, 227, 230, 235, 237
heimlich, the, 98, 106
Helen of Troy, 211, 221, 223, 230, 231
help, 179, 196, 254n16
helper: woman as, 196, 178
helping hand, 38; and signifier, 40
helplessness, 13, 17, 102, 136, 193, 217, 270n13; of body, 143; as fallenness, 138; and sentience, 103; and tragedy, 79, 82
heretic, 33, 156, 282n3
hermeneutics, 47, 53
hero, 109, 213, 230; tragic, 120
heterogeneity, 80, 109, 172, 233, 260n92; in courtly culture, 111; and homogeneity, 107, 270n9; sublimes group, 35
heterosexuality, 94, 187, 197
Higgins, Lynn, 225
historicism(s), 12, 41, 46; alterity of past in, 45; and desire, 52; ethics of, 45; Foucauldian, 50, 76; and Freud, 48; "new," 9–10; and psychoanalysis, 11, 47, 64; and utility, 241
historicists, 129
historicity, 67, 130, 262n9, 266n57
historiography: and courtly love, 19; ethics of, 56; medieval, 49, 57; popular, 49; and sentience, 18; and subliming of signifier, 57
history, 10, 16, 19, 32–33, 46, 55, 59, 62, 112, 123, 150, 153, 156, 175, 231, 236, 246, 252, 264n39; academic, 49; and chivalry, 63, 231; as communicative technology, 60; of courtly love, 12; English literary, 79; of enjoyment, 45, 74; as erogenous zone, 44; and fantasy,

69, 248; and Foucault, 50; of invention, 52; medievalism in, 247; and melancholy, 70–71; and memory, 70, 248; as pietas, 51; popular, 49; and responsibility, 175; of science, 52, 245; of signifier, 11, 20–21, 25, 34, 59; as symbolic order, 68; and tragedy, 127, 130
Holbein, Hans, 276n71
Holocaust: denial of, 45–46
homogeneity, 35, 77, 80, 107, 109, 111, 260n92, 270n9
honor, 174, 180, 182; and chivalry, 41; and sacrifice, 174, 235; and women, 289n34, 292n12
Horace, 88, 272n32
host, 285n28; Eucharistic, 73
Howard, Donald, 144, 214
Hûchet, Jean-Charles, 12, 64–65, 67
human: and inhuman, 13, 77
humanist, 236
humanities, 54, 56, 240, 243–47; and enjoyment, 241, 247; and medievalism, 45; and medieval studies, 53; and psychoanalysis, 10; as techniques of living, 69; and technology, 242; utility of, 241; and work, 242
humility, 51
hunt, the, 97, 133, 193
hypereconomy: Christian, 159, 173, 202; of mercy, 174, 291n7; vs. "old law," 159; of sacrifice, 155, 156, 163
Hypermnestra, 187

"I," 6, 18, 27, 101, 186, 191, 194; in mirror stage, 28; and neighbor, 39; as an other, 17
ideal, 48, 200, 236; groupifying power of, 99–100; and mourning, 249; of sacrificial rescue, 160
idealism: chivalric, 234; Christian, 71; philosophical, 76
ideality: and Schreber, 181
ideal object, 99

identification, 35, 37, 60–61, 71, 101, 149, 213, 259n63, n66, 264n26, 270n13; vs. becoming, 77; Christian, 32, 37; with dead, 56; enjoyment of, 38, 40; group, 32, 86, 142, 259n79; and image/imaginary, 28, 264n26; and *jouissance*, 31; in Mézières' *Tragedic Prayer*, 36, 87; and pity, 187; and repetition, 293n23; and sacrifice, 39; with signifier, 27
identity, 40, 66, 157, 166, 177, 182, 186–88, 190, 193; and alterity, 60, 63; group, 268n80; in historicism, 77; of knight, 205; particularity of, 27; and pity, 86; remade by *jouissance*, 7; and sacrifice, 32
ideology(ies), 68, 141, 162, 165, 168, 197
idol, 102, 125; and insentience, 14, 115
idolatry, 103
image(s), 5, 8, 26, 40, 59, 94, 139, 115–17, 161, 164, 170–71, 191, 195, 197, 200, 223–24, 226; Alceste as, 195; and altruism, 38; and attachment, 243; of beauty, 154, 186, 289n32; of Christ, 34, 37–38; of corpse, 94–95; of the dead, 250; and fascination, 273n36; and generalization, 104; ideal, 85, 180, 184, 193; identification with other, 28, 98, 104; of lost object, in mourning, 83; memory, 87; oneiric, 91; and particularity, 126, 271n21; prosthetic, 88; subject founded on, 28–29, 86; sublime, 34, 223; of suffering object, 196, 260n86
imaginary (register), 37, 60, 159–60, 240, 264n26
imagination, 121, 134
imago, 259n66, 264n26, 274n50
imitatio, 200, 260n82
imitatio Christi, 84
immensity, 88, 93, 95, 112; and courtly interiority, 276n63; in devotional subject, 87; and loss, 109; and psychic interiority, 88, 99; of world space, 272n30

inanimacy, 17, 83; of law, 151; of signifier, 251
incest, 214, 232
incorporation, 74, 170–71, 175; gift of death as, 30; of loss, 170; melancholic, 157, 166
indeterminacy, 156, 183, 194, 217
indifference, 13, 82, 89, 98, 105, 114, 116, 118, 129, 147, 223; and desire, 108; and Fortune, 138; and *jouissance*, 142; of law, 26; and object, 93, 134, 257n44; vs. particularity, 127; submission to, 110
influence, 200–201, 207
information, 114, 258n62
Ingham, Patricia, 11, 283n8
injury, 180, 203, 216–17, 284n19
Innocent III, Pope, 16
inscription, 59, 70–71, 88, 106; of subject by signifier, 162; by trauma, 227
insentience, 77, 91, 95; and crisis over matter, 14; as drive, 17; and Fortune, 125; and generality, 107; and indifference, 270n13; vs. justice, 16; and narrator of *BD*, 113; of signifier, 12, 57; superreal, 116; as tragedy, 137; of the "work," 88
insignificance: of Fortune, 122; in *NPT*, 122–23
insomnia, 91, 93, 96
inspiration, 66, 125
intent, 199, 205, 208
intention, 122, 200, 210, 227
intentionality, 44; of the law, 206
intercession, 166, 183, 187, 190
intercessor, 182, 289n33
interior, 77, 91, 93, 111, 132, 148, 172; courtly, 99, 106; of *finamen*, 113
interiority(ies), 24, 76, 88, 96, 166, 172, 208, 215, 220, 221, 257, 275n62; and body, 87; in *Boece*, 124; courtly, 79; of group subject, 84, 209; and history, 112; psychic, and prosthesis, 88; of sentience, 134; tragic, 90, 149
interiorization, 250; and sacrifice, 235
internal, the: as eternal, 89

interpretation, 47–48, 54–55, 110; sacrificial, of deaths of kings, 118; and signifier, 90
intertextuality, 54, 224, 227; and groupification of trauma, 226
intimacy, 106, 111, 112; as form of immensity, 87; and loss, 109
introjection, 34, 96, 149; and group enjoyment, 259n79
invention, 11, 46, 52, 55, 244, 262n7
Irving, David (biographer of Hitler), 46
iterability, 223, 225, 235; of identity, 27; of signifier, 142–43, 278n11

Jackson, Earl, Jr., 264n38
Jacobs, Jane, 68, 241, 262n7
Jameson, Fredric, 66, 265n47
Jeanne de Laval, 276n70
Jed, Stephanie, 236
Jesus, 74, 234
Jew(s), 156, 159, 202
John of Ireland, 214
John of Salisbury, 122, 285n25, 292n15
Johnson, Barbara, 21, 78
Jonson, Ben, 4
Joplin, Patricia, 295n48
jouissance, 6–7, 20, 23, 30–31, 34, 62–63, 71, 75–76, 79, 103, 141, 157–58, 161, 168, 175, 211, 220, 231, 245, 246, 247, 253n2, 254n10, 261n92, 269n5; and the arts, 240; and *ascesis*, 90; and beauty, 160; and courtly love, 120; court's claim to, 80; *dépense* as, 275n58; of discipline, 233; and exteriority, 164; feminine, 230; of form, 126–27; of Fortune, 123; of God, 182; and group, 37, 206, 222, 234; of judgment, 203; and the lady, 19, 22; of the law, 120, 163, 206, 229, 243; loss of, 195; and medievalism, 247; and melancholy, 95; of neighbor *(Nebenmensch)*, 38–39, 41, 85, 184; of order, 228; and particularity, 271n21; pearl of, 195, 290n53; and philology, 252; and potlatch, 256n92; and the real, 121; and renunciation, 73; and rescue, 156; and sacrifice, 30, 41, 204, 233–34, 254n14; and sentience, 18, 211; of shame, 186; and the signifier, 24–25, 63, 120, 161–62, 171, 229; as stranger within, 104; of submission, 29, 110; as suffering, 127; vs. surplus enjoyment, 278n16; of terror, 220; and the Thing *(das Ding)*, 167; of violence, 224; of war(rior), 160, 205, 216
jouis-sense, 165, 217, 221
joy, 99, 254n12
jubilation, 27, 186
judgment, 46, 121, 169, 200, 203, 220, 230; ethical, 177, 200; trauma of, 233
Juno, 94, 115–18
justice, 28, 40, 59, 78, 154, 175, 205, 240; of community, 59; and preservation of past, 250; as principle of animation, 16
Justice, Steven, 286n37

Kay, Sarah, 11, 257n48
Keen, Maurice, 294n35
Kelly, H. Ansgar, 82, 124, 127–28, 269n2, 270n14, 272n27, 278n12, 279n17
Kempe, Margery, 74–75
Kendrick, Laura, 286n32
Kieckhefer, Richard, 141
kinship, 23, 161
Kiser, Lisa, 274n51, 290n52
Knapp, Peggy, 144
knight, 292n14; Christ as lover-, 35–36; and courtly love, 164; of faith, 156, 157–58, 160, 164, 174; and gift of death, 160; and neighbor, 41
knighthood: Ramon Lull on, 35
knowledge, 44, 45, 62, 68, 77, 91, 141, 258n62; *ascesis* of, 163; of death, 91, 134, 170; and death drive, 119; and desire, 52, 267n68; gift of, 115, 118; and the group, 10, 46–47; historical, 44, 51; and indifference, 118; and the law, 46; love of, in medievalism, 56; mathematical, and signifier, 245; past as object of, 51; production of, 12, 55; sacrifice of, 163, 173; and symbolic order, 75

INDEX

Kristeva, Julia, 3–4, 19, 24, 66, 72–73, 152, 237, 243, 254n12, 262n4, 276n68, 282n2; on courtly love, 10, 257n51; on Freud, 282n76; on *jouissance*, 71; on psychoanalysis, 47, 70, 282n76

labor, 240; ethics of, 161; sacrificial, 58; of (self-)rescue, 186
Lacan, Jacques, 2, 11, 152, 168, 195, 258n57, 264n33, 284n20, 288n29; on altruism, 39; anamorphosis, 280n40; art, history of, 20; *Art of Courtly Love*, 23; beauty, 160, 194, 289n32; being-as-signifier, 250; charity, 184, 289n26; *Civilization and Its Discontents*, 38, 85; courtly love, 10, 19, 21, 120, 164, 266n55, 276n71; creationism, 287n3; *das Ding* (the Thing), 23, 28, 121, 285n23; death, 72, 194; death drive, 278n11; desire, 3, 228, 279n27; drive, 68–69; exchange, 242; *ex nihilo*, 182, 279n18; extimacy, 121, 289n27; the good, 185; group, 29, 211, 293n22; history of signifier, 255n25; iteration, 144; *jouissance*, 160, 254n14; the law, 25n13; medievalism of, 265n47; mirror stage, 7–8, 27–28, 156, 259n63, 264n26, 289n26; Nature's signifiers, 24–25, 258n63; *Nebenmensch*/neighbor, 40, 130, 153; pity, 171; real, 228; religion, 71–72, 75; responsibility, 127; sacrifice, 254n14; Sade, 260n86, 271n19; shame, 289n32; signifier, 57, 242; subject, 258n63; sublime, 258n61, 271n21; unconscious, 24, 132, 257n45, 278n14; utility, 241, 297n3; works, 256n33
lack, 69, 93, 99, 168, 179, 207, 221; in body of *finamen*, 183; and law, 5; in o/Other, 29–30, 234
Laclau, Ernesto: and Chantal Mouffe, 298n9
lady, the, 21, 23, 185–86, 258n59, 288n23, 289n31; in courtly love, 21, 183, 210; defines group, 41; and *jouissance*, 22; as inhuman partner, 162; and sublime, 18, 41, 162
Lady Philosophy: on Fortune, 26; shape-shifting, 134; and tragedy, 88
La Farge, Catherine, 159, 174
laity, 33, 142; lay body, 135
lamentation, 142, 169–70, 204; tragic, 143
Langton, Stephen, 27
language, 9–10, 14, 19, 44, 50, 66, 77, 246, 262n4; and courtly love, 19; generalizing power of, 120, 272n27; and sacrifice, 92; and sentience, 94; as signifying chain, 25; as tool, 53; unconscious structured like, 24
langue vs. *parole*, 54
Laplanche, Jean: and Jean-Bertrand Pontalis, 217, 256n29, 274n50
lapse, the, 101, 153
La Soufletiere, Ameline, 214
laughter, 114, 135, 223
lauzengier, 120–21
law(s), 5, 26, 28, 34, 57, 61, 76, 105, 142–43, 156, 159, 164, 168, 172, 205, 220–21, 249; arbitrary, 22, 53, 55, 160, 234, 270n18; in chivalry, histories of, 231; in courtly love, 80, 162; of death, 173; and desire, 4, 6–7, 10, 24, 35, 121, 158, 254n13; and drives, 119–20, 202; and enjoyment, 8, 162–63; form(ality) of, 137, 228; and Fortune, 128, 151; and gift, 15; of group, 9–10, 29, 41, 46, 95, 108, 110, 206; of Jews, 202; *jouissance* of, 163, 229, 233, 243; of knighthood, 36; of knowledge, 46; and living, techniques of, 52; obscenity of, 220, 259n72; oracular, 209, 237; and sacrifice, 136; senseless, 86; and sentience, 16; and signifier, 25–26, 77, 86, 162, 164, 229; submission to, 160, 162, 166, 173, 198, 259n72; as symbolic order, 278n14; and trauma, 208; of will, general, 185
legend(s), 49, 230, 235
Leicester, H. Marshall, Jr., 145

Leupin, Alexandre, 49, 65, 67
Lévi-Strauss, Claude, 25, 212, 258n63
Lewis, C. S., 218–19
libido, 25, 256n29
life, 14–18, 34–35, 53, 94–95, 98–99, 102, 118–19, 157, 165, 170, 178, 192, 252; artificing of, 80; and courtly love, 20; defense against, 88; fall into, 114; gift of, 17, 32, 157; of group, 62; hypersentient, 205; and image, 249; inner/interior, 87, 96, 215; and pain, 16; refusal of, 89, 128; renunciation of, 156; resistance to, 84, 122; and sacrifice, 30, 156; of signifier, 14, 263, 34–35, 237; and tragedy, 84, 128; and trauma, 127
limit(s), 29, 31, 170, 190, 196, 251; death as, 118–19; and desire, 186; and *jouissance*, 7; of life, 118–19, 192; of Other, 156; of subject, 64, 156, 184
Lionel, duke of Clarence, 131
literature, 69, 96; chivalric, 218; courtly, 63, 184; national, 67; and psychoanalysis, 65
living, 9, 58, 91; aversiveness of, 82; effects of dead on, 57; living on, 93, 102; and sacrifice, 4; techniques of, 4, 69, 76–77, 87, 259n79, and sentience, 12–13
Lochrie, Karma, 73, 262n13
lordship, 22, 29, 105
loss, 39, 45, 80, 109, 111, 151, 156, 169, 170, 200; and chivalry, 206, 235; and consent, 14; and cross, 34; denial of, 259n77; and gift of death, 37; and group, 85; of *jouissance*, 38, 196; and the lady, 210; and language, 92; and object, 18; past as, 55; and sacrifice, 156, 161, 217; sublime, 209; vs. universals, 179
love, 21, 24, 91, 75, 171, 183, 192, 194, 196, 204, 207, 221, 233, 239, 252, 258n57; of beauty, 89; Christian, 84; courtly, 10, 12, 18–24, 27–28, 40–41, 51, 63, 80, 99, 100, 112, 120, 162, 164, 167, 183, 186, 205, 208–9, 229, 231, 259n76, 266n55,

276n71, 288n25, 289n31; of enemy, 160; Freud's view of, 32; and neighbor, 86, 154, 156; of past, 251; of self/selfless, 158; and sexual difference, 63; submission to, 105; as technique of living, 31, 84
luck: and tragedy, 82
Lull, Ramon, 35, 260n89
lyric (poem), 19, 22, 63, 258n59

McCoy, Richard, 10
Macdougall, Norman, 49, 262n12
Machaut, Guillaume, 131, 274–75n55
Maclean, Ian, 183
magic, 141, 272n33, 278n15
magnification, 90, 112, 120; and tragedy, 88
Malory, Sir Thomas, 211, 222
Man in Black, 92, 97–99, 102–3, 123
mandate: of Other, 62, 157, 162, 259n76
mania, 164–65; megalo-, 179
Mann, Jill, 36, 290n34, 292n16
manners, 35, 100
Margherita, Gayle, 11, 292n16
mark, 122, 124–27, 144; and gift, 114; vs. meaning, 209; transmission of, by angels, 114
marker(s): guide drive, 70; and sacrifice, 15; as signifiers, 20
marking: and history of signifier, 255n25; memorial function of, 56; re-, 142; and showing, 258n57
marriage, 174, 212; as sacrifice, 175
Marx, Karl, 13, 66, 68, 241, 248, 298n9; and Friedrich Engels, *The German Ideology*, 266n59
Mary, Blessed Virgin, 23, 215
masochism, 19, 34, 51, 264n39; and sacrifice, 136
massification: of passional devotion, 87
maternity: prosthetic, 107, 276n68
matter: insentient, 14
Maurus, Rabanus, 33, 260n84
Mauss, Marcel, 171

medievalism, 64, 247, 252; academic, 45, 49, 248; antiutilitarian, 239, 242; gift of death of, 252; Lacanian, 265n47; popular, 49, 55–56, 58, 62, 247–48
Meilyr, 43–44
Méla, Charles, 67
melancholic, 259n77
melancholy, 56, 99, 93, 95, 111, 215, 234, 236–37; charity as, 32; love, 91; and mania, and cross, 34
memento mori, 152
memory, 57–58, 139, 165, 237, 263n25; craves what is delightful, 273n38; and the cross, 33; and devotion, 105, 273n39; and history, 48; and *imagines agentes*, 132, 263n25; and indifference, 91; interiority of, 105; and the lady, 96, 99; in medieval psychology, 121, 134; and particularity, 48; and pity, 187; and prosthesis, 252, 298n12; and sacrifice, 58; and signification, 250, 252; Simonides on, 89–90; and tragedy, 131; in unconscious, 70–71
Menocal, Maria Rosa, 12, 19
mercy, 156, 174, 183
messenger, 116, 220; angelic, 114
metamorphosis, 77, 180, 186, 265n40
metaphor, 54, 225
metaphysics, 140, 153
method, 9, 47, 50, 242
Mézières, Philippe de, 36, 87
Michael (archangel), 81
Michelet, Jules, 51–52, 56
Middleton, Anne, 66, 265n48
Mieszkowski, Gretchen, 293n23
militancy, 32, 156, 208
militia nova, 35
miniaturization, 98, 109, 112; and interiority, 88; tragic, 104
Minnis, A. J., 275n61
mirror(s), 7–8, 183, 204, 224; in *Babe*, 240; and charity, 289n26; for prince(sses), 178, 182–83, 287n9; stage, 27–28, 156, 264n26
Misyn, Richard, 260n81

mnemonic(s), 44, 59, 251; as signifiers, 20; technique, 57, 62, 67, 88, 200; technology, 58; traditional, 57
mobility: of desire, 24, 187
mobilization: of group, 28, 60
modernity, 45, 66; post-, 19
Mollat, Michel, 267n59, 287n9
monastery(ies), 55–56
monasticism, 41, 133, 135, 137
Monk (Chaucer's), 131–32, 136, 144–45, 152; portrait of, 133–35, 137–39, 145
morality, 3, 7–8, 145
Morpheus, 94, 96, 116–17
mortality, 51, 75, 205; and signifier, 192
mourning, 37, 55, 70, 88, 92–93, 100–101, 105, 117, 155, 166, 171, 236–37, 249–50; and attachment, 259n78; and body, 151; and courtly love, 167; for front, 160; and group, 33, 130, 229; and image of lost object, 83; and melancholic narrative, 70; and sacrifice, 155, 164; and signifier, 250; sovereign, 270n17; and subject, 164, 180; and trauma, 90
Muse(s), 123, 125–26

name: as signifier, 174
narcissism, 85, 120, 183–84
narration, 44
narrative(s), 66, 70–71, 236, 220; of sentience, 18; of sublimation, 232
narrator: in *BD*, 117, 132, 275n56; of *Canterbury Tales*, 135, 139; Chaucerian, 111, 118; of *The Legend of Good Women*, 190–91, 196, 198, 232–33
nation, 19, 109, 236
Nature: signifiers of, 24, 142, 258n63
Natureingang, 225
Nebenmensch, 184, 191, 194–95; in courtly love, 186; and *das Ding*, 121; extimacy of, 285n23; God as, 185; in subject, 20. *See also* neighbor(s)
necessity, 201, 241–42, 247; and chance, 122–23; and choice, 136, 164; and the state, 234

need, 241, 248, 266–67n59; Marx and Engels on, 68
neighbor(s), 39, 183–85, 261n92, 274n45, 289n31; and body of Christ, 37; Christian love of, 84; in courtly love, 80; evil in heart of, 192, 194, 197; and generalization, 274n45; and identification, 32, 38; and lady, 41; obligation to love, 38; Rickels on, 272n27; and sacrifice, 34; in subject, 20
Nichols, Stephen G., 252
Nietzsche, Friedrich, 16, 126, 155, 279n23
nom du père, 26

obedience, 4, 13, 26, 160, 162–64, 164, 183, 220; to command, 162; to the law, 163; military, 160, 163
objection, 203, 292n10
objectivity, 47
object(s), 13, 14, 23, 47, 89, 103, 114, 122, 133, 138, 180, 188, 196, 215, 228, 235, 251; and anticlimax, 93; anxiogenic, 217–18; apotropaic, 29; beautiful, 139; charitable, 195; of Christian love, 32; and codification, in *Art of Courtly Love*, 24; of desire, 5, 191; endurance of, 188, 195; erotic, 230; exchange of sentient, 9, 22, 24, 34, 202, 230; and Fortune, 102, 122; and gift of death, 119; as good, 16, 185; and group, 37–38, 293n22; of knowledge, past as, 51; and indifference, 118, 122; lost, 37, 52, 104; particular, 130, 229; persecuting, 218; raised to dignity of Thing, 21, 108; and sentience, 17, 22, 203, 204, 206, 209, 211; and the subject, 118; sublime, 41, 109, 162, 183, 190, 233, 237, 271n21, 293n22; and techniques of living, 18; in tragedy, 117; transience of, 153, 194; transitional, 97; traumatic, 162, 223
objet a, 108, 130, 164, 203; lady as, 100; sublime, 109
obligation(s), 173, 202, 206; to common good, 229; to love neighbor, 38, 184

obscenity(ies), 212, 236; Chaucer's, 236; of submission to law, 28, 220
Ockham, William, 31, 140, 178, 280n46
oikos, 161, 240
Olson, Glending, 285n30, 287n9
oneiric experience, 89; images, 91; unintelligibility, 96
opacity: of artifact, 13; of law, 26
oracle(s), 28, 43, 110, 162, 209, 271n18
oracular, 221
oracularity, 210; of signifiers, 226
order(s), 24, 159, 181–82, 205; and exchange, 228; of goods, 16; and group, 41; history as, 68; and imaginary, 264n26; of knighthood, 35; military, 292n12; and real, 257n56; of signs/the signifier, 22, 36, 57, 61; symbolic, 6, 20, 26, 29, 40, 75, 157, 211, 212, 222, 237, 254n10, 278n14, 292n12, 296n61; of things, 36
ordinance, chivalric, 29, 41, 115, 205
Origen, 90
origins: and psychoanalysis, 70
orphans, 29, 185, 204
other, the, 40, 59, 99, 101, 119, 156, 168, 173, 183, 185, 195–96, 239, 254n10; death of, 95; desire of, 7; and enjoyment, 38, 76, 264n26; first to go, 40; as the "I," 17; particular, 86; past as, 49; and pity, 187; rescue of, 29; as signifier, 250; subject founded on, 28, 86, 171, 185; suffering of, 3, 76; time of, 39; transmitted by history, 59
Other, the, 4–5, 29, 104, 251, 254n10, 278n14; as agency that rewards, 39; and gift of death, 82; imaginary, 123; one likes to be like, 86; and sacrifice, 37; subject as signifier in discourse of, 22
Ōther, the, 5–6, 29, 152, 156, 158, 210–11, 254n10, 278n14; desire of, 211; gaze of, 30; past as, 49; and signifier, 210, 250; structures subject, 156
othering, 9
otherness, 61, 65, 76

outside, 8, 77
overvaluation: of love object, 66, 180
Ovid, 93–94, 100, 115–18, 186, 277n7; *Tristia*, 80

pact, 56, 114, 205, 228, 237–38; of the group of two, 104
pain, 16, 30, 36, 44, 161, 188, 232, 256n29; enjoying, 126; and group, 38, 205; memory of, 33; and sacrificial body, 34; and sentience, 203
Painter, Sidney, 260n89
Palamon, 164, 167, 168, 174, 230; and exchange, 22; marriage of, 166, 173
Pandarus, 208, 210, 212, 218–20, 223–25, 232; logophilia of, 229; voyeurism of, 231
paradise, 97–98
Paradise Lost, 243
parapraxis, 25, 67
parliament, 229, 234
parole vs. *langue*, 54
Parsons, John Carmi, 288n24
participation, 139; unnatural, 64, 265n40
particularity, 27, 271n21; death establishes, 259n78; and indifference, 127; negated by Christian love, 84; of object, 99, 102, 108; negated by charity, 32
particular(s), 100, 200
partner: inhuman, 22, 162, 187
Pascalis Romanus, 91
passage, rites of, 63, 97
passion, 45, 245, 246; of Christ, knight's identification with, 36–37; and death drive, 142; Lacan on, 75; and the law, 6; vs. morality, 8; for number, 142; for Reason, 56; vs. restraint, 7; and signifier, 78; for technique, 244
passivity: and activity, in optics, 292n11; as destructivity, 231; and Fortune, 124
past, 44–45, 48, 51–53, 57–58, 60, 63, 69–70, 250; alterity of, 45, 48, 77; break with, 45, 51, 70; and desire, 43; and group, 71; historicism's responsibility to, 12; as lost, 55, 64; love of, 62; pleasures of knowing, 59; preservation of, 90; recording, 61; recovery of, 48, 251; signifiers of, 56
pastoral, 225, 239
pastourelle, 225
paternalism, 247
paternity, 236
pathos: of aristocratic subject, 183; Chaucer's treatment of, 149
Patocka, Jan, 175
patria, 29
patronage, female, 183; and queenship, 288n19
patron(s), 58, 79, 182; friendship with, 106
Patterson, Lee W., 56, 252, 282n74, 283n11, 292n16; on Theban repetition, 11, 295n55; on tragedy in *LGW*, 144
Paul, Saint: on the law, 6; on love, 32
pauper(s), 161, 200
payment, 34, 196
Payne, F. Anne, 144
pearl: and *jouissance*, 290n53
pedagogy, 123, 246
Pedro, King of Castile, 92, 130
penance, 291n6
penitentials, 201
performance(s), 54, 74–75, 167
performor: cross as, 34; past as, 55
Perrers, Alice, 214
persecution, 65, 282n3
personification: and *das Ding*, 20; and pain, 101
Peter I (Lusignan) of Cyprus, 36, 87, 131, 272n29
Peter of Blois, 259n68
petition(s): Alcyone's, 116; primal scene of, 119; queenly, 183; and sentience, 115
phallus: and pearl, 290n53
philology(ies), 64, 67, 243, 251; and Freud, 12; and medievalism, 252; "new," 251; in popular culture, 62; and religion, 72; Romance, 19
Philomela, 225–26

philosophy, 164, 168, 179
Philosophy, Lady. *See* Boethius
pietas: as enjoyment, 101; and memory, 90; and psychoanalysis, 70
piety, 125, 183, 187. *See also* pity
pilgrim(s), 33, 150; community, 144
pilgrimage, 34, 284n20; and the cross, 36
pity, 101, 111–12, 150, 171, 184; and befallenness, 146; and courtly love, 99; and crucifixion, 87; Dollimore on, 129; as enjoyment, 39; and gender, 290n34; and the neighbor, 189; and *pietas*, 58, 86, 184, 187, 192, 196, 290n35; and sentience, 115; and the subject, 129, 187; and tragedy, 87, 128, 272n27; transitivism of, 86, 171
Placidus, 88
plague, 40, 294n35
play, 46, 241, 244, 251; and history of technology, 262n7; of signifier, 232
pleasure(s), 10, 50, 55, 110, 172, 183, 191, 195, 211, 241, 245–46; of codification, in *Art of Courtly Love*, 24; of court life, 35; and death drive, 17; vs. duty, 4; and enjoyment, 246; and ethics, 254n14; Holkot and Ockham on, 31; and *jouissance*, 7, 254n10, 279n27; of knowing the past, 59; in learning, 244; of obedience, 220; and pedagogy, 246; principle of, 258n56; relation to the good, 253n6; and technology, 52; and trauma, 246
plus-de-jouir, 121, 164
poetics, 79, 122–23, 187, 194, 222
poetry, 94, 111, 213; courtly, 96
policy: Wallace on, 149
political subjects: and court culture, 110; signifiers, 284n19
politic(s), household, 182
poor, 39, 40–41, 155, 183, 261n97
pornography: on the Internet, 245; and medievalism, 63
poststructuralism: and medieval studies, 55

posttraumatic: grin, 147; laughter, 135
potlatch: and sacrifice, 256n34
poverty, 193–94, 267n59
power, 56, 58, 156, 187, 190, 192–93, 196–97, 202, 209, 214, 222, 245, 278n15; of alteration, 180, 184, 275n60; and attachment, 243; conceptive, 178–79; of fantasy, 248; and group, 37, 57, 94, 99, 117, 119, 205; and humility, 51; of images, 94, 99; of other, in history writing, 59; and pain, 38; and pleasure, 10; prosthetic, 236; queenly, 182; of rescue, 59, 179, 195; and signifier, 57; technological, 213; and Thing, 221
preparedness, 32, 60, 62, 102, 116–18, 138, 219, 229; vs. befallenness, 206; and the cross, 33; culture as cult of, 62; and death drive, 121; and enjoyment, 58; and Fortune, 125; as gift, 136, 145; and indifference, 105, 147, 270n13; of the knight, 36; knowledge of death as, 91, 119; and rescue, 89; and tragedy, 82–83, 87
presence, 57, 168, 250
present, 20, 90; effects of past on, 58, 64; and neomedievalism, 62
preservation: of past, 90; techniques of cultural, 62, 64
princes(ses): mirrors for, 178, 182–83
print, 58, 61
prisoners, 22–23, 230
privation, 5, 99, 108
Procne, 185, 224–26
production, 13, 54, 68–69, 244, 250, 256n40; of knowledge, 19, 44–45, 59, 65; and sublimation, 240
productions: desires in form of, 61, 242
productivity: of desire, 47; vs. pleasure, 241
prohibition(s), 6, 163, 197, 287n11
projection, 34, 270n13; and group enjoyment, 259n79
promise, 156, 187, 195; and credence, 188; and neighbor, 189; of rescue, 156

pro patria mori, 60–61
prosthesis, 93–94, 115–16, 136, 223, 245; and *ascesis*, 105; and courtesy, 100; as defense against Fortune, 81; and interior, 88, 97, 149; of maternity, 107, 298n12; and memory, 252; and sentience, 12, 256n29; subliming of, in *Boece*, 124; technology as, 298n12
protection, 222–23, 247
providence (purveiaunce), 129, 163, 166; and gift of death, 123; and the law, 124
prudence, 90, 158
psyche, 90, 99
psychoanalysis, 4, 11, 64–65, 72–75, 179, 243; and courtly love, 10; Derrida on, 153; on desire, 158; and ethics, 3; Foucault on, 265n41; and historicism, 12, 47, 71; and history, 152; Lacanian, 270n18; and the law, 158; and medieval studies, 12, 52; and medieval textuality, 67; and memory, 70; vs. religion, 73; and rescue, 29; resistance to, 52–53
psychology(ies), 65, 124, 140, 158, 201, 254n16; of falling, 112; medieval, 31, 121, 271n21
pugna pro patria, 60–61

quantification, 54, 139, 140–42
quantity, 140, 143
queen(s), 109, 182–83; charity of, 187
queenship, 288nn23–24; and patronage, 288n19
queerness, 63, 126

Ramazani, John, 134, 137, 139, 145, 147–48, 275n62, 280n38, 280n42
rank, 35, 100; in courtly love, 80, 120
rape, 203–4, 214, 224–26; and consent, 208
real, the, 12, 67, 159, 161, 167, 215; and *jouissance*, 121; and neomedievalism, 62; and sacrifice, 161; and signifier, 216; and the subject, 20; Žižek on, 257n56
reality, 179–81, 70, 75, 77

reason(s), 4, 28, 56, 121, 157, 163, 166, 172, 177–78, 182, 200, 254n10
reception: of Chaucer's poetry, 80
receptivity, 106–7, 190
reciprocity, 171, 225
reckoning, 40, 141
redeemer, 179–80, 196
redemption, 60, 73, 156, 165, 236
regimen(s), 12–13
relationship(s), 47, 69
relativism, 47, 245
relay, 98, 116; group power of, 37, 136, 205; in Mézières's *A Tragedic Prayer*, 36; and sacrifice, 235; technological, 107
relic(s), 23, 34
religion, 71–73, 268n80; and the neighbor, 153
remainders, of text, 49–50, 56; of past, 58
remembering, 96, 110; and rescue, 221
remnant(s), 167–68, 170; burnished, 9, 56; purified, 9, 30, 209
renovatio, 45, 66, 251
renunciation, 6, 73, 156; and the law, 164
repeatability, 143, 250
repetition, 21, 115, 150, 190, 211, 230–32, 250, 275n56; 293n23; compulsion of, 53, 142, 217; and the drives, 17; enjoyment, 200; and memory, 70; and trauma, 40, 233
replication, 21, 96, 100; technologies of, 64
repose, 185, 190–91
reposefulness, 108
representation(s), 11, 275n61; of death, 170; of enduring self, 83; historical, 50; and sacrifice, 41
repression, 9, 251
reproduction, 95, 100, 143; and death wish, 97; as indifferent, 127; power of transmission of, 133
reproductivity, 94
reputation(s), 196, 222, 224, 237

rescue, 100, 153, 171, 185, 190, 193, 195–96, 206, 219, 221; chivalric, 29, 160, 176, 184, 204; and enhanced identification, 60; fantasy of, 156, 168, 182; and history, in Caxton, 59; of neighbor, 38; of other, 89; power to, 158, 170; sacrificial, 160
rescuer(s): cross as, 34; self-, 35, 177, 186; women as, 196
resemblance, 110, 195
resistance, 52–53, 63, 75, 229; to life, 122; to psychoanalysis, 4
responsible subject, 278n13
responsibility, 13, 48, 135, 165, 200, 227; and the group, 205, 226; historical, 62, 66; and Oedipus, 127; and sacrifice, 158; and sentience, 205
restlessness, 185
resurrection, 190, 196
retrospection, 51, 216
return, 112; of death wish, 88; to origins, 70; of pleasure principle, 258n56
reward(s), 16, 156, 158
rhetorical gifts, 110
rhetorical prosthesis, 94
rhetoric(s), 99, 114–15, 245–46; of courtly love, 120; and humanities, 241; of loss, 169, 236; of responsibility, 248; of utility, 241; of *vanitas*, 5
Richard II, 131, 216
Rickels, Laurence A., 33, 80, 84, 89, 118–20, 129, 257, 259n79, 268n80, 272n27; on animation, 275n55, 277–78n9; on Christian church and group psychology, 32, 85; on indifference, 270n13; on Sade, 271n19; on sadomasochism, 118; on technology and the unconscious, 131–32
risk, 97, 198, 237, 245–47; in chivalric discourse, 235; and *jouissance*, 31–32; sublimed, 115
riskiness, 109
rite(s), sacrificial, 166, 205

ritual, 72, 183, 205; of ordination to knighthood, 35, 205; of submission to law, 198
rivalry, 102; *ascesis* of, 101
rival(s), 191–92; friendship with, 106
Robertson, Jr., D. W., 168, 173, 175–76, 286n43, 292n16
Rolle, Richard, 260n81
Romance of the Rose, The, 98, 105
romance(s), 62, 231, 265n47; chivalric, 29; medieval, 105; and rape, 227
Romans 7:7, 254n13
rulers: women, 182
rule(s), 116, 196, 218; and form, 137; that govern signifier, 25; and transmission, 118

Sacks, Peter, 296n61
sacramentum: and sacrifice, 284–85nn21–22
sacred, 9; and sacrifice, 284n21
sacrifice, 10, 15, 102, 135–36, 156–57, 160, 161, 167, 168, 202, 218, 229, 231, 236, 242; of belief, 208; and charity, 158; chivalric, 174; in courtly culture, 29; and the cross, 32; and desire, 4, 8–9, 156; economy of, 4, 119, 171; and enjoyment, 12, 158; and ethics, 201; and exchange, 31; and fallenness of object, 84; forecloses real, 161; Gothic relation to signifier of, 34; and the group, 205; and historicism, 12; and hypereconomy, 155–56, 162; *jouissance* of, 233; of *jouissance*, 32, 234, 254n14; of knowledge, 163; and law, 166; marriage as, 175; meaninglessness of, 164, 169; and memory, 90; and pain, 204; of the past, 56; relays suffering, 31; and rescue, 29; and responsibility, 158; and secrecy, 9; and sentience, 34; of Troilus, 235; women's capacity for, 196; and the "work," 14, 89
Sade, Marquis de, 196, 260n86, 271n19

Sadean object, 271n19
sadism: and courtly love, 164
sadist, 168, 170, 179
sadistic exteriority: of Monk, 149
sadomasochism: and the cross, 34; and the crucifixion, 37; and the double, 289n30; and the gift of death, 118; and Middle Ages, 63
safety, 39, 105, 211, 219, 221, 232
Saint David (monastery): in Gerald of Wales, 44
sameness: and dreams, 96; and history, 61
Sampson, 275n62
satisfaction, 6, 31, 69, 156; and the good, 15; impossibility of, 5; vs. *jouissance*, 7; of the neighbor, 37; of the subject, 23, 37
scandal: of ethics, 137; and form, 27; of the law, 163
Scanlon, Larry, 11, 106, 129, 228, 279n22
scapegoat: God as, 155; medieval studies as, 53
Scarry, Elaine, 16, 158, 203, 216, 256n29, 260n82, 284n19, 286n39; on creationism, 287n3; on the cross, 32; on sentience, 12, 15
scholarship: medievalist, 72, 76
Schreber, Daniel Paul, 190, 228
secrecy, 163, 169; affinity with sacrifice, 9
secret(s), 98, 170; of the dead, 119; and the law, 143; of otherworld, 118
self-extension, 107, 204
selflessness, 171
self-presence, 8
self-rescue, 29
self(ves), 181, 185; and "becoming," 77; care of/for, 4, 8, 58, 123, 125, 164, 253n5; and charity, 31, 171; double of, 289n30; and the friend, 106; and the other, in tragedy, 127; prosthetic, 120; re-creation of, 89
sense: feeling, and techniques of living, 12; moral, 3, 6

senselessness: of law, 28; sublimity of, 222; and submission, 162
sensibility, 101, 112; in courtly culture, 111
sensuality, 200
sensuousness, 12
sentience, 20, 24, 28, 31, 60, 74, 91, 105, 108, 115, 132–33, 151, 199, 204, 208–9, 216, 220–22, 236; as artifact, 18; and chivalry, 35, 204; and *das Ding*, 34; and the drives, 69; exacerbated by love, 207; and exchange, 22–24, 203; of group, 35, 37, 205, 219; heightened, 105; historicity of, 12; and insentience, 77, 83; and interiority, 220; and *jouissance*, 18; and language, 94; and loss, 99; magnified by history, 59; of the Other, 157; and pain, 16, 203, 206; and prosthesis, 81, 256n24; of subject, 30; sublime, 206; and war, 221
sentient work, 88
sentiment (sentement): in courtly love, 80, 120
sentimentality: and courtly love, 19
Sermon on the Mount, 161, 282n3
service, 16, 184, 229
set-apartness, 101, 107
sex, 178, 182, 234; in history of chivalry, 231; premodern, 50
sexual difference, 94. See also difference(s)
sexuality, 10, 50, 74; and charity, 176; of *fin' amors*, 183
Seys (Ceyx), 94, 96
Shahar, Shulamith, 214
Shakespeare, William, 50, 128, 145, 211–12, 213, 232, 245; *Hamlet*, 128, 143, 145; *King Lear*, 94, 285n26; *The Merchant of Venice*, 159, 285n26; *Romeo and Juliet*, 210; *Troilus and Cressida*, 293n23
shame, 186, 194; and beauty, 289n32; and chivalry, 179; and fantasies of rescue, 179; *jouissance* of, 186
shock, 217, 226

showing(s), 21, 36, 61, 258n57; in *Art of Courtly Love*, 24; charity as, 38; of signifier, 41
signification, 26, 73, 140, 183, 223, 250–52; *das Ding* as effect of, 20; as defense against life, 83; and embodiment, 12; and memory, 252; prosthetic, 125; and sacrifice, 208
signifier(s), 14, 23, 25, 27, 40, 45, 50, 56, 60, 62, 66–67, 73, 88, 90, 157, 167, 171–72, 182, 196, 209–10, 229, 234, 237, 250, 256n33, 258n57, n61, 259n76, 279n18, 297n67; arbitrary, 157, 221; and beauty, 164, 171, 188; and "becoming," 77; "being-as-," 22, 143, 174, 250–51, 281n57; circulation of, 243; as code, 258n62; of community, 233; and courtly love, 266n55; and death, 63; designs subject, 240; desire as effect of, 24; in discourse of Other, 22, 211; and drive(s), 226, 238; enjoyment of, 241, 246; and ethics, 152; and exchange, 23, 61, 213; gift of, 236; glory of, 60; groupified, as *genre*, 121; Helen as, 221; and historical analysis, 49, 60; history of, 20–21, 25, 59, 67–68, 78, 255n25; and humanities, 242; as humiliator, 15; and ideal woman, 289n32; and inanimacy, 83; insentient, 12–13, 85; iterability of, 278n11; and knight of faith, 174; law of, 86, 120, 162, 164, 170, 229; in literary studies, 241; as mark, 69, 197; and mathematics, 234–35; and memory, 69–70, 227; and mortality, 192; and mourning, 250; name as, 162; of Nature, 24, 258n63; and neighbor, 39; and omens, 57; oracular, 226, 235; order of, 22, 57, 63; passion of, 250; and persecution, 282n3; play of, 232; political, 284n19; and the real, 216; return of, 49, 51; role in history, 12; and sacrifice, 32, 34, 41, 237; and science, 245; seen from standpoint of Thing, 34; and sentience, 34, 38, 107; *showing*, 258n57; structures unconscious, 120; stylizes *jouissance*, 162, 229, 270n18; subject as, 23; sublime, 51; submission to, 20, 36, 170; suffering from, 168; as symbolic order, 6; over time, 51; traumatic, 225; and war, 221

sign(s), 117, 179, 228, 258n56; beauty as, 160; common good as, 179; and Fortune, 129; law of, 28; mnemonic, 273n38; and stereotypy, 130
Silver, Brenda, 225
similarity: in *BD*, 94
similar(s), 86, 178, 264n33
sin, 154, 178, 201–2
sincerity: of poets of fine love, 14, 120–21
sleep, 91, 147
Smith, Cyril Stanley, 242
Smith, D. Vance, 78
Snyder, Susan, 296n65
sociality, 106, 111–12, 240–41, 246
Socrates, 165, 250
sodomy, 186
sol iustitiae, 16
sorrow(s), 94, 190; aristocratic, 99; of Mary, 33; and techniques of living, 101
sources, historical, 49–50
sovereign, 75, 107, 172, 221, 260n92
sovereignty: female, 107, 109; and queen, 183
space(s), 98, 151, 208–9; body's entry into, 87; and immensity, 273n30; inner vs. world, 273n30; interior, 89, 209; mastery of, and tragedy, 81; organized by enjoyment, 24; private, 208; psychic, 97; upheld by cross, 33–34
specificity: as construct, 259n78; of living creature, 98; sublime, 108
specific(s): as interdependent with universals, 129
spectacle, 134; in chivalric culture, 41; of cruelty, 126; and tragedy, Augustine on, 136
specularity, 181, 194; of gift, 157
speech, 209–10, 239; sublime, 172

Spielrein, Sabina, 276n2
splendor, 36, 75
split, the: and charity, 38; and the law, 25; in subject, 7, 20, 29, 32
Stafford, Pauline, 182, 288nn18–19
Stanbury, Sarah, 11, 73, 261n96, 292n11
state, the, 27, 233, 236, 248; enjoyment of, 234
Statius, 219, 224
stereotypy, 127, 130, 142–44; of *genre*, 132; of the mark, 122; and pity, 129
Stern, Daniel L., 254n11, 256n29
story(ies), 54, 151; survivor's, 105; tragic, 109–10
strangeness, 49, 61, 73, 158, 161, 167; and consent, 215
stranger, 165, 185; and gift of death, 171, 173; and *jouis-sense*, 165; and the Lady, 186; within subject, 20, 104, 185
Strode, Ralph, 141
Strohm, Paul, 11, 182, 287n9, 289n33, 292n16
study(ies), 64, 69, 133; cultural, 72, 241–42; literary, 242; medieval, 45, 52–53, 64, 71, 78, 247, 252; Renaissance, 71
subject, 4, 15, 64, 76, 156, 165, 168, 170, 179–80, 187, 189, 193, 207, 215, 227, 234, 258n62; and anxiety, 217; aristocratic, 183; and artifact, 34; befallenness of, 81, 114, 209; and chance, 114; chivalric, 36, 206, 208; and choice, 49, 201; courtly, 80, 105; and *das Ding*, 20; and desire (of other), 3, 7, 30; dreaming, 96; and enjoyment, 162, 199; ethical, 177, 200; European, 156; and exchange, 61, 210; founded on image of other, 86, 156, 170; gendered, 198, 223; group, 20, 208–9, 219, 227, 230, 238; helplessness of, 115; in history of group, 170; in history of signifier, 20–21; hyper-, 204, 213; and image of other, 28; and impervious object, 258n60; inhabited by Thing, 161, 171, 184; interiority of hyper-, 84, 209; and language, 47; and the law, 120, 259n72; and *Lear*, 129; in medieval psychology, 201; militant, 156; in mirror stage, 8, 27; as necromancer, 119; obedient, 177; as object, 210; philosophical, 170; in psychoanalysis, 70; recoils from neighbor, 38; rescued/rescuing, 182; and responsibility, 175, 227; and sacrifice, 30–31, 156, 204; and sadomasochism, 118; and sentience, 22; and signifier, 13, 20–21, 162, 158, 194, 251; as signifier, 22–23; split, 7; strangeness to itself, 164; sublime, 213; submission of, 259n72; transformed by love, 180; and trauma, 223; women as, 22
subjection, 168, 178, 237; to signifier, 167
subjectivation, 86, 161, 166, 240, 269n82
subjectivity(ies), 7, 166, 181; aristocratic, 80; and the arts, 240; chivalric, 29, 237, 245; communal, 172; construction of, 85; in courtly culture, 111; and courtly love, 19; desire fundamental to, 2, 7; emerges from Thing, 23; ethical, 163, 177, 180; of *finamen*, 113; Foucault on, 64; group, 24, 71, 73, 166, 257n56, 267n68; and group body, 37–38; history of, 25; honor as mode of, 174; and *jouissance*, 18; prostheses of, 245; and prosthetic body, 26; and psychoanalysis, 64; religious, 71; and rescue, 39, 177; sacrificial, 164, 166; and signifier, 6, 10, 12, 25; and trauma, 217, 225
sublimation, 14, 72, 206, 216, 229, 231, 236–37; and the arts, 240; and courtly love, 18; desublimation, 203; groupified, 211; narratives of, 232; and philology, 251
sublime, the, 19, 80, 98, 114; nation as, 109; and the ridiculous, in Chaucer, 296n62
subliming: of dead object, 105; of targets of chase, 97; technology, 141, 258n61

sublimity, 72, 203, 222; Calchas lacks, 221; and the good, 203; of group, 219; of queen, 183; and tragedy, 110, 112, 209
submission, 163, 166, 205, 234, 237; to arbitrary law, 160, 162, 166, 170, 173, 172, 198, 215, 221, 259n72, 296n61; consensual, 220; and dominance, 119; enjoyment of, 164, 215; to form, 27; to indifference, 110; *jouissance* of, in chivalric culture, 29; to law, 28, 36, 259n72, 270n18, 278n16; and mourning, 171; to the signifier, 20, 34, 39; to the state, 229; sublime, 172
substantiation, 15, 284n19
substitution(s), 83, 100, 211–12, 230
subversion: and containment, 76
suffering, 32, 70, 165, 181, 195–96, 204, 275n62; amorous, 40, 80; caused by artifact, 34; and crucifixion, 37, 289n30; enjoyment of, 73, 76; and ethics, 3; as form of pity, 86; and Fortune, 128; as *jouissance*, 127; in *MKT*, 152; object's capacity to endure, 83, 185; of/for the other, 3, 98, 101; penitential, 44; and rescue, 59; and sacrifice, 31; and sentience, 206; and signification, 183; as spectacle, 126; and sublimation, 206; in tragedy, 125, 127; of tragic hero, 120
suicide, 104, 257n42; in Blanchot, 136
superexistence, 160, 165, 170–71
surplus, 30; and sacrifice, 212, 222
survival, 95, 170, 191; and anaclisis, 256n29; of death of beloved, 99; group, 222; of infants, economies of, 240; and *jouissance*, 222; of medievalists, 252; and memory, 40; and *objet a;* 109; techniques of, 205
survivor, 99, 105; of death of other, 95; nation as, 109; and pity, 86; voice of, 227
suspension, 98, 104; subject as effect of, 28
Suzuki, Mihoko, 293n23
Swift, Jonathan, 19–20

symbolic order, 68, 156–57
symbolity, 188, 244, 246; and enjoyment, 244; and mourning, 236; signified by beauty, 194
symbolics: of rebirth, 18
symptom: "I" as, 101; and truth, 153
system, open: signifying chain as, 25, 68

technique(s), 7, 13, 49, 64, 200, 251; and amorous suffering, 40; in antiquity, 89; aristocratic, 35; arts and humanities as, 69; of attention, 114–15; in chivalric culture, 29; Christian group identification as, 32; in courtly love, 41; and desire, 84; ethical, 58; of existence, Foucault on, 84; Freud on love as, 31; and group, 52; history as, 59; of knowledge production, 19; of living, 17–18, 30–32, 52, 56, 64, 76–77, 81, 87, 200, 253n5, 259n799; and medieval literary theory, 14; mnemonic, 273nn38–39; passion for, 244; recording, 60; and sacrifice, 4; and sentience, 12, 30; and sorrow, 101; of survival, 205; and tragedy, 131
technologization: and desire, 121; of psyche, 90
technology(ies), 107, 114, 140–41, 120, 141, 239, 242, 245; communicative, 58, 249; and enjoyment, 242; expressive, 91; and fiction, 52; history as, 60; and humanities, 242; and language, 53; and pleasure, 52; as prosthesis, 298n12; of repetition, 64, 250; and sentience, 12; subliming of, 141; of survival, 205; of transmission, 94, 118, 131; and war, 60
temporalia: as finite, 153; vanity of, and subject, 215
temporality: of fallen subject, 87; pleasures of, in courtly love, 183
temptation, 43, 152, 200
territory(ies), 60, 77, 98
terror, 40, 220
testimony, 45, 66, 120–21

Tetzel, Gabriel, 259n70
text(s), 21, 24, 49, 56, 58; and humanities, 54; and transmission, 96
textuality: of history, 10
theodicy, 178, 180, 182
theory, 13, 58, 66, 242–43; courtly love in, 12; medieval literary, 14, 80; neo-Marxist, 9; of probability, 53; and psychoanalysis, 65; psychoanalytic, 41; turn to language of, 10
Theseus, 157, 165–66, 171–73
Thing, the, 62, 159, 168, 202, 221; and anamorphosis, 276n71; and arbitrary law, 163, 167; in art, 23; Harry Bailey's missing, 135; "extimate," 161; and history of signifier, 20–21, 161; and the Lady, 63, 258n61; object raised to dignity of, 18, 108; relic as, 34; and sentient exchange, 202; in subject, 161, 170; and sublime object, 41. *See also das Ding*
thing(s), 15, 59, 244, 258n60, 265n40; order of, 36
thought: (anti)utilitarian, 242, 247; Aristotelian, Christianizing of, 14; and group, 9, 12; Platonic, 4
time, 89; Alcyone and, 117; of gift, 15; of group, 57; of neighbor, 185, 191, 196; and sacrifice, 210; of transference, 111; and vigilance, 111
timing, obsessional, 39
tool: exteriority of, 256n31; Freud on, 289n12
totality, 40
totalization, 152, 243
tournament: in *KT*, 166
trace, 87, 191
tragedian, 122, 142
tragedy, 80, 92, 104, 106, 109–10, 128, 146, 210, 221, 234–35, 237, 270n14; Aelred of Rievaulx on, 272n27; and anticlimax, 222; Augustine on, 86; Aquinas on, 88; and Chaucer, 79, 138, 269nn1–2; Chaucerian, and anxiety-management, 83; of Christ's passion, 37; courtly, 80–81, 111–12; crusader as subject of, 36; defined by the Monk, 138, 143; domestic, 112; and enjoyment of suffering, 125–26; Farnham on, 128; and Fortune, 84, 88, 123, 148, 279n17; and group, 117, 135, 209; history of, 127; in history of responsibility, 130; and immensity, 88; and love, 80; medieval, 96, 148; and memory, 131; and prosthesis, 94; as repetition compulsion, 142; and sentience, 137; and the Thing, 237; as warning signs, 227
tragic: nation as, 109
transference(s), 66, 93, 106; and anticlimax, 276n2; and catastrophe, 135; of death wish, 111; Freud on, 76, 274n50; and history, 152; and *imago*, 274n50; as "new editions," through sacrifice, 34; and stereotypy, 130
transformation(s), 77, 112, 180, 182, 191, 215; and love, 77; into otherness, 76; of suffering, 70
transgression, 44, 160; and enjoyment, 212
transience: of object, 153, 194
transitivism, 194; of charity, 185; in courtly love, 80; and pity, 86, 171
transitivist structure of friendship, 101
translatio, 235
transmission, 40, 59–60, 66, 95–96, 111, 118; between dead and living, 237; and death wish, 97; of desire, 112; enjoyment of, 117; and group, 117; of the mark, 114; of past, 58; and reproduction, 133; technologies of, 94; and tragedy, 131
transumptio, 66–67
trauma, 45, 90, 217–18, 220, 223, 225, 266n57; of aliveness, 16, 127; of befallenness, 126; of birth, 17; in chivalric literature, 218; as comedy, 222; of desire, 142; and enjoyment, 29, 208; and group, 47, 225; of identification, 38; of judgment, 233; and law, 163;

trauma *(continued)*, management of, 29, 40; and phobic language, 44; and pleasure, 246; and signifier, 224
trauatic figuration, 136
treachery, 187–88, 224
tristitia, 237, 265n65
triumph, 135, 209, 221, 252; and gift of death, 221; and mania, 160, 164; melancholic, 164, 170; of preparedness, 33, 83; of superexistence, 160
trobairitz, 22, 63, 258n59
Troilus, 204, 207–8, 210–11, 213, 218, 220, 228–29, 231, 234–36; enhanced sentience of, 236; exchanged by Criseyde, 230; melancholy of, 234; powers of rescue of, 223; sublime military body of, 224; submission of, to Trojan state, 205, 207
troubadour: joy of, 19; song of, 254n12
Troy, 96, 105, 230, 234–35; death drive of, 229
truth, 45, 140, 187; and consent, 208; and the Freudian symptom, 153; historical, 44; and humanities, 54; and philology, 72; and religious belief, 72; "tired with iteration," 212
tyranny, 163
tyrants: falls of, 145

Ugolino of Pisa, 131
Ultima, 55, 63
unconscious, the, 25, 257n45; as automaton, 162; designed by signifier, 24–25, 278n14; Freudian, drives in, 71; ignorance of death of, 96, 119; inscribed by trauma, 227; *jouissance* as prosthesis for, 245; memories in, 70; and negation, 132; structured by law, 163; and symbolic order, 254n10
undead, 89, 116
unexpectedness, 96, 102
unheimlich, 70
union(s), 109, 187, 196–97
unity(ies), 109, 123

universality, 88, 129, 188
universals, 107, 126, 129, 151, 179, 271n21
unpleasure: and discipline, 17
unrepeatability, 65, 250
utilitarianism: Lacan on, 297n3
utility: Bataille on, 297n3; and humanities, 241–42, 247; living being as beyond, 23; Marx on, 298n9

"vacuole," 186, 195, 290n53
value, 15, 122; of history, 59; of identity, 40; of representing the Thing, 258n61; of sentient objects, 23; of the "work," 18
Vance, Eugene, 64
vanitas, 5
vanity, 215
variability: of Fortune, 123
variation: and stereotypy, 144
variety: and forest, 98
vernacularity, 236
vessel, 5, 215
victim(s), 74, 229; body of, 168; and sadist's desire, 168; of torture, 203; tragic, 149
vigil, 16, 93, 105, 111, 133–34; as attention, 92; and awakening, 91; courtly, 99; of crusader, 37; and death, 99, 137, 158, 164–65, 170; and techniques of existence, 84; vs. sleep, 147
vigilance, 16, 32, 117; and subject, 30; and tragedy, 82, 87
Vincent of Beauvais, 275n61
violation, 227, 232; adjudication by signifier, 229; Criseyde's fears of, 219; and the law, 208; and traumatic shock, 217
violence, 204–6, 213, 224–25, 229, 232; and chivalry, 205; and consent, 238; and memory, 90; sacrificial, 34; sexual, 227; of state, 19, 236
virtual, 97, 112
virtue, 109, 123, 183
Visconti, Bernabo, 131

visibility, 99, 189, 197
vision: ethical stakes of, 194; and the gift of death, 90; *jouissance* of, 231; in tragedy, 81–44
vitality: and "affects," 256n29; and *anaclisis*, 256n29; of the lady, 99
vitalization: of object, 194
vulnerability, 18, 22, 31, 38, 88, 103

Wack, Mary, 274n46, 288–89n25
Wallace, David, 11, 66, 145–47, 149–50, 265n48, 277n8, 280n41, 289n93, 296n23
war, 55, 160, 164, 166, 171, 204, 218, 220–21; and chance, 236; conducted by women, 294n93; cultural fictions at stake in, 284n19; enjoyment of, 234; histories of, 216; Hundred Years' War, 204, 213, 216, 294n35; and international law, 205; and judgment, 203; just, 27, 161, 163; preparedness for, 60; and *showing*, 258n57; and technology, 60; Trojan War, 218; World Wars I and II, 45–46
warfare, 62; machine, 294n44
warrior: courtly, 29; interiority of, 208; *jouissance* of, 205; mourns, 206; and rescue, 222
Warton, Joseph, 296n62
wealth, 196, 240
weapon(s): cross as, 32–33; of mass destruction, 62
Weber, Eugen, 9
widows, 29, 185, 204, 214, 222
will, 4, 14, 140, 152, 172, 201, 204; and enjoyment, 199; general, 85, 150, 185, 261n98; indeterminacy of, 217; in medieval psychology, 200
Williams, Raymond, 50
Winkler, John, 227
wish(es), 3, 17, 116, 130, 134; death, 51–61, 88–91, 97, 118–20, 125, 128, 132; and beauty, 89; and memory, 105; and transference, 111

witness, 95; and grief, 112; as Other, 164; produced by group, 136
woman(en), 177, 223, 231; capacity for sacrifice of, 196; and exchange, 21, 212; heart of, 187; and *jouissance*, 22; and mourning, 170; pity in, 187; in "Theme of Three Caskets," 209
wonder, 89, 93, 97–98, 111, 141; Aquinas on, 276n65; mnemonic role of, 273n38; pleasure as threat to, 246; and tragedy, 147
wonderfulness, 96
Woodville, Elizabeth, 27
Woolf, Rosemary, 284n16
work, 13, 15, 55, 116, 152, 178, 196, 224, 234, 246; and befallenness, 126; benefit or cost of, 256n33; ethical problem of, 14, 83; and humanities, 242; and language, 10; of mourning, 92; of oneself, 29; sacrificed, 15; and sentience, 18, 88, 103; of signifier, 27
works, 16, 61, 182, 256n33; ethical ambiguities of, 246; and the signifier, 57; and tragedy, 126
wound(s), 33, 168, 207, 218, 264n29; Arcite's, 167–68; and chivalric culture, 216–17; in de Certeau, 51–52; and power to commune with dead, 221; and symbolic order, 216; and the Thing, 216

Yalom, Irvin D., 254n19
Yates, Frances, 263n25

Žižek, Slavoj, 30, 285n23; on acting "as if," 262n5; on courtly love, 10, 19, 51; on Derrida, 152; ideology, 168; the lady, 288n23; the law, 5, 272n24; masochism, 51, 264n39; on modes of enjoyment, 2, 62; *plus-de-jouir*, 121, 164; the real, 257n56; sacrifice, 298n16; "second death," 235; signifier, 164, 290n40; subjective destitution, 282n76; sublime object, 271n21; submission to law, 162, 164, 259n72; on the two fathers, 26

Medieval Cultures

Volume 28
D. Vance Smith
The Book of the Incipit: Beginnings in the Fourteenth Century

Volume 27
Edited by Glenn Burger and Steven F. Kruger
Queering the Middle Ages

Volume 26
Paul Strohm
Theory and the Premodern Text

Volume 25
David Rollo
Glamorous Sorcery: Magic and Literacy in the High Middle Ages

Volume 24
Steve Ellis
Chaucer at Large: The Poet in the Modern Ages

Volume 23
Edited by Barbara A. Hanawalt and Michal Kobialka
Medieval Practices of Space

Volume 22
Michelle R. Warren
History on the Edge: Excalibur and the Borders of Britain, 1100–1300

Volume 21
Olivia Holmes
Assembling the Lyric Self: Authorship from Troubadour Song to Italian Poetry Book

Volume 20
Karen Sullivan
The Interrogation of Joan of Arc

Volume 19
Clare A. Lees
Tradition and Belief: Religious Writing in Late Anglo-Saxon England

Volume 18
David Matthews
The Making of Middle English, 1765–1910

Volume 17
Jeffrey Jerome Cohen
Of Giants: Sex, Monsters, and the Middle Ages

Volume 16
Edited by Barbara A. Hanawalt and David Wallace
Medieval Crime and Social Control

Volume 15
Kathryn Kerby-Fulton and Denise L. Despres
*Iconography and the Professional Reader:
The Politics of Book Production in the Douce "Piers Plowman"*

Volume 14
Edited by Marilynn Desmond
Christine de Pizan and the Categories of Difference

Volume 13
Alfred Thomas
Anne's Bohemia: Czech Literature and Society, 1310–1420

Volume 12
Edited by F. R. P. Akehurst and Stephanie Cain Van D'Elden
The Stranger in Medieval Society

Volume 11
Edited by Karma Lochrie, Peggy McCracken, and James A. Schulz
Constructing Medieval Sexuality

Volume 10
Claire Sponsler
Drama and Resistance: Bodies, Goods, and Theatricality in Late Medieval England

Volume 9
Edited by Barbara A. Hanawalt and David Wallace
Bodies and Disciplines: Intersections of Literature and History in Fifteenth-Century England

Volume 8
Marilynn Desmond
Reading Dido: Gender, Textuality, and the Medieval "Aeneid"

Volume 7
Edited by Clare A. Lees
Medieval Masculinities: Regarding Men in the Middle Ages

Volume 6
Edited by Barbara A. Hanawalt and Kathryn L. Reyerson
City and Spectacle in Medieval Europe

Volume 5
Edited by Calvin B. Kendall and Peter S. Wells
Voyage to the Other World: The Legacy of Sutton Hoo

Volume 4
Edited by Barbara A. Hanawalt
Chaucer's England: Literature in Historical Context

Volume 3
Edited by Marilyn J. Chiat and Kathryn L. Reyerson
The Medieval Mediterranean: Cross-Cultural Contacts

Volume 2
Edited by Andrew MacLeish
The Medieval Monastery

Volume 1
Edited by Kathryn L. Reyerson and Faye Powe
The Medieval Castle

L. O. Aranye Fradenburg is professor of English, women's studies, and comparative literature at the University of California, Santa Barbara. She is author of *City, Marriage, Tournament: Arts of Rule in Late Medieval Scotland,* editor of *Women and Sovereignty,* and editor (with Carla Freccero) of *Premodern Sexualities.*